PROFESSIONAL GUNSMITHING

A Textbook on the Repair and Alteration of Firearms — with Detailed Notes and Suggestions Relative to the Equipment and Operation of a Commercial Gunshop

by

WALTER J. HOWE

Drawings by JOHN B. MOLL, JR.

INTRODUCTION

IN THE field of gunsmithing today, where the amateurs overwhelmingly outnumber the professionals, it is not surprising that most of the published books on the subject should ignore the commercial aspect of this old and respected profession. However, some of today's amateurs will be tomorrow's professionals and the change from "for pleasure" to "for profit" is often difficult for the aspirant who is not aware of, or prepared to cope with, the complications such a change brings about. The purpose of this book is to help those who wish to make this change not only to become skilled craftsmen but efficient businessmen as well.

The professional gunsmith must, in addition to being a first class technician, know how to deal with shooters *as customers* and to place a fair price on his services. He must also know when and how to refuse to work on a gun that is someone's pride and joy but actually an unsafe weapon. The practice of whiling away hours in idly discussing the merits of this gun or that cartridge with a fellow shooter is another little pleasure of amateur gunsmithing that the professional must learn to do without, at least during working hours.

Time, for which he had so little regard as an amateur, suddenly becomes important to the new professional. The idea of doing a job exactly as someone else demands it be done is not easy to get used to. And the strain of having every job finished and ready at a previously agreed to time . . . well, that frequently proves to be such a task that even seasoned gunsmiths hedge at a customer's, "When will my gun be finished?"

For the desultory novice or the highly inspired but unprepared amateur the field of professional gunsmithing offers little more than the possibility of unpleasant remembrances of the craft. The need for fair dealing and thorough repair work has always been great in this country where the benefits of mass production are seen in every home in the form of refrigerators, radios, electrical appliances, automobiles and, of course, guns. Good service at a fair price is all that any customer can and should expect of a repairman. However, common experience would indicate that the customer whose just expectations are fulfilled is among a minority. For the gunsmith who knows his work and renders good service the future holds only favorable promise, and the influx of competitors bothers him little.

In spite of some indications to the contrary, the average professional gunsmith's income is largely derived from repairing and modifying stock weapons. And it is this he should learn to do proficiently before attempting to improve on commercial standardized weapons and cartridges. Specialization in barrel work, stock making, metal refinishing, or any phase of gunsmithing is commendable, but something that should be given serious thought only after a basic knowledge and experience in general repair work have been thoroughly acquired.

In this text I have tried to combine the business and technical phases of gunsmithing so as to reflect their complementary relationship to efficiency and good work, and ultimately towards raising the standard of gun repair work to the high level it deserves.

It is my humble hope that this book will serve as an inspirational source as well as a technical guide to the student who is anxious to study gunsmithing but has been led to believe it is a craft that can only be mastered by old world teaching methods.

Professional Gunsmithing is the first of my books on the subject of firearms repair and modification. The second, now being written, will be concerned primarily with the problems of the amateur. Few books in any technical field are wholly original or revolutionary; rather, each in part records, in part augments, the gradual but positive progress of the profession. I can only hope this book fulfills its mission in that respect.

WALTER J. HOWE

Farmingdale, N.J.
October 1946

ACKNOWLEDGMENTS

ALTHOUGH it would be difficult to here thank everyone who has in some way helped to make *Professional Gunsmithing* a reality, I feel that this book would be incomplete without publicly saying, "It wouldn't have been possible without your help" —to my father, Mr. Walter A. Howe, whose lifetime encouragement has been priceless; to my wife, Nathalie; to the publisher, Mr. Thomas G. Samworth, whose name is legend in the gun book field; to the artist, Mr. John B. Moll, Jr., of Middletown, Delaware, whose work speaks for itself; and to Mr. Joseph F. Powers, of Berwyn, Pennsylvania.

Special thanks also to the following, each of whom best knows why he is mentioned: Mr. Cornelius Bertschinger, Mr. Harold J. Roddin, Detective John Trusch, New York City Police Department, Mr. Albert Purpura, Mr. Walter Chamberlin, Colonel Lewis R. Sussman CMP, Major Hugh Richter, formerly Office of the Chief of Ordnance, Captain Max Bearon, Ordnance Dept., Mr. Lou Smith of the Ithaca Gun Co., and last, but not least, Mr. Walter H. Bean, formerly of Springfield Armory, and at this writing with the Armament Shop at Fort Dix, N.J.

CONTENTS

CHAPTER ONE

Business Set Up and Customer Relationship

As IT is with all professions or trades where service is the chief commodity dealt in, a neat-appearing place of business is of the essence.

Aside from a few notable exceptions, as for instance where a genius, a master scientist or craftsman enjoys the somewhat dubious honor of pursuing his occupation in surroundings not commensurate with the decorum generally expected of such a pursuit, a mechanic is not infrequently judged by the appearance of his shop. This is as true for a gunsmith as it is for a doctor or pharmacist.

It is not for show alone that one keeps an orderly shop, for if it were, the least successful of all proprietors might have the best looking establishment (only of course so long as the original capital held out) and as such it would serve little purpose.

Actually, for a gunsmith a neat shop does not mean that he must have a floor that is clean enough to eat from or a work bench that looks like a polished dining room table. Rather, it means he should have a work place that is above all, well layed-out and large enough to enable him to carry on his normal business.

Size of Shop. Whether a gunsmith has his own store devoted entirely to gun repair and associated work, or shares a section of a sporting goods emporium, is of little importance. The important factor is that he have a place large enough to do his work with a degree of privacy second to none—privacy in the sense that he can retire to his work bench with repair jobs and be assured that the customer or kibitzer (so common to gun shops) will not stroll in and offer comments or suggestions. This does not necessarily call for a hermit's retreat or two-by-four enclosure but rather a work shop proper which is inaccessible (so made by railings or partitions) to all but those who are specifically invited to enter. Few gunsmiths can do their best work if the gun owner or the would-be helpful soul keeps interjecting hints as to how the particular job under consideration should be handled.

Privacy. That a gunsmith should enjoy privacy in his workroom is not suggested just to have him appear as a magician or secret worker, but rather for many practical reasons. As might be expected, a gunsmith is frequently presented with a gun, for diagnosis of trouble, that is not included in his repertoire of "weapons well understood." At a time like this the gunsmith, with the shop apart from his receiving counter, can graciously beg the customer's indulgence for a few moments while he takes the gun to his workbench and "looks it over under better light." In this manner the gun craftsman can more leisurely and freely learn of the gun's working characteristics and trouble. Then he can more confidently and intelligently discuss the problem with the customer, who will not feel he is entrusting his pet fire-stick to inexperienced hands.

Another decided advantage of having a somewhat private place for doing repair work can be appreciated by anyone who has had occasion to take a gun apart and, having left the many pieces scattered in a position of studied negligence to go to lunch or whatnot, returns to find a few pins serving as temporary toys for a waiting gun bug, idling away the moments by tapping them into the workbench top.

As a matter of precedent the gunsmith should exclude all persons from his workshop proper. This practice will pay dividends many times over in more ways than can be readily enumerated.

The Money Angle

To the professional gunsmith, either experienced or novice, his main purpose for being in business is to make money; while this fact would appear to a skilled mechanic of another profession as almost too axiomatic for mention, it is among some gunsmiths too frequently ignored. The business of gunsmithing, unlike most other mechanical pursuits, is often embarked upon by a man with such a love for guns and the sportsmen and shooters who own them, that he often ignores the money end of his profession until it is too late and he is forced into heavy debt. This condition is sometimes followed by an effort on the part of the gunsmith to regain his loss by slipshod work and short cuts in ethical procedure, all of which leads to ultimate failure in business.

Thus, we bring up a subject most important to every gunsmith, that is, the question of what to charge, or more technically expressed, uniform price determination.

Price Determination. To delineate a fixed chart of charges applicable to each and every job encountered in gun repair work would not only be impractical but well nigh impossible. In order better to appreciate the difficulty involved in attempting such an undertaking, one need only consider the number of various weapons handled by a gunsmith, plus the number of repairs possible to be made on each weapon, supplemented, of course, by the innumerable special jobs which defy classification.

Yet in spite of these specific barriers, there is a basic method of price determination that can be applied to virtually every type of repair work. Briefly it is this: The gunsmith must first place a value on his time, commensurate with his expected weekly income. Let us say, for example, the gunsmith spends 48 hours per week at his work and wishes to clear a minimum of $50.00 per week as a salary. Therefore, at first glance it can be seen that the hourly rate of wages alone must be approximately $1.05. But that is only part of the story, for there are other factors that must be taken into consideration, and first among them is the matter of overhead or operating expenses. Under this heading we list rent, gas, electric current, water, special taxes and license fees directly incident to the business proper, printing, postage, administration fees, et cetera. By totaling these expenses the gunsmith can get a very good working conception of his annual overhead, which in turn, when divided by 52, will give him the weekly figure. For example, let us take the following hypothetical gunsmith business of "The Marine Park Gun Works" on a yearly basis:

Rent	$480.	
Gas	72.	(Heats blueing tanks by gas)
Electricity	60.	
Water	18.	(Needed for blueing work)
Taxes & license fees	50.	(Permits, Occupancy Tax, etc.)
Printing & Administrative Costs	100.	(Local advertising and good will)
Depreciation on major tools and machine tools	100.	
(weeks) 52	$880.	Yearly overhead cost
	$ 16.92	Weekly overhead cost

To bring this figure of $16.92 per week down to a more workable medium it is necessary to divide this amount by 48 (the number of working hours per week), which comes to approximately 35¢ per hour. Now we must add the basic salary rate of $1.05 per hour to the 35¢ overhead per hour, giving a total of $1.40 per hour.

Under the heading of business overhead can also be included; premiums on health, fire and theft insurance, provisions for a reserve fund, telephone, and other items which can be best judged by the individual concerned. However, the important thing is to include everything that can truly be called overhead. To overlook any item, no matter how small, is to cut in on that very important thing known as profit.

The 48-hour work week is used as a basis for computation because it pretty well represents the maximum number of hours (eight per day in a six day work week) that any person should be expected to devote to his work. This work schedule allows the gunsmith a few hours leisure time to spend in working on his own guns or on experimental work.

For the man just starting in business, or for the good mechanic who has more work than he can handle in an eight-hour day, the 48-hour week might well be much too short. However, the exception (overtime and long hours) should not be used as a basis for figuring out anticipated revenue or the gunsmith will soon find out, much to his chagrin, that he has placed very little value on his time.

It is one thing to love one's work to the point where little else matters but it is another thing to starve. When money worries are plaguing the gunsmith he can hardly expect to do his best work and there is no reason why a good gunsmith should not be able to make a living at the work he likes best.

In price determination the next question posed is "What about the cost of parts?" "How should charges be made if it's just a question of installing a simple part in a gun?" Well, as a matter of fact, a great deal of the gunsmith's business amounts to just the installation of so-called simple parts.

Cost of Parts. Known well to dealer and customer alike is the fact that each gun company has available for distribution catalogs listing the name, number and price of parts for their make of weapons. Besides this, other large dealers like A. F. Stoeger & Co., Inc., New York City, sell general catalogs which list parts and prices for practically all domestic and many foreign made, rifles, pistols, revolvers and shotguns. Therefore, it is very easy for anyone to learn the official price list of parts used in gun repair. The official price list, of course, is the one issued by the manufacturer himself and it is these prices that should be quoted by the gunsmith in computing charges. And while the companies, as a rule, accord dealers and gunsmiths a discount of from 15% to 25% on parts, the gunsmith should charge list prices for repairs. This is no more than fair for if the customer were to buy the part direct from the factory he would have to pay list, in addition to postage and possibly packing expenses, plus money order fee.

The Time Factor. If a part lists for $3.00 and the gunsmith thinks it will require an hour to complete the job properly, he can pretty confidently tell his customer that the job will cost about $4.50.

In connection with parts replacement work, it is well to remember that few parts can be directly put into a gun without some hand fitting work being necessary. And often, especially in the case of revolver and double barrel shotgun parts, the money value of time consumed exceeds the price of the part. This is likewise true where it is necessary to disassemble and reassemble a weapon merely to replace a broken pin or simple spring which lists at only 25¢. Therefore, always bear in mind the importance of proper diagnosis of parts replacement work before setting a price for a particular job.

Of course, not all customers will insist upon knowing what it will cost to repair their pet shooting iron but it is well to be able to give them a rough inkling of what the job will amount to. This is highly important if the weapon being fixed is in need of extensive repairs, although it may only have cost the owner $12.00 when new, and is especially true of cheap foreign automatic pistols and inexpensive domestic varieties of .22 caliber plinking rifles. In this way the customer can decline having the gun fixed if, for a few more dollars, he can buy a new weapon.

With certain special work like sight making, action tune-up jobs, or stock refinishing, the gunsmith can justifiably add 10% to his regular estimate as a specialist's fee, to compensate for the added effort required for this type of work.

In the method here outlined for overhead cost determination and price setting, it must be remembered that it can be used successfully and fairly only if the gunsmith realizes his own capabilities and deficiencies. To illustrate: It would be very unfair for a gunsmith to take in a foreign make shotgun that he knows nothing about for repair and then charge for a few extra hours work time consumed in trying to put the gun together.

By the same token, it is unethical for a gunsmith to charge a customer for replacing a part broken while disassembling or assembling the weapon. This, of course, is not to be confused with the case of parts which are already broken on the inside of a gun and only come to the gunsmith's attention when he takes it apart for cleaning or inspection. That is one reason why a stipulated price should not be agreed upon with a customer until it is possible to take the weapon apart and make a complete diagnosis.

A good thought for any mechanic to bear in mind at all times is one that has guided many successful craftsmen in their business dealings: the job done right and delivered on time is worth any customer's good will and extra dollar, while the job done *almost* right is worth absolutely nothing.

Irrespective of how skilled a mechanic may be or how elaborate his place of business, he cannot very well expect to gain a reputation and prosper if he does not gain the confidence of his customers. The necessity for making a good impression on customers cannot be overestimated. A customer satisfied is not only a steady client but, more important, an active, every-day booster for the gunsmith. This sort of advertising cannot be bought—it is acquired and kept *only* through the medium of good workmanship, prompt service and professional-like manner. These three attributes are as necessary to a gunsmith's stock in trade as are his drill press, vise or screwdriver.

The Cardinal Rules

Customer confidence can be cultivated and developed if the gunsmith will but make a practice of following a few cardinal rules:

I. *Be exemplary in the handling of guns at all times.*

When a customer brings a gun in for repair, do not be rough with it.

Do not snap the trigger or open and close the breech, cylinder or bolt any more than is absolutely necessary.

Do not point the gun carelessly when it is necessary to pull the trigger for test purposes. Check to see that the gun is not loaded before snapping the trigger or making a diagnosis. After all, the customer may have brought the gun in because he couldn't get a cartridge out of the chamber (possible broken extractor), or perhaps, as often happens with revolvers, the cylinder has become frozen while shooting and refused to rotate, with three or four live rounds still remaining therein.

Have two rags handy at all times—one clean dry cloth for wiping off the gun after handling, and a lightly oiled cloth for rubbing over the metal parts afterwards. This procedure, which takes but a few seconds, will impress a gun lover very definitely. On observing this, he will naturally feel that the gunsmith is a person with whom his pride and joy can be trusted. The love of a gun by most sportsmen is a truly deep affection, and the gunsmith would do well to bear this in mind at all times.

Have a rack or other suitable contrivance in which to stack rifles or shotguns which are in for repair. Most especially, have a safe place where guns can be put after they have been repaired. Nothing is more disconcerting than to repair a gun and have it be damaged just because it happened to fall from some perilous perch where it was resting after "fixin."

II. *Don't make promises that can't be kept.*

While it would seem offhand that a gunsmith is not a person who has many promises to make and live up to, actual analysis reveals many facts quite to the contrary.

Too often the gunsmith thoughtlessly promises a customer that his gun can be finished on a certain day, only to realize a few hours before the agreed-to time that it will be impossible to complete the job. It is at a moment like this that the gunsmith must start thinking up excuses as to why the gun is not finished. Fortunately, the average gunsmith's repertory of excuses is usually only exceeded by his ability to fabricate new stories to suit various seasons or the temperament of the person owning the gun. And, while the talent of alibi manufacturing cannot be totally discredited, it is far better to keep faith with customers by having the gun ready when promised.

To bring about the habit of prompt delivery, a gunsmith should always allow himself ample time to perform any repair job, and when in doubt it is wiser to overestimate the time needed for completion rather than underestimate it.

If parts are needed and they are not in stock at the moment, ample time should be allowed in order that these can be purchased, either from local sources or the factory. At any rate, it is well to get in the habit of ordering parts as soon as the need arises for them. In this way much worry can be avoided.

To aid in parts ordering, the gunsmith will be a better business man if he has a complete set of all the latest factory catalogs on hand. Order from these catalogs and always give number, proper name and list price of the part. In addition, it is good to give serial number and caliber of gun if part is for model of weapon that is old type or akin to similar models made by the company.

As a gunsmith's trade warrants it, the practice of stocking certain parts is to be highly recommended. Just what parts should be stocked and what minimum quantity of each should be on hand is a matter which the individual gunsmith knows best. If, in certain localities there is a preponderance of one type of gun, say, for instance in a rural community where a few makes of double barrel guns predominate as armament for the local hunters, the gunsmith can safely and profitably stock a few of each of the parts that in his experience have proved to be most likely needed for replacement: on shotguns (of the double barrel type), firing pins and flat type main, or sear springs are very liable to short life; on automatic pistols, magazines and barrels most frequently go bad; on revolvers, hands, main springs and grips are the parts most commonly replaced. This is, of course, just to mention a few. For all popular make and model weapons, small coil and flat springs are definite musts for stock. This is especially true of Iver Johnson and Harrington & Richardson revolvers. While the initial cost of these parts is very small, the dividends reaped by having them on hand are great.

III. *Keep abreast of all the latest models and calibers of guns; also be well informed on the latest methods of repair technique and technical developments in the arms and ammunition field.*

As a highly skilled mechanic, the gunsmith should and must be well informed as to the latest matters going on that affect himself and his customers. One of the best means of achieving this goal is to be on the mailing list of all the firearms, ammunition and accessories companies that manufacture and distribute these respective products. The second way (a supplementary rather than an alternative method) is to subscribe to all the sporting magazines that carry articles and advertisements on firearms, ammunition and accessories. One of these publications worthy of special mention is "The American Rifleman," the official magazine of the National Rifle Association. This monthly publication is a true thesaurus of material for every gun lover.

To round out the information garnered from current magazines, a valuable store of facts both theoretical and practical can be learned from books on gunsmithing, cartridge loading, shooting and elementary ballistics.

The importance of being able to discuss the more technical side of firearms and ammunition will become increasingly evident to a gunsmith as time goes on. Knowing the why and how of gun operation is not only valuable as a means of impressing customers, but, more important, as an aid to gun trouble diagnosis. Also, with a technical background, a gunsmith can develop and experiment with possible improvements and new ideas connected with guns or gun repair work.

IV. *Know and live up to all the laws regarding traffic in firearms, ammunition and components thereof.*

In recent years, there have been many laws and ordinances enacted relating to dealing in firearms and ammunition, and in large cities legislation specifically affecting gunsmiths has made an appearance.

As an idea of what particular phases of the gun business are affected in various localities, the following list is given, and while some states, cities and towns have very few laws regulating this business, it would be well for the gunsmith to learn from the police and fire departments of his own business territory what licenses and permits are necessary if he is to conduct it as a law-abiding citizen:

1. Federal Firearms Act
2. National Firearms Act
3. U.S. State Department Regulations concerning importing arms and ammunition
4. Pistol Permit Laws
5. Fire Department permits to store ammunition
6. Licenses for dealing in firearms
7. Licenses for dealing in second-hand firearms
8. Licenses regulating the storage of explosives and primers

9. Licenses regulating manufacturing of firearms and ammunition
10. Regulations dealing with use of U.S. Post Office facilities for shipping and receiving guns, ammunition and component parts
11. Laws regulating the sale of guns and ammunition to minors, certain types of undesirable people, i.e., habitual drunkards, drug addicts or persons known to have been convicted of certain crimes.

In connection with this phase of the gunsmithing business, it might not be amiss to point out that a gunsmith or gun dealer can avoid a great deal of trouble if he will but comply with all legal matters regulating his profession and livelihood. Whether or not the gunsmith or gun dealer agrees with, or believes, the particular laws he must function under are just and fair, is of small import. The fact remains that they are there and, as with all laws or regulations, must be complied with until such time as they are modified or legally erased from the statute books.

As a final word on this subject, it is almost needless to say that gunsmiths or gun dealers who make a practice of selling, repairing or modifying weapons for underworld persons or suspicious characters are worthy of the most extreme punishment that can be legally meted out. It is men of this ilk who have given the gun business most of the adverse publicity that it has received.

V. *Do not compromise with safety in repair work.*

From the popular .22 caliber rim fire cartridge, developing pressure of approximately 15,000 pounds per square inch, to the powerful Government .30/06, with its better than 50,000 pounds pressure, are to be found cartridges of virtually every conceivable caliber and ballistic property.

Some of the weapons made to shoot these many cartridges were designed in the days when black powder was the only propellant for small arms projectiles. With the advent of smokeless powder, certain model weapons had to be redesigned to accommodate the additional strains imposed by this new gunpowder. Still, and unfortunately so, there do remain even to this day not a few shotguns which are totally unsuited for firing modern commercially made loads. Manufactured with barrels known variously as damascus, twist or laminated steel, such guns are regarded by experts as a definite hazard when used with high velocity or extra-range loads. Yet, in spite of continued warnings from magazine gun editors and authorities on the subject, many shooters continue to employ this suicide combination for hunting and shooting.

During the course of a gunsmith's business he will be called upon frequently to repair many different types of weapons, from the aforementioned kind to the most modern and best made rifles, pistols and shotguns. Upon these weapons he is expected to do only one kind of work—the very best. For when dealing with a contrivance so powerful and potentially dangerous as a firearm, there can be no halfway measures in repair work. It must never be forgotten that the force of an expanding gas is distributed equally in all directions—that the same force which sends the speeding bullet on its way is also pressing against the chamber wall and bolt, or breech face, with comparable pressure. This is a most important fact to remember when working on the breech locking mechanism of any gun, as well as when replacing bolts in bolt action rifles. (See Chapter Thirteen.)

Firing pins, of which there are so many sizes and shapes, are directly concerned with safety too, for if they are not properly shaped at the nose or are too long or short they can be a very dangerous part in a gun.

The application of heat to the receiver of a rifle or cylinder of a revolver, or for that matter any part of a weapon which is subject to the direct strain of firing, is a practice that is to be avoided unless the repairman has the technical knowledge and facilities to reheat treat any part in which the temper has been destroyed. (See Chapter Fifteen.)

In making special parts which are subject to shock, stress or strain (hinge pin of shotguns, firing pin bushings, et cetera) the gunsmith should always be certain of the steel to be used and know the proper heat treatment required for the part after it is machined.

Never work upon a gun which may afterwards be unsafe to shoot. In this respect there is no in-between status. Either a gun is or is not safe to fire. The only exception to this rule is in the case of firearms which are to be used solely for display or collection purposes and such guns should not be over-embellished or altered lest their period authenticity be destroyed. There are today entirely too many collectors of antique firearms and dealers who are engaged in this nefarious practice.

VI. *Do not undertake to work upon jobs that are beyond abilities or facilities.*

Every mechanic or engineer, no matter how skilled or well versed, has certain specialties, and, by the same token, certain limitations.

Not every automobile mechanic is a master of every phase of car repair any more than every physician is capable of performing delicate brain or eye operations. Rather, in these fields there are specialists—men who have made an exhaustive study of one, or maybe even a few, phases of their respective calling and devote their time and talents to their specialty.

These specialists are necessary in every field of scientific and technical endeavor, for the amount of knowledge needed to operate successfully, in these professions, is so extensive as to preclude each mechanic being an expert in every phase of his business.

In order to capitalize on a particular operation in gunmaking or gun repair work, certain skilled machinist-gunsmiths specialize in barrel making and fitting barrels to actions, while others with special cabinet making training do only stock making and inletting work.

Both of these specialties require a high degree of knowledge and skill not usually possessed by the general gunsmith, plus investment in special tools, jigs and fixtures which is only warranted by a large volume of business.

To attempt any major repair or alteration job on firearms, for which special tools, equipment or skill the gunsmith does not possess are needed, is not only conducive to poor customer relations but also results in a loss of time, which to any repairman is money.

This, of course, does not mean that the gunsmith should shun taking on difficult repair or alteration work merely because he hasn't a completely equipped machine shop or isn't a past master, but rather he should learn to know his own capacities and just what jobs he can perform profitably and correctly. And if a gunsmith believes he is capable of inletting stocks or making barrels, he should not restrain himself from finding out. However, the best way to ascertain this is to experiment on an old gun that does not belong to a customer. Then a failure will not mean a customer's gun ruined or paying a specialist to do the job correctly.

VII. *Know the customer.*

Knowing the customer does not necessarily mean that the gunsmith must cultivate a friendship with each person that chances to bring him work, or probe into his personal business. Rather it means that the mechanic must develop an "approach" so to speak, and learn to listen.

Although it is common knowledge that many gun owners know little about their weapons, other than how to load and fire them, there are not a few gun cranks, target shooters, hunters and arm chair ballistics experts who possess considerable knowledge about firearms. The mere fact that individuals in the latter group bring their weapons to a gunsmith for repair, adjustment or modification is not an indication that they do not know how to do a particular job or what can be expected. They bring their guns to a gunsmith because they want a job done correctly by a man who has the tools and time to do it. This practice alone quite frequently distinguishes them from those who know little or nothing about guns and bring their completely disassembled "shootin iron" to the professional only after it has proved to be easier to take apart than to put back together.

For business purposes, all customers should be treated with equal courtesy and attention, but always sound each customer out before making any rash or controversial statements, and at all times the gunsmith would do well to keep personal opinions to himself unless specifically requested to evaluate some particular gun or gun accessory ; in which case, all statements made should be based upon accepted fact and reasoning.

So that no doubts will be set up in the customer's mind as to the knowledge and ability of the gunsmith, the latter should, when presented with a strange scope or accessory for installation, be the apex of politeness, and by subtle questioning find out how the damn thing works and where and how it should go on the gun. The same precaution also goes for guns with which the gunsmith has scarcely a nodding acquaintance.

Smart, or otherwise, however, no customer should be given free reign of the shop or be permitted to assume the status of official "hanger around." No mechanic can fully concentrate, or do his best work when he has someone, other than an employee, wandering about the shop. During business hours the gunsmith should devote himself to work and service and not to answering a lot of questions or keeping one eye on a would-be gunsmith who took up some other profession and has a lot of spare time on his hands.

A gunsmith's shop is a very fascinating and interesting place for a gun lover to visit and he usually picks a time to visit it when the "old master" is up to his neck in work (which is always) and thinks nothing of idling away a few hours. As tempting as it might be to talk over last hunting season or the merits of lever action rifles with a loquacious customer, this sort of chit-chat should be discouraged. At $1.40 per hour, the profit on a small job is quickly turned into red ink on the ledger book if much over-the-counter gossip is engaged in with visitors.

All of this should not be construed to mean that the gunsmith must be anti-social or assume the role of a disinterested money grabber, but rather that he should employ a great deal of discretion in his dealings with customers. There is no one over-all rule applicable to all of them. As individuals they have their likes and dislikes; their outstanding points and shortcomings. And while it is not necessary to make a psychological study of each customer it is good business policy to be able to size each one up and act accordingly. When in doubt remember the old adage: *"It is better to keep one's mouth closed and be thought a fool than to open it and remove all doubt."*

Within this chapter I have tried to outline, with just so much detail as necessary to give a logical reason for each suggestion, the side of gunsmithing about which little is written. The thoughts expressed in this chapter are written from experience, some costly—and other ideas passed along to me from gunsmiths and gun dealers who have used them with success.

For in the final analysis a gunsmith's worth can be fairly judged by his following of customers and his income derived from satisfying these customers.

CHAPTER TWO

THE SHOP AND ITS EQUIPMENT

WHILE tools and equipment alone do not raise a novice gunsmith to the status of first class mechanic, there is a certain group of basic tools (from which others can be fashioned) that come under the heading of being "absolutely necessary" to do repair work correctly and economically. To be sure, there probably are tools and machines other than the ones herein listed, eminently more satisfactory for certain types of work, but since the gunsmith's initial capital is assumed to be limited, he must invest in the most versatile equipment.

This aspect will be covered in more detail as it specifically applies during the course of the chapter. For both easier listing, and as an aid to future reference on the part of the reader, tools and equipment will be listed under four specific headings, and then subdivided accordingly:

Shop Furnishings (work bench, racks, closets, tool cabinets)
Shop Machines and Accessories
Hand Tools (common)
Metals, Materials and Shop Supplies

Shop Furnishings

The Work Bench. To attempt an exact description of what constitutes the ideal size and shape of work bench would not only be nigh impossible, but worst of all, useless, for the varying sizes of men and shop room available are so diverse that only a lengthy compendium on work benches would be sufficient to scratch the surface. Yet there are a few fundamental rules concerning construction of this most important piece of shop furniture that must be followed if one is to have a suitable "operating table" for guns.

Above all, a work bench must be sturdy and firm. Certainly one cannot expect to do fine work on a bench that sways back and forth with each stroke of a file or hacksaw. To help achieve this sturdiness, the work bench should be amply reinforced with bolted-on crosspiece supports. Legs and main top supports should be made of 4 x 4 wood rather than 2 x 4 because the additional weight and base cross section area of the larger pieces makes for excellent stability.

The top of the bench should be made of jointed board (screwed, not nailed, to the main beams) and then covered with a seamless piece of fiber board, or Masonite Presdwood. It is very important that the top of the work bench be seamless, for in this way the gunsmith will never have to bemoan the loss of a small pin, screw or spring that fell down between cracks and disappeared. Only those gun repairmen who have searched for hours on hands and knees below a work bench with seams just wide enough to allow the very smallest pins to drop through can attest to the absolute necessity for a seamless-topped work bench. Furthermore, a composition-topped bench, especially when varnished or shellacked, does not absorb oil and moisture as does a plain wood-surfaced affair.

Although many prefabricated commercial type work benches are so designed as to accommodate a drawer or two, this writer does not believe there is any particular need for drawers in a gunsmith's bench. Usually such drawers (ostensibly made to hold the not too frequently used tools) soon become repositories for miscellaneous junk and other unclassified gadgets for which no other hiding place can be found. And, more frequently than not, these underslung compartments become weighed down to the point where they sag and are just about movable.

Small drawers, with compartments, have a definite place in a gunsmith shop for storage of gun parts that might otherwise become mixed up, but these should be in a special cabinet rather than attached to the work bench.

For the average size man, a work bench should be from 35" to 38" high and for best over-all results, the bench should be as long as shop space permits. At busy times a fifteen-foot work bench does not seem long enough.

The width of the bench depends to a great extent upon what other things besides work (parts, boxes, tools, racks, etc.) are to be placed on it. However, it is nice to have at least 26" of free working width on any bench.

In addition to the main work bench, it is very handy to have an auxiliary bench for use in connection with special work, such as disassembling a strange gun, or doing a hurry-up job when the "big" bench is covered with wood shavings and linseed oil. An old kitchen table (properly reinforced so it doesn't wobble), with a chair to suit the table height, makes an ideal auxiliary bench.

It is surprising how helpful one of these small benches can be—especially when one is confronted with a particularly tough problem in reassembly work. Often by sitting down at the small bench with a few essential tools and the "works," the gunsmith, a little more relaxed, can see some things he couldn't while standing over the cluttered-up main work bench.

The Vise and Attachments. Since the greater part of a gunsmith's work requires operations to be performed on guns and parts that must be held rigidly in processing, the bench vise is an important consideration.

Although vises for bench use are made in many varying sizes, the gunsmith's vise should have jaws about 4″ wide and be of the universal type. In other words, the base of the vise as well as the rear jaw should be movable. This type of vise will accommodate tapered barrels, and also can be swung in a radius of 360°, thus allowing the gunsmith to file, saw, or cut from the most advantageous angle.

Soft (copper, brass, lead)

Leather

Wood

VISE JAWS

FIGURE 1

In order to prevent marring of blued and finished surfaces, the bench vise should be equipped with removable copper, leather and wood vise jaws. The accompanying illustration (Figure 1) should serve adequately to guide the gunsmith in making special jaws to fit whatever size of vise he may have.

Besides the main vise, a small one for holding little parts is a very handy addition to the work bench. Its worth is doubly appreciated when the big vise is being used to hold a major repair, and a part that must be installed needs to be subassembled in a vise.

Though the common practice among mechanics is to have their main vise mounted on the work bench, this writer has seen large vises mounted on a pipestand arrangement as in Figure 2. This sort of setup seems to have many advantages for gunsmithing work where long barrels must be held at various angles

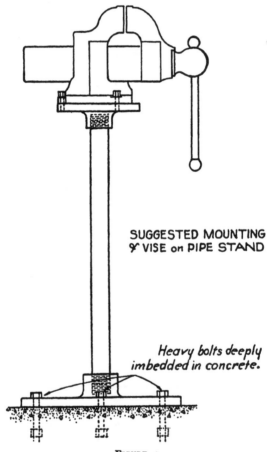

SUGGESTED MOUNTING
9" VISE on PIPE STAND

Heavy bolts deeply imbedded in concrete.

FIGURE 2

to do some of the jobs that are encountered from time to time.

An ultra deluxe version of this pipestand vise holder would be one in which a universal joint arrangement, that could be loosened and tightened by a screw, was incorporated. Such an improvement would permit the vise to be swung to any compound angle position. Plain or fancy, though, it is imperative with such a setup that the base be securely moored to the floor.

Carpenter's Vise. Although it is inexpensive, and can be installed on any type of work bench, the gunsmith's need for a carpenter's vise is actually very slight. There is practically no phase of stock work where the main vise, with a pair of wooden jaws, will not suffice. (A special set of wooden vise jaws, *with felt facing*, should be kept on hand to be used when a finished stock must be held in the vise.)

Racks for Holding Tools. When an efficiency expert comes to a factory or shop, where production methods of assembly or repair are being used, one of the first things he considers is the position of the tools in relation to the operation being performed. Often these experts find that a mechanic wastes a good portion of the time he spends on a repair or assembly task looking for tools to accomplish his work.

To correct this constant time-consuming fault, which benefits neither owner, worker nor consumer, the efficiency expert usually suggests that the most frequently used tools be placed so that they are within easy reach as needed, and yet not so crowded as to affect easy identification of similar tools.

There are various corrective measures which are suggested to remedy this situation, often involving a specially built semi-circular work bench with rotating bins within arm's length of the repairman. For the gunsmith, however, who must be constantly on the move from his work bench to the store front or elsewhere about the shop, one of the most practical setups devised is illustrated in Figure 3. Modifications can be made by the individual to suit his own particular needs and tastes.

It should be noted that under this arrangement all tools are in full view and can be easily selected as needed. Tools which are not used very often can be stored in a rack or cabinet placed adjacent to the work bench. To stop certain tools from rolling to the bottom of their respective compartments, guides in the form of brass pins or wooden dowels can be placed at points where they will do the most good.

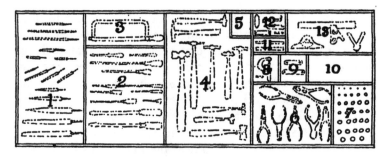

1 General size files.   4 Hammers.
2 Screwdriver.   5 Needle files
3 Hacksaw.   6 Pliers.
7 Drift punches, center punches, etc.
8 Micrometer.
9 Thickness gages and thread pitch gage.
10 Scale, combination square, center head, etc.
11 Small honing stones for trigger pull work.
12 Firing pin protrusion gages.
13 Special small tools used frequently.

A SUGGESTED TOOL RACK LAYOUT FOR WORKBENCH

FIGURE 3

Containers for Gun Parts. Like work bench designs, a specific layout for keeping gun repair parts is very difficult, for shop space limitations, and the amount of parts that different gunsmiths feel inclined to stock, precludes a good basis for almost any extensive commentary on what the ideal setup should be. Nevertheless, whatever arrangement the gunsmith does decide upon, he should remember the importance of labeling or marking each drawer or compartment in a manner that will enable him to find the part he desires with a minimum of rummaging and disrupting of other parts.

If partitioned drawers or boxes are made to hold small pins or springs, the partitions should be made so as to fit snugly at all joints; otherwise small items might easily become lodged between adjoining compartments or even slip to another compartment when the drawer is moved back and forth.

Transparent plastic boxes, of the kind used by fishermen to keep dry flys and hooks in, are ideal for holding small pins, parts and springs. In Figure 4 the most practical (for gunsmiths) size and compartment arrangement of these boxes is illustrated.

When ordering any of these boxes for parts storage use, always specify that they be of "Nitrate" stock, in as much as

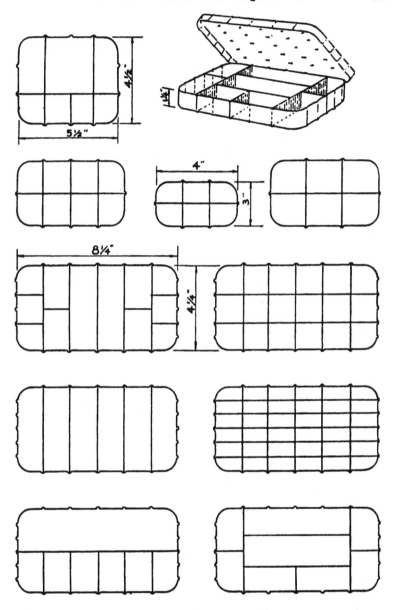

SIZE AND COMPARTMENT ARRANGEMENT OF
TRANSPARENT PARTS BOXES

Figure 4

this material is less liable to crack in cold weather than the "Acetate" stock, of which they are also made.

All points considered, De Witts Pyra Shell transparent boxes are very inexpensive, since they are strong, light containers and do not promote rusting of steel parts as do boxes made of wood.

The advantage of a transparent box should be obvious to anyone who has searched through old envelopes, match boxes and cigar boxes (the more common repositories for parts) for a part needed in a hurry.

Parts, no matter how or where stored, should at all times be covered with a film of grease. Light oil usually does not offer sufficient protection against corrosion, especially when parts are stored in contact with wood or cardboard, for these materials quickly absorb the thin film of oil, leaving the part an easy prey for rusting.

Shop Lighting. Few things are as provocative to short temper and inevitable carelessness on the part of any mechanic who must see what he is doing, as the handicap of poor lighting.

Poor lighting does not necessarily mean that an insufficient number of electric lamps is used, but more accurately, that they are not placed in such a manner as to provide maximum illumination where it is actually needed. It is for this reason that particular attention should be paid to the location of lights around the shop. In addition to a bright but soft light over the work bench (the fluorescent type is ideal for this purpose) a gooseneck type lamp, which can be moved around as needed on the bench, is a must item.

Wall sockets for plugging in motors, soldering iron, a small glue-heating stove, and many other electric appliances, should be generously and advantageously placed, for their true worth is too frequently realized only when these outlets have not been previously installed.

Though this writer does not profess to be an expert electrician, he does know from experience that electrical wiring, fuse boxes, motor controls, etc., are very important considerations from the standpoint of business and safety.

An improperly hooked up motor, a fuse that is too strong for the wiring it is supposed to be protecting, or an overload on the wiring system, can often be the cause of a gunsmith's losing many dollars and hours as a result of a fire or burned out equipment. All of which means that the local electric company or a competent electrician should be consulted before any extensive array of motors, heating units, lights, et cetera are hooked up to the building's incoming electric line.

Shop Machines and Accessories

The Polishing and Grinding Head. This is the absolute number one essential power-driven tool of any gunsmith shop. On it much work can be done that will save the mechanic many hours of hand work and for most operations it will do a better job than can be done by the hands alone. For a complete description of this item see the "Grinding and Polishing Equipment" section of Chapter Sixteen.

The grinding and polishing head is used not alone for sharpening tools but more often with special wheels for grinding and buffing guns to be blued (See Chapter Sixteen) and putting a fine finish on moving parts. And, when a heavy wire wheel is attached, excellent dulling of a metal's surface can be accomplished where it is desired to put this finish on sight ramps, or similar places where a non-reflective surface is wanted.

The Bench Grinder. Although the polishing and grinding head can be fitted with a dry stone wheel of almost any size, shape and texture and used for all around tool shaping, a bench grinder, of the type made by Atlas, is one of those machine tools which the busy gunsmith finds almost indispensable.

For putting a point on a center punch, for grinding a screwdriver in a hurry, for touching up a drill point, the compact, two-wheel (one coarse, one fine) bench grinder, while not an absolute must, is thirty-odd dollars well invested.

The Drill Press. Little need be said to point out the necessity for this machine in the gunsmith shop. From sight mounting jobs to stock work, in addition to the innumerable incidental operations connected with everyday gun repair work, the drill press figures prominently.

There are many companies which manufacture drill presses and most all of them turn out machines that are suitable for gun work. The preferred type, however, seems to be one having a $\frac{1}{4}$ or $\frac{1}{3}$ horsepower motor with a step cone pully and V belt drive. The chuck should be of the detachable type and have a capacity of from zero to $\frac{1}{2}$".

As manufactured, most drill presses have the conventional finger flip type switch for turning the power on and off. The gunsmith will find the arrangement unhandy at times, however, since often both hands are needed to hold the work being done. With a bit of ingenious rigging, this can be changed to a foot controllable switch. Too, with such an arrangement the gunsmith can exert a more instantaneous control over the power, in as much as he need not contend with the time lag of reaching over to manipulate the switch at times when the power must be shut off quickly in an emergency.

For use with the drill press, a good selection of high speed twist drills is imperative. Although somewhat expensive, one of the best selections of drills can be had by assembling a set of what are known as "Wire Size Drills," consisting of 80 drills ranging in size from .0135" to .2280", plus a set of 26 "Letter Size Drills," ranging in size from .2340" to .4130".

These two sets of drills are best bought in metal holders that indicate the size of each drill in progressive order. In the long run it is more economical, and conducive to finer repair work, if these drills are bought in cased sets rather than individually as needed. For one thing, a mechanic seems to be more careful in using things he buys in sets or groups, for the simple reason that he prides himself on his complete set rather than just a box full of assorted drills. Too, at times when a certain size is needed in a hurry, it might not always be available at the local source of supply, and thus someone's gun must lay around while one can be procured.

The larger size drills (from $2\frac{7}{64}$" to 1"), chiefly for stock work and making special tools or accessories, can be very adequately covered by having the following basic sizes: $\frac{7}{16}$"—$\frac{1}{2}$" $\frac{9}{16}$"—$\frac{5}{8}$"—$1\frac{1}{16}$"—$\frac{3}{4}$"—$1\frac{3}{16}$"—$\frac{7}{8}$"—1".

When the drill press is equipped with a chuck having a $\frac{1}{2}$" capacity, all drills above that size will of necessity have to be purchased with $\frac{1}{2}$" shanks, and if this is not possible, then the shanks can be turned down, on a lathe, to that size.

Of course, the gunsmith should not go ahead and cut the shank on every drill down to $\frac{1}{2}$" just so that it will fit the drill press chuck. This cutting down is recommended only when the drill press (with its $\frac{1}{2}$" chuck) must be used for a job.

Generally, drills over $\frac{1}{2}$" in diameter have a tapered shank made to fit into the tailstock of a lathe, or the spindle of the larger type, heavy duty drill presses.

A set of two V blocks, hardened and ground, are absolutely

necessary when drilling holes in gun barrels (for sight mounting) and other round work.

For square and irregular shaped work that must be held firmly while drilling, a universal drill press vise is needed, preferably of the type that can be bolted to the table. The universal compound vise is without doubt the finest type for gunsmithing use. With it, work can be held in almost any position on the drill press table, and by working either or both feed handles the point to be drilled can be brought under the drill exactly.

Although not recommended as a general practice, a drill press can be employed to great advantage in many phases of woodwork where it is necessary to remove wood from the inletted portion of a stock or forearm. By using a router, conventional T-slot cutter, or end mill in the drill press and running it at highest possible speed, a nice smooth job can be accomplished. Naturally, this type of work places a great thrust strain on the machine and tends to decrease its precision for hole drilling. However, if used carefully for light routing work, and not too often, no appreciable degree of damage will be done.

The Lathe. Lathes vary in size from the small jeweler's style for making fine watch parts, where the operator must look through a magnifying glass while working, to the mammoth machines for turning down 16" seacoast cannon where the machinist rides along on a seat watching the cutter peel off 1" metal ribbons.

In between these extremes are many models of varying lengths and capacities. Some are especially suited to production work, others for screw cutting, and still others for general work.

Under the latter heading an ideal size for the gunsmith would seem to be one that can accommodate at least 36" between centers, and having a 9" swing. It should be equipped for thread cutting and have automatic cross feed.

Also, where it is anticipated that much barrel work (chambering) is to be done, the headstock spindle should have a hole in it that is at least 1-⅛" in diameter, so that a "rough" barrel blank can be held close to the chuck face for chambering and the like.

Generally speaking, one does not find the small precision-type lathe equipped with a headstock spindle having a hole much larger than 1" (about ¾" seems to be average) in it. Therefore, it is necessary for the gunsmith to make a choice. For all around work, it would seem that the smaller, high-speed bench lathe, for which almost every type of accessory can be bought at a price within reason, is the best bet unless the gunsmith plans to do much chambering work, in which case the bigger lathe is almost a must.

Each type lathe (i.e. the big vs. the small) has its advantages and disadvantages, and the final decision to purchase one or the other should be made only after the gunsmith has thoroughly and truthfully analyzed his abilities, anticipated specialty, and most probably future desires.

For example, suppose a gunsmith is not very good at lathe work and will use whatever lathe he buys for making firing pins, plungers, et cetera, and has no particular ambition to branch into conversion work. His best bet, without a doubt, is to purchase a small lathe.

On the other hand, suppose a gunsmith is a crackerjack machinist, but sees little prospect of doing any appreciable amount of barrel work in his locality, though he would like very much to do it if he could. Now this sort of problem requires a little thought. If this gunsmith truly feels he can drum up a worthwhile mail-order trade in due time, or stir up local interest so that shooters will want to have their .30's converted to shoot his ".107 phonograph-needle-atom-zippo-special" then he should not hesitate in buying the larger type. However, if it is all wishful thinking, based on what *might possibly be done*, then it would seem that the additional expense, and relative inadaptability to "small work," of the "big lathe" would scarcely justify purchasing the latter.

Methods for holding work in the lathe are: by chucks, collets, or between centers (using face plate). Some lathes are so equipped as to accommodate all three methods. Others, as manufactured, can only be used with two, three or four jaw chucks, or between centers.

Good chucks are expensive, and not every gunsmith just starting up can afford to purchase both a three and four jaw type (the two jaw chuck has no place in gun work). Yet one chuck is an absolute necessity because much of the gunsmith's work is of such a nature that it cannot be turned between centers or held in a standard-size collet. And while a four jaw chuck is more flexible for all types of machine work, the writer would, from personal gunsmithing experience, choose a universal three jaw chuck over the independent four jaw type, if a choice had to be made.

Collets, which can be adapted to many standard make lathes by the use of a draw-in collet chuck attachment, are an excellent means of holding standard size round stocks ($1''$ in diameter and smaller) from which very accurate parts must be turned. If a gunsmith has one of the smaller bench or floor lathes and intends to do semi-production work on hard-to-get parts, then investment in a set of collets and a draw-in attachment should be given serious consideration.

Although the purchase of a lathe represents a sizable investment, and it often goes unused for days at a time, the gunsmith who wants to be equipped to take care of all general repair brought to him cannot very well afford to be without one. For the making of special tools and parts, for experimental work, for turning down odd pins, or duplicating simple factory parts that must be made in a hurry, it has no equal. Nor in versatility has it a peer, for with commercially procurable attachments it can be converted to do boring, milling, reaming, drilling, precision grinding, knurling, threading, spring winding, besides turning work of virtually every sort.

It is not infrequently that a mechanic will rack his brain for an easy way to make a part or perform an operation, only to be looking at the machine that can probably be of great help; that machine is the lathe.

While it is within neither the scope nor intent of this work to go into detail regarding the methods or extent of lathe operation, the author hopes the interested reader will avail himself of and consult the suggested works on machine shop practice listed in Chapter Twenty. As a matter of fact, this applies to all the general machine tools outlined within this chapter, for to know the versatility of one's tools is to know a great deal.

Milling Machine, Shaper, and Automatic Hacksaw. While these three machines would certainly be a worthy addition to any gunsmith's shop, they do not come under the heading of must tools.

For all practical purposes, the only one of these which is worthy of serious consideration is the milling machine, in as much as it is very handy in connection with parts making and the fabrication of special tools for repair work.

Purchasing the milling machine itself is only part of the story, though, for it must be remembered that there are such items as table vise, dividing head, angle plate, and, most important and expensive of all, cutters, that must also be bought if the machine is to be used to any extent in an efficient manner.

All factors considered, it is this writer's humble opinion that the best type of miller, for the gunsmith who needs such a machine in order to do his specialty work, is one of the table models equipped with power longitudinal feed. There is very little milling work that the gunsmith will be called upon to do that cannot be done on one of these small machines. For the mechanic who can make use of one, and who has the ever-required cash, the table milling machine, with attachments and a selection of cutters, will certainly convert many a back-breaking job into a rest period.

As far as the shaper or automatic hacksaw is concerned, this writer can only say that the real need for them in a small gunsmith shop has yet to be demonstrated, unless, perhaps, the mechanic turns out a specialty item or does some super conversion on a production basis, in which case the need would be obvious.

Other Power Machines. In addition to the machines just discussed, the gunsmith who does a great deal of specializing might find it necessary to buy: a surface grinder (for highly finishing flat metal parts to close tolerance); profiling machine (for turning out hammers, triggers and the like); or power-driven woodworking machinery (band saw, circular saw, router, jig saw, et cetera).

When it becomes necessary to purchase any type of special machinery to go into production on a certain specialized item or process, the gunsmith should not hesitate to write to a machine tool manufacturer or dealer and ask their advice. In this modern age, new machines for doing special work are developed so rapidly that no one but a person connected with the machinery business could very well keep abreast of them.

As a bow-out to this little dissertation on shop power tools, it might be well to mention that the mere acquisition of a drill press, lathe, et cetera does not mean very much unless they are properly set up, discriminately used, and periodically cleaned and lubricated.

It is surprising how many "mechanics" will invest $500 in a lathe and drill press, set them up on any old table, without regard to their being level, pound them harder than they should be, and complain to the manufacturer when unoiled bearings and grit-laden parts cause the machines to break down.

Hand Tools (common)

Aside from the special tools, jigs and fixtures (covered in Chapter Three and elsewhere in the book) which must be fashioned by the gunsmith himself to accomplish various operations incident only to gun repair work, he must have a well rounded selection of common hand tools. Common, though, only in the sense that they can generally be purchased as stock items, for in some instances they must be somewhat modified to be fully suitable for gunsmithing purposes.

In the following list covering these tools, comments will be made where it is deemed necessary; for the others, no comment is needed.

Taps and Dies. From machine screw size 1–64 to National Fine 1/2"–20, these important thread cutting tools should be purchased in the beginning as tap and die together rather than separate units. Then when it is necessary to enlarge a threaded hole that has been damaged or crossed, a new screw body can be lathe-turned and threaded to fit.

Sizes most commonly used are:

Machine Screw Sizes

1–64	4–48	8–32
2–56	5–40	8–36
3–48	5–44	10–24
3–56	6–32	10–32
4–36	6–40	12–24
4–40	6–48	12–28

Fractional Sizes

1/4"–20	5/16"–24	7/16"–14
1/4"–28	3/8"–16	7/16"–20
5/16"–18	3/8"–24	1/2"–20

Occasionally a metric thread is found in foreign guns that must be recut (chased), but this is usually so rarely encountered that having a selection of this type of taps and dies on hand is scarcely necessary. Over a period of time a gunsmith usually does acquire quite a selection of metric taps and dies, which he finds necessary to purchase as the need arises.

In Chapter Nineteen there is a rather complete listing of some metric taps and dies, as well as the regular type, with recommended tap size and body drill dimensions.

Tap Holders and Die Stocks. There are many models and sizes of tap holders and die stocks available commercially, and the gunsmith will probably find it necessary to purchase two or three different sizes of each to accommodate the various sizes of taps and dies.

Screwdrivers. In the gunsmith's tool kit, the screwdriver is king. Yet, for his purposes, there are very few commercially made screwdrivers which are, as manufactured, suitable for gun repair work. To be of proper shape for working on guns, screwdrivers, as purchased, must be reground. Figure 5 illustrates a screwdriver bit as regularly ground, and the shape of a bit as reground for gunsmithing work.

The necessity for this regrinding can be better appreciated when we look at the screwdriver slot in the head of any screw and take notice of the shape of this slot. It is straight from top to bottom, and of uniform width. By putting a taper-ground screwdriver in this slot, chances are that if any force is required to dislodge or seat a screw, the slot will become enlarged at the top. And nothing is more indicative of poor workmanship than burred or battered screw heads. Aptly, they are often referred to as the "apprentice's trademark."

A good stock of various size screwdrivers is absolutely necessary, ranging in size from the small jeweler's type, used in removing precision-type sight screws, to the heavy duty-type for dislodging rusted-tight stock and receiver screws.

Screwdrivers can be made from drill rod and then hardened and tempered, but usually, for all practical purposes, a "near right size" one can be bought locally and reground to the needed size. Good commercially made screwdrivers (not the ten-cent store type) will last indefinitely and the gunsmith should not hesitate to invest anywhere from 50¢ to $1.00 for each one.

Making screwdrivers is something that this writer can only recommend as a last resort, for they must be heat treated properly if they are to be of any real worth, and the time required to do this, in addition to making the blade, handle, and ferrule, and assembling them, brings the cost per tool well above the $1.00 mark.

Pliers. When properly cared for and used on work for which they are designed, good pliers should last for many years. A practical assortment consists of one pair each: Standard Side-Cutting Pliers; Long Needlenose Pliers; Short Needlenose Pli-

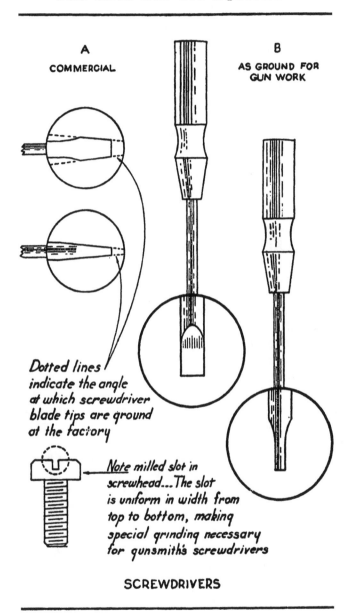

A
COMMERCIAL

B
AS GROUND FOR
GUN WORK

Dotted lines
indicate the angle
at which screwdriver
blade tips are ground
at the factory

Note milled slot in
screwhead...The slot
is uniform in width from
top to bottom, making
special grinding necessary
for gunsmith's screwdrivers

SCREWDRIVERS

Figure 5

ers; Barrel and Tube Pliers; Slip-joint Combination Pliers; and the Bernard Parallel-action Pliers, which is almost a one-hand vise in that the jaws hold pins, parts, et cetera so firmly with a minimum of applied hand pressure.

Hammers and Mallets. The conventional machinist's ball-peen hammer, in 3 oz., 6 oz., 8 oz., 12 oz., and 16 oz. weights, is the backbone of the hammer department. For some jobs a copper, lead, fiber, or plastic hammer is a necessary adjunct.

For woodwork, a wooden mallet and a rawhide mallet are equally desirous.

Files. For all general purposes, files can be classed under nine headings. They are: Pillar, Taper, Round, Half Round, Square, Slim Taper (Triangle), Flat, Hand and Mill. Besides these there are special files for gunsmithing work, such as Slotting, Checkering, Knife-edge, Heart-shape, Sear-notch and Screwhead.

All of these files, in both groups, are made in different lengths, widths and degrees of coarseness.

In a short time the mechanic learns to know exactly how many and what kind of files he must have in order to accomplish his work efficiently. Aside from a general selection bought at the beginning, additions should be made as the type of work one does make them necessary. This is the surest method of selecting and buying files.

When files become dull they should be retired from service and put aside for future use to be ground into scrapers, chisels or similar special tools.

Here is a little suggestion that might help to keep files from getting dull before they should. When breaking in a new file, do it on a piece of brass or bronze. Also, never start a new file on a thin piece of steel or iron. The narrow edge tends to snap off the points of the teeth.

Wood Chisels. Needed in widths of $\frac{1}{8}"$—$\frac{1}{4}"$—$\frac{3}{8}"$—$\frac{1}{2}"$—$\frac{3}{4}"$—$1"$ for ordinary stock repair and alteration work; plus a set of gouges in sizes $\frac{1}{4}"$—$\frac{1}{2}"$—$\frac{3}{4}"$—$1"$. Good chisels are cheaper and better in the long run—don't be penny-wise.

Hacksaw Frame. Preferably the adjustable type which can accommodate blades of different lengths, plus a supply of blades ranging from 14 teeth per inch, for sawing heavy stock that requires plenty of chip clearance, to the 32 teeth per inch type, for use on tubing and other fine cutting work.

Wood Saws. One each of rip, crosscut and back saw should fill this order adequately. Also, a coping saw and keyhole saw are time-savers if very much stock making is anticipated.

Drift Punches (Also called Pin Punches). Ranking in importance with screwdrivers and files, drift punches, while simple, must be of high quality as well as of great variety. And while this common tool, in its sizes from $\frac{1}{64}''$ to $\frac{1}{4}''$ in diameter, can easily be turned from drill rod on a lathe, the writer strongly recommends the purchase of these items from commercial sources because of the difficulties involved in properly hardening and tempering them. When an emergency repair situation requires a size of punch that is not available, then, as always, necessity becomes the mother of improvisation and a special punch can be quickly turned out that will serve the purpose.

Although there is a great sense of satisfaction gained from making tools that are used day in and day out by one's self, the gunsmith would do well to bear in mind that there are some tools, many in fact, that are well made by reliable manufacturers and sold at a fair price. Drift punches are in this category. For a list of the names of drift punch manufacturers, as well as fabricators of other tools mentioned in this and other chapters of the book, see Chapter Twenty.

Brace and Bits. For stock work and general shop maintenance, a good ratchet type brace with $\frac{1}{4}''$—$\frac{3}{8}''$—$\frac{1}{2}''$—$\frac{3}{4}''$—$1''$ bits is very helpful. The brace can also be fitted with special adapter rods for holding emery cloth or steel wool, which are in turn used for polishing rifle chambers, revolver cylinder chambers and shotgun bores.

For loosening up very stubborn screws, a brace can be fitted with a screwdriver bit and used to exert a great deal of properly applied force. The screwdriver bits for this sort of work are commercially procurable.

Reamers. These are very expensive items and a set which included: the taper pin assortment from #3/0 to #6; straight reamers from $\frac{1}{16}''$ to $1''$ by sixteenths; and the most often needed sizes of adjustable and expanding reamers, would be perfect, but the price would run to three figures. Therefore, the man with limited capital should buy only those he must have as the occasion requires. In this connection, though, do a little forethinking. If a job is presented that will require a reamer, buy or order it before it is actually needed. Sometimes the local dealer might be closed or "out of stock" when the gunsmith arrives with that "I must have it now" look in his eye.

Breast Drill or Hand Drill. Either one of these will serve well when it is necessary to drill a hole in some part of a gun (wooden or metal) that cannot or need not be put on the power drill press. Also very useful in connection with holding brass balls and countersink for barrel crowning work.

Center Drills. For use in lathe, drill press, and breast or hand drill.

Countersinks. Have a few of different sizes and angles (60° and 82°) for both wood and metal work.

Measuring and Layout Tools. The following listing includes all the tools and instruments of this category that are essential to good gunsmithing. Some of these precision items are a bit on the expensive side when one has to go out and buy them all at one time, but considering the years of good service they will render, if properly handled, one can scarcely consider them as being really costly.

Precision measuring tools eliminate guess work and in the field of gunsmithing, where an ill-guessed measurement might easily mean the difference between a safe and an unsafe gun, the gunsmith should have no doubts about investing in tools that will help him to do safer and better work.

Micrometer Caliper (Outside). Having 0 to 1″ capacity with a thimble graduated so that readings down to a ten thousandth of an inch can be taken.

Micrometer (Depth). Equipped with three interchangeable rods giving a range of measurement from 0 to 3″ by thousandths of an inch.

Vernier Caliper (Inside and Outside). Having a capacity of at least 6″ and equipped to give a reading in thousandths of an inch.

Steel Rules. In 6″ and 12″ lengths, graduated in 8ths and 16ths on one side, and 32ths and 64ths on the other. A rule graduated in 10ths of an inch is very useful for scope-mounting work. For working on foreign guns a steel rule, about 15 centimeters long, and graduated into millimeters, is essential.

For stock work and general measuring where lengths over 12″ are common, a flexible steel rule about 6 feet long, of the kind that can be pushed in or pulled from a small case, is almost indispensable.

In Figure 6 there is illustrated a little item that comes in very handy at times. It is a product of the L. S. Starrett Company, who make precision tools of all types. (Send for their catalog— it's a worthy addition to any shop library. Their address is in Chapter Twenty.) The Starrett outfit needs no publicity from this writer but their holder, with insertable rules, is so good that it deserves special mention. It is a dandy tool for making measurements in out-of-the-way places and the rule can be inserted at any angle. One holder is good for all rules, since any of the latter can be replaced easily and quickly by one of another size or having other graduations.

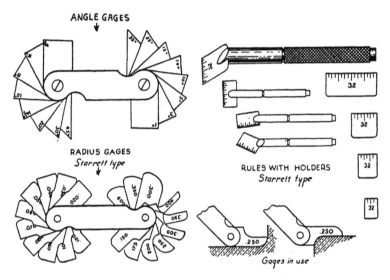

FIGURE 6

Squares. For stock work and general woodwork, a carpenter's square is best. For general layout work on metal the combination square with protractor head and center head is required, plus a pair of tool maker's squares for sight-mounting work.

Levels (or spirit levels, as they are frequently called). Used in connection with scope-mounting work. A pair of small levels (about 2″ long) will fill the bill in this category. The larger level, while of little use for gunsmithing work directly, is necessary when it comes to setting up power tools, such as lathe, milling machine, et cetera. However, the machine dealer will usually lend one of these out when he makes a sale so hold out for this favor when buying.

Universal Bevel (also called adjustable try square). Used for testing surfaces that are not at right angles to each other.

Screw Pitch Gage. For measuring the pitch of screw threads.

Angle Gage. For measuring angles. The individual ground leaves are arranged in a little holder, as are the leaves of a screw pitch gage.

Radius Gage. For measuring radii in small parts. A great help to the mechanic who does much part duplicating.

Thickness Gage. Of the kind having 25 leaves ranging in thickness from .0015″ to .025″ by thousandths.

Taper Gage. Used for measuring the diameter of small holes. The leaves of these gages are so made that measurements from .010″ to .500″ by thousandths can be taken. Excellent for getting the size of bores (at the muzzle), revolver chambers and the like.

Center Gage. For checking the points of tool bits used for thread cutting. Also used to check position of a tool bit in relation to chucked work that is to be threaded.

Universal Surface Gage. Although not absolutely necessary for everyday work, this layout tool, when used on a flat, true surface (surface plate or piece of plate glass) is very helpful in doing sight-mounting work.

Marking Gage. For use in stock layout work.

Scriber. The type having one end bent at 90° for getting at inside "places," and the other end straight for conventional marking work seems to be as good as any.

Center Punches. Buy them or make them, but be sure that the point is ground at the correct angle and that it is concentric to the body of the punch.

Some mechanics like the automatic center punch which makes a mark without being struck by a hammer. Good for layout work where the gunsmith has only one free hand.

Prick Punches. Same comment as for center punches.

Outside Spring Calipers. A pair each of the 3″ and 6″ size will take care of all normal requirements.

Inside Spring Calipers. Same comment as for outside spring calipers.

Spring Dividers. For gunsmithing work the 4″ size is large enough.

Hermaphrodite Calipers. Not used too often in gun repair work but it pays to have the 4″ size available for use.

Parallels. Used in connection with setting up work in a drill press or milling machine. On a surface plate or a piece of plate glass they are used to make the job of scope-mounting easier and more exact. Get a pair in the ½" x ¾" and the ½" x 1" size and keep them in a felt-lined (oil-soaked) box when not being used.

Surface Plate. In discussing and evaluating some of the above precision tools, they were mentioned as being used with a surface plate because of the flat, true, hard base that a surface plate affords. In short, a surface plate is a true, common base for making comparative measurements or layout on a subject piece that is placed upon it. For lining up sight blocks and taking certain accurate measurements, such as the height of a cartridge case, the surface plate is more than handy—it is necessary.

If the gunsmith does not feel he can afford to purchase a surface plate, then he should at least buy a 2' x 2' piece of ⁵⁄₁₆" plate glass and use it as a fair substitute.

Bunsen Burner. For heat treating and coloring pins or small parts. An alcohol lamp will serve the same purpose if gas for a Bunsen burner is not available.

Cold Chisels. Small sizes for chipping work. (See Figure 7.)

Oilstones. One large India double-faced stone for sharpening chisels, scribers, et cetera; also an assortment of the small square, round, and triangular shapes for trigger pull work and for removing burrs from inaccessible places in gun frames and receivers. See Chapter Seven for details.

Soldering Coppers (or Soldering Irons, as they are more popularly known). One of the electrically heated type and a pair of light-weight flame heated soldering coppers, chiefly for doing sight and parts duplicating work.

Wood Planes. For stock work the gunsmith should have a low angle block plane for fitting butt-plates and recoil pads, and a jack plane for general work around the shop and on forearms.

Spoke-Shave. Helpful in connection with rough-shaping stocks and forearms.

Draw-Knife. Same comment as for spoke-shave except that it takes a lot more skill to use a draw-knife efficiently.

"C" Clamps. These come in so many useful sizes as far as gunsmithing work is concerned that it is difficult to recommend anything but a pair each of "C" clamps having a jaw opening of: from 0 to 2"; from 0 to 4"; from 0 to 6"; and from 0 to 8". As special need arises, other sizes can be bought. There are innumer-

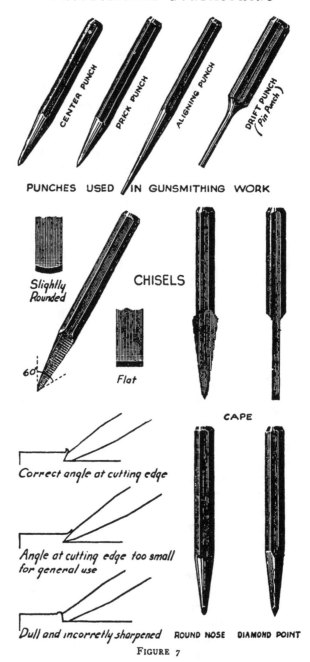

PUNCHES USED IN GUNSMITHING WORK

CHISELS

Slightly Rounded

60°

Flat

Correct angle at cutting edge

Angle at cutting edge too small for general use

Dull and incorrectly sharpened

CAPE

ROUND NOSE   DIAMOND POINT

FIGURE 7

able uses for "C" clamps around a gun repair shop, from holding sight bases in place temporarily, to fastening work to a drill press table.

Toolmaker's Clamps (or Parallel Clamps). These are excellent for holding scope blocks to a barrel while the holes are being drilled. Two of these clamps are all that are needed for the gun repair shop.

In Chapter Three the manufacture and use of special clamps is discussed and illustrated.

Scrapers. One flat scraper, and one three-corner scraper (made from files having the serrations ground off and then drawn to straw color) will be needed to dress down a part, chamber edge, or receiver recess where no other tool will do. (See Figure 8.)

FIGURE 8

A scraper is a very efficient tool and can be used to true up a surface or dress down an edge like no other hand or machine tool can. It behooves any gunsmith worthy of the name to learn how to use the different types of scrapers.

Metals, Materials and Shop Supplies

Incident to the making of special parts and tools, and the repair and refinishing of stocks, the gunsmith must have in his shop at all times at least a limited but varied stock of metals, oils, solvents, finishing compounds and other general hardware supplies. The following list, of course is by no means complete, but it should serve as a good indication of the basic requirements in this category.

Drill Rod. Made in round, square and flat shapes. It would be wonderful if the gunsmith could have a length of each type in every size. However, since the cost would be prohibitive, to say nothing of the space required to store it, the next best thing is to have a few feet of the popular size round stock in $\frac{1}{32}''$, $\frac{1}{16}''$, $\frac{1}{8}''$, $\frac{3}{16}''$, $\frac{1}{4}''$, $\frac{5}{16}''$, $\frac{3}{8}''$ and $\frac{1}{2}''$ diameter. From these pieces almost any size pin for gun repair work can be fashioned.

Tool Steel. For making gun parts (sears, hammers, links, et cetera) flat tool steel is necessary. Buy three-foot lengths of this metal in the following sizes: $\frac{1}{8}'' \times 2''$; $\frac{3}{16}'' \times 2''$; $\frac{1}{4}'' \times 2''$; $\frac{5}{16}'' \times 2''$; $\frac{3}{8}'' \times 2''$; $\frac{1}{2}'' \times 2''$; $\frac{5}{8}'' \times 2''$; and ask the dealer what the particular steel's carbon range is; this is important information when it comes to doing heat treatment of a part fabricated from steel.

Although other thicknesses and widths might be a bit closer to the size of a part being duplicated, if the above sizes are on hand at all times almost any emergency request can be met in a professional manner.

For making punches, chisels, and tools for shop use, tool steel in round, hexagon, and square shape is desirable.

Cold Rolled Steel. Good for such parts as barrel ramps, barrel ribs and sling swivel bases. Can be case-hardened, and therefore is suitable for parts which require a hard surface and somewhat flexible core.

Best sizes to stock are three-foot long squares in $\frac{1}{4}''$, $\frac{3}{16}''$, $\frac{3}{8}''$, $\frac{1}{2}''$ and $\frac{3}{4}''$ sizes. Buy other lengths as needed.

Brass and Copper Rods. A few feet of each in $\frac{1}{4}''$, $\frac{3}{8}''$, and $\frac{1}{2}''$ will always be found useful in making punches, bushings or screws for certain antique weapons.

Solder. A roll each of acid core and rosin core solder will usually suffice for all gun repair work.

Emery Cloth, Crocus Cloth, and Sandpaper. Sheets of each in the various grades from roughest to finest grit are absolutely necessary.

Powdered Emery. Three pounds of the various grits, from #90 to flour of emery, will last the gunsmith for some time. Its main use is in dressing fiber, felt or canvas wheels for polishing parts prior to blueing. For details, see chapter on Grinding, Polishing and Blueing.

Pumice Stone. A few pounds of this abrasive will be found very necessary in stock polishing work.

Glue. The flake type to be heated in a double boiler; a bottle of iron glue and caseine glue are very handy for quick jobs. DuPont Household Cement (in tubes) has proved its worth as an all-purpose glue for a long time. It is an adhesive worth trying.

Spar Varnish, Lacquer (DuPont), **Shellac** (white), **Linseed Oil,
Japan Drier, Turpentine, Wood Alcohol, Varnish Remover, Wood
Filler, Wood Stains** (oil base), **Tung Oil, Beeswax.** These are the
gunsmith's minimum needs for stock finishing. After he has
practiced for a while, he will no doubt have 66 other liquid compounds, each adding a special something to the "secret formula"
stock finish he has developed. This acquisition comes only with
time, though, and serves as a bit of "window dressing" to impress
those gun owners who honestly believe in the superiority of "specially concocted" stock mixtures. Just so long as no one gets
gypped or handed an inferior job, this "hocus-pocus" practice
cannot be condemned. After all, there is a bit of witchery in most
of us and what Barnum said applies to everybody in some way or
another.

Oils and Greases. After a gunsmith has cleaned or repaired a
gun he should, of course, as a matter of policy, lubricate it. If a
gun is to be stored away the gunsmith can, if requested, prepare
the weapon for this hibernation. In either case he should use only
the best compounds for the purpose, and of the many products on
the market for these purposes, some are excellent and others—
well, are just not as good as they might be. Therefore, it behooves
the gunsmith to purchase and use only oils and greases that are
made especially for the purpose and bear a reliable trade mark.

For lubricating internal moving parts, such oils as Fiendoil,
Hoppe's Gun Oil, or oils made by Winchester, Remington, Savage, and Ithaca are quite satisfactory. (For additional comments
on oils see Chapter Eighteen.)

For preserving weapons prior to extended storage, Hoppe's
Gun Grease, Stoeger's Barrel Grease, or grease marketed by
Winchester or Remington can be relied upon.

For the latest and most complete technical information on gun
oils, solvents and greases, follow the Dope Bag column of The
American Rifleman. If in doubt about some particular lubricating or preservative compound he intends to use, the gunsmith
should not hesitate to write the Editor of this column and ask
what N.R.A. tests on the product have brought to light.

Aside from the metals, greases, oils and abrasives mentioned
above, there are other special abrasives, glues, et cetera that are
required for special phases of gunsmithing work, and in the best
interest of complete understanding are described in various chapters under appropriate headings.

CHAPTER THREE

SPECIAL TOOLS AND FIXTURES

IN AS much as gunsmithing is a very specialized mechanical business, there is, naturally enough, a need for a good many gadgets, tools, jigs and fixtures that cannot always be commercially procured and must, therefore, be made by the gunsmith himself.

Some of these items are simple in construction and easily made from scrap material. Others, while not as simple or easy to make, are, nevertheless, worthy of the time and expense required to construct them, for in the long run they make easier and less hit-or-miss many of the everyday phases of gun repair work.

Within this chapter several of the more necessary special tools and fixtures will be described and illustrated. Needless to say, not all of them are original, but they will prove helpful and should give an indication of the possibilities of special tools.

Necessity will be the mother of invention when the gunsmith finds it difficult to replace certain springs, pins or parts in a weapon. For it is important, when confronted with such a situation, that he analyze the problem and reason out the why of the difficulty, with an eye towards a method for making the task easier.

Although there is not, as a rule, any commercial market for the sale of special tools for gun repair work, an exceptionally simple contrivance which might have an appeal to the home tinkerer or repairman can be written up in article form with suitable illustrations and often sold to a sporting or gun magazine; by the same token many good ideas on the repair of guns are to be found from time to time in the pages of these publications.

As a last resort, on very knotty problems of adjustment, disassembly or assembly on a particular make and model of gun, it might not be amiss to write the manufacturer of the piece concerning the problem, requesting whatever information or literature that might be available.

.22 Caliber Headspace Gage. A complete layout of the very important gages for checking headspace on rifles (See Chapter Thirteen) is expensive and for ordinary gunsmithing not really necessary. Yet a pair (minimum and maximum) of these gages for the .22 caliber rim fire will be found to be very handy because of the great numbers of this caliber weapon in general circula-

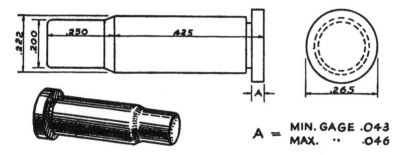

A = MIN. GAGE .043
MAX. ''   .046

HEADSPACE GAGE FOR .22 CAL. RIM FIRE GUN

FIGURE 9

tion. Although a dimensional drawing (Figure 9) is given here, it is better to purchase items of this nature from a factory or have them made by a toolmaker who can turn, harden and grind them to the very close dimensions required, unless, of course the gunsmith knows he can do the job himself—and correctly.

Firing Pin Protrusion Gages. Gages for measuring firing pin protrusion (Figure 10) are best made from flat steel stock, which should be hardened, polished and marked with an electric pencil as to what type weapons it is to be used on. Variations of this gage, other than those illustrated, can be made for getting at certain firing pins which, by virtue of their location, are not accessible, or present some particular problem.

In using one of these gages, it is imperative that the firing pin be pushed forward to its maximum protrusion and that the gage be held perfectly flat against the bolt face. To that end, the face of the gage which rests against the bolt face must be perfectly true and smooth so an accurate reading will be obtained.

Tool for Colt Cylinder Ratchets. The tool illustrated in Figure 11, used for removing cylinder ratchets (ejectors) from any modern Colt revolver, is one that the gunsmith will find far superior to a pair of needlenose pliers, which usually mar up the

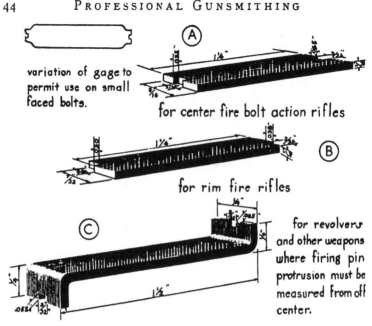

variation of gage to
permit use on small
faced bolts.

for center fire bolt action rifles

for rim fire rifles

for revolvers
and other weapons
where firing pin
protrusion must be
measured from off
center.

FIRING PIN PROTRUSION GAGES

FIGURE 10

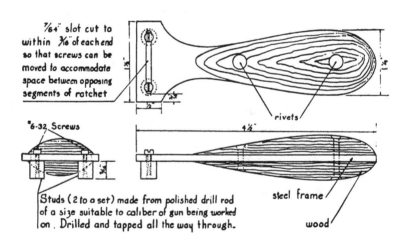

⁷⁄₆₄" slot cut to
within ³⁄₁₆" of each end
so that screws can be
moved to accommodate
space between opposing
segments of ratchet

rivets

"6-32 Screws

Studs (2 to a set) made from polished drill rod
of a size suitable to caliber of gun being worked
on . Drilled and tapped all the way through.

steel frame

wood

TOOL FOR REMOVING RATCHETS FROM COLT REVOLVERS

FIGURE 11

part badly when any amount of force is required to screw the ratchet off or on.

The body of this tool is made from sheet iron, or sheet steel, about ⅛″ thick and fitted with two pieces of walnut shaped so that a comfortable handle is formed. The walnut pieces can be riveted to the frame in the same way as are handles on a kitchen knife.

One special note—on the Colt D.A. 38, which was used by the Army for a few years prior to the adoption of the .45, the ratchet has a left-handed thread. Therefore, when loosening one of these, turn it in a clockwise direction, in other words, opposite from what you would expect.

Recoil Plate Tool. For fixing recoil plates into place on revolvers the tool illustrated in Figure 12 makes this otherwise hard

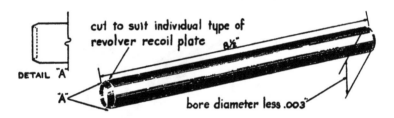

cut to suit individual type of
revolver recoil plate

DETAIL "A"

bore diameter less .003″

TOOL FOR SETTING REVOLVER RECOIL PLATES IN PLACE

Figure 12

job very easy. No exact dimensions are given for the setting end of the tool because of the different sizes of plates that are encountered in different models of Colt and Smith & Wesson revolvers. The proper dimension for the setting size of the tool is best determined by measuring the collar ridge around the recoil plate and adjusting the tool to that size.

The tool should be made of drill rod, hardened, and tempered to a dark blue (See Chapter Fifteen). While the tool illustrated is for a Colt revolver, the same type of tool is used on Smith & Wesson revolvers, except that the formed end of it must be made smaller to fit the small recoil plates common to Smith & Wesson revolvers.

The entire tool should be finished to a high scratch-free surface so that the bore will not be injured when the tool is put into it.

The 8½" length is suggested because a tool of such a size will fit any particular type of revolver it is designed for, irrespective of the barrel length.

Stock Bolt Screwdriver. For loosening those stubborn long bolts which are used in many types of shotguns to fasten the stock to the receiver, the gunsmith will do well to make himself a screwdriver of the type illustrated in Figure 13. Make from ⅝" drill

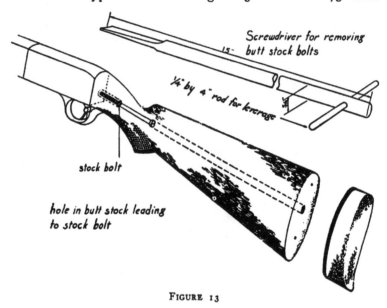

Screwdriver for removing butt stock bolts

¼" by 4" rod for leverage

stock bolt

hole in butt stock leading to stock bolt

FIGURE 13

rod, forged at one end, ground to final shape, and then hardened and drawn to a dark blue. The leverage afforded by the long shank and 90° handle will be appreciated when one of those rusted-in screws is being dislodged.

Bore Examination Mirrors. One of the operations most frequently performed by the gunsmith is that of bore examination. With weapons in which the bore can be removed quickly for close examination, or observed directly from either breech or muzzle end, no special accessories are needed. However, this condition exists only with some weapons; for the others an indirect method of observation must be employed. Two tools for accomplishing offset bore examination are illustrated in Figure 14. The dental mirror, readily procurable from a local dentist or dental supply house, can be used on any type of gun, while the bore reflector is best suited to big bore weapons (caliber .30 or over).

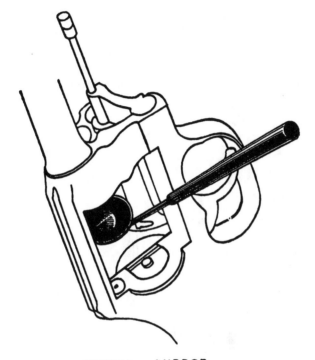

DENTAL MIRROR

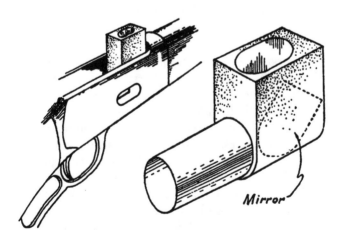

BORE REFLECTOR

Figure 14

Hammer Nose Tool (Revolver). When removing firing pins (hammer noses) from either Colt or Smith & Wesson revolver hammers, there is always the danger of bending or breaking the hammer if it is held in a vise to accomplish this operation. By using the fixture illustrated in Figure 15, one not only eliminates

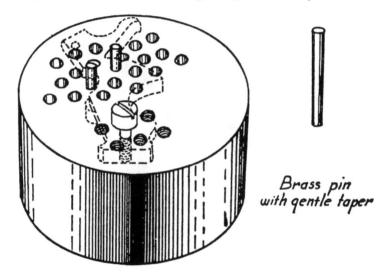

Brass pin with gentle taper

BLOCK FOR HOLDING REVOLVER HAMMER

FIGURE 15

this disturbing possibility, but also makes easier the removal of the hammer pin with a minimum of effort. A series of holes can be drilled in this fixture so that it will accommodate all the different sizes of Colt and Smith & Wesson hammers.

Hand Grinders (Motor Driven). Under the heading of Shop Machines and Accessories, a most versatile machine tool was not included, because it belongs more correctly under the heading of Special Tools. Known under various trade names, the most popular of which is Handee Tool, it is composed of a small high-speed motor enclosed in a casing which can be held in the hand, and equipped with a chuck having a ⅛″ capacity. This tool can be used to great advantage for removing burrs from the inside of frames or receivers of guns, or enlarging the hole in a peep sight, just to mention a few of its capabilities. By using dental burrs, small drills, and mounted abrasive wheels in its chuck, this high-speed hand tool will more than pay for itself in a short time. It is not made to take the place of the drill press or grinding head, but rather is a special tool in its own right without peer.

A motor-driven flexible shaft equipped with a chuck will perform tasks akin to those accomplished by the hand grinder, but the latter's comparatively slow r.p.m. places it as a bad second.

In using either the drill press, hand grinder, or flexible shaft, however, the gunsmith will find wide use for the dental burrs previously mentioned. Procurable from the local dentist without cost when they have become dull for his purposes, they are still more than keen enough for many phases of metal cutting work.

Front Sight Fixture (.45 Automatic Pistol). For installing and staking into position a front sight on the .45 automatic pistol the fixture illustrated in Figure 16 should be of no small help. After the old sight has been removed, the new blade is placed in position, and the slide is then laid between the jaws of the fixture. The back end of the slide is supported parallel to the front end by a piece of hard wood placed under the former. Then the front sight stud projecting through the slide can be peened over with a drift punch and the excess metal cut off with a fine round file.

Plunger Tube Rivet-set. (.45 Automatic). Although it is not very often that one encounters a loose plunger tube on a .45 automatic pistol the pin and rivet-set arrangement, as illustrated in Figure 17 provides a safe and efficient way to do the job. Make the rivet-set and the pin that goes in the tube opening, of drill rod, hardened, and tempered to straw color. The rivet-set handle is best made from cold rolled steel.

Dummy Pins for Assembly Work. When it is necessary to subassemble parts before fitting them into a frame or receiver where, in turn, a pin holds them all in place, the gunsmith will find it advantageous if he has a collection of special short pins handy to hold these subassemblies together while the main pin is driven into place. These special pins should be made from drill rod with a slight taper on each end. After being turned, tapered, and highly polished, they must be hardened and then drawn to a dark brown or light purple. Figure 18 shows the proper shape and typical use of these pins.

Rifle Rack. A very handy rack for holding rifles and shotguns which are being worked on is illustrated in Figure 19. The crank at the butt end of the rack is used to tighten up a leather-faced wooden jaw against the stock of the weapon, thus holding it

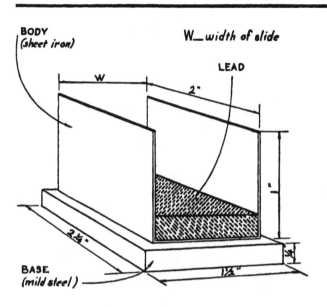

BODY
(sheet iron)

W—width of slide

LEAD

BASE
(mild steel)

FIXTURE FOR SUPPORTING 45 GOVERNMENT
PISTOL SLIDE WHEN INSTALLING FRONT SIGHT

TO CONSTRUCT

1. Fold piece of sheet iron to given dimension to form body.　2. Rivet body to the base 3. Block both ends with sheet metal and pour in lead to form a cushion about ¼" deep 4. Remove temporary sheet metal ends and trim off excess lead.

NOTE

'Body' should be light gauge sheet iron not heavier than 015'. In this way the body of this device will be flexible enough to accommodate slides that are slightly oversize—

FIGURE 16

y in place. Care should be taken, of course, not to apply too
1 pressure against the stock when tightening, lest the stock
h be marred. More de luxe versions of this rack can be made
e gunsmith sees fit, and attachments can be made which will
:ase its versatility for gun repair work.

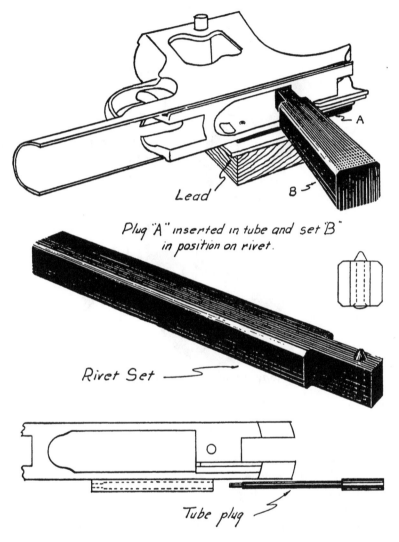

Plug "A" inserted in tube and set "B"
in position on rivet.

Rivet Set

Tube plug

PLUNGER TUBE RIVET SET

FIGURE 17

Tap for Thread Chasing (Revolver). If a gunsmith expects to fit many revolver barrels to either of the two famous makes of American six-shooters, he should make or have made up for him special taps, to be used as thread chasers, for cleaning out or slightly enlarging the threads in the revolver frames. To obtain

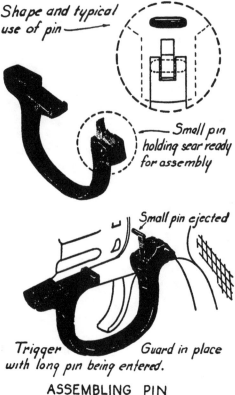

Shape and typical use of pin

Small pin holding sear ready for assembly

Small pin ejected

Trigger with long pin being entered.

Guard in place

ASSEMBLING PIN

FIGURE 18

the proper dimensions for these special taps, one need only "mike" the outside diameter of the threaded barrel and then cut a tap on the lathe having a .006″ taper in its length. Thus, the further the tap is run into the frame, the more metal will be removed. Figure 20 indicates the steps in the making of a typical tap.

The particular dimensions must be supplied after measurements of diameter and pitch have been made. Great care must be exercised in using these taps lest too much metal be removed, and a resulting loose fit be the result. With this, as with all phases of parts fitting work, it must always be remembered that it is easy to remove metal but nearly impossible to replace it. Let caution and common sense always be partners to the gunsmith in his every task.

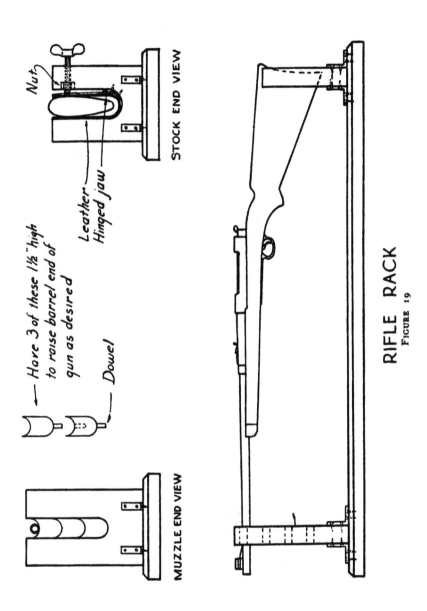

Nut

Leather

Hinged jaw

STOCK END VIEW

— Have 3 of these 1½" high
to raise barrel end of
gun as desired

Dowel

MUZZLE END VIEW

RIFLE RACK

Figure 19

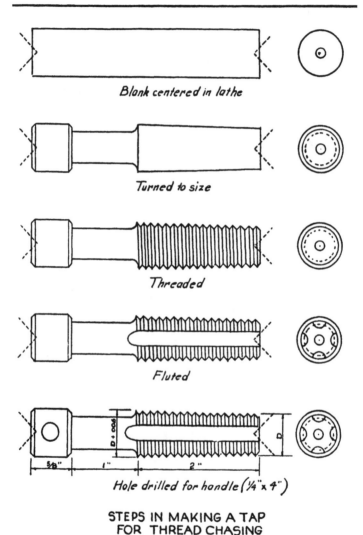

Blank centered in lathe

Turned to size

Threaded

Fluted

Hole drilled for handle (¼" x 4")

STEPS IN MAKING A TAP
FOR THREAD CHASING

Figure 20

Barrel Dent Removers (Shotgun). In Figure 21 are illustrate
few suggested styles of shotgun barrel dent removers. The d
ensions given in these drawings are those which have been a
pted by the manufacturers of American shotguns. Therefor

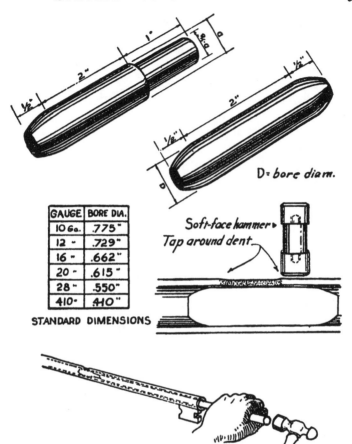

D= *bore diam.*

GAUGE	BORE DIA.
10 Ga.	.775"
12 "	.729"
16 "	.662"
20 "	.615"
28 "	.550"
410 "	.410"

STANDARD DIMENSIONS

Soft-face hammer ▸
Tap around dent

SHOTGUN DENT REMOVERS

TAPER FOR REMOVING MUZZLE DENTS

FIGURE 21

it is imperative that the sizes of the gunsmith's dent removers do not exceed these figures.

Dent removers should be made from high quality tool steel, turned within .006″ of final dimension, hardened, and tempered, and then precision ground to exact size. They should be devoid of tool marks and any other surface imperfection that would tend to scratch or mar the mirror-like finish of the best shotgun bore. After each usage they should be carefully wiped dry of all traces of foreign matter and covered all over with a heavy grease to preclude any possibility of rusting (see Chapter Fourteen concerning the proper use of dent removers).

Brass Punches. For knocking out parts that would be damaged if a steel punch were used, the set of brass punches illustrated in Figure 22 is recommended.

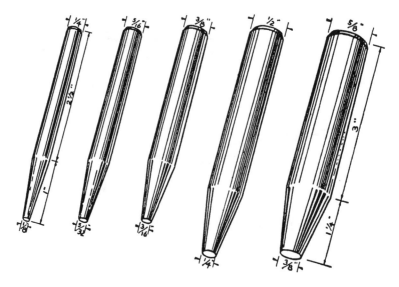

SET ℴ BRASS PUNCHES

FIGURE 22

This writer also suggests that punches of the 3/16″ and 3/8″ dimensions also be made from copper—to be used on especially light or delicate parts where the softness of copper would be desirable.

Clamps. Aside from the clamps mentioned in Chapter Two, the gunsmith will note as he does a greater volume and wider variety

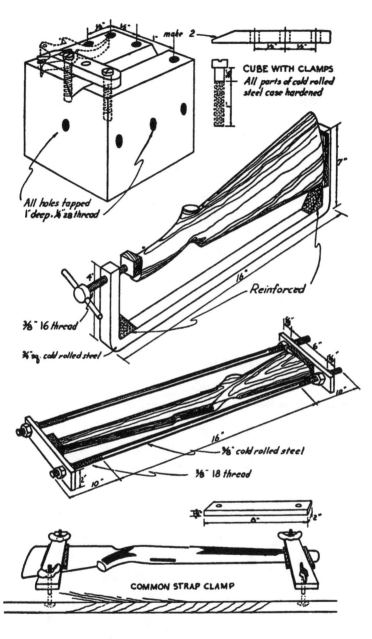

make 2

CUBE WITH CLAMPS
All parts of cold rolled
steel case hardened

All holes tapped
1" deep. ¼" 28 thread

4"

⅜" 16 thread

¾" sq. cold rolled steel

7"

16"

Reinforced

16"

6"

10"

2"   10"

⅜" cold rolled steel

⅜" 18 thread

6"   2"

COMMON STRAP CLAMP

SPECIAL CLAMPS

Figure 23

57

of work, the need for clamps of every sort. Figure 23 shows a few special style clamps and some ways of using them.

Those illustrated should give the novice an idea of what can be done with a few pieces of metal and an assortment of bolts and nuts.

On clamps of the general "C" type, it is most advisable to weld or bolt some sort of reinforcement at the bent sections so that "give" or "spring" will be held to an imperceptible minimum.

Vise for Holding Pins. Although it is possible to hold small diameter pins ($\frac{3}{16}$" and under) in a regular vise without marring them, it more often than not involves wrapping the pin in emery cloth or putting lead jaws on the vise to insure that the pin will not be deformed when the "squeeze" is put on. Even with "padding" around it, a pin is still apt to tip to one side or another when being filed or honed because of the light jaw pressure on it. In Figure 24 is illustrated a vise that does away with all the preparatory and "kid glove" work generally associated with holding small pins.

Construction details are simple and should be obvious from the drawing. All parts are of cold rolled steel. They should be case-

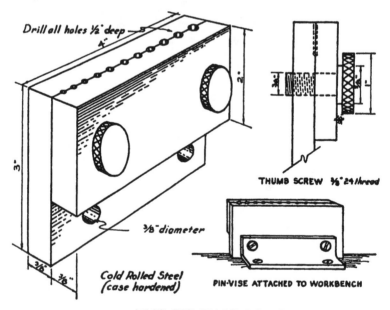

VISE FOR HOLDING PINS

Figure 24

hardened, however, after being machined. Another point to note: do not drill the holes for holding the pins until after the blocks have been drilled and tapped for the thumb screws, and the latter are tightly in place. Then mill or file the top of the two blocks true, while they are held together. Finally, center punch for the pin holes and drill them.

There is no fixed rule as to what size the pin holes in the vise should be. The gunsmith can "mike up" (measure with a micrometer) various samples of the most frequently encountered pins and use number size drills to make the holes.

This writer's pin holding vise has the following size holes in order: $\frac{1}{16}$"—$\frac{1}{32}$"; and number drill sizes: 60, 55, 52, 48, 43, 38, 33, 30, 28, 24, 20, 17, and 13.

To use the vise, just drop the pin to be held in a hole nearest the pin's size and tighten up on the thumb screws.

No spring arrangement is needed to force the vise jaws open in as much as the jaws are never opened more than $\frac{1}{64}$".

A pair of tweezers are handy to have near the vise for getting a grip on a short pin that drops down almost to vise top level when inserted in a hole.

Variations of the illustrated vise can be made to suit each individual's requirements and personal taste—(Oh, what mistakes are covered in thy name!).

Bottoming Chisels. If the gunsmith expects to do very much stock inletting, he will need a few bottoming chisels. Basically, a bottoming chisel (or bottoming tool if you prefer) is nothing more than a regular chisel that is off set. Figure 25 illustrates the general lines of two types of tools and also a few of the most frequently used cutting edge shapes. Although drill rod makes a satisfactory tool, when hardened and tempered correctly, tool steel makes a still better tool that will hold an edge longer and its use is recommended.

Bottoming Rasps. The bottoming rasps illustrated in Figure 25 are forged from drill rod or tool steel, ground to shape (square, half round, etc.) and then serrated. The teeth should be cut sharp and deep so that there will be plenty of chip clearance.

These rasps can be formed to any desired shape and, when hardened and tempered correctly, are of great assistance in inletting stocks and forearms. A tooth pitch of about 20 to the inch will leave a smooth surface, free from the "mouse-teeth marks" left by an ill-handled bottoming chisel.

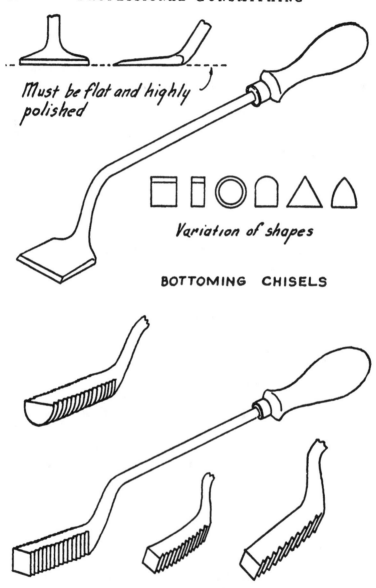

Must be flat and highly polished

Variation of shapes

BOTTOMING CHISELS

BOTTOMING RASPS

FIGURE 25

Magazine Dent Remover. In Figure 26 there are illustrated two methods of constructing a magazine dent remover.

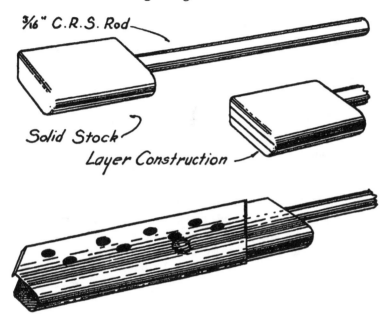

MAGAZINE DENT REMOVER

FIGURE 26

A magazine dent remover need not be fancy, milled from any special type of steel, or heat treated, but it must be right size for the magazine it is to be used in.

Although a dent remover fashioned from a solid piece of steel is the preferable type, the layer method of construction produces a very serviceable tool, which can be made quickly by soldering together pieces of flat stock whose combined dimensions are near to the desired finished size. In making a layer type dent remover, always place the two thickest pieces of stock on the outside so they, rather than the thin pieces, will be taking the pounding.

The ideal remover should be at least 2″ long and have a fairly smooth finish on the surfaces that contact the walls of the magazine.

Before using a magazine dent remover, always make certain that it and the inside of the magazine are clean and free from any particles of abrasive material that might cause the magazine to become scarred.

The secret of a good dent remover is its nearness to the shape and size of the magazine it is to be used in. Tolerance should run about minus .005" and plus zero.

After a dent has been removed, the magazine should be loaded to capacity with live cartridges and then inserted in the gun. The magazine should go into the gun easily and drop out readily (from weight of cartridges) when the magazine catch is released. If any "stickiness" or "sluggishness" is felt as the magazine is inserted or withdrawn, the chances are that the dent was knocked out a bit too hard, causing a bulge in the body of the magazine. Iron out any of these bulges or high spots before putting the job aside as being well done.

As a final check, run the cartridges from the magazine through the gun by operating the slide by hand. (Keep your fingers away from the trigger and point the gun towards a tub of sand while doing this; remember—safety with firearms is one of the few habits that is good for everybody.) This test will show up any tendency of the magazine follower to stick as it passes the area where the dent was.

As a general practice, dent removal should be confined to those magazines which are designed to be readily disassembled through their bottom, e.g., Walther, Luger, Mauser, C.Z., et al. It is very difficult, if not near impossible, to do an efficient dent removal job on a magazine which must be disassembled through its top, without injuring the lips. (See Chapter Twelve for importance of magazines.)

Dummy Cartridges. At not a few points in this book the use of dummy cartridges is recommended in connection with testing the mechanism of a gun or magazine.

As the name suggests, dummy cartridges are inert, and as such there is no chance of accidental discharge should the trigger be pulled while they are being run through the gun during the course of a functional test.

While it is possible to make a dummy cartridge by pulling the bullet, emptying the powder, firing the primer of a live round, and then reassembling the bullet into the case, this writer does not believe that dummies so made are of any worth unless the work is carried out by a reloader who has the shell-resizing and bullet-seating equipment to do the job correctly. Even at that, there is always the possibility that the case might be resized by a worn die which would produce an oversized case.

Oversized dummies as well as undersized dummies are no good since they are apt to lead the gunsmith to believe that something is wrong with a weapon being tested, when actually the cartridges are at fault.

Good dummies are best made from new components (unprimed cases, standard bullets) purchased from any of the companies which sell these items. The Pacific Gun Sight Company sells these components and it is reasonable to believe they will assemble dummy cartridges if a sufficient quantity is ordered. Write them for details.

Good dummy cartridges are essential and the gunsmith should not hesitate to make or order at least 20 in each of the most popular calibers he has occasion to work with. This list should include shotgun cartridge dummies made of brass (full length) and reinforced inside with a $\frac{1}{32}''$ tube extending from base to mouth.

A few final notes on dummy cartridges: they should be as near in weight to a standard, fully loaded cartridge as possible; the neck cannelure should be extra deep so that the bullet will not be forced into the case from continual usage; a piece of black rubber (from a tire) should be cemented in the primer pocket to cushion the firing pin blow.

Aside from the special tools described under this chapter heading, there are many others described and illustrated in other chapters of the book, which, because of their application to a particular phase of repair work being discussed, are more appropriate there.

CHAPTER FOUR

The Gun in for Repair

I T IS often remarked that a task well begun is half done. While this simile may be a bit overdrawn, it serves well to convey a very worthwhile bit of information.

In gun repair work the importance of beginning a job correctly with a definite plan of operation in mind is of the essence. This does not mean that a gunsmith must approach each repair project as a surgeon does a major operation, but rather he should know exactly what is wrong with a gun before he starts to fix it; and when he begins the actual repair work he must have a definite plan in mind to follow.

Naturally, after a gunsmith has plied his trade for a few years, he has gained enough experience on certain types of gun repair jobs to go ahead and process them in an efficient manner without any special thought or effort being necessary.

For the novice gunsmith, and even the experienced one who from time to time is called upon to trouble-shoot on a weapon foreign to his talents, there are some simple yet efficient procedures that can be followed, which should prove to be very helpful towards the making of a smooth-running and profitable shop.

Not infrequently a gun owner will bring his weapon to the gunsmith's shop and, with some degree of casualness, inform the mechanic that such and such is wrong with the gun, just how it should be repaired and exactly what it should cost to fix it.

Then there is the average type of customer who, appreciating that the gunsmith most probably knows more about gun work than he does, respectfully gives his gun over for repair, volunteering only such information as he believes necessary to guide the gunsmith in his diagnosis. Thus it behooves the gunsmith to institute a uniform system of perfunctory inspection to be performed upon each gun that is offered to him for repair. As a matter of fact this inspection, which can usually be completed in a few minutes, will make a very good impression on the customer and, more important, afford the gunsmith a very good idea of what *is* wrong with the piece. With such knowledge, the gunsmith can more accurately forecast the time required to complete the job and, if necessary, roughly estimate the repair cost.

General Inspection Procedure

Preliminary Examination. The inspection ritual, which will naturally vary with different weapons, should include a look through the bore of the gun for bad pits, obstructions, excessive wear or bulges and examination of the chamber for smoothness and possible deformation of extractor slots cut in the barrel. With *dummy* cartridges the feed mechanism, extractor and ejector can be tested. Further visual inspection should include a look at the firing pin nose, locking lugs and locking recesses and for the presence of burrs or cracking on all parts. The woodwork of the gun should be checked for cracks, splits or looseness on the piece and, finally, the general exterior appearance of the weapon with attention to the finish and condition of any attached accessories (recoil pads or special sights).

Uncovering Additional Defects. Often such an inspection will reveal defects or potential sources of trouble in addition to those that motivated the customer to bring the gun in for repair. When informed about these facts, the customer might decide to defer having the additional work done at the time if it is not absolutely necessary. That, of course, is his privilege; nevertheless, the gunsmith should feel satisfied in the knowledge that he has acted in an ethical manner. Furthermore, the customer will have little basis for complaining that the gunsmith did a "bum job" if one of the deficiencies pointed out at the inspection time, which he did not want taken care of, develops into an actual breakage later on.

Strange Guns. If a gun which is new to the gunsmith is presented to him for repair, as might be the situation in the case of some foreign or old style domestic weapons, he should, with great tact, ask the customer to show him just what he believes is wrong with the gun. In this way he can note how the gun is opened, and possibly even how it is broken down into its major assemblies. If, even after this demonstration, the gunsmith is somewhat in doubt as to the exact functioning of the piece, he can beg the owner's indulgence for a moment while he takes it into his private shop "to examine it under better light" or feign the need for some special tool or inspection device to aid in the diagnosis. Within the confines of his sanctum-sanctorum the mechanic can, without benefit of critical overseeing eyes, more leisurely observe the general design of the gun. Bearing in mind the main points of operation of any type of gun as to opening, cocking, loading, firing, extracting, ejecting and closing, he can then face the customer with greater confidence and feel more qualified to discuss the gun under consideration.

With a strange gun, or for that matter, any gun with which the gunsmith is not too familiar, the matter of cost estimating should be dealt with very carefully. To underestimate the cost for repairing a gun is very bad, for it means that when the customer returns to pick up his pet fire stick and is told he has to part with a few more hard earned dollars than he expected, he not infrequently feels that the gunsmith is trying to overcharge him. The truth of the matter, in most instances like this, is that the gunsmith is not even making a fair margin of profit; for in realizing that he must charge more than the agreed upon figure, he holds to a very minimum the increase in price.

Disassembling the Strange Gun. When taking apart a gun that is not too familiar to his talents, the gunsmith should proceed very slowly and then only after having studied the weapon's system of operation very carefully. Avoid the haphazard method of loosening all screws in sight and knocking at all pins that seem to be holding some part in place. Often this careless practice leads only to jamming a number of parts together and further complicates disassembly of the gun, to say nothing of the damage to the parts and the receiver.

In weapons where there do not seem to be any visible screws or bolts holding the stock on (especially true of shotguns), remove the butt plate of the gun. More than likely there will be a deep hole in the butt end of the stock which houses a stock bolt (See Figure 13). When this bolt is unscrewed, the stock can be taken off, thus revealing a part of the gun mechanism.

Where possible, it is always advisable to remove spring tension from a part when removing it. By doing this, the gunsmith can avoid having to search all around his shop for the part that jumped out and bounced off everything in sight. Where it is not possible to relieve spring tension, as for example is the case with some double barrel shotgun hammers, then the pin or screw upon which they rotate should be dislodged slowly, at the same time holding finger pressure against the part so as to preclude the possibility of its jumping out when the holding pin is moved clear.

Since the disassembling of any gun, no matter how difficult it might prove to be, is usually much easier than assembling, it is the wise gun craftsman who observes very carefully the position of each part as he removes it from its correct position. On strange guns one of the best ways to assure one's self of proper assembling of the piece is to employ a layout system when disassembling. Utilizing such a method does not denote the gunsmith as a novice, but rather as an experienced hand.

In using the layout method, one need only note very carefully the location of each part as it comes from the gun relative to a basic fixed assembly and lay it on a piece of paper marked with a number indicating the order in which it was removed from the gun. On these little papers notations can be made where applicable, indicating the exact position of a part or spring which might be so made as to allow its being replaced in an alternate but wrong position.

While on the subject of taking guns apart, it might be well to point out that little or no purpose is served by disassembling a weapon any more than is actually necessary. Aside from consuming extra unpaid-for time, there is always the possibility of breaking or losing a part which might prove very difficult and expensive to replace and refit.

The old adage about a place for everything and everything in its place should be borne in mind when taking any kind of gun apart. As each part is removed from the weapon it should be so placed that it cannot roll off the work bench and in such a location that it will not be swept away and mislaid if the work bench must be made available for another job of the hurry-up type. Lost or mislaid parts mean lost time and, sometimes more important, an unexpected delay in delivering a customer's gun, chiefly because the missing part cannot be replaced in time to meet the promised delivery.

Ordering Parts. After a gun has been diagnosed as needing a new part or parts which can be secured from usual supply or factory sources, the gunsmith should without delay order them, giving as much information as possible to the supplier as to make, model, serial number and caliber. By including all this information in his request for parts he is assured that the proper parts will be delivered with a minimum of delay.

Installing a New Part. When installing new parts in a gun, the mechanic must proceed with caution, since often the new part will be a little large (plus tolerance) all around in contrast to the worn parts with which it must fit and work. If a new part seems sluggish or binding in its movement, no attempts to correct this condition should be made until the part, in relation to the rest of the mechanism, has been studied and the source of the trouble has been ascertained beyond a doubt. Often at a quick glance, a new part seems to be binding at a particular point, while in actuality, detailed study reveals the source of the interference to be at another place. This is especially true of revolvers and repeating type rifles in which certain parts function on a timed basis, i.e., one part performs more than one phase of operation during different stages in its path of motion. Metal should be cut off new parts a little at a time and with a very fine file or, preferably, a small correctly shaped honing stone. All traces of filings or grit should be removed each time before trying the part for fit.

Making Parts. If it is necessary to make a part for a gun, as might be the case with a foreign or obsolete type, the first consideration is the type of steel to be used. It is an out and out waste of time, material and effort to go ahead and make a part for a gun from a steel which cannot be hardened and tempered or from a hardenable steel which does not have the proper alloy content to stand up under the particular stresses and strains imposed by operating conditions. Naturally, it cannot be expected that the gunsmith has at his disposal the necessary equipment and technical charts to make involved metallurgical tests for determination of the exact type of steel needed for a replacement part from the old one. Nor is it practical for the gunsmith to have a stock of the various alloy steels in the numerous sizes and forms for making such parts.

However, by studying the chapter in this book on Heat Treatment, he should be able to apply the general information contained therein to good advantage in turning out a part that will stand up under all normal operating conditions. With a small assortment of the more popular square, round and flat sizes of drill rod, tool steel and cold rolled steel on hand at all times, the gunsmith can be quite confident that he will be ready to make any and all small parts that cannot be procured commercially.

In making a replacement part the gunsmith should be guided

by the purpose it will serve in the gun and the amount of what type wear the part must endure. If a part is subject to constant pounding (as a gun hammer), it should be made from tool steel, then hardened and tempered so as to be hard enough to withstand the sear or trigger wear against the engaging notch; and still not so hard as to be brittle, which would cause the face of the hammer to crack after it strikes the outside breech face or firing pin a few times.

In some domestic and in many foreign revolvers it will be noticed that certain parts, such as hammers and triggers, are made of mild steel which is in turn case hardened. Parts so made are quite satisfactory if the hardening is accomplished in a uniform manner throughout the piece (See Chapter Fifteen).

As the new gunsmith has the opportunity to examine the many different makes, models and grades of firearms, he will soon learn to recognize the difference between parts of good quality and those which are but formed pieces of metal. This not only augments his technical knowledge but, more important, inspires him to do finer work and be a craftsman rather than just another mechanic.

Barrel Replacement Precautions

Replacement of barrels is a phase of gunsmithing work which can be a nice source of revenue if the gunsmith realizes his own capacities for this type of work and does not attempt to change barrels in guns for which he does not have the proper holding fixtures or gages.

Automatic Pistol Barrels. As a general rule automatic pistols present little or no problem when it is necessary to remove the old or replace a new barrel. At most it is usually only necessary to stone the engaging lugs on pocket type automatic pistol barrels when they are very difficult to turn into the receiver.

Barrel and Frame Blocks. With barrels of the style that screw into the receiver and must be drawn up tight to achieve sight alignment, there is some chance for trouble if the gunsmith does not use suitable tools and holding devices when accomplishing removal or installation. As can be readily appreciated, gun barrels must be screwed up very tightly into the receiver in order that they may retain a firmly fixed position during the strains and stresses of operating conditions. To dislodge a barrel so fixed, great force must be applied and in the process of exerting this pressure the frame of the gun must be rigidly held in a vise. And, since the frames of many weapons are merely steel shells, they in turn must be protected from deformation by the use of supporting blocks. As a rule these supporting blocks are nothing more than carefully machined pieces of steel or brass which can be inserted in the gun frame so that the latter can be squeezed tightly in the vise without fear of bending.

The Luger automatic pistol, which has a screw-in type barrel, also has an extremely light frame, and if an attempt be made to dislodge a stubborn barrel from it the frame will most certainly be bent and twisted, often to the extent that it will require many hours of hard work to get it restored to operating condition again.

Because of its unusual construction the Luger receiver can accurately be described as being "weak" as far as removal and installation of its barrel is concerned. For that reason the gunsmith who expects to do barrelling work on this type of pistol, should, by all means, have internal and external receiver blocks.

The internal block should be made according to the dimensions taken from the pistol's breech block and should be as long as the open section of the receiver in which the breech block operates. This block should be constructed so that a pin can be placed through the rear link holes of the receiver and the internal receiver block itself.

The external blocks need only be two pieces of flat brass, about 0.25" thick and machined to fit around the outside contour of the receiver. With the inside block in place the two brass blocks are placed around the outside of the receiver and the whole works clamped between the vise jaws.

For all practical purposes the best way to make Luger receiver blocks is to get a Luger pistol in working order, study its make up, and work out the dimensions and problems incident to their construction by the cut-and-try method.

Revolver Barrels. When removing revolver barrels it will usually be found more advantageous to hold the barrel being removed in the vise and, with an oak or similar hardwood handle inserted in the frame, to apply the twisting force here rather than holding the frame and wrenching the barrel loose (See Figure 27). Even when using this method there is always a possibility of springing the sideplate loose from the frame and in the event of an extremely stubborn barrel it is a good plan to

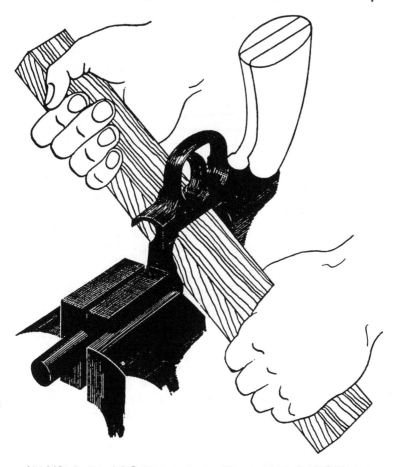

HANDLE IN POSITION FOR REMOVING BARREL

FIGURE 27

place a parallel clamp around the frame where the sideplate is located. Needless to say, a piece of felt or leather (rosin coated) should be placed in between the jaws of the clamp and the blued surfaces so the latter will not be marred.

On Smith & Wesson revolvers, the pin which passes through the frame and barrel should be pushed out before attempting removal of the barrel. Occasionally, when a new barrel is put in an S&W revolver, it is necessary to run a drill through the frame and across the top threads of the barrel in order that this pin can be driven back in proper alignment.

Rifle Barrels. Rifle barrels, especially those of the military class, are, as a rule, very tightly drawn up against the receiver face and often resist even the most forceful efforts at dislodgment. Figure 28 illustrates a typical special wrench used to

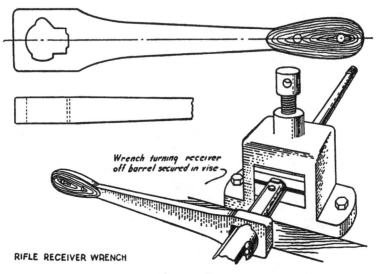

RIFLE RECEIVER WRENCH

FIGURE 28

remove and install barrels in bolt action rifles. Similar wrenches can be fashioned to accomplish the same task on most any type of rifle.

If the gunsmith does not have a barrel vise he should adjust the rear jaw of his bench vise to accommodate the taper shape of the rifle barrel. However, the Pacific Barrel Vise, which is especially made for this work, is a worth-while investment to any small shop which does barrel work.

The procedure for installing barrels is similar in all respects to that of their removal, except that the installation phase requires a great deal more care to prevent marring—plus exact fitting to achieve proper headspace and sight and extractor alignment.

Summed up then, barrel removal and installation, when properly performed, is a phase of gun repair work that requires the gunsmith to be on his toes during the entire job. It is a most important task and one that does not leave any allowance for halfway or "good enough" work.

Final Inspection

Before a gun, which has been in for repair, leaves the gunsmith's shop he should check and double check the work he has performed on the gun to ascertain that it is done as well as possible; and in addition make an overall check of the weapon to make sure of its general condition with an especially keen eye towards its safeness. Where possible, screws that have badly burred heads should be taken out and the burrs removed, polished and quick blued by dipping them in oil and holding them over the Bunsen burner or other flame until a dark coloring is imparted to the head. This operation consumes only a few minutes and the gunsmith will be more than repaid in the long run by return customer trade and mouth-to-mouth reputation as a thorough and skilled mechanic.

As a final touch the gunsmith should clean and oil the bore of the repaired gun and rub a light film of oil over the exterior metal surfaces to prevent any possible rusting should the gun lay around the shop for any appreciable time or be put aside for a few days by the customer after he takes it from the shop.

Good will and reputation for the gunsmith and his shop is made up of many factors—fairness in repair charge, promptness of delivery, quality of work and overall dealing with the customer. If the gunsmith strives to excel in all these phases there is little that can hold him back from being successful. If he fails to realize the importance of any or all of these, his chances for success will be greatly lessened and his daily progress will be marred by many discouraging turns of events.

CHAPTER FIVE

FUNCTION AND TIMING OF PARTS

TO BE able to properly diagnose gun troubles and execute the repairs necessary to correct their deficient condition, the gunsmith must have, in addition to his knowledge of tools and machines, a basic theoretical knowledge concerning the operation of all types of small arms. True enough, it is possible to work on guns without possessing any appreciable theoretical background, but for anyone starting in the business, the day-to-day problems incident to repair work can be more confidently approached and easily handled if he has such an overall knowledge.

Theory of Operation

All breech-loading small arms, irrespective of make, model, type or caliber, are designed and made to accomplish, by various systems, the discharge of a missile, or pattern of missiles, from a tube sealed at one end. For the accomplishment of this task all guns are made. And to do it in a manner which will provide a maximum of safety, convenience and accuracy for the user, the modern firearm has evolved into a fine but complex mechanical instrument.

In order that the gunsmith might better understand the purpose and function of the many parts and assemblies that contribute to the making of the modern gun, the pages of this chapter are written, and so that there should be no gap in the continuity of understanding, more than a few elementary points will be covered. From those who feel some of the material is so obvious as to be almost superfluous, the writer begs indulgence, feeling that in the overall picture the little additional reading time will not have been wasted.

The Cartridge. Before considering the gun itself, we should first examine the reason for the gun's being, viz., the cartridge. The cartridge is made of four components, all of equal importance: the case, the primer, the propellant (gunpowder), and the bullet.

74

Assuming the cartridge to be locked in the firing chamber of a gun, let us, as if peering into a glass weapon, observe just what happens. When the trigger is pulled, it disengages itself or a connection (sear) from the hammer or firing pin, which is under spring compression. Thus released, the hammer is driven forward by spring force and brings the firing pin down sharply on the primer. Being of such a nature that a sharp blow affects its chemical make-up, the priming composition jets a spurt of flame into the cartridge case, where the propellant is ignited. Upon ignition, the propellant generates a tremendous volume of gas which, because of its limited confinement in the cartridge case, exerts a pressure equally upon all surfaces with which it is in contact. The bullet, being only crimped in its case, offers the path of least resistance to the force of the equally expanding gas, and so is driven at high speed through the bore of the gun towards its mark.

To accomplish this projection of a bullet in a safe manner, a locked breech block or bolt is provided, and to facilitate withdrawal of the fired case from the chamber an extractor is incorporated in the gun mechanism. To throw this extracted case clear of the weapon, an ejector is included. To facilitate convenient holding, a stock or grips made to fit the shoulder or hand is an integral part of the weapon. And to aid in directing the bullet towards its mark, metallic or telescopic sights are attached to the top side of the rifle, pistol, revolver or shotgun.

Thus, from the simple tube closed at one end, the firearm is evolved into a fine mechanical instrument, through the medium of added refinements. To understand the purpose of these various refined additions is to have a working knowledge of any and all small arms.

The Chamber. The firing chamber on all types of weapons, except revolvers, is an integral part of the barrel itself. In either case, however, the chamber serves the same purpose, namely, to hold the cartridge in place prior to and while it is being discharged. The chamber, at the time of manufacture, is reamed to very close tolerance and finished as smoothly as is practicable under the conditions of modern fabrication methods. When a live cartridge is introduced into the chamber of a gun it fits rather snugly, but under normal conditions not so tightly that it cannot be withdrawn by hand. At the instant of firing, however, the cartridge case, under pressure of the powder-generated gas, expands, so that its exterior surface presses very tightly against the chamber wall, which is replete with many minute surface depressions put there by the reamers used to shape and finish the chamber to size. And, although the cartridge case does spring back somewhat to pre-fired size after the pressure has been completely relieved by the bullet's exit from the gun, it is usually so tightly bound in the chamber that a special effort on the rim or groove of the cartridge case must be exerted to dislodge it. To effect this dislodgment is the primary function of the extractor.

As can be readily appreciated, the extractor is subject to a great deal of strain and if the chamber of the weapon becomes rusted or scored, an additional strain is thrown upon the extractor because the expanding fired case will enlarge to fill any and all depressions in the chamber. It is for this reason that gun experts do not recommend the firing in any gun of a cartridge which has a case that is shorter than the full length of the chamber, viz., .22 caliber rim fire shorts in a weapon chambered for the .22 caliber long rifle cartridge (See Figure 29A).

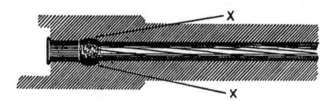

22 RF *short cartridge in barrel chambered for 22 long rifle cartridge*

X..NOTE EROSION CAUSED BY FIRING SHORTS

FIGURE 29A

If a gunsmith is presented with a gun which the customer says has faulty extraction, he should, after careful examination of the extractor, look into the chamber of the gun and take note of its surface. If the surface appears to be rough, scored, eroded, or rust-pocked to a degree that cannot be corrected through the efforts of crocus cloth or 7/0 (fine) emery abrasive action, then it is best to recommend to the customer that he have a new barrel, or cylinder in the case of a revolver, installed in the gun or suffer the inconvenience of ripped cartridge case heads or unreliable extraction of fired cases.

Function of Parts

When polishing out a chamber with emery cloth, care must be taken to see that neither an excessive amount of metal is removed, nor the shape of the chamber altered. Either condition will only increase extraction trouble, due to cartridge case expansion, rather than correct it.

The Extractor. In addition to its primary function of withdrawing fired cases, the extractor, in many types of repeating weapons, also serves to guide each live round of ammunition as it is stripped from the magazine and carried on its way to the chamber. When a complaint is received concerning the feeding of cartridges from magazine to chamber, the extractor should be looked over very carefully and tested with dummy cartridges to ascertain whether or not a deformed or burred extractor is preventing the rim of the cartridge from being raised into place upon each actuation stroke of the gun mechanism.

The Magazine. In partnership with the extractor on matters of feeding are the lips of the gun's magazine. The magazine lips, when manufactured, are so shaped that the cartridge, while being stripped therefrom, will be released at the proper instant and jump into the bolt's path, to be guided on into the chamber. Naturally, after a long period of service, the magazine lips are inclined to spring or wear out of proper shape and thus allow the cartridge rising from it to jump free before the bolt has moved far enough forward. This latter condition is conducive to poor feeding and subsequent "jams." While it is frequently possible to squeeze the lips of a magazine together to equal the original size, it is, generally speaking, a poor policy, for it is usually only a matter of a short time before the magazine again becomes faulty and must be replaced with a new one. Normally a magazine costs only a fraction of the original price of a gun and yet it is just as important as the weapon itself. Therefore, magazine repairs should be confined only to emergency conditions when a new magazine is not procurable and the old one must be continued in service.

The Ejector. With the possible exception of the Enfield .30 caliber rifle (M1917), most weapons have very sturdy ejectors. (The main trouble with this rifle's ejector is that it has a spring, which is an integral part of it, that too often breaks off and does not project the ejector out far enough to flip the cartridge from the extractor claw.) Yet, from time to time, the gunsmith will receive complaints from customers whose guns do not seem to eject properly. This is especially true of automatic pistols, and autoloading rifles and shotguns, in which the ejection mechanism plays a very important role.

In cases of ejection trouble, the extractor again comes in for scrutiny, for often the extractor is damaged in such a manner as to hinder or prevent the ejector from flipping the cartridge case from the extractor's grip at the proper instant. Then, when the bolt or slide reaches its maximum rearward position on the recoil stroke and the case has not been ejected clear of the mechanism, on the forward travel stroke the fired case will prevent the bolt or slide from going into battery, thus causing a jam.

A loose extractor or ejector will interfere with the proper function of the latter; so will a worn or loose ejector fail to throw the spent cartridge clear of the weapon in a positive manner.

When an ejector is repaired or replaced, the gun should be test fired, rather than just running a few dummy cartridges through the mechanism by hand. Only the actual stress and timing of firing can give the ejector a true test.

The Firing Pin. In the chapter before this we spoke of the firing pin, and under other chapters it will be commented upon further as specific discussion warrants; actually, an entire detailed work could justifiably be written on this, the "spark plug" of the gun. It is the firing pin that is the connecting link between the gun as a mechanical instrument and the live cartridge.

This link, which is subject to a combination of strains, should come in for very careful examination when a gun owner complains of inaccuracy, hang fire, delayed ignition, pierced primers, misfires or any form of erratic cartridge ignition.

Aside from actual breakage, a firing pin can wear on the nose, after considerable use, to the point where it becomes shortened, so that it fires the cartridge only occasionally, or perhaps not at all. Long, thin firing pins sometimes bend or buckle in their length, if the pin is not properly tempered. As can be appreciated, even a slight bend in a firing pin will shorten its length to the extent where it will not protrude far enough through the breech or bolt face to insure denting of the primer sufficiently.

The proper protrusion of a firing pin is .060″, the minimum

being .055″ and the maximum .065″. In Chapter Three the gages for measuring firing pin protrusion are described and illustrated.

A firing pin that is longer than it should be is a potential source of danger to the shooter, and occasionally even an innocent bystander is injured by bits of minute flying debris that are scattered about when the long firing pin *pierces* a primer. A pierced primer can also be caused by a firing pin whose nose is badly marred or pointed, rather than smooth and carefully rounded. In either case the results are similar. When a primer is pierced the ignition of the gun powder is accomplished, but through the hole pierced in the primer the evolved gas within the cartridge case jets out at high pressure back into the mechanism of the gun and the face of the shooter. Gas so released can, and often does, inflict irreparable damage to a weapon, to say nothing of the injury to persons nearby.

The Firing Pin Spring. In certain models of guns a spring is fitted around the firing pin. The purpose of this spring is to return the firing pin to a fixed position after each discharge. These springs are of the coil type and, while very durable, do at times break under the constant strain to which they are subjected. Often such a broken spring will continue to function in the proper manner because of its confinement within the firing pin channel. Nevertheless, it is apt at any time to become twisted or turned within this channel and either prevent the firing pin from hitting the cartridge or cause the firing pin to project from the breech face. While neither condition is desirable, the latter is definitely more dangerous, since there is the possibility of a cartridge being fired prematurely, as the breech is closed and before it is locked. Certain double barrel shotguns are very bad offenders in this respect, and as such should be checked whenever the fired shells show evidence of scratches on their head in a direction from the primer to the lower edge of the rim, when positioned in the gun chamber.

Rim fire cartridges, of which the popular .22 caliber is probably the best known, do not have a separate primer assembly as do center fire cartridges. Rather, the inside of the entire rim is coated with primer composition so that no matter what segment of the rim is struck by the firing pin, ignition will take place.

Rim Fire Cartridge Make-up. In a center fire cartridge there is a small, separate anvil (See Figure 29B) which serves as a firm base upon which the priming composition rests. Thus, when the firing pin strikes the exterior face of the primer, the priming chemical is compressed between the latter and the anvil. On the other hand, rim fire cartridges do not have this integral anvil. Instead, the rear face of the barrel is called upon to serve in

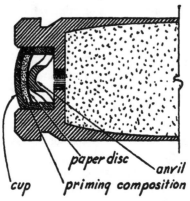

paper disc

anvil

cup　priming composition

DETAILS OF CENTER FIRE
CARTRIDGE PRIMER

(Separate Anvil Primer)

FIGURE 29B

this capacity. It is for this reason that owners of rim fire weapons are always cautioned against snapping the trigger when a live cartridge or dummy round is not in the chamber. Otherwise, a slightly oversize or floating type firing pin will tend to peen over the rear face of the barrel, which causes double trouble; primarily because the area where the pin strikes will in a short time be dented lower than the rest of the rear face, producing a condition of no support for the underside of the rim to rest on; and secondly because that portion of the edge of the chamber in this area tends to turn inward, and makes insertion and extraction of cartridges very difficult, if not near impossible.

From the foregoing little discussion on the firing pin, one can readily appreciate its importance. Further on in this book even more detailed aspects of it will be considered for, broadly speaking, one can scarcely say enough about it, and even at that, each individual case of firing pin trouble that the gunsmith encounters will add more to his knowledge of this small but vital gun part.

Firing Pin Bushings. Close in kinship to the firing pin itself is the firing pin bushing, or, as it is called in some types of weapons, the recoil plate. Under either nomenclature, however, it is the same part and serves a similar purpose. Generally, it is made of a harder grade of steel than the breech face and is somewhat larger in diameter than the cartridge primer designed to be fired in the gun.

In revolvers and other hammer-type guns, where the firing pin comes through the breech face at an angle, the firing pin bushing not infrequently becomes burred up. These burrs, which are turned outward on the breech face, have a tendency to drag against the rear face of the cartridge. With revolvers this is most undesirable since it makes cocking of the weapon very difficult. These burrs can be filed off at times, which will preclude the necessity of installing a new bushing. When the firing pin hole in the bushing becomes enlarged to an appreciable extent, however, the old bushing should be removed and a new one installed. Otherwise the entire purpose of the bushing's presence will be defeated.

Both Colt and Smith & Wesson revolver firing pin bushings (recoil plates) are easily driven out from the hammer side of the gun. Other makes of revolvers have the plates screwed in, and a spanner or split-type screwdriver is used when removing them. This operation is covered in detail under a heading in Chapter Eleven.

Springs. Unless it be some experimenter's dream or an impractical weapon, there is no small arm in general usage that does not have springs, either of flat or coil type, as an integral part of its mechanism. As a matter of fact, most guns require a number of springs of different sizes to accomplish the various phases of loading, locking, firing, extracting and ejecting. The Colt .45 Government automatic, for example, has six springs; the Smith & Wesson .45 revolver (M1917) has 10 springs; and the Model 1897 Winchester Sporter shotgun has 12 springs. Of these three weapons, only the shotgun has two springs within its own mechanism that are interchangeable. All others in each of the weapons are of varying sizes and shapes and as such do not lend themselves to interchangeability.

Springs are put in various places in a gun for a definite purpose. Manufacturers do not arrive at the size or design of these springs in a haphazard fashion. Rather, from prepared tables and engineering experience, they know just how much force is required to move a certain part or assembly through a required distance. Further, within the limitations of working space that the gun mechanism allows, they know what size of spring need be used to actuate the part or assembly in a positive manner under normal operating conditions.

When it is necessary to replace a spring that has become broken, or lost so much of its tension that it no longer works in the proper fashion, a new spring, procured from the manufacturer, should be used. For only by using a spring having dimensions exactly the same as the original can the gunsmith be sure that he is doing this particular job as it should be done.

Coil springs, when made to specification, are referred to by a series of dimensions (See Figure 30). A variation from *any* of

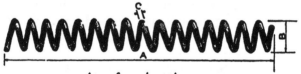

A .... free length
B .....free outside diameter
C .... wire diameter

COIL SPRING DIMENSIONS

FIGURE 30

these dimensions changes the spring's capacity for performing a specific function.

A spring that has the same outside diameter as another, and is "just about as long" cannot and should not be considered as a substitute, for often in cases of this sort it will be found that the wire diameter and number of coils per inch are at variance with each other.

The ends of coil springs should always be regarded with a keen eye, for if they are bent out or turned in to any appreciable degree, the spring will have a tendency to bind on a plunger, or be forced into uneven compression. Usually rounding out the tip of the last coil on each end of a new spring with a small honing stone will preclude the possibility of the ends catching on a plunger or guide on which it moves.

Coil springs used in firearms are usually very inexpensive. Therefore, when a spring shows the first signs of fatigue, kinking, or deformation, it should be replaced by a new one.

Flat springs of the tapered variety, when heat treated properly, have, over a long period of gun manufacture, proven themselves to be quite satisfactory. However, certain of them found in cheap weapons are so poorly finished, i.e., the surface is marked with deep tool marks, as to provide many points of potential breakage. This latter condition can be somewhat lessened by removing the spring from the gun and, with fine emery cloth wrapped around a small file, carefully abrading a few thousandths from all surfaces, until the spring is smooth and free of tool marks. This operation should be done so that the strokes of the emery cloth are made in the lengthwise direction of the spring.

When removing or installing springs, great care should be employed, for a spring can be rendered useless by rough handling. With coil springs the greatest danger is encountered when removing them from holes or wells in which they may have become rusted or gummed. Frequently this condition gives rise to the use of force on the part of the gunsmith, who uses pliers, picks, or anything with which he can get a grip and effect a dislodgment. Occasionally, this method proves effective, but more often than not the spring unwinds a few coils before becoming loose. Net result—an absolutely worthless spring.

Flat springs, especially of the heavy V type, should not be over-compressed when being removed or installed. Nor should pliers or makeshift spring removing tools, which have a tendency to slip and mar the spring, be used. Flat springs should be compressed and allowed to return to normal "set" position gradually. Compressing them suddenly or allowing them to snap from complete compression to normal "set" is not to be recommended; rather, all pressure on the tool being employed should be gradual and uniform.

In due time, most every tinkerer and gunsmith discovers that the action of a gun can often be lightened by cutting a coil or two off various springs which act upon the firing mechanism. Within certain limitations this practice can be carried out with beneficial results. Yet it can easily be carried to an extreme. For example, the trigger rebound spring in a Smith & Wesson revolver (swing-out cylinder type) can be reduced by a coil or two and still actuate the gun mechanism under normal conditions. Yet this will have a tendency to slow down the speed of the trigger's return to the forward position. If too many coils are removed from the spring, the trigger will have a tendency to catch at a cylinder stop. This latter condition will prevent the cylinder from being unlocked automatically between shots. Naturally this is most undesirable, to say the least.

No specific rule can be given to indicate just how much of a standard spring can be removed and still leave the gun operating properly. Generally, though, it can be said that spring modifications should be held to a minimum, and even then the gunsmith should extensively test any action in which he has occasion to reduce spring tension.

The Breech Bolt. Various names are given to that assembly or part of a gun which supports the rear face of the cartridge case. In lever action and trombone action weapons it is called the breech bolt; in automatic pistols it is the slide; in falling block guns it is the breech block, and in military shoulder arms it is the bolt. In other types of weapons, such as the revolver or double barrel shotgun, the receiver serves as the standing breech.

Almost needless to say, the breech mechanism of any gun must be considered *first, last and always from the standpoint of safety*. When making repair or replacement on the breech bolt of any gun, there is no room for anything but first class workmanship, parts and knowledge. After all, it is this part which has about as much force directed against it as does the bullet itself. Never must this part be substandard in any way for if it is, the bullet may no longer be the mass offering the path of least resistance.

Alterations, modifications, heat treating or skeletonizing should never be made on the bolt, stationary breech face, locking lugs or locking lug recesses of a gun, unless advice of the manufacturer can be obtained.

To be on the safe side at all times, a gunsmith should not undertake to fit a new bolt to a gun unless he has a method of accurately checking the headspace of the piece. To better appreciate the necessity for this reasoning, a careful reading and complete understanding of the following paragraphs on headspace is recommended:

Headspace. The whole tale of headspace hinges upon the tolerance to which various cuts are held in the manufacturing stage, coupled with wear on locking points in the receiver and barrel of a gun. Added to this is the difference encountered in size of the same caliber cartridges marketed by various manufacturers.

Although headspace measurements made through the use of gages are recorded in two different terms, the reason for and importance of each is based on the same theory. For rifles shooting a rim-type cartridge (British .303, .22 et al.) this headspace is recorded as the distance between the face of the bolt and the inner rim of the cartridge when seated and locked in the chamber of a gun. For rimless cartridges (.30/06, etc.) headspace distance is measured from the shoulder of the cartridge to the face of the bolt. Gages for headspace are of the "go" and "no-go" variety, and are referred to as minimum and maximum. The bolt of a weapon must close and lock on the minimum gage. If a bolt does not close on a minimum gage it means that great difficulty will be experienced in locking a standard cartridge in place.

To remedy this condition in a rifle shooting a rim-type cartridge, a few thousandths must be turned off the rear face of the barrel. In the case of a weapon chambered for a rimless cartridge, the chamber must be reamed out a bit deeper—or, when available, another bolt can be tried. This latter practice is usually possible only at the factory, or in a government arsenal or military armament repair installation.

The real danger in a gun, however, is excessive headspace. With the gun-cartridge combination the brass cartridge case is definitely the weak link. As we all know, a cartridge is stamped out, in various operations, from a sheet of high-grade brass and, like all other metals, brass will stretch just so far before it breaks. When a cartridge is fired, the gas which is evolved not only drives the bullet from the gun, but also exerts an equal amount of force or pressure on all surfaces of the cartridge case. This pressure forces the thin side walls of the brass to press the tightest against the walls of the chamber, whose surface is scored with minute circular tool marks as a result of reaming. The forward part of the cartridge case, being thinner than the rest, very readily expands to fill these tool marks, scratches and cavities, and holds tenaciously so long as the pressure is maintained. At this same instant, the gas is exerting a pressure against the inside head of the cartridge case and causing it to move backward towards the bolt face. This combination of factors results in a more or less stretching of the cartridge case.

If the head of the bolt is not too far from the rear face of the cartridge case, this stretching is arrested and everything is O.K. On the other hand, should the headspace of the gun be excessive (and a few thousandths of an inch at this point may mean everything), the brass will continue to stretch towards the rear, and when it passes its elastic limit the case will rupture, freeing to the rear the pent-up gas that might possibly blow the gun apart.

While on the grim side of what can happen if experienced advice is not taken, it might be well to point out that grease or oil in the chamber of a gun raises the pressure enormously, by virtue of the fact that the cartridge case is prevented from holding onto the wall of the chamber at the instant of explosion. When a cartridge case does not cling to the chamber walls, the whole thrust of pressure is placed against the bolt face and then transmitted to the locking lugs. Constant pounding of this nature on the locking lugs leads to metal fatigue and then some fine day, when least expected or bargained for, the lugs give way and another weapon is relegated to the scrap pile. And, as often happens, the shooter or someone standing nearby is seriously injured.

As they come from the factory, guns made by reliable manufacturers have already been properly headspaced and in most cases will continue to be safe from this standpoint, provided that no bolt-swapping is engaged in between shooters who have the same kind of rifles. Obsolete or used military weapons, however, which are purchased other than directly from a government arsenal (through the Director of Civilian Marksmanship) should be headspaced before using, because bolts in weapons of this class are often interchanged among military personnel in an endeavor to secure a "smoother action," or better trigger pull.

One of the sure signs of excessive headspace in any gun is ruptured cartridge cases. The break in the case usually occurs near the rear end of the cartridge in the bottle-neck type, since this is the thick portion of the case which does not cling as tenaciously to the chamber wall as does the thin portion.

Other Parts. Aside from the parts common to many different types of weapons heretofore considered, there are other parts and assemblies too numerous for detailed discussion. Some of these are of simple construction, such as plungers, pins, stirrups, et cetera, and scarcely warrant any special comments under this chapter heading. Others, however, are more complicated and require much care and forethought when being repaired or replaced.

Representative of this latter group is the rebound lever found in all modern-type Colt revolvers. Held between two lugs located midway in the grip section of the frame, the rebound lever has freedom of motion in an up-and-down direction, since it pivots between the frame lugs on a pin. In addition to guiding the hand in proper angular position during the cocking phase, the rebound lever, by virtue of a small projection on its inside face, also engages and releases the bolt from the cylinder notch, thus allowing the hand to rotate the cylinder to the next chamber. Before this next chamber achieves its alignment, however, the bolt slips from the projection on the rebound lever and is ready (by virtue of spring tension) to engage the next cylinder stop notch.

From this brief delineation it can readily be seen that the rebound lever serves a dual purpose and as such must receive special attention when being considered for replacement. By the same reasoning, the replacement of a hand or bolt, both of which are actuated by the rebound lever, must be regarded in relation to the latter when being adjusted or replaced.

Similarly, the trigger on a modern Colt revolver serves in more than one capacity: it functions to engage and hold the hammer in a cocked position; in operating the gun double action it engages the hammer strut and actuates the hammer; when operating for single or double action, it serves to move the hand. From Figure 31 it should be noted that the trigger must move through a definite minimum distance if the hand is to completely rotate the cylinder a full $\frac{1}{6}$th revolution at each cocking of the gun. If the trigger is shortened at Point "A," then the hammer notch will engage the trigger before the cylinder has reached its proper alignment. When this condition exists a revolver is said to be "out of timing," a most undesirable and dangerous fault.

From time to time, as the gunsmith encounters new weapons, he will see parts which are common only to certain guns. However, by possessing a thorough working knowledge of general gun mechanisms, he will find it easier to diagnose the exact function, or functions, of these parts. No mechanism should ap-

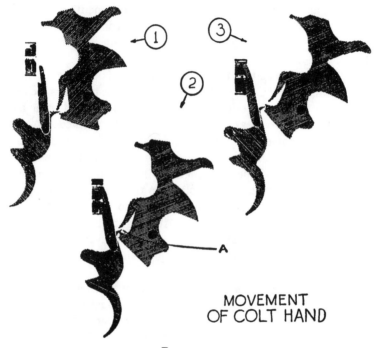

MOVEMENT
OF COLT HAND

FIGURE 31

pear so complicated that it defies understanding for, as the writer has attempted to explain in this chapter, every weapon is made up of a definitely related group of necessary parts and assemblies, each of which performs one or more definite tasks. In proper combination and timing, all of these parts together make up the gun, whether it be pistol, revolver, rifle or shotgun —single shot, repeater or autoloader.

CHAPTER SIX

Cleaning Actions and Removing Bore Obstructions

O F THE many lubricating and preserving oils on the market, very few, if any, are of such a nature that they do not, after some extended period, become gummy and tend to make a gun action sluggish. This condition is not alone caused by oxidation of the lubricant, but also from dust and moisture combining with the oil to produce a hard-to-dissolve residue which clings tenaciously and continues to build up on parts, in holes, and between the coils of springs.

When this residue accumulates to any extent, as it does particularly inside the mechanism of double barrel shotguns and similar compact action weapons, it tends to increase the trigger pull, slow down hammer and firing pin action (causing misfires and hangfires), and make the gun generally unreliable and difficult to operate. Often a gun in this condition is brought to the gunsmith by a customer who imagines the piece to be on its last legs and beyond repair. Inspection in such instances will usually reveal that the parts of the gun are so coated with a pitch-like substance that normal freedom of movement is impossible and springs cannot function as they were designed to. There is only one remedial action for a gun in this condition and that is a complete cleaning. No amount of light oil or super special solvent can be used to do the job—the gun must be cleaned with boiling water and a detergent if it is to be done thoroughly and correctly.

Cleaning the Action

Disassembly. Assuming the weapon in question to be a double barrel shotgun in need of such thorough cleaning, the following simple but effective process should be employed:

1) Break the gun down to its three basic sections, i.e., stock and action, barrels, and fore-end.

2) Disassemble all moving parts from the barrel group, such as extractor, ejector, cocking cam or levers, et cetera.

3) Disassemble all parts from the action, being careful to dislodge all small springs gently so as not to stretch the coils, which might be firmly "glued" in their well.

4) Fill a pan or metal container with enough water so that the receiver, or biggest part to be cleaned, will be completely covered, and add enough Oakite or similar commercial cleaner (that does not contain lye), procurable at most any grocery store, to make a good strong solution.

5) Allow the parts being cleaned to boil in the solution until all traces of foreign matter are removed, adding water when necessary so that the parts will always be completely covered.

6) When, after continuous boiling, the parts appear to be perfectly clean, they should be removed with pliers, one at a time, and shaken free of all excess water clinging to them or remaining in recesses, and then plunged, while still hot, in a pan of light oil. High grade acid-free S.A.E. 10 motor oil serves nicely for this purpose. Large or unwieldy parts, such as the receiver, which cannot safely be swung around on the end of a pair of pliers, should be laid on a piece of absorbent cloth to dry before being plunged into oil.

7) If any parts show signs of superficial rust, it should be removed by rubbing them across a piece of No. 3/0 emery cloth tacked to a smooth and true wooden board. If the rust has progressed to the stage where deep pitting has resulted, then no effort should be made to grind the surface down to the depth of the pits, or the parts will no longer be within prescribed size limits. Light burrs and similar deformations on parts and around holes should be filed or stoned smooth, as needed.

8) After parts needing it have been treated as described in Step 7, all parts and springs should be cleaned in a solvent like benzine or kerosene, to remove all traces of the oil that was applied after the boiling treatment. Application of this solvent will also float away any metallic or abrasive chips gathered during the burr removing operation.

It might be well to note here that commercial automobile gasoline contains traces of acid and therefore should not be used on blued parts since acid has a detrimental effect on blueing.

After cleaning with solvent, a fine grade of gun oil should be applied by means of a small artist's brush to all parts, springs and surfaces. Except for reassembly, this second and final oiling completes the entire operation, and while at first thought it might seem a bit foolish to dip parts in oil after boiling and then clean them off following the smoothing up process, there is reasoning behind it. If the parts were taken directly from the boiling water and allowed to cool in air, a great deal of time would be wasted, to say nothing of the fact that the parts would immediately start rusting. To put a good grade gun oil on the parts after boiling would be a very expensive and unnecessary action, inasmuch as most of it would have to be wiped off preparatory to burr removing or reassembling.

9) Reassemble the gun, exercising caution so as not to mar or damage any of the parts that must be put in place by force. Finally, wipe off all excess oil from the receiver, as it would have an adverse effect if it were to drip into the inletted portion of the stock and rot the wood.

Within the detailed outline of the foregoing process, the double barrel shotgun has been used as an example chiefly because it represents what is generally regarded as the most difficult of all small arms to work on.

In the case of weapons from which the barrel cannot be easily removed, it is most advisable to immerse only the receiver in the cleaning tank while the barrel remains outside.

Handling of small parts and springs can be greatly facilitated by wiring them together before immersion. This system can be employed if the gunsmith is not too familiar with the weapon he is working on, by separately wiring parts of each group or assembly together.

It is poor policy to attempt this complete cleaning process by only partially disassembling a weapon, since much of the residue lodged in holes and recesses will not be cleaned out, thus defeating the main purpose of the operation.

Cost Factors. When contracting with a customer to do a complete cleaning job, the gunsmith must base his fee upon the amount of time he will have to spend taking apart and reassembling the gun, since it is anticipated that no parts will have to be replaced. However, to play safe, the gunsmith should have an understanding with the customer that if parts or springs are needed they will be replaced, but, of course, at additional cost. This latter factor cannot be too greatly stressed, for occasionally a gun that seems to function all right will be brought to the gunsmith for cleaning, only for him to discover upon disassembling it that some pin, spring or part is cracked and has functioned only because it has been contained within its operating space by virtue of supporting plates or parts. Needless to say, the gunsmith cannot ethically replace such a defective part and return the gun to its owner as being repaired. Therefore, his only alternative is to contact the customer and explain the situation truthfully and recommend that the new part, or parts needed, be installed. Few customers will find cause for complaint when a mechanic acts in this commendable manner.

Bore Obstructions

In spite of the warnings constantly sounded by gun column editors against the practice of trying to shoot out the bullets, rags and whatnot that become lodged in gun bores, there are countless shooters who feel such admonitions do not apply to them, and proceed accordingly. Occasionally these would-be mechanics blow up a gun, but more often only succeed in damaging the rifling or pounding the obstruction more firmly in place. Eventually, these battered firearms reach the gunsmith and he must be prepared to salvage them from an ever-beckoning junk heap.

Although no expensive equipment is needed to remove bore lodgments, there are a few special tools which every gunsmith should have on hand so that he will not be tempted to use makeshift or inferior equipment if it is necessary to do a rush job for an anxious hunter.

Cloth in Rifle Bores. Figure 32A shows a tool which is used to cut cloth patches and would-be patches from the bore of a rifle.

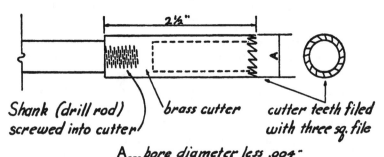

Shank (drill rod) screwed into cutter   brass cutter   cutter teeth filed with three sq. file

A...bore diameter less .004″

TOOL FOR CUTTING CLOTH OBSTRUCTIONS FROM BORE

FIGURE 32A

It is recommended that this tool be made up for .22 caliber, .30 caliber and .35 caliber bores. These three sizes will pretty much take care of all the popular model sporting and target rifles that the gunsmith might normally encounter. Tools for other weapons can be made if enough local shooters possess special caliber weapons.

There is another simple accessory which, while not absolutely necessary, can be used to great advantage with the patch cutting tool. It is nothing more than a piece of brass turned to the shape illustrated in Figure 32B. This bore guide, with a hole drilled

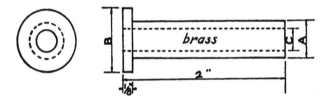

A....bore diameter, less .002"
B.... diameter of barrel at muzzle
    (1" is ideal for all purposes)
C.....shank diameter, less .002"

BORE GUIDE FOR PATCH CUTTING TOOL.

FIGURE 32B

through its length, serves as a guide for the tool shank as it is rotated by hand. The guide minimizes any bowing or bending of the shank and consequently keeps the patch cutter on center during the operation.

For the .30 caliber and .35 caliber patch cutters, ¼" drill rod or cold rolled steel should be used as a shank. More than one shank will be needed, for not all obstructions will be lodged the same distance from the muzzle and a shank that is too long is very inefficient. Therefore, it is well to have three shanks; one should be 12" long, another 20" long, and the longest about 24". One end of each of these rods should be of reduced diameter and threaded. The threaded portion should extend about ½" from the tip and be of a size that will fit into the female threaded portion of the tool.

To use the tool, proceed as follows:

1) Select the proper size shank, after determining how deeply the obstruction is lodged in the bore, and screw it into the proper caliber cutting tool. Insert this assembly into the bore of the gun, as far as it can be pushed by force of hand.

2) Slide the correctly suited bore guide over the shank and push into the muzzle of the gun.

3) Place the protruding end of the shank in the chuck of a breast drill, or carpenter's brace, and tighten it in place.

4) Without exerting too much forward force, start turning the drill until it begins to bite into the obstruction. Then speed up the turning operation until resistance becomes so great that continued rotation of the tool is nearly impossible. Remove the tool from the bore and clean out any fragments of cloth that have been cut loose. Check the cutting edges of the tool to see if they are becoming dull or bent. If so, sharpen them with a three-square file and proceed again.

5) After all the cloth that can be cut loose is removed, withdraw the tool and cork up one end of the barrel, fill with solvent or oil and allow to stand for a few minutes.

6) Remove cork, pour out oil and run a near-caliber-size cleaning rod through the bore. This will force out any loosely set particles of cloth.

7) Attach a brass or bristle brush to a cleaning rod and vigorously push it back and forth through the bore. Finally, run a lightly oiled patch through the bore and the job is done.

Cloth in Shotgun Bores. Removing cloth obstructions from shotgun bores is a task differing from the same job on rifles only in that a worm type tool rather than a cutter is used, since the amount of material to be removed is usually so great that cutting it loose would be a time-consuming operation. The worm illustrated in Figure 33 can easily be made from a length of ½" diameter drill rod with a tapered spiral ground on one end. The handle provided at the opposite end is made of ¼" round stock and serves to turn the worm into the bore obstruction.

Double pointed worms can be purchased commercially from any gunsmith supply house and serve as well as the homemade variety.

Before using these wormers on a shotgun bore obstruction, the bore should be flooded with some type of light oil, preferably penetrating oil, and allowed to soak overnight. The oil should be poured in both from the muzzle and the breech so that all sections of the obstruction will be wetted. Corks can be used to plug both ends of the bore so that a minimum of oil will leak out when the barrel is placed in an upright position.

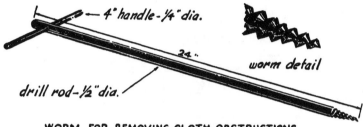

WORM FOR REMOVING CLOTH OBSTRUCTIONS
FROM SHOTGUN BORES

FIGURE 33

When using the wormer, do not attempt to drive it too deeply into the obstruction or it will do nothing more than expand the lodged cloth, and then neither it nor the obstruction will budge. Just turn the wormer in a little bit at each attempt, until it starts to grab hold, then pull out. In this way a little bit of the cloth will be removed at each try. Occasionally, when it is one large piece of cloth that is stuck, the wormer will catch one end of it and the entire piece can be unraveled and pulled out.

Never attempt to pound out a cloth obstruction from a shotgun, for the barrel walls are so thin that they might bulge as a result of the obstruction expanding while being pounded. While speaking of precautions incident to this type of work, it would be well to remember that shotgun bores, with their highly polished surfaces, show very clearly all scratches and marks inflicted by metals harder than itself. Therefore, it behooves the gunsmith to exercise extra care when inserting, turning and withdrawing the wormer, so that its sharp edges do not come in contact with the surface of the bore. The possibility of bore damage by the wormer can be greatly lessened if a breech guide is used. The breech guide is nothing more than a piece of brass or steel turned to the shape and dimensions (Figure 34) of a shotgun shell, with a guide hole drilled through it to accommodate the wormer shank. This breech guide, like the bore guide for rifles, helps to keep the wormer on center at all times and prevents bowing of the rod.

When removing any obstructions from the bore of a shotgun, the gunsmith must bear in mind that walls of shotgun barrels are always thinner near the muzzle end, and if any forcing or tapping is done it should be directed from muzzle to breech. At that, however, all tapping should be held to a minimum, and then done only when all other methods have failed.

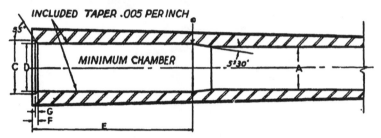

STANDARD BORE & CHAMBER DIMENSIONS FOR SHOTGUNS.

GAUGE	BORE	CHAMBER					
	A	B (A)	C	D	E	F	G
10	.775	.841	.933	.8554	2.875	.074	.026
10 MAG.		.8379			3.500		
12	.729	.798	.886	.8118	2.750	.072	.026
12 MAG.		.7968			3.000		
16	.662	.732	.820	.7458	2.750	.065	.026
20	.615	.685	.766	.6988	2.750	.060	.024
28	.550	.614	.688	.6284	2.875	.060	.022
.410	.410	.463	.537	.478	3.000	.060	.020

(COURTESY, ITHACA . GUN CO.)

FIGURE 34

Bullets in Rifle Bores. On a par with dislodging cloth and patches from gun bores is the equally tough job of removing bullets. Usually by the time a weapon in the latter condition reaches the gunsmith's emporium, it has been worked upon for no few hours by the sad owner, who still cannot realize how a bullet can become so stuck as to resist the best efforts of his pounding.

There are a few methods commonly used by professional gunsmiths to clear bores of stuck bullets which, when used separately or in conjunction, usually result in eminent success. This does not automatically make the task an easy one, but the proper tools in a cautious gunsmith's hands should make possible the removal of any bullet, no matter how tightly it is wedged in place.

Before commencing the actual work incident to removing a lodged projectile, there is a preliminary factor that should be taken into consideration.

Preliminary Work. Find out from the gun owner what type of projectile is lodged in the bore, i.e., lead, metal jacket, flat nose, pointed, et cetera. Also, it is helpful to know if there is more than one slug in the bore, or possibly any other lodgments, such as cleaning rod tips, or pieces of broken cleaning rods; and if such a combination of impediments is present, how are they located. That is to say, is the bullet lodged between two pieces of rod or is there a cleaning rod tip lodged between two bullets—in short, what is in the bore and in what approximate relative position? Knowledge of this information is important, for it affords the gunsmith an idea of what unusual conditions he might ex-- pect to encounter and enables him to prepare accordingly.

Some customers tend to act coyly when asked just what oddments are lodged in an obstructed gun bore, but will immediately become very helpful (and truthful) when the gunsmith informs them that the longevity of their firestick depends on his knowing, since a slip of the removing tool on some unexpected object might hack a few lands from the rifling.

Presuming the gunsmith to be in possession of the foregoing knowledge, the gun being worked upon should be disassembled to the extent that the breech end will be accessible for insertion of rods, drills and other tools needed to do the job. In the case of a bolt action rifle, this usually involves only the removing of the bolt. With lever action, trombone action and falling block guns, it is necessary to take down the entire action before the breech can be uncovered. At times it is also advisable to remove the stock and forearm, so that oils and cleaning solvents that might have to be put in the bore will not soak into the wood and discolor it.

If a gun is of such construction that the breech end of the barrel is not accessible in a straight line from the axis of the bore, then all the work will have to be done from the muzzle end. If it is not feasible to work from this end, the only alternative is to remove the barrel from the receiver. This procedure can scarcely be recommended, considering the difficulty and extra work involved, unless, of course, no other way seems practicable.

After the gun has been firmly clamped in the vise, in such a position that there is at least four feet of working space at both breech and muzzle end, a rod of any size that will fit loosely in the bore is pushed in from the breech end and a pencil mark made on the rod indicating the depth it has gone into the bore. This marked distance is then transferred to the outside of the barrel, showing the position of the obstruction from the breech end. Repeat this same procedure from the muzzle end of the barrel and the space between the two lines on the outside of the barrel will be the size of the bore obstruction. Thus the gunsmith can tell at any time how he is progressing during the operation of tapping or drilling out the obstruction, by taking measurements and comparing these new marks with the ones originally made on the outside of the barrel.

Pounding It Out. If there is only a bullet, and no other obstruction, such as rods, et cetera, lodged in a bore, then the first attempt at removal should be by the old reliable pounding-out method. After determining which end of the barrel the bullet is stuck nearest, shoot a few squirts of oil along the path the bullet will have to follow in being forced out. Naturally, the path chosen should be the shortest one of travel, unless other extenuating factors preclude this course. Next, select a piece of drill rod of a size about .005" less than the bore diameter, true up one end, and slightly chamfer the edge on this end so that no cutting edge will score the bore should the rod go off its course.

Note: Under no circumstances use brass or other soft metal for a driving-out rod. Such type of rod is not only useless, but often swages the obstruction more firmly in place or becomes swaged in place itself.

The proper diameter rod having been selected and faced off, push it up to the obstruction. At this point, *and this is important*:

No More Than Six Inches of the Rod Should Project Beyond the End of the Gun.

If the rod selected allows more than this length, all in excess should be cut off, even though the remaining length will not go all the way through the bore. The piece cut off can be utilized to make up this difference in length after the bore obstruction has been pushed farther along. However, at no time during the operation should more than six inches of unsupported rod be pounded upon. This, as stated before, is most important, if not the whole secret of performing a successful job, because it prevents bending of the rod and consequent failure to move the lodgment.

Before describing the proper method of procedure for the next step of actually hammering out the obstruction, perhaps it would not be amiss to comment on the theory behind the action so that a more complete understanding of the situation might be gained.

Bullets for modern weapons are, as a general practice, made slightly larger in diameter than the bore of the gun through which they are to be fired. For example, the bore of the Springfield rifle is .300" in diameter and the rifling is cut to a depth of .004". Thus it can be seen that the "across the land" measurement of the bore is .300" and the "across the groove" measurement is .308". The bullet, however, is .309" in diameter. Now let us consider another fact based on experiments conducted at Springfield Armory. These experiments showed that it requires in excess of 1,000 pounds per square inch of pressure to force a maximum diameter bullet through a minimum diameter bore.

From this it should be quite evident that light blows from a light hammer on a rod do nothing more than cause the lodged bullet to expand and become more firmly swaged in place. Therefore, when attempting to pound a lodged obstruction from the bore of any weapon, other than a shotgun, each blow delivered must be of sufficient force to move the bullet rather than just upset it; use a heavy hammer and "sock it"!

After the bullet is forced along the bore about 5", the rod should be withdrawn and a 5" piece of the same diameter rod, with *both* ends trued up and chamfered, pushed into the bore. Then reinsert the main rod and resume pounding. As the bullet is pushed down the bore about 5", another short rod should be put in place, until the lodgment is knocked out completely. Any fragments of lead adhering to the interior bore surface can usually be freed by a vigorous bore scrubbing with a bronze wire brush held in a cleaning rod.

The small rods, or as a matter of fact all rods used for removing bore obstructions, should be cleaned after use, treated with a coating of grease and put away for future use. In this way the gunsmith will not have to run around looking for a miscellaneous collection of rods each time he is faced with a job of this sort.

If the gunsmith expects to do much bore obstruction removal via the rod and hammer method, he might well spend a few hours making up a set of rods as illustrated in Figure 35A. If properly cared for, they will outlast the gunsmith and help him to make many an honest dollar with a minimum of bruised knuckles. A main handle and five lengths of rod for .22 caliber, .25 caliber, .30 caliber, and .35 caliber should take care of all

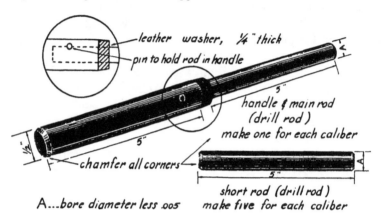

leather washer, ¼" thick

pin to hold rod in handle

handle & main rod
(drill rod)
make one for each caliber

5"

chamfer all corners

A...bore diameter less .005

short rod (drill rod)
make five for each caliber

HANDLE AND RODS FOR POUNDING OUT BORE OBSTRUCTIONS

FIGURE 35A

normally encountered weapons. The leather washer shown in the drawing is very important since it will act as a cushion and prevent marring the muzzle or receiver of a gun if the lodgment gives way suddenly under pressure from a well directed blow.

Drilling It Out. An alternative method of removing lodged bullets is to drill them out of the bore. This procedure is to be recommended only when all attempts to drive them out have proved to be of no avail, for at best it is a task that requires a great deal of skill, understanding and patience.

After selecting the proper size drill (.010″ less than bore diameter) for the caliber of gun being worked upon, regrind the point to a 30° angle and proceed as follows (Figure 35B):

1) Put the drill in a lathe chuck or collet, making sure that the chuck jaws contact the shank part of the drill and not the flutes, and turn the shank down to ⅛″ diameter for a length of about ½″.

2) Take a 6″ piece of smooth, straight, brass rod that measures .003″ less than bore diameter and face both ends off true. Drill a ⅛″ hole to a depth of ½″ at each end and chamfer the corners.

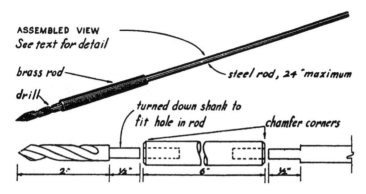

TOOL FOR DRILLING OUT BORE OBSTRUCTIONS
FIGURE 35D

3) Select a piece of cold rolled steel or drill rod about .010" in diameter less than bore size, and 24" long, and turn one end to ⅛" diameter for a length of ½".

4) Tin, with acid core solder, the turned end of the drill shank, the turned end of the 24" rod, and both holes in the length of brass. Then, with a Bunsen burner or alcohol torch, heat first one end of the brass piece and the tinned drill shank, and sweat the latter into the former. Do the same to the other end of the brass section and 24" rod, and sweat them together.

Used in a hand or breast drill, this type of drilling tool will maintain its center in the bore while cutting, because the near bore size brass piece serves as a constant guide and is not thrown off by any slight bending of the main rod.

Whatever bit of bullet remains in the bore after drilling out the main part can be driven out with a bore size rod, and then the bore should be completely cleaned with a brass brush.

In removing types of obstructions other than those specifically covered here, the gunsmith must evaluate each job at hand and decide just what is the most practical and safest way to do it. In all instances, though, it must be remembered that improper tools in the hands of an expert are just about as useless as the best tools in the hands of a novice.

Stuck Cartridge Cases

Fired Cases. If a fired cartridge case is just stuck in the chamber and not ruptured, it is best to insert a long rod of near caliber size in the muzzle and tap it gently at first, so as to reduce the possibility of breaking the case in two. If light blows do not effect removal, increase the force with each subsequent blow until the case comes loose.

When a stuck case comes free from the chamber with very little effort, then check the extractor on the gun, for it is probably broken or bent; or the spring that holds it in place is either missing or defective.

Before proceeding with the aforementioned method to remove cartridge cases, always check on the following points:

1) See that the breech block or bolt is open, so that the pounding is not being directed against a closed or locked breech.

2) Make sure that the case being removed does not have a live primer in it. This may sound a bit odd, but after all, the owner of the gun may have pulled the bullet from a live cartridge, emptied the powder out and inserted it in the chamber for some reason or other. This has happened more than once to the writer and it is being passed along because primers pack a dangerous wallop and sometimes resent being tapped on from the inside.

3) Have the gun firmly held in a good vise so that it does not wobble or shift as each blow is struck. This is a point which can hardly be stressed enough. When a gun cannot be held tightly because the stock or some part is in danger of being crushed by the vise jaws, then remove the stock and place the gun in the vise in such a way that it can be held securely.

RUPTURED
CARTRIDGE CASE
EXTRACTOR

Marble type.

FIGURE 36A

Ruptured Cases. Ruptured cases, which are usually an indication of excessive headspace (See Chapter Five), can usually be removed by one of three methods. Either the first or second method to be described should be tried before resorting to the third, for this last is one that requires the patience and dexterity of a skilled surgeon:

1) The ruptured case extractor illustrated in Figure 36A is

much simpler to use than it is to make, and for that reason this writer recommends that it be purchased from a gun supply house rather than made. To use it, just insert it in the chamber so that the lip will engage the mouth of the cartridge case; then put a rod in the muzzle of the gun until the end rests upon the tapered piece of the shell extractor and gently tap on the rod until the case comes out. If the shell extractor does not grip the rim of the shell mouth after a few tries, it is useless to proceed further, for the mouth of the case is either so damaged or so thin that it provides no bearing surface for the extractor lips.

2) To remove a ruptured cartridge case by the tap method requires more forethought than it does actual work, for it involves nothing more than selecting a fine pitch tap of such a diameter that the threads will bite into the brass case without cutting through and scoring the chamber. Thus it is obvious that great care must be exercised in making a choice of the proper size tap for each different caliber of shell, lest a ruined chamber be the sad aftermath of a would-be well done job.

No definite size of tap for each size shell can be listed here for when dealing with tapered shells the amount of case remaining in the chamber governs the size of tap that must be used.

Always select the finest pitch commensurate with the size of tap being used; then the tap does not have to be forced too far forward in the case in order that sufficient holding surface for the tap teeth can be obtained. When dealing with cartridge cases having a fast taper, proceed cautiously, bearing in mind that the first eight or 10 teeth on a #1 (taper) tap are shorter than the main teeth. As a matter of fact, for best results a #3 (bottoming) tap should be used when possible. This partially precludes any chamber scoring as a result of underestimating the true diameter of the tap.

Using the proper size tap, it is only necessary to have five or six teeth biting into the cartridge case in order to achieve sufficient holding power. With the tap firmly screwed in the cartridge case a barrel-length rod inserted from the muzzle and acting against the front of the tap, should be struck with light hammer blows until the cartridge case breaks free.

3) Methods 1 and 2 having proved to be non-workable, the gunsmith must resort to chiseling, or cutting the case from its seemingly unmovable position. The proper type of chisel for this sort of job is illustrated in detail in Figure 36B. In using this

chisel it is advisable to proceed slowly and employ only that amount of force which can be applied by hand. *Do Not Use a Hammer.*

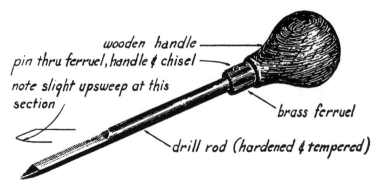

wooden handle

pin thru ferrule, handle & chisel

note slight upsweep at this section

brass ferrule

drill rod (hardened & tempered)

CHISEL FOR CUTTING RUPTURED CARTRIDGE CASES

FIGURE 36B

Aside from the special caution required in carrying out this operation, it will, in most cases, be necessary to remove the barrel before any cutting work is performed. This is not a happy prospect but after the gunsmith has been plying his trade for awhile he will learn that it is easier in the long run to start a job right and see it through to a successful conclusion, than to do makeshift work and always wind up behind the eight-ball.

With the barrel held firmly in a vise, move the chisel in a straight line along the lower part of the case, from the breech end towards the muzzle, making a fine cut with each stroke. On long bottle-neck type cases, cut no further than the shoulder, and *always blow away all chips* turned up so that the depth of the cut can be judged. When the case has been split, take a piece of $\frac{1}{8}''$ square brass rod, sharpened in the manner of a wood chisel, and force it under the split so that the cut edges turn up, affording an area large enough to provide a surface for the jaws of needle-nose pliers. Before using the pliers to pull the case loose, pry up all the case that is possible and squirt a liberal quantity of penetrating oil between the cartridge case and the chamber walls. Let this stand overnight in an upright position so that the oil gets down into the less accessible spaces near the front end of the case. Then, with needle-nose pliers, pull the case out, using a back-and-forth motion. Do not attempt to twist the pliers in a

circular fashion as the brass of the cartridge case may uncurl
or break off.

After a ruptured cartridge case has been removed from any
type of weapon, the gunsmith should attempt to determine what
underlying causes have occasioned such a malfunction.

As stated previously in this chapter and in Chapter Five, most
ruptured cartridge cases come about as a result of the weapon
having excessive headspace. The customer should be warned
when this condition exists, for another ruptured case might result in the gun blowing apart or loosing a jet of high pressure
gas into the eyes of the shooter. A new bolt or, in some cases, a
new barrel, will be needed to correct this condition of excessive
headspace.

When either a stuck or ruptured case is encountered, the possibility of a rusty, pitted or scored chamber must not be overlooked, as this condition can and does cause cartridges to stick,
because the soft brass of the case expands to fill all depressions,
no matter how small, at the instant of explosion. If a chamber is
found to be so badly marred that removal of the scoring would
make for a very loose chamber, then a new barrel is indicated.
When only light scratches or superficial rust is present, a dowel
rod, fashioned to chamber shape and slit to retain a piece of crocus cloth, can be turned inside the chamber by means of a hand
drill.

Unfired Cases. Now and then a rifle is presented to the gunsmith in which there is a loaded cartridge stuck in the chamber.
Sometimes it is a comparatively easy proposition to remove it,
while other cartridges prove near impossible to dislodge. Easy
or difficult, the task is at best a tricky one, for loaded cartridges
must be treated with respect, especially ones that are stuck and
might well have an indented primer.

The first step towards removing a stuck loaded cartridge is
to check the extractor of the gun and see if it is in good operating order. If it is not, then replacing or repairing it might be
the answer to the problem. If a properly operating extractor does
not pull the case free, then chances are that it is stuck very
tightly and more forceful methods must be employed.

Fill the bore of the gun with light oil and let it stand overnight with the muzzle of the gun pointing upwards. After it has
remained this way for the required length of time, again try to
extract the case by means of the extractor. If the extractor rim

of the cartridge case is ripped off or deformed where the extractor grasps it, a hook or claw should be formed from brass or soft steel and hooked under the rim. In short, try to pry the case loose, being careful not to turn in metal around the edge of the chamber.

When this means fails, it is often fruitful to fill the bore completely with a light oil and then push a rod, having one end fitted with leather washers (exactly the same size as the bore), slowly into the bore. This little contraption (Figure 37) works on the

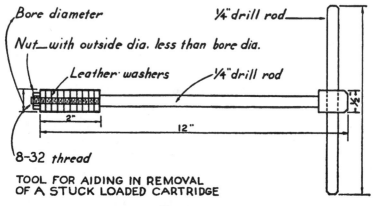

TOOL FOR AIDING IN REMOVAL
OF A STUCK LOADED CARTRIDGE

FIGURE 37

hydraulic principle and considerable pressure can be exerted on the cartridge with it. The important thing is to have the leather washers perfectly circular and the same size as the bore. In this way very little oil will be allowed to squeeze past the washers and all the compression force will be exerted against the bullet and case.

In using this tool, make certain that it is started into the bore straight and push on it very, very slowly. As pressure is applied on the handle of the tool (note that the handle is made especially large to stand up under pushing and pulling), the oil will be forced into every minute space between the stuck case and chamber walls; and at the same time a pushing force is brought to bear against the cartridge.

If good compression is achieved, the gunsmith will find that he cannot push the tool very far into the bore by hand. At this point, then, it is permissible to deliver a few sharp blows on the end of the tool. Often the sudden application of pressure of this sort will jar the cartridge loose, or at least force enough oil between the case and chamber walls so that extraction from the rim end of the case is possible.

If none of the previously suggested methods produces results, then the only thing left to do is to pound the cartridge out from the muzzle end of the gun.

A safe way to do this is to drill a hole through the bullet (from the muzzle end of the gun, of course), using a small diameter drill (⅛″), in an arrangement similar to the one suggested for drilling out lodged bullets. Empty the powder out of the case through this hole by pointing the muzzle of the gun towards the ground, first having made sure that the bore is dry so that powder grains will not stick inside it. Having done this, next introduce a small tube or pipe into the bore down as far as the bullet, and pour a small quantity of water through this tube. If this setup is all right, the water will flow into the cartridge case and seep through the vent hole into the priming composition, rendering it somewhat insensitive. Let the water remain in the case for at least a few hours, but meantime dry out the bore with a patch so the rifling will not become rust-specked.

Next, take a piece of drill rod (bore diameter minus .005″ and long enough to reach the bullet tip, plus about 5″ for holding and pounding) and drill a hole in one end so that it will cover the bullet for a length of about ¼″. Coat the rod with oil, push it in until it rests against the bullet, and start pounding. Start off with light, sharp blows and increase their force until the case breaks free.

If the bullet recedes into the case during the pounding process, think little of it and keep on hammering. This is bound to happen unless the case is dislodged after the first few light blows.

After the case has been freed from the chamber, examine the latter and find out if that was what caused all the trouble. Any of the following defects could cause a case or cartridge to stick:

1) Undersized chamber
2) Deformed chamber
3) Rusty chamber
4) Metal turned in around the edge of the chamber
5) Metal turned in around the extractor groove
6) Oversized chamber (in guns shooting rimless cases)
7) Gun loaded for long period of time, permitting cartridge to corrode and "freeze" to chamber.

The wrong cartridge (for example, an 8 mm Mauser in a gun chambered for the .30/06), can cause a loaded cartridge to stick. Also, handloaded cartridges that are not held to minimum or maximum tolerance have a tendency to bind in a rifle chamber.

While a gunsmith cannot compel a customer to refrain from putting inferior handloaded cartridges into his gun, he can, if the chamber is damaged, suggest that it be repaired before the gun is again used.

In outlining the various methods of removing a loaded cartridge from the chamber of a gun, this writer has not touched upon the idea of firing the cartridge and then knocking out the empty case inasmuch as it is assumed the gunsmith will give this method first thought. The cartridge should not be fired, however, if it is not the proper one for the gun or if it is so deep in the chamber that the breech bolt face will not support it. It is better to spend a few hours easing a stuck cartridge out of a gun than to fire it and have a doctor spend many hours picking fragments of a rifle receiver out of one's face. Besides, customers do not like to have their guns blown up—especially by gunsmiths.

When working on stuck cartridges or cartridge cases in a .22 caliber rim fire weapon, the greatest of care must be exercised because the walls of a .22 case are very thin and soft, and tear very easily. Also, a few scratches on the chamber wall and that gun will forever after be a headache as far as extraction is concerned. There is no room for slips or mistakes when prying and pounding a cartridge from a .22 rim fire gun. If a gunsmith hasn't the tools, knack or know-how to do the job on this caliber gun, he might better turn the job down than attempt it with makeshift tools or methods.

CHAPTER SEVEN

Adjustments and Considerations

A CUSTOMER does not always bring his gun to the gunsmith because it is actually broken but possibly because it is in need of tuning up.

Perhaps a man may have an inexpensive double barrel shotgun which, while not defective in functioning, has nevertheless a very rough operating mechanism. And although this latter deficiency is common to most cheap mass-produced guns after very little use, it does not mean that they are beyond redemption. While the gunsmith cannot expect, or be expected, to turn them into super-smooth operating weapons simply by employing a few tricks of the trade, he can do much in the way of improvement.

Disassembly of one of these coarse operating guns will usually reveal, in addition to the accumulated grease and foreign matter (which must be cleaned off before proceeding any further), deep and irregular tool marks on the moving parts and the fixed surfaces which these parts contact when in motion.

Action Improvement Work

Uncovering Defects. The first step, after the sideplates have been removed and the mechanism has been cleaned out, is to operate the mechanism of the gun and observe the points at which excessive friction is being caused by parts rubbing against each other. In addition, look for scratch marks and tears on the parts and sideplates, which also indicate improper contact between parts. Parts which rotate on pins should be checked for excessive play between the pin and hole in the part.

Wear Between Pin and Hole. Few defects can be the cause of so much rough action operation as excessive play between a pin and the hole of a moving part. Where possible, a new pin of hardened and highly polished steel should be substituted for the undersized or eccentrically worn pin. If circumstances are such that it is not practical to put in a new pin, then the hole in the part which fits on the pin might be rebushed, providing, of course, there is enough metal surrounding the hole to allow for reaming out and inserting the bushing.

Bushing a Part. Putting a bushing in a moving part is not an exceptionally difficult job but it is one that requires the employment of utmost accuracy throughout. For if a bushing is installed in an improperly reamed hole, or if the hole in the bushing is not absolutely concentric to the outside of the bushing, the path of motion of the part will be thrown out of line and impose undue stress on all other parts that it works in conjunction with, to say nothing of making the action worse than ever.

To rebush one of these parts proceed as follows:

1) Enlarge the original hole with a drill about 0.022″ larger in diameter than the hole.

2) Ream out the drilled hole. Reamer should be about 0.004″ larger than drilled hole.

3) Chamfer the corners of reamed hole, on each side of the part, with a countersink.

4) Select a piece of drill rod slightly larger in diameter than the reamed hole and turn a length down 0.0625″ longer than needed so that when finish-turned it will be about .002″ larger than the diameter of the reamed hole.

5) Drill and ream a hole in this piece so that when finished it will just move freely on the pin.

6) Cut the bushing off and face both ends so that the remaining piece is a few thousandths longer than the width of the part it must fit into.

7) Harden and temper the bushing and press it into the part.

8) Finish off the protruding ends of the bushing by grinding or stoning, so that they are flush with the operating width of the part.

As can be seen from the foregoing description, making and installing a bushing does require more than a few minutes time. It should not be attempted if a new part is procurable at a price which would make this operation impractical or more costly, or when the part to be bushed is otherwise worn at points where remedial action is impossible or impractical. However, when a part cannot be replaced or is so complicated in design that fabrication of a whole new unit would be too costly, then bushing it is often the answer to the problem.

In cases where the size of the part does not allow for installation of bushing that is strong enough to withstand being inserted by press fitting, a thinner one can be made and carefully sweated in place.

Smoothing Marred Parts. Where the surfaces of parts are scarred from contact, these parts should be removed and checked for hardness by trying a file against the metal. If the file does not bite in, then in all probability the surface is case-hardened and a file cannot be used to deburr or refinish the part. Instead, an abrasive-coated grinding wheel, as described in Chapter Sixteen, should be used. In using these wheels, care must be exercised so that too much metal will not be removed, causing excessive play between parts. Parts being ground should also be held against the rotating wheel in such a manner as to preclude the rounding of sharp corners or the grinding of surface hollows.

After all deep scratches have been ground out, the part should be rubbed back and forth on a piece of fine emery cloth tacked or glued to a flat, smooth board. This operation will aid in producing a true, flat, uniform-grained surface. Final polish should be put on by buffing the part against a leather or felt wheel coated with Lea Polishing Compound.

If previous inspection has revealed the part being refinished to be of mild steel, it should be case-hardened after final polishing and fitting. This will insure, to a great degree, the part retaining a scratch-free surface and smoother operational qualities over a long period of usage. However, before attempting the hardening process, the gunsmith should make certain that no further work, except perhaps a bit of hand stoning, is necessary. For once a part is properly case-hardened it will resist all attempts to be filed, sawed or machined.

In connection with this type of work, it might be well to point out that while there is room for improvement on certain types of guns, much damage can be done if the utmost caution is not exercised when grinding or filing parts. Engaging notches, locking lugs, locking recesses and the like should not be filed or ground, other than to remove definitely formed burrs. Even buffing on the back surfaces of a bolt's locking lugs is something that just is not done. Remember, a few thousandths of an inch can mean excessive headspace.

On Colt Revolvers. On Colt revolvers the action can be greatly improved by smoothing up the side of the hand which contacts the sideplate and the top of the rebound lever where the mainspring rubs on it.

Where an overall lighter action is desired on a standard Colt revolver to be used for target work, other improvements can also be effected.

The end of the mainspring can be bent as in Figure 38, and the bottom flat of the bent portion ground on a soft-back wheel and polished to a mirror finish. Bending of the spring should be done with a pair of wide-jaw pliers. The edge of the spring (Point A) should also be rounded so that it will not dig into the tip of the rebound lever.

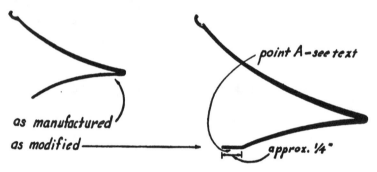

point A—see text

as manufactured

as modified ⟶ approx. ¼"

COLT REVOLVER MAINSPRING

FIGURE 38

The bolt spring can be removed and one a bit longer, but made of finer gauge wire, substituted. This is not a change that should be accomplished without a bit of experimenting, however, for if the substituted spring is too weak it might result in the bolt not jumping into the cylinder recess on time. Such a defect would be very serious and could bring about misfires.

The end of the bolt which is actuated by the rebound lever can be bent in towards the frame so that the rebound lever will not have to drag too much against it. This bending should be carried out with care and understanding, so that the bent end will not be depressed to the extent where the tit on the rebound lever will fail to fully actuate the bolt.

The underside of the trigger (Figure 39) can be polished to a mirror-like finish by means of fine emery cloth, followed by crocus cloth. Very little metal need be removed to achieve this finish, and polishing strokes should be in a lengthwise direction. Be careful in doing this so as not to change the angle on the end of the trigger which engages the cocking notch of the hammer, as this might tend to increase the trigger pull and affect the timing of the gun.

If the sideplate of the revolver shows signs of wear where the hand rides, refinishing of the hand will correct this.

If the sideplate shows signs of wear at the radius where the rebound lever moves, and slight polishing of the offending side of the lever does not correct it, then the pin which holds the lever in place is probably undersized and should be replaced.

surface A

COLT REVOLVER TRIGGER

FIGURE 39

Possibilities. From the foregoing descriptions the gunsmith should be better able to visualize the possibilities of action improvement work by means of grinding, polishing and hardening of parts. The examples just cited are by no means a representation of the limitations of this sort of work. Rather, they are singled out to illustrate the general course of action that should be followed. Work of this type has almost limitless possibilities of application and can provide the ingenious and foresighted gunsmith with a profitable means of income, besides adding to his reputation as being more than just another gun mechanic. However, the gunsmith cannot expect to be regarded as a specialist in action work until he introduces an improvement for which a genuine need exists, or at least expertly carries out a phase of action improvement originated by other specialists, e.g., short-action on revolvers, accuracy improvements on the .45 automatic, cockeyed hammer on revolvers, et cetera.

Action improvement work as a rule is born of a thorough understanding of the shortcoming of a particular gun, which comes from shooting the gun or analyzing shooters' complaints, plus a knowledge of the gun mechanism. This does not mean that the gunsmith must be a crack shot or a mechanical engineer; rather, it means that he must be able to recognize a true "bug" in a gun's design (as differentiated from an opinion on the relative killing power or shape of a stock) and know how a practical improvement can be made at a reasonable price.

Undoubtedly there is a "bug" or two in every commercially-made gun and only relatively few users ever awaken to the fact that there is room for improvement. However, now and then an alert gunsmith or mechanic with a commercial turn of mind comes to life and presto! the public is offered an improved type safety, a speed action mainspring made of square wire, a barrel bushing with three little ball bearings in it, a shotgun-type safety for a rifle, and a few other items which appeal to the shooter because he sees that they will make his scores better or his hunting trip more fruitful.

Chamber Defects

Extraction. In Chapter Five, under the topic of inspecting the extractor, mention is made of the importance of a smooth chamber in a gun. Here again it might be well to point out that this portion of a gun barrel should receive special attention when making inspection of a semi-automatic arm where complaints of sluggish extraction or ruptured cartridge cases are made.

It should be borne in mind that a fired cartridge case expands into every pit and tool mark of a chamber, and this adds up to a great deal of resistance which can appreciably slow down the extraction phase and put added strain on the extractor claw. This is especially true in the case of .22 rim fire weapons, where the cartridge case is of thin and soft metal.

Often chamber pits and scars are so bad that the amount of metal which must be removed to restore complete smoothness will enlarge the chamber to a degree where it might be greatly oversized. In such cases it is best to recommend a new barrel for the gun. If the customer does not wish to make an expenditure of this sort, then do the next best thing and smooth up the chamber as much as possible by means of very fine emery cloth, followed by crocus cloth. Both of these abrasive cloths should be used on a dowel rod cut to the approximate shape of the chamber and of such a diameter as to permit wrapping one thickness of the abrasive medium around the rod (see paragraph on Lead Fouling in Shotgun Bores).

Substitute Work

When returning a gun on which a secondary or alternate job has been performed at the customer's insistence, the gunsmith should explain the true facts of the case so that he will not be accused of doing a slipshod job. However, where safety to the user of the gun, or anyone who might be standing near, is involved *no alternate or substitute work should be attempted*. Rather, explain to the customer that there is only one way to do the job and that any makeshift repair would serve no purpose other than to create a period of worry for all parties concerned and possibly eventually culminate in an accident.

Judging Bore Condition of Rifled Weapons

Almost invariably the first thing a prospective purchaser of a used gun looks at when inspecting it is the bore. As a matter of fact, almost everyone who even thinks he knows something about firearms not infrequently judges the shooting value of a weapon by casting an appraising glance down through the rifled tube and is guided in rendering a decision solely by what he imagines he saw. If the bore is somewhat worn but is clean and shining, a favorable verdict is usually given. On the other hand, if mild pitting is present to the extent where the bore appears dull, then the opposite conclusion is reached, i.e., "This gun is no good."

While it is not within the scope or intention of this book to directly attempt education of the mass of individual gun purchasers, it is important that the gunsmith should be qualified to appraise the apparent qualities of a rifled gun bore and inform his customers frankly and honestly when asked for a professional opinion.

Rifling Characteristics. Ever since rifled guns have been in existence, there has always been a great deal of controversy as to the relative merits of different types, pitches and depths of rifling. By means of involved mathematical computations and years of experimenting, certain fundamental theories have been arrived at which are today carried out as standard operating practice by the commercial manufacturers of firearms, although at this writing new and somewhat revolutionary (remember, the gun field is an ultra-conservative one) types and methods of rifling are being employed. For example, the rifle, U.S. Caliber .30 M1903*A3* (the old M1903 Springfield slightly revamped) is made with two lands and two grooves, as compared with the conventional four lands and a like number of grooves in the bore of the parent weapon. Too, the freeboring system, in which a section of the bore directly in front of the chamber is reamed free of rifling, is making its appearance on rifles modified by companies specializing in this type of work. However, indications are that the conventional system of boring and rifling will be with us for some time to come before free-boring and two-groove rifling are generally and commercially adopted.

Rifling Nomenclature. As is quite obvious to anyone who has looked down the bore of a gun for more than a fleeting instant, rifling is nothing more than a number of spiral grooves cut in the bore, leaving an equal number of apparently raised segments known as lands. The spiral direction of the rifling is referred to by its rate of progression, and except for a few special guns having a progressive twist, this rate of progression is uniform. The third factor which enters into the determination of rifling classification is the direction of the twist, i.e., right-hand or left-hand. Thus, to classify the rifling characteristics of a Springfield rifle, U.S. Caliber .30 M1903 it would be correct to say that it has four lands and four grooves having a uniform right-hand twist of one turn in 10″.

The purpose of the twist in the rifling is to impart a spinning motion to the bullet as it travels down the bore and keep it rotating on its longer axis as it goes through space. A football player imparts the same motion to a football when throwing a forward pass.

The groove depth of the rifling, which is expressed in thousandths (or ten-thousandths) of an inch, is not the same for all weapons. It varies from 0.0025″ to 0.005″, depending upon the type of bullet designed to be fired in the weapon. However, in some guns the grooved depth will be found to measure as much as 0.009″. This latter is especially true of foreign made pistols and old large bore guns.

Factors Affecting Bore Condition. Present generally accepted theories as to what makes a gun good or bad, on the basis of bore condition, can be summed up as follows:

1) If the bore is free from bulges (ring bore), bends, deep pits, excessive wear of rifling just forward of the chamber, and the lands appear sharp and distinct, it is reasonable to assume it is in good condition.

2) If the bore has a bulge at any point in its length, it is absolutely unserviceable and beyond the stage of practical repair.

3) If the bore is pitted to the extent where a large pit 0.25" or longer crosses an entire land and groove, then the barrel should be considered in poor condition and not conducive to even fair accuracy. In this condition it will become fouled easily and allow passage of gas ahead of the bullet.

4) If the condition of the lands is affected to the extent where they no longer have sharpness on their driving edge, then it must be assumed that many rounds of ammunition have been fired through the gun, or it has been neglected, and the remaining accuracy might be somewhat doubtful. Extensive light pitting in the rifling can also produce similar results.

Pitted Bores. Nowadays, with modern non-hygroscopic powders and non-corrosive primers, pitted barrels as an after-effect of combustion products residue is very uncommon. However, American military ammunition in both caliber .30 and caliber .45 is not equipped with non-corrosive primers. Much of this ammunition gets into the commercial market and is used extensively in peacetime by hunters and target shooters. If a gun in which this ammunition is fired is not cleaned soon after firing and for another two days following the initial cleaning, the bore will soon show extensive deposits of rust. And where there is rust there is pitting.

The introduction of non-corrosive primers was a wonderful innovation but with it there came an invitation to carelessness. Many gun owners now consider it absolutely unnecessary to clean bores after firing, since the products of combustion are not deleterious to the rifled tube. In some instances this is a justified assumption. However, in damp climates cleaning and oiling of the gun bore should be an accepted practice. As a matter of fact, the life of any gun bore can be better guaranteed if cleaning and oiling of the bore is done after the gun has been fired and is ready to be put away until the next time.

The Human Element. Evaluating bore condition is at best nothing more than high class guess work because of the many preconceived notions each gunsmith has (as to what constitutes a bad bore) before he looks down the rifled tube. That is, of course, presuming the inspector has a basic knowledge and is familiar with the defects (ring bore, cracked barrel, et cetera) that automatically render any barrel unsafe and unserviceable. However, aside from these generally accepted disqualifying defects there is more than one school of thought as to the extent pitting, muzzle wear and erosion can be tolerated before a barrel ceases to be accurate enough for practical use. Therefore, it is important that the gunsmith know how good or bad a gun shoots before he condemns a barrel on the basis of erosion or pitting.

It is quite surprising how well some badly eroded barrels shoot, and equally surprising the groups made with M1 rifles in which the muzzle is so enlarged that a 0.308″ gage can be inserted to a depth of 0.75″. When one sees barrels that are, according to one theory or another, no better than a hose, deliver shot after shot into the black of an "A" target at 300 yards, then one cannot help but wonder if some extensive research on the subject of "barrel life" is not needed in this era of scientific exactness.

Metal Fouling in Rifle Bores

Lead Fouling. In weapons which fire non-jacketed (lead) bullets, pits act to collect minute particles of lead and the bore often becomes leaded to the extent where accuracy of the piece is appreciably reduced. Weapons so afflicted can be deleaded by placing a cork in the breech of the gun and filling the bore from the muzzle end with metallic mercury. Then a cork should be placed in the muzzle and the mercury-filled bore allowed to stand for a few hours or, better still, overnight, until the lead and mercury become amalgamated. After all the mercury is poured out of the bore, the latter should be scrubbed with a brass bristle brush to loosen and remove any flakes remaining. Follow this with patches soaked in bore cleaner, and finally oil. While this treatment will remove practically all of the accumulated lead in a gun bore, it will not prevent a recurrence of the same condition.

Metal Fouling. Metal fouling, chiefly the nickel from the old style nickel bullets, is not too often encountered in gun bores nowadays. However, when someone digs up some old ammunition and runs a few boxes of them through a barrel he is apt to be quite surprised with the "flake-plating" the bore gets.

Metal fouling can be removed with denickeling paste, sold by Stoeger, or by corking up the chamber at the origin of the rifling and filling the bore with standard metal fouling solution. This old Army formula calls for one ounce of ammonium persulphate mixed with 200 grains of ammonium carbonate, to which four ounces of water is added. After the solids have dissolved in the water, six ounces of 28% ammonia is added and the solution allowed to stand for one hour before using. Because a batch of solution deteriorates in a month or two, it should be prepared only as needed and in small quantity (one-fourth of the above quantities).

Before the standard metal fouling solution is introduced into a bore, the latter should have been cleaned with solvent and wiped dry. Metal fouling solution should be allowed to remain in the bore not more than 20 minutes and should not be spilled on any other metal surfaces of the gun. It should never be poured into a hot barrel. After a metal fouling solution treatment the bore should be flushed with water, dried and oiled. It should also be checked the next day to make sure that the solution has not caused a rust to form in the bore.

Lead Fouling in Shotgun Bores

Shotgun bores which are constantly becoming lead fouled can be lapped out, providing that the causative pits or tool marks are not so deep that their complete removal would weaken the tube.

To lap a shotgun bore, choose a piece of dowel rod long enough to pass through the entire length of the barrel and of appropriate diameter (0.625″ for 12 gauge; 0.50″ for 16 gauge; 0.375″ for 20 gauge). Slit one end for a distance of 3″ to accommodate a wrapping of emery cloth. Turn the other end of the rod to such a diameter that it will fit in the chuck of a hand drill or a portable power drill. Put a length of emery cloth in the slit in such a manner that the turning of the drill will tighten the abrasive cloth on the rod as it is being rotated. Individual cases will be the determining factor as to what grit of emery cloth should be used. However, under no circumstances should any coarser than No. 1 cloth be used. A bit of light oil should be applied to the bore as the lapping is done, and the rod should be moved in gradually as it is rotating. A mark or stop should also be put on the rod so that no cutting will be done on the choke portion of the barrel. The point at which the choking starts in the barrel should be determined before commencing the lapping operation. As the bore is made pit-free from the use of the coarser grit emery cloth, finer grades should be substituted until No. 3/0 wet or dry abrasive cloth is reached. After this, crocus cloth should be employed, until the bore has a uniformly high polish throughout its length.

Although it is possible to accomplish the lapping of a very lightly pitted shotgun bore with a hand or breast drill, the results achieved will be inferior to one done by means of a motor powered polishing unit. If a portable power drill is not available, the tailstock assembly can be removed from a lathe and the dowel rod inserted in the lathe chuck. By running the lathe at high speed excellent results can be achieved.

Gloves should be worn when performing this lapping job on the lathe, for the barrel heats up readily to the degree where it cannot be held in the bare hands, and the gunsmith must be protected and comfortable as it takes a minimum of an hour to do one tube. If a portable power drill is used, there is no necessity for the gloves, since the barrel is held in a vise rather than the hands. But whether a lathe or portable power drill is used, the barrels should be stripped from the rest of the gun. Probably the most important thing to remember when lapping a shotgun tube is to keep the lap moving forward (or backward on the return stroke) while it is rotating. In this way no high surfaces or low surfaces will be caused as a result of the abrasive acting too long in one place. Too, if there are dents in a tube, they must be completely removed before any lapping is done. Otherwise the abrasive will cut heavily into the raised portion on the inside of the bore and weaken it to a dangerous thinness at this point.

Cannibalization

As applied to the gun repair business, cannibalization means that one gun of a certain type is sacrificed to provide parts for another gun of the same type. However, it is a practice that should be resorted to only when repairing obsolete or foreign guns for which parts are unobtainable or expensive to make.

As an illustration, this writer frequently buys up old Savage automatic pistols, Smith & Wesson automatic pistols and similar obsolete weapons that are badly in need of repair and which can be bought for a few dollars at most. Then when a person who has, say, a Savage automatic in splendid condition except for a broken grip, is willing to pay a couple of dollars for a replacement grip, it can be taken from one of the old guns, polished up a bit, and installed on the customer's pistol. Now charging a couple of dollars for a grip that originally listed at 50¢ might sound like a bit of sharp business practice but it is not, for the gunsmith will find, in buying up old guns for cannibalization purposes, that he will accumulate a majority of certain parts that never sell and be short of others which are most frequently broken. Therefore, in order to realize a fair profit on his investment (and often it will be months, even years, before some of the parts will be called for) the gunsmith must get a good price for all parts sold.

Cannibalization, which was a common practice in the Ordnance Department during the early days of World War II when spare parts were short and complete weapons in serviceable order were needed badly, should not be practiced on guns for which parts can be bought or readily made. Taking parts from one gun (for which parts are available) for the purpose of fixing another of the same type, because the gunsmith "forgot" to order the needed parts, is not cannibalization, it is just plain bad business.

When a gun is bought for the purpose of cannibalization it should be completely disassembled and each part carefully examined for excessive wear, cracks, deformation, or any defect which would render it unfit for use. Naturally, when dealing with used parts, a certain amount of wear on them must be expected, but no part should be considered serviceable if it will not, when properly installed, function as it was designed to. Special inspection should be given the "vital parts" of a gun, i.e., sear, safety, firing pin, which, if not up to working standard, might conceivably be the cause of an accidental discharge. Though the majority of accidental discharges with firearms are due to human failings, no gunsmith wants to, or can afford to, be known as having fixed up a gun that failed because of mechanical reasons.

After the inspected parts have been segregated, the serviceable ones should be cleaned up, touched up with a stone to knock off burrs, et cetera, reblued if necessary, cataloged, preserved and put away. This is the efficient method of handling parts from cannibalized guns and a way which will make it easier for the gunsmith to know just what he has on hand at all times in the line of hard-to-get parts.

Frames from guns that have been stripped of all parts should be cleaned up, oiled and laid aside—never can tell when some shootin' feller will advertise in "The Rifleman" for just such items. After all, a cleaned up gun frame that brings a five spot is more to the gunsmith's credit than one laying in the corner of the shop covered with a delicate red rust, forgotten for years.

The importance of tagging parts from old or unfamiliar weapons cannot be stressed too strongly. Good business practice demands it and the fact that one easily forgets which spring or pin goes in what gun after a few years of their being stored in among a pile of miscellaneous scrap makes it imperative.

Cataloging such parts makes it possible for the gunsmith to determine very quickly whether he can fix an obsolete weapon presented to him for repair. Also, it affords him a better means of utilizing the services of a helper, who can be referred to the records of "parts on hand" rather than a heap of rusty guns when the latter wants to know is such and such a part available. Some fellow summed it up pretty well when he said, "A place for everything and everything in its place."

Adjusting Trigger Pulls

How often we hear a person complaining that his gun is no good because it has a poor trigger pull. In many cases such a condition exists because the owner either has a cheap gun which came from the factory with a bad pull, or he has tried to do a little trigger pull adjusting, lacking proper tools or skill—or both. Occasionally it is the result of wear between engaging parts. However, no matter what the cause might be, the practicing gunsmith will find that adjusting trigger pulls is work which calls for a good deal more thought than action. And while it is impractical, if not virtually impossible, to outline the proper and more efficient method of adjusting the trigger pull on each make and model of gun, by approaching the problem from both a theoretical and practical point of view the subject can be quite adequately covered.

To correct bad trigger pulls, the gunsmith must first understand the way in which trigger mechanisms work. As the first step in that connection there are illustrated in Figure 40 four common basic trigger release mechanisms.

Types of Mechanisms. *The first* (H&R) is that type of design in which the hammer is directly engaged by the trigger. Generally in this type the mainspring is connected by some means to the hammer and the trigger is brought in the path of the hammer notch by means of a light spring, or raised by the action of the hammer. Both Colt and Smith & Wesson employ this type mechanism in their modern swing-out cylinder revolvers. It is also used on other revolvers, single shot rifles and shotguns extensively. For purposes of future reference, we can refer to this as the direct contact trigger mechanism.

FOUR TYPES OF TRIGGER RELEASE MECHANISM

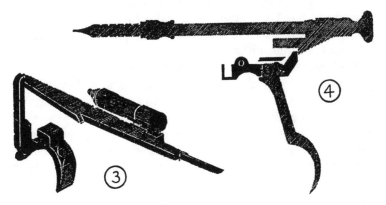

FIGURE 40

The second type, in which the hammer is engaged by a sear, is best represented by that mechanism incorporated in the Colt .45 Government Automatic pistol, as well as other automatic pistols, shotguns and rifles. This is a common type of trigger mechanism.

In *the third* type illustrated (Luger Pistol) the sear engages the firing pin (striker) directly since there is no hammer in mechanisms of this sort. This system is most often found in foreign automatic pistols, as well as our own Colt .25 Automatic.

The fourth type, let us call it the bolt action trigger mechanism, is basically close to type three but nevertheless is so widely employed in military rifles that it is worthy of special listing. The mechanism of the Springfield M1903 rifle is used to illustrate this type of mechanism.

These four types of mechanism were selected for illustrative purposes not only because each is a representative type, but also because they are parts of guns which the average gunsmith sees quite frequently, or at least can lay his hands on for purposes of study. But whether it be one of these mechanisms or any other that he is likely to be confronted with, the gunsmith should bear in mind that with all of them, no matter how many or what style of links, cams or sears they are comprised of, his task is to adjust the various contacting surfaces so they pass across each other smoothly and break away from each other sharply and positively.

Before going more deeply into the matter of pull weight (weight of pull) and other factors affecting a trigger mechanism, perhaps it might be best to first consider the tools used in this phase of gunsmithing work.

Tools for the Job. Second in importance in the matter of trigger pull work are the tools required for the job, and they are comparatively few. A file, a few small honing stones and a magnifying glass about fill the bill.

Files. In connection with using a file on surfaces, notches and points which govern trigger pull, this writer must caution all those who would do a successful job to bear in mind that only the finest cut (dead-smooth) file, having two safe edges (uncut edges), should be used.

Two or three light but definite strokes with an 8″ dead-smooth, narrow, pillar file will usually suffice to remove all the metal necessary to correct an improper angle or smooth off a deep mark from an engaging surface or point.

For purposes of absolute clarity and understanding, a pillar file is illustrated in Figure 41. Also, in connection with the words "fine cut" in reference to a file suitable for trigger pull work, let it be noted that such a file is very much smoother than a common fingernail file. As a matter of fact, the cut on this type of file is so "smooth" that it can be rubbed vigorously across the skin of a clenched fist knuckle without removing any skin or causing any pain. If a file the gunsmith has in mind does not measure up to this standard, then he had better be content to use a stone until such time as he can secure the correct type of file.

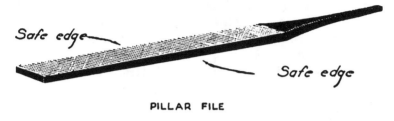

PILLAR FILE

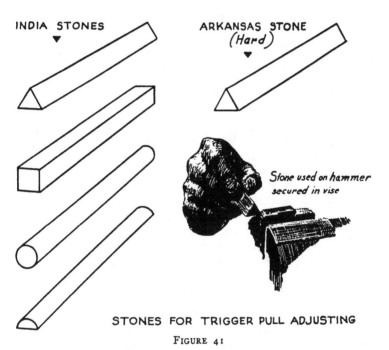

STONES FOR TRIGGER PULL ADJUSTING

FIGURE 41

Needle files as a rule are unsuited for most any phase of trigger pull work, except possibly deepening or reshaping a half-cock notch, because they are quite flexible and tend to round off corners when pressed down on with any appreciable degree of force. Also, only three shapes of needle file, i.e., equaling, slitting and round-edge joint, have parallel sides—a must for a file that is to be used for trigger pull work.

Why all the detail and ado about a file for trigger pull work, the gunsmith might ask. Well, this writer can say from his experience that the correct file in trained and cautious hands can be made to form angles and surfaces far superior to those produced by oilstone alone. To better appreciate this it should be remembered that the best oilstone must be handled lightly and gingerly; if it is not, it will snap in two. Certainly the thought of an oilstone snapping off when "too much" pressure is applied tends to make the mechanic "go light" when he is using a stone on a surface that is usually quite small. Hence, he cannot bear down with the amount of force necessary to hold the stone on an even plane throughout its length of travel. On the other hand, a file can be borne upon as heavily as deemed necessary for trigger pull work, and no thought need be given its ability to stand up under applied pressure.

All of which affords a good opportunity to point out that most of the success in using a file for this type of work lies in:

1) Using the correct file—(do not bother with a handle; it really is not necessary for this job).
2) Knowing what amount of metal must be removed from what surface to produce a desired angle (and using a guide to help achieve this angle).
3) Employing a few definite, bold strokes to achieve the desired results—(do not drag the file back across the work, and clean the file teeth *after each stroke*).

Like most everything else, it takes practice before one is able to make a file do the bulk of some trigger pull jobs, but the gunsmith who masters the technique will often wonder how he managed previously by just using an oilstone.

In all fairness, it must be pointed out that a file cannot be used on the trigger release mechanism of all weapons. For example, the hammer and trigger of Smith & Wesson revolvers are surface-hardened and resist all attempts at filing. Similarly, the cocking pieces on most military rifles are so hard that they cannot be touched by a file.

There are many weapons which will come to the gunsmith for trigger pull adjustment which, while having parts capable of being filed, should not be filed unless it has been established that the engaging surfaces are in need of appreciable change.

Oilstones. For smoothing contacting surfaces that will better the quality of a trigger pull, and for smoothing surfaces that have been filed, the various small oilstones illustrated in Figure 41 are without peer.

For maximum usefulness and efficiency, stones used for trigger pull work must be free from surface or shape irregularities, i.e., a triangular or square stone should have sharp edges so that these edges can be employed to get into corners formed by the juncture of two contacting surfaces. Also, these edges should be free from nicks or depressions that might tend to tear or groove a surface.

Generally, these small oilstones are about 4" long and of two classes: India oilstones, and Arkansas oilstones. For trigger pull work there are four shapes—square, triangular, round, and half-round—that are most useful.

The India stones come in three degrees of grit: coarse (CF), medium (MF), and fine (FF). There is little need for the gunsmith to use anything coarser than the MF grade on trigger jobs, and if MF is employed for cutting or smoothing, then a fine stone should be used to tone down the surface scratches made on the metal by the coarser stone.

An Arkansas hard stone is always used to put the final touch on a trigger pull job, since one of these stones can be made to produce a steel surface so smooth that oil will barely adhere to it.

For the money that can be earned with them, and the service they render, these little stones are truly worth their weight in gold. In addition to the ones especially suitable for trigger pull work, there are others of various shapes and sizes which lend themselves admirably to all sorts of fine adjustment work on gun mechanisms where a needle file it too coarse and fine abrasive cloth is not firm or substantial enough. In the tool section of the Stoeger catalogue, all these stones are illustrated and identified. For $5.00, more or less, one can purchase a versatile set of these stones that will last for many years if they are handled sensibly and stored in a place where they will not be subject to having hard objects thrown on them. Although they are very hard, these small oilstones are quite brittle and will snap easier than an equivalent size piece of glass under similar handling.

If the edge on one of these stones breaks or becomes chipped to an appreciable extent, then it is possible to restore the edge by shaping it on a power-driven grinding wheel. In shaping the edge of a small oilstone by this method, wear goggles or a face mask and hold the stone against the rotating wheel so that a straight and true edge will be produced. Final lapping of the stone should be done by rubbing it across a flat, true piece of cast iron or brass that has been charged with a fine grade of powdered abrasive and oil.

In addition to careful handling, the only special attention required by these stones is that they be cleaned in gasoline or a similar solvent occasionally to float away the metal dust and matter that tend to clog the pores and reduce its efficiency.

As harmless as the finest oilstone might look, it is in the true analysis a tool for removing metal—and this it does. Too many mechanics are prone to underestimate the cutting ability of a small oilstone. This underestimation of the stone's potentialities has been the ruination of many a trigger pull and worse—the reason for having to scrap triggers, sears and hammers that have been honed away by the "foolproof" oilstone.

A good thought for the gunsmith to bear in mind is this: if a small stone can, in the course of being properly stroked over a particular metal surface a dozen or so times, reduce a trigger pull from six to three and a half pounds on a revolver, the same stone can, in the same number of *indiscriminate* strokes, raise the pull from six to nine pounds.

The impression seems to have gotten around, aided by lip service from some who have never collected an honest two bucks for doing a customer-satisfying trigger pull job, that little oilstones are good for beginners to practice with because very little harm can be done. This is pure legend and the sooner the gunsmith realizes that the small oilstone can do as much harm as it can good, the closer he is to being an "old master" on trigger pull work.

There is no particular position that must be assumed when stoning a trigger point or sear notch, though some mechanics do have a small table with vise attached, to which they can draw up a chair and calmly stone, examine and try; stone examine and try, until the desired results are achieved.

Because these stones are quite short (about 4"), they do not afford as much holding surface as a file does. Nevertheless, no matter how the stone is held and moved, it is imperative that the edge or surface which is doing the cutting be in full and even contact with the surface being cut. Any half-baked, would-be mechanic can keep a 4" stone flat on a 4" surface, but it takes a real gunsmith, worthy of the name, to keep a 4" stone squarely on a trigger notch surface that is 0.375" wide at most, and less than 0.03125" deep.

No, there is no secret "old country method" by which one learns to correctly use a small oilstone on the engaging surfaces of a trigger mechanism. It is just a matter of going slowly at first, and experimenting with the various grits and shapes of stones until one knows the qualities and limitations of each type as used on different notches and surfaces.

In using any of the small oilstones, the beginner's greatest weakness usually is "wobbling." By this is meant the tendency to round off corners and edges as a result of uneven pressure on the stone, as it is moved back and forth. Novices are guilty of this practice more than others since they are not quite sure of themselves and tend to move the stone while mentally weighing the pro and con of heavy versus light strokes, and the outcome of the job in general.

In using either a file or stone on parts controlling trigger pull, one of the most important considerations is to have the part being worked upon firmly held in a vise in such a way that the angle of the surface being filed or stoned is parallel to the top of the vise jaws (see Figure 41). In this way the gunsmith can more easily check any tendency the file or stone might have towards cutting in a plane not parallel to the desired angle.

For the mechanic who has done little or no trigger pull work, with either file or oilstone, the writer recommends practice on some old gun or his own personal weapons where the damage done will not be known to others who might be given to saying unkind words if the finished job is not what it should be.

The Magnifying Glass. Because the very shallowest scratches and tool marks can adversely affect the quality and weight of a trigger pull, it is frequently necessary to inspect a sear end or trigger notch through a magnifying glass. Though there are no exacting specifications as to how many power a glass for this purpose should be, it must be powerful enough to clearly show up surface irregularities on trigger mechanism contact points that are not visible in detail to the naked eye. Other than that, it can be of any description because it need only be used a few times during the course of any trigger pull adjustment job. A magnifying glass, or jeweler's loupe, has its place in this phase of gun repair work but the gunsmith should not feel called upon to scrutinize a hammer notch or trigger point through the magnifying glass each time he takes a few strokes with a stone or file.

The magnifying glass is very handy, if not necessary, when

examining the appropriate components of a gun which has a gritty pull. After a job has been completed the glass can also be used to show up any particularly rough edges that should be touched up. Other than these times, using the magnifier during the operation serves only to confuse the gunsmith and causes him to work with an exaggerated picture of the surfaces.

Summed up, this writer is trying to point out that the magnifying glass has a place in the gunsmith's tool box, but its usefulness is necessarily limited and will not make up for lack of knowledge of trigger pull work or ineptness at using the file and stones.

Measuring Trigger Pull

As a standard of comparison, trigger pulls are referred to in pounds and half fractions thereof, and range in pull weight from one and a half pounds for the target revolver to as high as 10 or 12 pounds on cheap shotguns and revolvers.

In Figure 42 there is illustrated the setup of weights that is most commonly used to measure trigger pull. Although the method of measuring should be quite clear from the drawing, the gunsmith should remember that a true reading can be obtained only when the gun is lifted gradually and uniformly. He should note also from Figure 42 that the position in which the gun is held likewise has a bearing upon the accuracy of the reading.

The weights can be turned from cast iron, cold rolled steel, or brass, the latter being preferred because of its resistance to corrosion. The hook section should be made of drill rod and bent while hot, and the base weight on each wire should be bolted on tight so as to prevent its coming loose.

Trigger pull pressure can also be measured with a small accurate lift-type scale, though this writer does not believe a scale is as handy and manageable as the weights.

As a rule, the lighter the pull, the less will be the resulting movement of the gun as the shooter applies pressure to the trigger. However, it is neither safe nor wise to have the pull on all weapons as low as mechanically permissible because of the human element involved.

On pocket pistols and revolvers the pull weight is usually kept between four and five pounds, so that in a moment of excitement the tense user will not accidentally discharge the piece. On hunting rifles the pull weight should also be kept a little above four

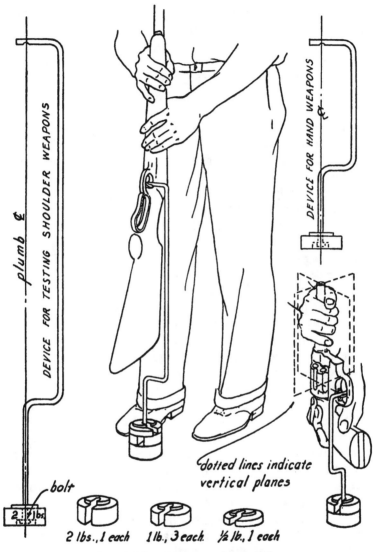

TRIGGER PULL WEIGHTS

FIGURE 42

pounds, so that a nervous hunter will not be inclined to fire the gun before he has fully gathered his wits and has his game properly pictured in the sights. On certain auto-loading guns, such as the Government .45 Automatic pistol, the pull weight must be kept slightly above four pounds so that the rapid movement of the slide will not jar the hammer from the sear, thus momentarily converting the weapon to full automatic.

Yes, this writer knows that some individuals boast of having a pull of less than four pounds on their Government model, but with such a light pull the probability that the gun will "follow through" at a crucial moment is too great for all-the-time mental ease. Of course, in these days of special improvements on handguns it is not beyond the realm of possibility that some fellow will come forth with a very simple sear block that will permit reduction of the pull on automatic pistols to that found on target revolvers.

Weight of Trigger Pull. With most trigger release mechanisms the matter of achieving a good pull in terms of applied pressure (pounds) resolves itself into having the two main contacting surfaces free from all surface irregularities and engaged at a desired angle. Now let us break that thought down and discuss in more detail these requirements.

"Free from Surface Irregularities." Surface irregularities as far as trigger pull work is concerned relates to those scratches and tool marks whose presence makes the passage of one surface across another perceptibly rough to the trigger finger. Generally there are such tool marks on the trigger mechanism contacting surfaces of all the low and medium price stock weapons. If the gunsmith can polish these tool marks away with a fine Arkansas oilstone, without changing the angle of the surface he is working on, then the pull weight will be reduced slightly and the feel of the pull improved tremendously. However, if, in the course of "smoothing up" contacting surfaces their angles are changed, the pull is often made worse in spite of the fact that the surface irregularities are eliminated. It is for this reason that all novices in trigger pull work are urged to leave alone the work of improving the pull on a factory-new gun and concentrate on those weapons where the contacting surfaces are already well worn and in need of slight recutting.

Practice alone in handling the tools (stones and file) for trigger pull work is an important step in the education of a student gunsmith, and practice on guns where even a slight improvement is quickly noticed is preferable to practice on those guns where a gunsmith's gunsmith is expected to gild the lily. Unlike a slip of the chisel on an inletting job, which can be corrected for all practical purposes by the addition of a little stick shellac, a slip of the stone or file in trigger pull work can mean the gunsmith must foot the bill for a ruined part or have the wrath of an irate shooter heaped upon him.

As illustrated in Figure 41 (and mentioned elsewhere in this chapter) the part being polished with a stone should be held in the vise at such an angle that the top of the vise jaws act as a guide for the stone as it is moved back and forth. The importance of keeping the stone (or file) fully on the surface being stoned cannot be over-emphasized, even when the finest Arkansas hard stone is being used to remove surface irregularities. Sometimes it is possible, depending upon the shape of the part being worked on, to hold it between the vise jaws so the ledge, or edge, to be polished is even with the top of the vise jaws (see Figure 43A).

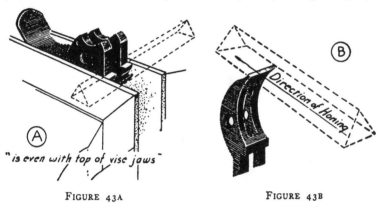

FIGURE 43A   FIGURE 43B

Then the top of the jaws can be used as a rest for the stone. Of course, to realize the full benefits of using this method, the vise must have fairly even jaws that are not covered with grooves and notches from years of usage. This writer feels it pays some mechanics who find it difficult to keep a notch or sear end true while polishing it, to invest a few dollars in a small vise to use just for trigger pull work.

Though it is not possible to do it that way on all sears, stoning on contacting surfaces should be done in the same direction as the part normally moves when it is in the gun (see Figure 43B).

When endeavoring to improve the quality of a trigger pull by smoothing off the contacting surfaces (and that is the first step that should be taken before any rash filing or intentional angle-changing is done) best results are obtained when all (usually only two) surfaces are polished to equal fineness. To polish one surface and leave rough the other it contacts is a poor practice since the latter will generally scar the former in due time, thus bringing about a change in the pull weight and character.

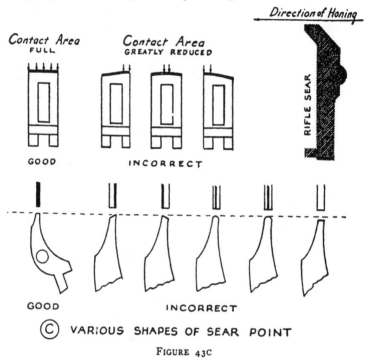

FIGURE 43C

After the contacting surfaces have been polished sufficiently (this will be evident by the nickel-plated appearance of the metal) they should be freed of any adhering abrasive particles by being immersed in benzine or a similar solvent, then wiped dry and oiled.

If testing reveals that the polishing has not improved the quality or character of the pull, close examination of the contacting surfaces should be made to see if there are any high spots that must be leveled off before full contact area between surfaces is achieved. Sometimes incorrectly controlled stoning will alter the shape of a sear nose so that only a section of it rests in and passes across the ledge of a hammer notch. It should be obvious to the gunsmith that a reduced area (from the standard size) on a sear nose is something less than desirable, especially when it takes the form of those illustrated in Figure 43C.

Up to a certain point polishing of contacting surfaces is the most practical and sensible way of improving a trigger pull; beyond that point (when a high polish has been achieved) it is just a slow method of changing the angles. The gunsmith should bear this in mind when, after a few polishings and tests on contacting surfaces, he notes little or no improvement, or possibly even a worsening of the pull.

"Engaged at a Desired Angle." In Figure 44 there is illustrated the trigger and hammer of a direct contact mechanism in which the contacting surfaces are shown engaged at different angles.

Contacting surfaces in Position 1 are at such an angle that a heavy pull would be experienced. The hammer would be cammed

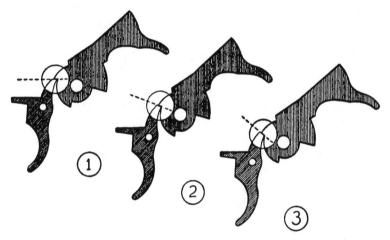

TRIGGER POINT AND HAMMER NOTCH ENGAGEMENT

FIGURE 44

back against the mainspring as the trigger is pulled. Though this angle is not undesirable from a safety standpoint, all the polishing in the world would not materially reduce the pull weight. On old guns in which there is much play between the parts and the safety is not too reliable, this angle between the trigger (or sear) and hammer (or firing pin) will at least minimize the chances of the gun going off if it were dropped.

In Position 2 the parts are engaged at a desired angle. When the trigger is pulled the hammer will not be cammed back, nor is the angle such that the slightest touch or jar on the trigger will give the hammer the mechanical advantage and force the trigger out of engagement, as is the case with the parts in Position 3.

Whether the parts he is working on are trigger and hammer or sear and firing pin, the gunsmith should study the angle at which the contacting surfaces rest and pass across each other and see if it cannot be reconciled to compare with one of those illustrated in Figure 44. Once that is done corrective action should be easier. Any mechanic can do a job more efficiently and better when he knows exactly what is wrong with something and how it should look and operate when it is in perfect operating order.

Changing the angle between contacting surfaces should only be done after the gunsmith has decided whether it is better to do the cutting on one surface or another, or possibly both. Generally in most mechanisms the cutting is done on the hammer notch. However, this does not always preclude the necessity for touching up the trigger (or sear) a little.

On revolvers it is a poor practice to take any off the end of the trigger because in shortening it the timing of the piece is apt to be adversely affected (see Chapter Eleven). Revolver mechanisms are very sensitive in this respect and the sooner the gunsmith becomes aware of the clannishness that exists between revolver (Colt and Smith & Wesson in particular) parts, the fewer new triggers he will have to buy, for customers' guns.

In changing the angle on a contacting surface, the gunsmith will often find that he has to cut away so much metal that the hammer's position will be shortened to the extent that the parts meshing with it no longer function as they should.

Yes, the ramifications of trigger pull work are many and this writer makes no attempt to convey any thoughts to the contrary; still it is not so difficult a phase of gunsmithing that a student gunsmith should consider it as being beyond his ability to master. It is a type of work where few tools are needed but where errors in judgment are costly. When doing a trigger pull job the gunsmith must be observing and note any unusual changes in the operating smoothness of a gun after a job has been done. If the pull seems unusually light, the gun, after being cocked, should be tapped and generally vibrated to see if the hammers can be jarred off—if they can, well that is a very bad condition and should be remedied without delay. No trigger pull job is worth a penny if it leaves the gun in an unsafe or unreliable status. A light trigger pull is desirable but not at the expense of the gun possibly going off when it is dropped.

The pull on double barrel shotguns, which figure more than any type of gun in hunting accidents, should never be reduced any lower than good sense dictates (i.e., the type of person using the gun, and the basic mechanism design). Too light a pull on a double gun can cause it to "double" when it is fired. Doubling (the other hammer jarred off as a result of vibration set up by the first shot being fired) is bad, not only because the shooter is surprised and frightened beyond description, but also because the second shot may be discharged in a direction where injury to another person is possible. It goes almost without saying that the only way in which a gun can be tested for doubling is to take it out and fire it. Load one barrel at a time and see if the other hammer falls.

Surface-hardened Parts. Surface-hardened parts of a trigger mechanism which are stoned to the extent that the surface hardening is removed, must be re-hardened or the contacting surfaces will quickly change their shape, and possibly wear to the point where they are unsafe.

Creep. Pull weight alone, however, is not the sole criterion of a good trigger pull, for the quality of the pull must be taken into consideration. For no pull, irrespective of how light it might be, can be passed up as being good if creep, or drag is present.

Creep as a deficiency in some mechanisms should be distinguished from the long pull or "take up" which is found on most military bolt action rifles that are purposely made that way. Aside from the latter class of guns, creep as a deficiency factor is generally encountered in old worn guns or in new guns where a novice gunsmith has done too much stoning or filing. In either case it is the exception rather than the rule that the creep can be eliminated without installing at least one new part (sear, trigger or hammer). However, it is the gunsmith who must make a proper decision in each case as to whether a part can be salvaged by working on it or if it must be discarded in favor of a new one.

In Figure 44A the hammer and sear of a Colt .45 Automatic pistol are shown engaged in ways that would cause creep if either one were in the poor condition as indicated. The Number 1 combination of this group would not only cause creep to be felt but also the gunsmith would find it difficult to achieve a permissibly light, smooth pull because of the relatively small contact area of the sear point. As can be appreciated, a very narrow engaging surface (point) on a sear or trigger tends to produce a pull

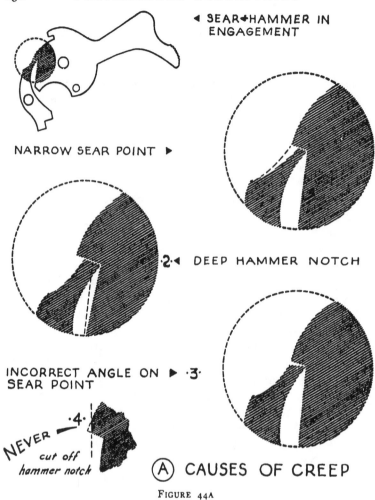

◄ SEAR⊕HAMMER IN
ENGAGEMENT

NARROW SEAR POINT ▶

·2·◄ DEEP HAMMER NOTCH

INCORRECT ANGLE ON ▶ ·3·
SEAR POINT

NEVER ·4· cut off hammer notch

Ⓐ CAUSES OF CREEP

FIGURE 44A

basically heavy in character and often ruins the hammer notch it engages because it acts as a scrape cutter each time it is pulled across the notch. If the hammer notch is surface-hardened, it is not affected by a too narrow sear point, but the sear point will wear quickly and thus the quality and weight of the pull is constantly changing. This latter situation is found to occur most often in cheap shotguns and revolvers after the surface-hardening is ground or filed off the sear. The best remedial action when a condition of this sort is found to exist in a good weapon is to discard the defective sear.

The Number 2 view of the Colt .45 Automatic sear and hammer shows how a deepened hammer notch can be the cause of creep. The only proper corrective measure indicated if the notch is deep is to replace the hammer with a new one. When a new hammer is not available or the customer cannot wait while one is being procured, then it is often possible to partially compensate for the depth of the notch or thinness of the sear by installing a pin or two in the hammer, as indicated in Figure 44B. The pin

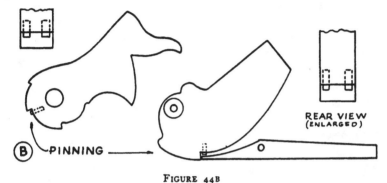

REAR VIEW
(ENLARGED)

(B) PINNING

FIGURE 44B

used should be of drill rod and be about 0.0625" in diameter, more if the size and construction of the hammer permits. Although this method (and its variation in which a small rectangular piece of steel is sweated into a hacksaw-made slit) of "fixin' up" an excessively deepened hammer notch has been given considerable publicity, the novice should not feel inclined to be careless in working on hammer notches knowing that he can fall back on pinning if all does not go well. Actually, pinning is one of those little tricks of the trade that it is well to know but should not be employed too often. Simple as it may look, it takes a good mechanic to fit a small diameter pin in a hole that must be drilled smaller than the pin by a thousandth or two. Also, the pin must be so tightly fitted that it cannot possibly work loose and project out too far and interfere with full engagement of the sear. If the gunsmith must resort to pinning, he should work very carefully throughout. After having fitted the pin and stoned it so it projects the desired length, the hammer should be tested in the gun to make certain the sear (or trigger) is not prevented from fully entering the notch because the pin is too long.

Although pinning is here discussed in literally the same breath as the hammer of a .45 Automatic pistol, it might be well to clarify the situation and point out that some hammers, because of their design, cannot be pinned—and the Colt .45 Automatic hammer is one of these. No listing of these hammers whose notch depth cannot be decreased by pinning is necessary because they will be obvious to the gunsmith when he encounters them.

Number 3 of Figure 44A shows a sear which has been stoned or filed to such an angle that it has only a very small contact area near its back edge. This will produce a creep in the pull and also make for a very hard pull. It is possible in certain cases to restore a sear so shaped to a different angle and still have the gun working properly. However, some types of sears are held to very close tolerances and when they are stoned just a little bit too much they no longer engage the hammer properly, and so contribute to a dangerous situation whereby the gun butt being smartly dropped or placed on the ground will jar the hammer off. A short sear can also cause a gun to misfire or hang fire if the gun has a hammer equipped with a half-cock or safety notch.

Number 4 shows the notch of a hammer filed off in a manner which the non-thinking beginner often does to compensate for a creepy pull brought about by a too deep hammer notch. This is an example of what *should not be done on hammer notches*. A notch so altered will help to lessen creep all right, but it will result in hang fires or misfires because the half-cock notch will either strike the rear end of the sear point or engage it completely. Remedial action in a case of this type calls for a new hammer and sometimes a new sear if the latter has been abused much by the half-cock notch.

In this commentary on causes and cures of creep, the hammer and sear of a .45 Automatic pistol are used for an example, not because they are more given to developing a creepy pull than any other combination, but because they are parts from a gun that most every gunsmith can buy and examine. In short, they are good models for this purpose. Also, the gunsmith should understand that the remarks pertaining to the causes of creep and bad pulls with these illustrated parts apply with equal force to all hammer-sear and hammer-trigger combinations whose method of contact and release can be similarly resolved.

In Figure 44C there are illustrated some of the commonest means whereby the creep in a military type bolt action trigger mechanism can be lessened.

In Sketch 1 (Figure 44C) the dotted lines indicate approximately the portion of the cocking piece that should be ground off. The exact amount that should come off must be determined by the gunsmith for each individual weapon he works with. There is no such thing as using a rule-of-thumb for this sort of work where a few thousandths one way or the other can mean accidental discharge of a rifle. This portion of the cocking piece has to be ground off because an ordinary file will not touch it. Before grinding this piece the gunsmith should take care to see that the face of the wheel is dressed true so the surface on the cocking piece will be flat and smooth. A hand stoning, to remove any burrs raised by grinding, should be done as a final operation.

In Sketch 2 (Figure 44C) arrows indicate the area on the trigger fulcrum which should be ground slightly and then highly polished on one of the wheels described in Chapter Sixteen. As a matter of fact, any of the comparatively large surfaces which must be highly finished can be done with the wheels and compounds described in that chapter. As excellent as some of these wheels and methods are, though, the gunsmith should remember that the part being polished or buffed must be held firmly and pressed against the wheels carefully or some of the edges and surfaces (that must be perfectly square and flat) will be rounded and rippled.

In this same figure the front end of the trigger that rests against the underside of the sear is shown as built up slightly. This build-up can be accomplished by hand-soldering a piece of steel on the surface indicated, or by means of a small diameter pin or screw. Wear on this section of the trigger and on the corresponding flat of the sear will be the determining factor in each case as to how much the build-up should be. Ordinarily 0.015″ is sufficient and 0.025″ maximum.

In employing the method suggested by Sketch 3 (Figure 44C), the long trigger creep is prevented rather than eliminated since the piece of sheet steel (cold rolled, case-hardened) riveted or silver-soldered to the guard acts as a stop to keep the trigger from coming all the way forward. Hence the sear is kept from full engagement. Here again this piece must be fitted, cut and tried until a safe amount of projection is arrived at that will not allow the sear to be held too far down in the cocking piece channel of the receiver.

Before the gunsmith who does not completely understand how the trigger mechanism of a military bolt action rifle works, undertakes to do any of the jobs suggested above, he should sit down with the gun to be modified and scrutinize its mechanism. He should note how the sear must bear the brunt of arresting the cocking piece as the latter rapidly moves forward under the force applied by a not gentle hand (that of a hunter or target shooter absorbed in watching game or a target). He should also note and remember that if this sear is lowered too much (Sketch 4, Figure 44C) it is apt to allow a worn cocking piece to by-pass or trip it and possibly cause the cartridge being fed to fire. A remote possibility? Yes, but a possibility, nevertheless, that no gunsmith can dare to ignore. Familiarity may breed contempt in some situations but it does not breed anything except good, safe workmanship when it concerns a gunsmith and trigger pull work.

Too many writers on the subject of gun repair are in the habit

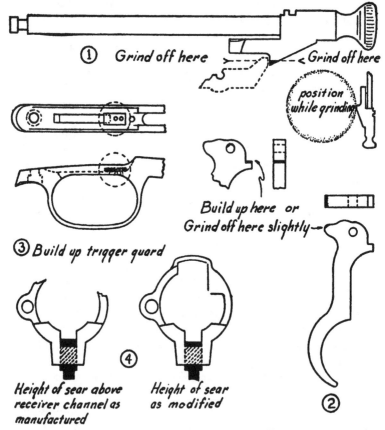

REDUCING CREEP IN BOLT ACTION TRIGGER MECHANISM

FIGURE 44C

of prefacing their instructions with the thought that they know many trick ways of reducing pull, eliminating creep, et cetera, but because some gunsmiths (would-be or practicing) might hurt themselves or somebody else if these esoteric short cuts were used, they cannot be divulged. That attitude is strictly the bunk as far as this writer is concerned. After all, when a man makes up his mind to be an amateur or professional gunsmith, he has at least reached the age of common-sense reasoning where he can be held responsible for his acts, either by his customers, or, if necessary, legal authorities. Truth of the matter is that there are no dangerous secret ways of changing or adjusting trigger pull other than a job carelessly done and represented to a customer as safe.

Though nothing herein is suggested that is a dangerous modification there always is the possibility that a misinterpretation of instructions, brought about by hasty reading or preconceived ideas of the reader, can result in his doing something to make a gun potentially dangerous. Hence this writer's constant admonition to the novice gunsmith that he know what he is doing before he does it. It is not enough to look at Figure 44C for example, and quickly note that creep can be lessened by grinding off a bit of metal here or building up there; instead the novice should try to figure out why the author chose that method, and whether it is not possible to accomplish the same purpose in another and possibly better way. The reader of this book, or any technical book, for that matter, should not take everything that is printed in it as positive unchanging fact. Much of any technical textbook represents the particular author's way of doing various jobs— many of these ways are the same that previous writers evolved or discovered—the remainder are the author's own which he has worked out and found to be efficient. It is for this reason that the student gunsmith with a limited but solid background in things mechanical should not hesitate to question any suggested method of trigger pull adjustment if he has reason to believe there is a better way of doing the job. We would still be doing a great number of jobs the hard way, the old way, if some fellow along the line had not stopped and asked himself, "Why cannot that be done another way? I think I know a better method."

Engraving and Etching

There are very few good doctors who are also good lawyers, and by the same token there are very few good gunsmiths who are also good engravers—and for the same basic reason. Being any one of the four is a full time job of itself, requiring years of study and preparation to attain a degree of skill whereby a living can be made at the chosen profession.

Although one must be quite versatile, and skilled in many crafts to be a good gunsmith, it is scarcely necessary that he be an engraver. Rather than spend a great deal of time in trying to master the art of metal carving, the gunsmith would do well to advance his talents in a more practical phase of gunsmithing.

Engraving. Because engraving in the true sense serves little or no practical purpose on a rifle, shotgun or handgun, it is first and mainly a means of beautifying a gun. Therefore, it is not a field in which there is even elbow room for a professional-novice. Good, genuine engraving is a thing of beauty, and doubly beautiful on a gun of deserving quality. And anything but good engraving is not engraving, but rather an assortment of unharmonious nicks, lines and scratches, that detracts from even the basic appearance of a cheap gun.

Engraving on jewelry, where one sees some little examples of the metal cutter's skill, is child's play compared with engraving on guns, where the hardest and toughest of steels are encountered. As a matter of fact, some rifle and shotgun receivers cannot be properly engraved unless they are annealed, and then must be heat treated after annealing. All of which prompts this writer to recommend that the gunsmith act only as middleman when a customer wants his gun engraved.

The problem of where a gun should be sent to be engraved, in this writer's opinion depends largely upon the type of gun being engraved and the extent of the proposed engraving. If a revolver is being readied for a retiring law enforcement officer and a few appropriate words are to be engraved on the sideplate or backstrap, then it is permissible to have such work done by a local engraver or jeweler. However, if a high-powered sporting rifle or a shotgun is to be decorated with engraving and relief work or inlays, then it should be sent to the factory where it was made, or to one of the gun engravers advertising in "The Rifleman." And because there are only a few gun firms or engravers who have the knowledge and equipment to heat treat and engrave firearms, this writer prefers to deal directly with the respective manufacturer of a gun. Winchester, Remington, Ithaca, Colt, Smith & Wesson, and others all undertake to engrave and do similar special decorative metal work on their own guns, and it goes almost without saying that these firms would not do anything to their guns which would in any way weaken them or tend to make them less serviceable than a non-engraved gun.

Engraving on Foreign Guns. Many an otherwise well informed gun lover or gunsmith is often tempted to overestimate the value of a foreign gun or inexpensive domestic product because it is embellished with engraving. This is an unfortunate and sometimes expensive delusion to labor under when one pays a goodly sum of money for a highly ornamented weapon that is basically of poor materials and inferior workmanship.

The gunsmith who does much buying and selling of foreign guns should learn to be a bit of a connoisseur and closely study the engraving on Spanish, Belgian and French weapons. Not infrequently engraving is put on some continental weapons to cover up sloppy fitting work and to draw attention away from their less desirable features. This caution, however, should not be construed to mean that engraving on a foreign gun automatically makes that gun no good. This is not necessarily the proper conclusion, but it is correct in so many cases that the gunsmith should be wary.

Etching. Etching is a phase of metal decoration at which any gunsmith can try his hand. The trying should, however, be confined to pieces of metal and guns from the shop junk pile until a degree of proficiency is attained which might justify commercializing of the newly acquired talent.

Even if the gunsmith does not become skilled enough to decorate firearms with etching, he might find it handy in permanently marking special tools and fixtures which cannot, because of their shape or size, be stamped with letter or number dies.

Before a piece of steel or iron can be etched it must be thoroughly cleaned with alcohol or gasoline to remove all traces of grease or oil. Next, the entire surface of the unit to be etched must be covered with an acid resisting substance ("ground") and then the desired design or writing scribed through the ground to expose the naked metal underneath. The unit is then placed in a glass, crockery or enamel-ware pan in which has been dissolved enough nitric acid and water in equal proportion to completely cover the immersed article. The article is allowed to remain in the bath until the acid has eaten deeply enough into the metal to form a pattern of desired depth and tone.

One variety of ground can be made by mixing together dried shellac and wood alcohol until a mixture of brushing consistency is achieved. To give color to the mixture a few grains of potassium permanganate may be added.

Another "ground" is beeswax placed in a piece of cheesecloth folded five or six times to form a container or "mop." To apply the ground the work must be slightly heated and the wax-filled cloth rubbed over the metal, thus causing the wax to melt and transfer onto the metal.

Although professional etchers use many different sizes and styles of needles to cut through the ground, the beginner should concentrate on a simple one made from a scriber with the point well stoned to a smooth, round point.

In order to get a little practical experience with etching, and to encounter first hand the troubles that are bound to spring up, the gunsmith should select a small piece of steel, say about 2" square and, after preparing it properly, trace a simple flower design or initials onto the ground. Then, with the etching point, cut through the ground over the traced lines and finally immerse the piece in acid. By doing this the gunsmith will learn first hand about the importance of covering all surfaces with ground, the necessity for a sharp but smooth needle, the difficulty of cutting completely through the ground at all points, and the rapidity with which acid will etch the softer grades of steel.

As the gunsmith learns more about etching and decides that his artistic background is sufficient to warrant further study, he can fashion many sizes and shapes of needle points from old dental burrs and experiment with different grounds and other acids, such as hydrochloric and acetic acid.

While the deleterious effects of acid on blueing, and iron and steel in general, are discussed in detail in Chapter Sixteen, the writer cannot but sound another reminder at this point.

Matting. On sight ramps, sighting surfaces, tangs, backstraps, et cetera, matting is done to reduce light reflection, provide a better gripping surface, or produce a contrasting finish against polished blueing.

Matting can be done with a prick punch and hammer but requires a great deal of practice before a uniformly pocked surface can be turned out every time. Part of the success in good matting by the punch and hammer method lies, it would seem, in learning to hold the punch loosely and still have it under control. A light hammer is also desirable since deep punch marks make a far less attractive matting job than does a uniform surface of shallow ones.

Matting can also be done with the more specialized tools, as illustrated in Figure 45. By using these tools separately or in combination, the gunsmith can make some very distinctive patterns and designs that are both attractive and practical. The tools should be forged from round tool steel, ground, and filed to shape, and the serrations filed or machined on a smooth, true face. Hardening and tempering should be done carefully because the edges of these tools must stand a great deal of abuse. Tempering color should be light purple. Before using any of these tools on a rib, sight, or receiver, the gunsmith should test the metal with a file to make certain that it can be worked. Some receivers, particularly those of military weapons, are often quite hard and will wreck a set of matting tools; and since this writer does not see the necessity of annealing a receiver or grinding away 0.015″ of it, the only alternative is to suggest matting by the acid method (see Chapter Sixteen).

Vibro-Tool. For doing matting on small parts such as sight discs and front sights, as well as on larger subjects, the Burgess Vibro-Tool is the answer. It is an electrically operated vibrating unit which can be held and moved like an oversized fountain pen. It has a little chuck into which can be inserted knives, cutters, needles and similar attachments (including tools made from high speed steel and tungsten carbide) which, when actuated at about 7,200 reciprocations a minute, can be made to do very fine work. The tool is priced at about $8.00 at this writing, and is money well invested. The Burgess Vibro-Tool can be purchased at hardware stores or from Frank Mittermeier, the gunsmith supply man (see Chapter Twenty for address).

After Matting. After a piece of metal has been matted, checkered, or similarly tooled, it is generally rough looking in appearance and sometimes covered with burrs that are objectionable to the touch. In such cases it is generally advisable to brush over the matting with a wire wheel. A wire wheel having the general specifications of the type used for carding (see Chapter Sixteen) is recommended because it will smooth down rough edges and impart a brushed finish without polishing the surface.

Damascene (Damaskeen) Work or Engine Turning. On the wheels and parts of many imported watches one cannot help but

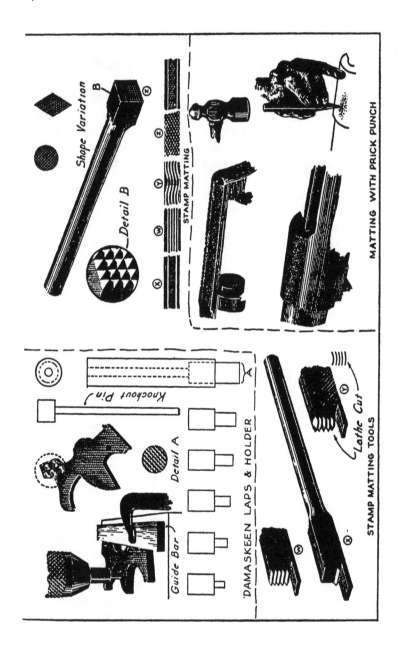

notice the little concentric circles which seem to flash and turn as the watch is tilted in any direction. These little circles, or engine-turnings as they are often called, not only beautify a part or surface on which they are put but also serve as a means of holding a slight film of oil.

On rifle bolts, magazine followers (bolt action type), and revolver hammers, engine-turning can be done as a means of dressing up these otherwise plain-looking unblued parts. The only special tool needed is illustrated in Figure 45 and can be made from a piece of cold rolled steel with the inserts made of fiber, hard rubber or bakelite.

In using this tool the gunsmith should select the size insert that will look and work best on the part to be engine-turned. For example, on a rifle bolt it is best to use an insert no wider than 0.1875" or the circles will appear incomplete due to the small area of the bolt that is contacted at each time. On flat surfaces (revolver hammers) where the insert has full surface contact, a larger insert can be used.

The part to be worked on should be placed on the drill press table and a guide provided so that it can be moved along in a straight line until one complete row of circles is made; then the guide should be moved over and another row of circles started, but alternate in position to the first row.

On round surfaces it is often better to hold the part in the hand and press it against the end of the whirling rod rather than bring the rod to bear against the work, as is the case when parts are damaskeened on the drill press table.

Flour of emery (No. 220 grit or finer) combined with oil to the consistency of a flowing mixture, is coated on the surface of the work and the drill press should be run at a fairly low speed so as not to wear out the high points (that make the circles) of the insert.

The pressure that should be exerted in order to insure the formation of circles rather than one frosted-appearing circular area is something that the gunsmith will have to work out for himself, depending upon the type of insert he uses and the hardness of the metal being worked upon. Safe to say, though, this writer's experience has convinced him that best results are usually forthcoming when a constant finger pressure is maintained on the drill press handle.

CHAPTER EIGHT

SELECTING AND MOUNTING SIGHTS

IRRESPECTIVE of how much a gun costs or how finely embellished with engraving or checkered woodwork, its true worth as a "shooting iron" lies in its ability to place shots in an aimed at target. Whether this target be paper, a tin can, charging lion or sitting woodchuck is of small moment; the important thing is that the target be hit when it is aimed at and fired upon.

To bring about the hitting of a target, three general factors enter into the picture; first, there is the inbuilt accuracy of the weapon itself; secondly, the almost incalculable human element; and last, but of no less importance, the sighting equipment. It is with this latter factor that we shall be primarily concerned in this chapter—not forgetting, however, its connection with the other two.

The practicing gunsmith soon learns from experience that the mounting of sights, both metallic and telescopic, constitutes a sizable portion of his year round business. He is frequently called upon to advise and select for the customer the proper sight or combination of sights that should be mounted on any gun from an inexpensive .22 single shot rifle to a left handed shooter's target rifle.

The task of selecting the correct sights for a gun is on a par in importance with the actual mounting of them and as such requires that the gunsmith should be well informed as to the different types and makes of sights and the purposes for which each is best suited. Some types are very versatile and therefore widely adaptable, while others are designed to fit and give worthwhile results on only one make and type of weapon. At times it is also necessary to take into consideration the eyesight of the person who will shoot the gun, since some men beyond middle age and others with an optical defect might have need for a special size notch or aperture, or perhaps even an unusual rear-front sight combination.

Thus it can be seen that the selection of sights for a gun is not merely one of attaching any sight that happens to be in the gun-smith's stock or of haphazard choice, but rather the result of care-ful thought, reference to sight and gun manufacturers' catalogs and discussion with the one who will use the gun.

If a customer has his mind made up as to exactly what type of sight he wants, then there is little need for any further discus-sion with him along these lines. However, this is not always the case and it behooves the gunsmith to have a fundamental work-ing knowledge of gun sights. This knowledge must necessarily include a theoretical background covering the aspects of bullet drop due to gravitational attraction and the suitability of dif-ferent type sights for hunting and target shooting, in addition, of course, to knowing what standard sights can be fitted to vari-ous makes and models of gun. The latter information is to be found in catalogs which should be referred to whenever the matter of sight selection arises. These catalogs should be kept up to date at all times, and the best way of insuring this is to request the various companies that manufacture these items to put you on their mailing list.

Bullet Drop

Although the subject of bullet drop has been discussed count-less numbers of times in sporting magazines and allied publica-tions it is so vital to the understanding of sight adjustment that it is worth reviewing in this chapter.

Sir Isaac Newton, the famed British scientist, is credited with recognizing the fact that gravity exerts a uniform attraction upon all falling bodies. Although this attractional force varies with latitude, longitude and elevation, it is considered for all practical purposes to be constant and equal to 32.2 feet per sec-ond. In other words, a falling object will increase its velocity at the same rate each second, the increase being 32.2 feet per second. Thus if any object is dropped from a height it will fall instantly towards the ground due to the force of gravity. It will start to fall slowly but will gain momentum and increase its velocity the farther it falls.

When a bullet is discharged from the barrel of a gun held some distance above but parallel to the ground, the bullet starts to drop the instant it leaves the support of the bore. It falls just as fast as it would if dropped from the hand at the same height. However, since the gun-projected bullet is travelling forward at high velocity and is speeding towards its mark, it will be some distance in front of the gun muzzle before it strikes the ground. Figure 46A illustrates this drop and forward movement, which,

FIGURE 46A

in combination, forms a path of movement known as the trajectory. The particular trajectory illustrated represents the flight of a 150-grain .30/06 government bullet having a muzzle velocity of approximately 2,700 feet per second. Actually, this bullet does not cover 2,700 feet in one second, for its forward velocity is decreased by air resistance. Consequently, at the end of the first second the bullet has dropped more than 12 feet and moved forward about 650 yards.

To compensate for this bullet drop so that distant objects can be hit, it is necessary to elevate the muzzle end of the gun, causing the bullet to leave the bore at an ascending angle. Then does a fired bullet assume a flight path as seen in Figure 46B.

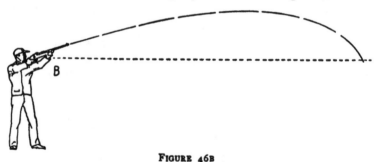

FIGURE 46B

Naturally, for bullets of various weights and speeds this angle of elevation is different, and is expressed in terms of minutes of an angle; a minute being approximately 1.00″ per 100 yards. To be more exact the deviation at 100 yards for one minute of angle is 1.044″.

Thus, to raise the point of impact 1.00″ at 100 yards it is necessary to adjust the elevating slide or scale on a rear sight for one minute of elevation. If a bullet drops 4.00″ at 100 yards, then elevation correction of four minutes must be made, and so on for different ranges. The amount of bullet drop, expressed in minutes for most standard American cartridges, can be found in folders and catalogs issued by arms and ammunition manufacturers.

Windage Correction

Although provision for making lateral adjustment (windage correction) is made on most sights, it is more often than not used to correct any lateral deviation that might occur as a result of consistent human error or off-center mounted sights. Windage scales are usually marked off in minutes, and as with elevation adjustment or micrometer sights, ¼ minute clicks on either knob will allow for finer corrections.

Generally speaking, most hunters and plinkers give very little consideration to the matter of windage unless a wind is blowing from either 3 or 9 o'clock of the shooting position. Otherwise it is usually difficult to make a quick and correct adjustment that would affect shooting at ranges up to 200 yards, and most hunting is done at ranges far short of this distance.

Serious target shooters on the other hand, who shoot from one fixed position for a half hour or more at one time, make good use of windage adjustment on a windy day by getting off a few "sighters" and noting the point of impact to the left or right of the bull. If the wind in such instances is blowing from one direction at a near constant speed then corrections made at the time are noted in a score book the faithful have for such occasions and serve as future references when shooting in a wind of the same velocity. Hunters, however, cannot very well use this system for they are not usually in one position long enough to take advantage of previous calculations.

Pro and Con

In the matter of choosing the sight, there are some thoughts which are worthy of any gunsmith's consideration. But, as can be appreciated, with such a controversial subject, not all persons are in complete agreement. Nevertheless, the following opinions represent the most up-to-date ideas on the subject, based on the writings of a majority of the experts in the field of guns and gunning in these modern days.

Metallic Sights

Rear Sights. Metallic sights can, for all practical purposes, be considered in two categories, viz., open sights and peep, or aperture, sights. Each has its particular advantages and disadvantages. However, the latter type is gaining in popularity by leaps and bounds. The latest type military small arms such as carbine, Garand rifle, and M3 submachine gun, are all so equipped, whereas during the last war our armed forces had only one shoulder weapon—an M 1917 rifle—in general usage with an aperture sight alone as standard equipment. Yet for any manner of target work nowadays a peep sight is a must on a rifle.

Young people with good eyes can "catch an aim" at short ranges more quickly with the open type rear sight than they can with the aperture style. Older people with failing eyes, however, find open sights a detriment to good shooting, chiefly because of the blurred picture they get while trying to line up rear and front sights on the object being fired upon. Shooters experiencing this latter difficulty can be greatly aided if they will but change to the peep sight, which is usually mounted much nearer the eye than the open type, and use a disc with a large hole in it. Although the large aperture is preferrable for hunting and fast shooting, the small aperture is preferred for target work since in this latter type of shooting it is necessary to see only a small portion of the shooting field.

It might be well to note that with any size of aperture, it requires special effort to use the rear peep sight *incorrectly*. Shooters who are accustomed to using open style rear sights, invariably, when using a peep sight, bring the front sight down to the bottom of the aperture when aligning the sights on a target. In using the peep sight the shooter should just look through the peep hole at the target and bring the front sight into alignment with the center of that peep aperture. No special effort is necessary, for the normal eye will naturally focus through the center of a small circular opening.

Front Sights. A front sight should be selected only after determining what type rear sight will be used. A very narrow front sight blade will not give best results with a wide rear sight notch. Three of the most popular style front sight blades, from which designs most others are made by addition of colored beads or cutting off here or there, are illustrated in Figure 47.

THREE TYPES OF FRONT SIGHTS

FIGURE 47

Before Mounting Sights

Responsibility. Owning a rifle equipped with a telescopic sight is an ambition cherished by many gun owners, both hunters and targeters. A telescope equipped rifle has many advantages too well known to mention, along with certain disadvantages. A telescopic sight is definitely a delicate instrument and cannot take the abuse one ordinarily heaps upon iron sights. The gunsmith must always bear this in mind when he is entrusted with a weapon that has such a sight affixed or during and after installing one.

When a telescope equipped rifle is brought to the gunsmith for repair work other than on the scope or mount the telescope should be removed, if practicable, and given to the customer for safe keeping. In some cases this will not be expedient or desirable to the customer, for it will be necessary for him to rezero the gun. However, when possible this practice should be followed for it will pay dividends to the gunsmith in the long run as he will be relieved of the worry of having to pay for or repair at his own expense a telescope that becomes damaged while in his possession. If a customer prefers leaving his rifle with scope intact, then the gunsmith should check the scope, in the owner's presence, to see that it is being received in good condition. If the lenses are dirty, chipped, marred or reticules broken, this should be called to the customer's attention, and noted on the repair tag, so that he will not hold the gunsmith accountable when he returns to claim his gun after the repair work has been completed.

The Customer's Choice. Often a customer will bring to the gunsmith a sight or set of sights, which he has purchased directly from the factory, to have mounted on his favorite shooting iron. Before agreeing to mount sights so presented, the gunsmith should check them and make sure that they are for the particular make, model and caliber weapon to which they are to be affixed. Furthermore, be sure that all the necessary components are included with the sights, such as screws, shims or special tools. With telescopes check and double check the mounts, for a scope is worthless if it is not affixed to the correct type mount.

Modifications. Occasionally, before mounting certain telescopes, it will be found necessary to modify the bolt handle or safety on some bolt action rifles so that, in being actuated, these parts will not strike the delicate scope or mount. In instances of this sort the customer should be told just how much alteration will be required and approximately the additional cost to be incurred. Perhaps he might not choose to have the weapon modified, preferring to select another style of mount or scope which can be mounted without necessitating alterations to the gun. If another type mount is not available, then the gunsmith should assure himself, before contracting to do the job, that practical alterations can be made on the interfering parts.

Likewise, when mounting types of metallic sights where a small portion of the stock must be cut away to make room for the sight body, the customer's permission should be secured so that he will not be surprised, upon returning, to find that his pet hand-rubbed stock has been altered.

Always Fill Old Holes. Where an old barrel sight or receiver sight is removed after mounting a metallic or telescopic sight, the gunsmith must remember that he should fill up the dovetail or unused tapped holes with a dummy of some sort so that these fastening points will not be marred or ruined. The cost of these dummy dovetail blanks or headless screws should be included in computing the price for a sight mounting job.

Working with Dovetail Base Barrel Sights

Removing Them. Front or rear dovetail sights are driven in from right to left, and therefore should be driven out from left to right, that is, with the barrel pointing away from the operator. If an old sight is being driven out, a length of square copper or brass, about 3.5" long and 0.25" across, should be used as a drift. Lay one end of the rod squarely against the side of the dovetail and tap the other end of the rod gently with a hammer, increasing the force of the blows gradually until the sight starts to move. Then continue to tap with just enough force to push the sight out completely. It is not necessary or advisable to wallop a dovetail sight so hard that two or three blows will send it spinning across the shop.

Installing Them. The work incident to inserting a dovetail base sight, and it is generally a new or good one that is being installed, must be done with a bit more care and consideration than that accorded a removal job so that the sight will not be marred or forced into the barrel slot at an angle. Before tapping the sight in place, the barrel slot and surrounding area, as well as the sight itself, should be cleaned of all foreign matter and any small burrs present filed off. After having done this, start the sight in place by hand if possible; if the fit between the sight base and dovetail is too tight to permit this, then guide the sight with the fingers of one hand and start it in place by tapping with a rawhide hammer. Once properly started, the sight can then be driven fully in position by using a fiber or hard wood drift.

Do not use a brass punch under any circumstances since it is apt to mar the sight base. A short piece of aluminum or copper can be used if the sight proves to be very difficult to move. If either of these rods will move the sight, then it should be tapped out and high spots on the slot noted. File off the high spots with a small needle file or, better still, use a smooth cut three square file having two of its cutting sides ground off. Such a file will enable the gunsmith to enlarge either side of the dovetail while still maintaining the proper angle and not removing any metal from either the base or the other side. However, no matter what sort of file is used, only a very little bit of metal should be removed before trying to fit the sight again.

With Loose Fits. Some sights, instead of being a very tight fit in the dovetail, will be so loose that they can be slid through from side to side by finger pressure. There are two ways to correct this condition, each, however, being better suited to certain individual conditions. For example, if the barrel slot is not of standard size, as is the case with some foreign and old domestic guns, then a gib should be cut from cold rolled steel, fitted, then blued and put in place so that a snug fit will be achieved between sight base and slot. On the other hand, if the looseness is only due to a few thousandths difference in size between the surfaces, then a shim of brass can be cut to size and installed.

On inexpensive rifles, where the making and fitting of a shim might tend to increase the cost of the job out of proportion to the value of the gun, then it is permissible to peen down very slightly the top of the dovetail slot on the barrel. This operation is done most neatly when a copper or fiber rod is interposed between the hammer and barrel so that the latter will not be noticeably marred. Too, experience will teach the gunsmith that only very little tapping is required to achieve the desired results. However, this latter method should not be employed on any weapon where even the slightest disfigurement would depreciate the value or appearance of the piece.

Holding the Gun. When removing or installing a sight on a gun that must be driven in or out, there is always the danger of bending the barrel. To preclude this unhappy possibility, the gun should be placed in the vise between padded vise jaws so that the section of the barrel being worked upon is fully and directly supported against the jaws. To secure this setup on rear sights, it will generally be necessary to remove the stock of the gun. Such a disassembly operation, which usually requires only a few minutes, should not be regarded as unnecessary or a waste of time, for actually in the long run it makes removal of the old sight and installation of the new one an easier and quicker task. This is one of the tremendous trifles of repair work that so often makes the difference between having a repair job turn out correctly on schedule, and a bogged down job where everything goes wrong and ends up with the gunsmith being behind the financial and reputation eight-ball.

When They Are Stubborn. Although it is not the practice among manufacturers of guns to solder or pin in dovetail base sights, this writer has had occasion to work on a few guns where the sights were held in place by either one or both of these methods. If the truth were known, such sights were probably put in by a novice gunsmith who thought it easier to resort to these methods rather than use a shim. Therefore, when a dovetail sight resists all normal efforts at removal, the gunsmith should lay aside his tools for a moment and look for any pins or slotless screws that might be present. If such is found to be the case, and the pin or screw cannot be drifted out or unscrewed, then the only recourse is to place a center punch mark at the estimated center of the holding medium and drill it out with a drill that is a few thousandths larger than the estimated size of the pin or screw. In doing this be very careful and do not drill any deeper than is absolutely necessary lest the wall of the barrel be weakened or pierced.

If no pins or screws appear to be present, then there is always the possibility that solder has been used. Here the gunsmith should apply heat to the sight and barrel dovetail area and constantly tap on the sight base after the melting point has been reached. This should dislodge any sight so affixed. If it does not, then a quantity of penetrating oil should be squirted between the sight and dovetail joint and allowed to stand overnight. This will loosen up any rust that is acting as a barrier to removal. Should none of these suggested methods prove to be conducive to easy removal, then the gunsmith has no other alternative than to use a steel drift punch on the sight and pound upon it until it comes loose. Since this sort of pounding will no doubt scar the sight very badly, it should only be employed as a last resort.

Attaching Receiver Sights

For no few years now the receiver type micrometer sight has enjoyed an enviable degree of popularity among shooters who appreciate and benefit by its advantages of affording nearness to the eye and a longer sighting radius. Many good rifles coming from the gun factories today are equipped with these sights, or if not actually equipped the receiver is at least drilled and tapped to receive a Lyman or Redfield micrometer type sight. Attaching the correct sight to a gun so prepared is a matter of a few minutes work requiring only that a few screws be tightened in place—unless, of course, the stock has to be cut out to accommodate some overhanging portion of the sight, in which case another fifteen or twenty minutes will be required.

On the other hand, when the gunsmith is called upon to set up, drill and tap, and mount one of these sights, his ability as a mechanic will be put to a real test on the first few jobs. Easy as it might appear to drill and tap two holes in a rifle receiver exactly where wanted, there is little doubt but that the beginner will only too quickly realize how deceiving such a task can be.

Nevertheless, by proceeding with caution and using the proper tools, the gunsmith will soon find that he can tackle this sort of work without wishing that he did not have the job to do.

Lining It Up. After the gunsmith has positively ascertained that he has the proper sight for the make and caliber of the gun (this applies especially when the customer brings his own sight in for mounting) the weapon should be stripped of its stock and any other parts that might interfere with holding, drilling or tapping. However, the old rear sight should not be removed, nor should the front sight be touched (if it is to be changed at all) until the new rear sight is in place, for it is the original sight setting that will serve as a guide in lining up the sight being installed. Lining up of the new sight is best accomplished by placing the gun in a vise and extending a length of fine wire across the top of the front sight and passing through the notch on the old rear sight (See section on cutting down revolver barrels in Chapter Eighteen). At this point the new rear sight should be held by hand at its approximate correct position and then aligned exactly by further extending the wire so that it can be drawn through the aperture of the disc. (Note: Make certain that the aperture of the rear sight is set on center on the windage scale.) By manipulating the sight, in respect to the extended wire, the former can be brought into correct alignment and held there while three short lines are scribed around the sight body near that part of the sight (usually the bottom) which comes closest to the stock. In this way the scribed lines will hardly be noticeable when the sight and stock are in place.

Once these guide lines are scribed, a "C" clamp can be used to hold the sight against the receiver while the center punch marks are made. The center punch used for spotting through the sight screw holes should not be of the conventional tapered shank type but rather of the kind illustrated in Figure 48. The diameter of the punch at its lower section should be of such a size that it will just fit through the hole in the sight body and the point on the punch must be absolutely concentric to this section. To achieve this the punch can be turned from tool steel or drill rod on the lathe and the point cut by using the compound rest. Inasmuch as there are not very many different size screw holes, the gunsmith will probably find that six specially made punches will take care of all the different sights he will have occasion to work with. As with all special tools, these punches should be used only on the job they were made for and stored carefully when not in use.

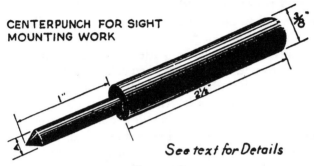

CENTERPUNCH FOR SIGHT
MOUNTING WORK

⅜"

1"

2¼"

See text for Details

FIGURE 48

Drilling. Having made the center punch holes, the position of the sight, relative to the scribed lines, should be checked again to make certain that it has not shifted. If the sight has shifted, then reset it and tap lightly again on the center punch in case the shift occurred during the original center punching operation. Next select a drill that is a few thousandths of an inch smaller in diameter than the screw hole in the sight, and with the sight still in place spot drill the receiver. However, only spot drill one hole. Without disturbing the set of the work on the drill press table, change drills. i.e., remove the body size drill and put the tap size drill in the chuck and drill deeply enough into the receiver so that sufficient full threads for good holding can be tapped in. On most rifles it is usually possible to drill completely through one side of the receiver without causing any injury to the gun, and where this is possible it should be done for it will make the subsequent tapping operation very much easier than tapping in a shallow bottom hole.

Tapping. Still using the drill press setup, the starting, or number one tap, should be put in the drill chuck and started into the drilled hole by rotating the chuck by hand. Do not attempt to speed things up at this point by switching on the drill press motor. The only reason it is suggested that the tap be started in by means of the drill chuck is because this method offers the best way of starting the tap in straight. Once the tap has been started in the hole, the drill chuck should be unloosened. This will leave the tap properly started and the thread cutting operation can be finished with the hand operated tap holder. To insure a nice smooth finished thread the tap should be advanced slowly, i.e., rotate it a half turn forward at a time, then back-tap slightly to break off the chips. A little oil or cutting compound squirted in the hole and on the tap will also reduce the possibility of the tap sticking and breaking.

Too many words cannot be written on the importance of proceeding slowly and with caution when using small diameter taps, for it only requires the slightest bit of improper or careless pressure on a tap to break it. And in spite of all the marvels of this atomic and radar age, it is still one hell of a tough job to extract a broken tap without ruining the threads and surrounding metal. Therefore, when the gunsmith is tapping a sight screw hole and feels the tap tightening up, he should stop immediately and count ten—just to allow himself a few seconds recess. Then squirt some more oil into the hole and gently unscrew the tap. Before starting it in again, recheck the tap drill to make sure it is the correct size; also check the tap for sharpness of the teeth. If any of them are dull or broken, another tap should be brought into play.

Another danger sign that forewarns of a tap about to break is a squeaking noise emitted each time the tap is turned in or out during the thread cutting operation. If the application of oil does not suppress this noise, then a new tap should be employed. This same noise is also apt to be heard when the metal being tapped is too hard, in which case spot annealing (See Chapter Fifteen) of the metal in the immediate area of the hole must be effected before going on with the job of tapping.

Getting back to our job of mounting a typical receiver sight, we already have one hole drilled and tapped and ready to receive a screw which should be put in and tightened up. At this point the clamp which has been holding the sight in place temporarily can be removed. Again check the sight's position relative to the scribed lines and if necessary loosen up the screw and make corrections. Reset the gun, with sight attached, on the drill press table and repeat the operations carried out when the first hole was drilled, i.e., spot drill, drill with tap drill and tap out the hole. Finally, put in the second screw and with a smooth cut file, of a style (flat, round, et cetera) best suited to the contour of the section being worked upon, file away any screw projection or burrs raised during the drilling and tapping operations, that protrude beyond the normal surface on the inside of the receiver. After filing, use a small stone or fine emery cloth attached to a stick so as to finish the surface off smoothly.

After It Is Mounted. When the sight is mounted, check its position by placing the gun in a vise and sighting against a small target fixed about 10 feet from the muzzle of the gun. First check the setting of the old sight on the target and make a small pencilled cross (+) at that point, then look through the new rear sight and note any appreciable lateral deviation in alignment. Slight lateral error is often due to the receiver not being in perfect conformity to the shape of sight body where the two are together. This condition can sometimes be corrected by unloosening both screws and then tightening one up fully, and noting if any appreciable space exists between the receiver and the back of the sight near the other screw hole. If such space is noticeable, then a small brass shim type washer can be inserted behind the other screw so that when it is tightened up the sight will not be canted. Incidentally, resorting to sight shimming usually indicates that the ole debbil carelessness has had a hand in the job; let's be more careful, huh?

If a sight is so badly mounted that shimming will not correct the defect, then the gunsmith has no other alternative but to move the sight either forward or rearward far enough to tap and drill new holes. Before doing this, however, the old holes should be plugged with headless and slotless screws and ground or filed to blend in with the general contour of the receiver.

This writer has suggested using the front and old sight as a medium of securing alignment for the new rear sight, for the reason that the gunsmith generally receives a gun from a customer with the sights set in the position (laterally) that are best suited to the peculiarities of the gun and customer. However, if the gunsmith is called upon to mount a receiver sight on a gun where either the front or rear sight, or both, are conspicuously set off from the normal center of the bore, then he should find out from the customer if such a setting is necessary to achieve normal lateral zero. If it is, then the gunsmith can confidently proceed to mount the new sight, using the original sights as a guide. On the other hand, if the customer admits that he is not too good a shot or just resorts to Kentucky windage to compensate for the offset of the sights, then the new sight should be mounted dead center on the gun and thus allow the customer to use the windage scale on the new sight to compensate for such "things."

Mounting Telescope Sights

Prelude. In his very excellent book, "Telescopic Rifle Sights," Colonel Townsend Whelen has a chapter entitled "Mounting Scopes on Rifles." The second paragraph of this chapter reads as follows:

> "But first of all let me say a word about mounting by local gunsmiths. Not all gunsmiths are competent to mount scopes. I have seen some horrible work done by small local gunsmiths as well as by some careless amateurs. Scope blocks put on all 'cockeyed'; scopes mounted so far off center and out of line with the axis of the bore that it was utterly impossible to sight them in on the target; and screw holes drilled completely through the barrel into the bore. Be sure your gunsmith is competent before you entrust your pet rifle and scope to him."

If this statement had emanated from some gun factory executive or person with a possible axe to grind it might well come under the heading of propaganda with an eye towards personal gain. But coming from a man who has the respect and admiration of shooters, gunsmiths, gun manufacturers, publishers, editors and fellow writers, it is a statement worth heeding.

Colonel Whelen is not exaggerating the situation one bit when he states that "not all gunsmiths are competent to mount scopes." All of which means that the mechanic who does a really good job of scope mounting stands a very excellent chance of having the shooters from miles around beating a pathway to his door.

There is more to scope mounting than drilling and tapping a few holes, though it must be admitted that the gunsmith who can do these two operations with ease and skill has a great deal in his favor.

When a shooter comes to the point where he is willing to invest, or has invested a few days (maybe weeks) pay in a scope and mounts, he is generally an esteemed member of the clan and one who has given no little bit of thought to the matter of sights and sighting. Naturally, when one of these members comes to the gunsmith with his rifle and glass sighting equipment he expects that he will have a very nice little discussion with the gunsmith as to the advisability of using x mount with y scope, et cetera, ad infinitum. The gunsmith who is on the ball, or who does a great deal of experimenting, can immediately answer most all of the customer's questions and perhaps make a few suggestions that will benefit him no small bit. However, the gunsmith who knows scopes only by their wholesale price stands very little chance of inspiring customer confidence.

To be able to mount a scope correctly, the gunsmith should know the difference between various types of scopes and what mounts each can be used with. He must know why high power scopes are good for target work but poor for use on moving game. He must be able to visualize the combination that a certain rifle, scope and mount will result in, and whether this combination will be good for the type of shooting the customer has in mind. He must be able to show the customer how to make windage and elevation adjustments on the scope of the latter's selection and show him how to care for it, if requested to.

Scopes and scope mounts are real precision items only when they are selected for, and mounted correctly on, the gun that they were designed to fit. Also, they must be accurately placed to suit the physique and manner of shooting of the shooter.

Within this chapter the mechanical phases of scope mounting are covered in such detail as is needed to give background for doing a good job. The matters of how a scope works and what makes a certain type mount desirable or otherwise for a particular gun is something that *cannot* be dealt with in a condensed version. Evidence of this is in the fact that it took Colonel Whelen 200 pages to cover the subject in his book. For the mechanics who thoroughly understand scopes, mounts, and their adaptability to different weapons and conditions, this writer advises that they not bother with Whelen's book—for the other 95% there is no better complement to this chapter.

Good shooting calls for good scopes and good mounts, and these cost plenty. If the mounting job is not done correctly, even after having taken into consideration such matters as eye relief, proper scope, et cetera, then the whole outlay of the shooter's hopes, money and time is nothing more or less than a total loss. And certainly no gunsmith seeking to build or perpetuate a good reputation can afford to trifle with the ambitions of an inspired shooter.

Aligning Scope Blocks. Although the actual installation of telescopic blocks or mounts is somewhat similar to that of mounting a receiver sight in the operations of drilling, tapping and shimming (horrors forbid) if necessary, the matter of initial alignment is not quite so easy for, as can be appreciated, the wire method cannot very often be used as a direct means, although in some cases it can be of help in locating the sighting center along the bore and receiver.

On an octagon or "straight throughout its length" round barrel, locating the top center of the barrel is a comparatively easy job wherein the wire method can be employed advantageously to aid in indicating the center for drilling. Once the top barrel center is located, the base or bases upon which the scope is to be mounted can be temporarily fastened to their correct position by means of a "C" clamp or parallel clamp. Then the holes can be drilled and tapped in the same way as recommended for the receiver sight except that the drilling operation must be attended with greater care so that the drill does not penetrate the barrel and ruin it. To positively preclude this happening, the gunsmith should predetermine the depth that the drill must go, and set the stop on the drill press accordingly.

Too, in tapping out these blind holes, the utmost in caution must be exercised so that the tap will not be snapped off as a result of its end hitting the bottom of the hole. The number one tap should be used to start the threads in the hole and the number three or bottoming tap then used to cut the threads to the bottom.

As an aid to spacing scope blocks correctly, the gunsmith who anticipates very much scope mounting work should provide himself with a drill jig that has holes in it spaced so that distances of 4.5", 6", 7.2", 8", and 8.2" between blocks can be brought about.

Figure 49 illustrates the general design of one style of such a jig. In using this jig on a barrel that has a very extreme taper in its length, it is good practice to shim up one end of the jig to conform with taper.

Drilling jigs for use in connection with the installation of side mounts, such as the Weaver "T" series, or the Griffin & Howe, are very desirable and are one of those items upon which the gunsmith can while away a few of those slack hours that are prone to occur during the mid-summer months.

In making any sort of a drilling jig for scope mounting work, use drill rod flat stock that will resist all normal wear incident to clamping, rubbing, et cetera but do not attempt to harden and temper the jig unless previous allowance is made for shrinkage, warpage and over-all shape distortion. All factors considered, this writer can see little advantage in hardening and tempering scope drilling jigs of the type used in small gunsmithing shops.

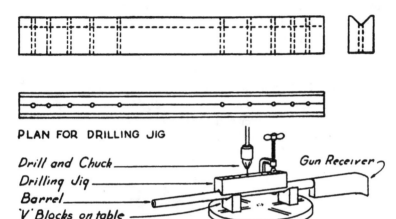

PLAN FOR DRILLING JIG

Drill and Chuck

Drilling Jig

Barrel

'V' Blocks on table

Gun Receiver

JIG IN POSITION ON DRILL PRESS TABLE

DRILLING JIG FOR USE IN SCOPE MOUNTING WORK

FIGURE 49

Another method of scope block alignment is illustrated in Figure 50. This method is predicated on the idea that there is at least one surface on a barrel-receiver assembly that is absolutely true and flat, and that this surface is perfectly parallel to an imaginary line drawn across at the center of the barrel (180° rotation).

SCOPE BLOCK MOUNTING

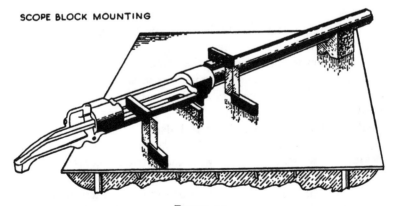

FIGURE 50

A surface plate or large piece of plate glass is employed to provide a true base upon which a pair of "V" blocks, or one "V" block and one steel parallel are laid. Upon these blocks the barrel-receiver assembly is placed and the "squaring up" operation can then be performed.

If one does not have a surface plate or piece of glass, there is little advantage in trying to do the job on a work bench top. In the absence of a surface plate, it is better to place the gun barrel between felt vise jaws that have been slightly oiled, and use a small level on the receiver and the barrel to achieve proper block location (See Figure 51). The purpose of the oiled felt jaws is

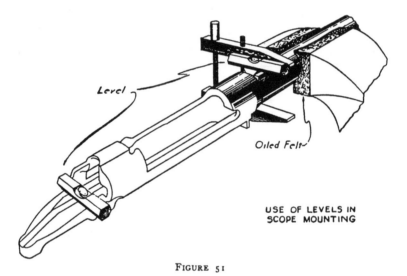

Level

Oiled Felt

USE OF LEVELS IN
SCOPE MOUNTING

FIGURE 51

so the barrel, while rigidly held in the vise, can be rotated slightly to aid in the leveling process.

In addition to each being on the perfect center of the barrel, the blocks of a telescope sight must be spaced correctly (here is where a drilling jig comes in handy) so that no part of either one will protrude beyond the ends of the fitting on the scope itself. Improperly spaced blocks will also interfere with the locking of the scope mount on the blocks in many cases because the locking screws will not align with the notch or recess provided for them in the blocks. This can lead to a condition where the scope will shake loose after a series of shots have been fired from the gun. Such a setup can scarcely be conducive to the accuracy which is to be normally expected of a rifle having a mounted telescope sight on it.

The height of scope blocks is also of the utmost importance when it comes to mounting work since the entire usefulness of a telescope can be reduced to naught if it requires all the normal internal adjustment to zero-in the weapon. Sometimes the standard block for a particular scope-rifle combination proves to be near worthless if the weapon has a special barrel on it (having a non-standard outside diameter), or if the receiver has been modified at the point where a block would ordinarily be affixed.

This is just another one of the small items that the gunsmith must probe into, check, double check, and check again before he starts drilling and tapping. Yes, sir, there are a lot of ifs, ands, buts and details to scope mounting. To the man who knows his stuff, though, they are mere routine; to the other fellow who does not realize what study and experience mean, they are mystery factors to be dealt with only with crossed fingers and silent prayers.

Side Mounts. When mounting scope sights which are affixed to the gun by means of mounts attached to the side of the receiver, a parallel clamp should be used to hold the mount against the receiver during the operation of alignment. This clamp should be so positioned that it does not cover any of the holes in the mount, for when alignment is achieved, only after much loosening and tightening of the clamp and moving the mount, it is most disheartening to have to move the clamp in order to make way for the drill.

A side mounted scope is a bit more difficult to line up correctly than is any other type because, in addition to being set on horizontal center, the mount must also be so placed that it will not cause the scope to be held at an angle of elevation or depression. In short, the scope must be parallel to the axis of the bore or any adjustments made on the scope's elevation knob will not be in keeping with the deviation expected from normal zero of the rifle.

Figure 52 illustrates one of the most efficient methods of properly locating the side plate of a side mounted scope.

Bridge Type Mounts. Bridge type mounts are fitted to the top of a rifle receiver and are mounted in the same way as barrel scope blocks. However, this type of mount cannot be recommended for the low number Springfield rifle with its case-hardened receiver or for any rifle which has a surface-hardened receiver. There often are other styles of scope mounts commercially available which can be mounted on such a gun, by means that do not require sections of the all important receiver to be annealed, so that the gunsmith need not suggest or encourage selection by a customer of a bridge type receiver mount. This same admonition goes for all rifle-telescope combinations where one type of mount is not as well suited to the gun as are any one of many other styles. Under such circumstances the gunsmith should earnestly try to show the customer why a certain type of mount is far less suited to his gun than are many other available mounts.

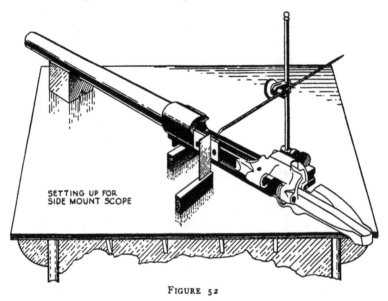

SETTING UP FOR
SIDE MOUNT SCOPE

FIGURE 52

When a customer complains that the telescope mount barrel blocks are always coming loose, it is possible to correct this condition by sweating the blocks to the barrel. To do this, use a piece of fine emery cloth and polish all the blueing from the bottom of the blocks and the area on the barrel where the blocks rest. Tin these surfaces very lightly and screw the blocks tightly in place. Then apply heat to the blocks until the solder melts, tighten up the screws fully while the solder is still molten, and let cool. This operation should only be undertaken after the owner's permission has been secured because many dyed-in-the-wool gun cranks change the sighting equipment on their gun every time something new appears on the market, and, therefore, like the sighting appendages so affixed on their weapons that they can be quickly removed and without any globules of solder remaining on the barrel. In practice it is not very often necessary to solder mount blocks to the barrel of a gun; still it is well for the beginner gunsmith to know that such a practice is not frowned upon by professional gunsmiths.

Although it is to be expected that a mechanic as versatile as an experienced gunsmith should have a working knowledge of rifle telescope construction, this writer is of the opinion that the job of telescope repair and adjustment should not be undertaken by a gunsmith unless it be of a very minor nature and must be done in a hurry. Otherwise, in the interest of rendering better service and avoiding trouble, this writer further recommends that the gunsmith act only as middle man and send all telescopes requiring repair back to the factory where they can be fixed properly by experts who have the special tools needed for the job, and a reputation as telescope makers to maintain. This course of action not only relieves the gunsmith from a good deal of responsibility and worry, but also permits him to render first class service to his customers and realize a modest profit that most likely would be a loss if he had attempted to do the job himself.

In the same category with repairing telescopes is that of making special mounts for telescopic sights. Although it is within the pure mechanical ability of an experienced mechanic to fashion blocks and mounts for a particular scope-rifle combination, the project can hardly be considered as practical unless the gunsmith is working on a cost plus basis (which is unlikely) in the interest of some customer who fancies himself to be developing the mount for which the shooting world has long been waiting.

For the gunsmith to attempt to duplicate a factory made commercial-type mount with some slight modifications just to suit some customer's particular taste in unusual scope-mount combinations is very poor business, unless the customer is prepared to spend at least twice as much as a similar conventional stock item would cost. If a customer is insistent upon having a special mount made but the gunsmith does not feel he has the time or necessary experience to undertake such a job, then the best plan for him is to contact one of the specialty gun companies like Stoeger Arms Corporation, New York, N.Y., and find out what they would charge to make and affix a mount of the kind desired by the customer. Here again a few dollars can be made by acting as middleman.

On all deals where the gunsmith acts as middleman, he should as a matter of good business practice get a deposit equal to at least one half the cost of the project so that the customer will not be too inclined to back out merely because he is dissatisfied with some small detail. This does not mean that the customer, by putting down a deposit, is legally or ethically bound to accept the finished product of his own design if it is not up to specifications, but it will help to bail the gunsmith out financially if the special mount does meet original specifications but does not, for some trivial and non-correctable condition, suit the customer enough so that he will accept it. Nor should a held deposit be used to force a customer to accept anything he would not ordinarily be expected to if the held money was not in the picture.

Special Sights

Although this writer has recommended in many places throughout this book that some tools, parts and accessories are better bought than made by the gunsmith, this should not be construed as an overall rule-of-thumb against making anything, but rather as an invitation to analyze each situation where the alternative of "buy ready made or make it yourself" exists and make a decision accordingly that will favor both his reputation and pocketbook. And in connection with sight work, there are some special sights which can be made by the gunsmith that will favor both of these conditions.

Revolver Sights. First there is the matter of special sights for revolvers and it should not be difficult to imagine how much room for personal expression there is along these lines, to say nothing of the improvement that can be made in the shooting qualities of the gun.

A good rear sight for revolvers, which, while not adjustable, will aid in snap and target shooting, is illustrated in Figure 53. Actually, it is nothing more than a thin piece (about $\frac{1}{32}''$) of steel with a notch in it and cut to such a shape that it will conform with the general lines and dimensions of the frame. This blade is fitted into a hacksaw-made slot in the frame and is held in place by solder. However, it should be sweated in only after it has been cut to finished dimensions and blued. A word of caution at this point—do not make the slot more than $\frac{1}{16}''$ deep,

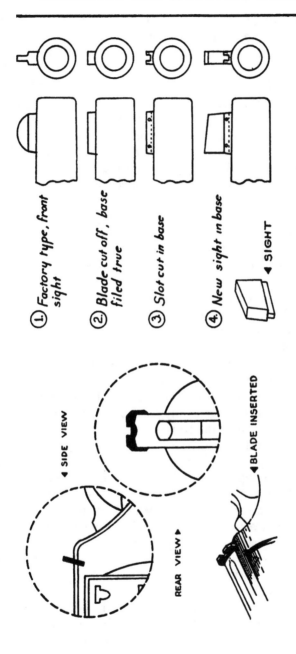

1. Factory type, front sight

2. Blade cut off, base filed true

3. Slot cut in base

4. New sight in base

◄ SIGHT

INSTALLING BLADE IN REVOLVER SIGHT BASE

◄ SIDE VIEW

REAR VIEW ►

◄ BLADE INSERTED

INSERTED REAR SIGHT BLADE FOR REVOLVER

less if possible, for this point on a revolver is subject to a good deal of strain and should not be unduly weakened. A shallow slot is all that is necessary and will serve just as well as a deep one to hold the blade.

A front sight that will enable the shooter to get the full benefit from the suggested rear sight is illustrated in Figure 53. The details of construction are illustrated in sequence of operation and can be carried out on any of the modern Colt or Smith & Wesson revolvers with the possible exception of a few of the latter's top break models. If the gunsmith does not choose to pin the sight in place he can sweat it in place, or, if deemed necessary, both solder and pin can be employed.

The type of front sight shown in Figure 53 is not necessarily the best or the only type of front sight but merely used as an illustrative medium. And since there can be as many different styles as the gunsmith's imagination conceives, any attempt to suggest others would be a bit superfluous. The main thing to be borne in mind when making one of these is the purpose for which the gun will be used. That is, if the revolver belongs to a detective or peace officer and will be carried in his pocket, then neither the front or rear sight should be too high or have pronounced sharp edges that might catch on the pocket lining. Also, the eyes of the person who is going to shoot the gun must be taken into consideration. For example, a man who has some astigmatic condition or weak eyes, generally requires a narrower front sight blade in proportion to the rear sight notch width than does a man with near perfect eyesight.

The "pick-up" qualities of a front sight can be greatly improved by inlaying a piece of ivory, mother of pearl, colored plastic, gold, silver, brass or aluminum at its tip. The rear sight blade can be similarly improved for dusk or night shooting by indenting with a small chisel around the notch and applying white, or better still, luminous paint in this indent. The indent need not be very deep for its only purpose is to retain the paint below the exposed surface of the sight and thus protect it from being rubbed off.

On short or cut down revolvers, a ramp sight of the style illustrated in Figure 54 is often quite desirable since such weapons are most often pocket guns used for defense work. The ramp can be cut from almost any type of steel that can be easily machined and will take a blueing (this, of course, eliminates stainless steel

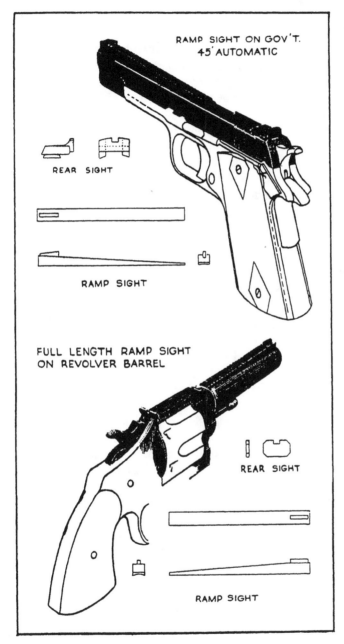

RAMP SIGHT ON GOV'T.
45' AUTOMATIC

REAR SIGHT

RAMP SIGHT

FULL LENGTH RAMP SIGHT
ON REVOLVER BARREL

REAR SIGHT

RAMP SIGHT

FIGURE 54

or steel having a high percentage of either nickel or chromium in it). The most important factor in making a ramp sight is to cut the curvature on its base so that it will fit over the barrel in such a way as to appear as if it were part of the barrel itself. Other than that the shaping of the ramp, or the method of matting is largely a matter of personal taste of either the gunsmith or the customer.

Because of the comparatively thin wall of a revolver barrel, the ramp can neither be pinned nor screwed in place and therefore must be sweated on. This operation does not pose any particular problem if the frame is to be blued after the ramp is sweated on, for under such circumstances the gunsmith need not worry if a bit of solder or flux oozes on to the side of the barrel and in being removed takes a bit of blueing with it. However, if the gun is not to be blued, then the flux and solder must be used very sparingly and, in addition, a light film of oil should be applied to all surfaces of the barrel except where the solder is tinned on. Although this oil will undoubtedly send up a bit of smoke as heat is applied to the barrel, it will act as an inhibiting agent against surplus solder and flux that runs from between the joint.

A "C" clamp is used to hold the ramp sight in place while it is being sweated on and a sharp narrow chisel used to gnaw away any traces of solder showing from between the ramp base and barrel.

Pistol Ramp Sight. The sighting equipment on an automatic pistol, most especially the .45 Government Model, which is used quite often for match shooting, can be improved by installing the Colt Adjustable Rear Sight and a ramp front sight similar to the one illustrated in Figure 54.

The rear sight, if the Colt type is desired, is procurable from that company and is driven into place after the dovetail slot on the slide has been enlarged to receive it. If a non-adjustable rear sight is preferred for use with a ramp front sight, then the conventional rear sight can be retained and its notch enlarged and squared at the bottom (this is not necessary if the new type A1 rear sight is already on the gun) or a new sight of the gunsmith's or customer's design can be made from cold rolled steel, incorporating such desirable features as a wide square notch with a relief cut around the front face of the notch, and having a dull finish. The method for putting this finish on is described in detail in Chapter Sixteen on Grinding and Blueing of Guns.

The ramp sight on the automatic pistol illustrated in Figure 54 has a flat bottom and is fitted into a milled slot extending from the extreme front of the slide to the front end of the ejection port. The depth of the milled slot need only be about $\frac{1}{32}''$ and the ramp can be sweated, taper pinned, or screwed in place. If either of the latter two methods is used, then the gunsmith must make certain that no part of the pins or screws protrude below the inside surface of the slide to interfere with the latter's free movement. In shops where a milling machine is not available, a flat can be filed on the slide top or the base of the ramp can be cut with a radius to fit the curvature of the slide. Here again the etched dull finish can be imparted to the ramp surface or equally spaced file cuts (about .03125'' apart and .010'' deep) can be scribed in the manner of steps across its face. Some mechanics even see certain practical and beautifying advantages in covering the ramp with closely placed prick punch marks.

While it would be very nice if it were practical to install a ramp sight on an automatic pistol slide without having to reblue the entire unit, experience has shown this writer that such is very rarely the case. For in spite of the very best efforts and methods there are, as a rule, slight corrections either in the height or width of the sight blade that must be made after the sight is affixed to the slide. Too, whether pins, screws or solder are used, there are almost always some little sections that must be filed, polished or adjusted, thus leaving an exposed bright metal surface. So in the interest of turning out an A-1 job rather than one that is almost first class, this writer strongly recommends that, where at all possible, the slide of an automatic pistol be completely reblued following the installation of special sights. Surely the slight additional time required to refinish a so-simple-to-blue item as a Government Automatic pistol slide will not reduce the gunsmith's profit on the entire job by very much. As a matter of fact, the gunsmith should include the time required to refinish the slide as part of the sight fitting job, unless, of course, the customer expects it gratis, in which case the cost of this item can often be added to the cost of making the sights themselves or included in the cost of the overall job without specific reference to it in the itemized bill.

Shotgun Sights. Although one does not ordinarily associate shotguns with nail driving accuracy from a standpoint of sighting and aiming, there is little doubt but that this angle of the gun's equipment has been given some serious thought by the specialty makers in recent years. In addition to raised ribs, ventilated ribs, special colored beads and ring type sights, at least one enterprising manufacturer has seen fit to market a one-power telescope sight for shotguns, and another has brought out an optical sight that projects a ring and dot around a target. Just how popular these sights have proved to be cannot be attested by this writer. Nevertheless, it does indicate a trend towards more accurate pieces of sighting equipment on shotguns. Thus, in these days of seven league strides in scientific development, the public demand for replacing the old with something new is very great and even the tradition-embedded art of gunsmithing must be ready to meet that demand. This is not too hard to understand, especially since the public has been told how radar enables an anti-aircraft gun crew to knock down a plane that cannot even be seen.

All things in their time, however, and for the present the gunsmith should, and probably will, be quite content to master the task of screwing in a brass front sight on a shotgun without having the sight look as if it had been mashed between two moving gears. One way of avoiding this marring of the sight is to drill a small hole, say $\frac{1}{16}''$ diameter, down through the center of the sight and square out the hole with a needle file or square punch. A small square wrench, a la Allen wrench style, can be made from mild steel and used to tighten the sight in place. After the sight has been seated, a piece of brass cut square, with a slight taper, can be tapped into the hole in the sight and filed down to blend with its top. While this method of performing such a simple task might seem to be complicated and time-consuming, it is, in the last analysis, a positive and comparatively quick method of doing the job neatly.

If the gunsmith does not choose to employ the above method, then he has no other choice but to turn the sight in place with a pair of serrated jaw pliers and file and polish away the engraving that the pliers leave. On inexpensive or battered-up guns, this latter method might be permissible but on good or new guns where even an odd shaped front sight (as a result of dressing up) tends to spoil the overall appearance of the piece, the gunsmith should not consider the few extra minutes required by the former method to be ill-spent or wasted. Scratches and scars on newly installed parts are truly the apprentice's trademark and surely no professional gunsmith cares to be regarded as a beginner.

Ivory or plastic bead sights which are so often used in pairs (a large one at the muzzle end of the gun and a smaller one near the middle of the rib) generally have a tapered shank which fits into the rib of the gun. These sights are very brittle and consequently will break when anything very hard is brought to bear against them suddenly—for example, the head of a hammer. Therefore, when putting these sights in place, a piece of soft wood, having a hole a little larger than the diameter of the sight, should be placed over the sight and the hammer force applied against the wood. Even with this precaution the blows delivered should be only hard enough to set the sight in place. Small square reamers are available, and usually supplied with ivory sights so the hole in which they are to fit can be reamed out to correct size before the sight is put in. These reamers are not decorations or fancy drift punches and therefore should be used before any attempt is made to install the sight.

And so we come to the end of this chapter. Within it the writer has tried to cover the points that puzzled him and other gunsmiths, both professional and amateur, when they were getting started. Almost needless to say, there are probably some points that have been overlooked, while others have been overstressed. However, in any event, this writer has tried to present the important things, those problems and their solution that most often confront the mechanic who is trying to make an honest living at the thing he wants, knows and likes best, in a way that enables him to turn out good work at a profit.

To read this chapter over once and feel disappointed that the answers to some particular problems cannot be found should not discourage the gunsmith, for perhaps if he will but peruse it again and do a little combining of thoughts contained under somewhat unrelated sounding subject headings, he will be enlightened.

CHAPTER NINE

MAKING SMALL PARTS

ALTHOUGH this writer firmly believes that most gun parts are better bought than made, it goes almost without saying that World War II brought about a situation which makes modification of this policy a necessity for almost every small shop gunsmith.

Shotguns, rifles, pistols and revolvers—single shots and repeaters—from points east and west, the war souvenirs have been brought into this country by returning servicemen and mariners. While yards of regulations, laws, stipulations and manipulations will drain a great many of these foreign-made small arms from general circulation, there will still be thousands of them around for years to come, with a large proportion in which missing, broken or worn parts must be replaced.

In addition to the demand for foreign gun parts, few of which will be coming from the demilitarized European countries, the gunsmith will also be called upon from time to time to make parts for obsolete American guns, or special parts (e.g. tool steel links, and hand fitted barrel bushings for the .45 Government Automatic) for modern weapons.

Basically, the making of small parts for guns is a phase of machine shop work and, therefore, the gunsmith with a knowledge of lathe, milling machine, shaper and drill press operation has an advantage over the gunsmith whose forte is stock work. Be that as it may, though, it is possible for any thorough mechanic with an analytical mind, and the talent to sit down and think a problem out, to make small parts—for the trick in parts making is not as much actual cutting of steel as it is in devising an efficient and practical method by which a piece of metal can be trimmed to a given shape or set of dimensions.

With unlimited time, and a machine shop full of tools, almost anyone with a mechanical turn of mind can turn out a serviceable small part. However, since the small shop gunsmith is in a competitive business and the price charged for a custom-made part is in direct proportion to the time element involved, it is necessary that he be familiar with certain facts, tricks and kinks incident to this sort of work. To that end the thoughts in the following pages are directed, and while few dimensions or exact methods for making particular parts are given, this is because a broad approach to the subject is more effective when one considers the numerous and varied gun parts that the gunsmith can be called upon to make.

The main purpose of this chapter is to acquaint the gunsmith with the fundamental phases of parts making and to stimulate his imagination, for the gunsmith with a practical imagination (call it ingenuity, if you prefer) can do more with a drill press and file than a less imaginative individual surrounded by tools.

The Safety Factor. When the gunsmith undertakes to make a working part (as differentiated from a non-functional part, such as a front sight, a sling swivel, a ramp, et cetera) for a gun, he must remember that he is putting himself in a position where guess work, good intentions and the "that's good enough" attitude can very likely cause a misfire, hangfire or backfire. And the backfire can be of the double barrel variety if an irked customer sees fit to consider legal action or writes a justified letter to the N.R.A. suggesting that the gunsmith be given a rebuke through the columns of "The Rifleman"—and this has been done, too. Of course, while fear of being caught up with and censured should not be the factor deterring a gunsmith from turning out sub-standard parts, it is mentioned here because not all mechanics fully realize their responsibility to the legitimate shooting public.

No gunsmith should have the audacity to install a working part he has made unless he is technically confident that the part is as safe and strong as it should be for the function it is to perform. It is no disgrace for a mechanic to turn down a repair job on a gun that will require a specially made part if he knows that he has not the knowledge or equipment to make the part. But it is a disgrace and a low in true sportsmanship if the gunsmith undertakes to do such a job and then when stumped by the difficulty of making a part effects a temporary repair that is potentially unsafe and undependable.

Unsafe Guns. Elsewhere in this book this writer urges that a gunsmith should not put his reputation and other people's safety in jeopardy by agreeing to repair guns which are basically unsafe. It is to be appreciated that not every gunsmith wants to go out on a limb and call a shooter's pet pot metal Spanish pistol or post World War I bastard Mauser a menace to long life and good eyesight. Nevertheless, the gunsmith should not hesitate to refuse any gun for repair that he has reason to believe will, when repaired, be of doubtful strength to handle the modern ammunition for which it is chambered. That is a gunsmith's prerogative and, from a public safety standpoint, his duty.

However, when the gunsmith declines to service a gun because he earnestly believes it to be unsafe, he should tactfully but positively explain to the customer his reasons for not repairing the gun. Some customers, not necessarily a majority, unfortunately, will have a great deal of respect for the mechanic who puts ethics and safety before dollar-grabbing. Others, usually less technically-minded individuals, who believe that steel made 50 years ago is superior to the alloys produced today, will either scoff at the gunsmith, act insulted, or explain how "this gun was killing black bear before you were born and shoots harder than any damned pipe you ever fixed" et cetera. If this sort of customer is allowed to cool gradually he will frequently soften up to the point where he can be reasoned with at greater length and coerced and cajoled into facing the fact that his heirloom belongs over the fireplace where it can be admired as a second "Killdeer."

Damascus and Twist Barrels. In spite of warnings, admonitions and near threats sounded by experts who know best and who have no axe to grind, there are still thousands of hunters who go afield every season with shotguns that have *damascus* or *twist barrels*. This is a serious and lamentable situation because people who shoot modern shells in damascus or twist barrels are flirting with trouble, for these old steels just were not made to stand up under the pounding that *any* modern shell dishes out. Yet, because the guns that do blow up are not advertised around, the average damascus barrel shotgun owner figures that since his gun has not blown up, all the warnings are so much scare talk designed to make people buy new guns.

Of course the thousands of damascus barrel shotgun owners who think this way are all wrong but their being considered wrong does not materially improve the situation because they continue to shoot their guns until the weapon blows up or breaks down. If it blows up, the owner buys a new gun (if he is still interested in shooting). If it breaks down, then he brings it to a gunsmith, whereupon the gunsmith, who is not given to servicing any potentially dangerous gun says:

"Sorry, Mr. Breves, but I do not think you would be wise in spending any money to have this splendid old shotgun repaired. It was a good gun in its day but please believe me when I tell you that every time you fire this gun you are one shot closer to the time when it will blow up. I do not doubt you for one minute, Mr. Breves, when you say you have fired a couple of dozen boxes of high speed shells through this gun, but all I can say to that is that you have been mighty lucky. Fact of the matter is that the leading gun companies will not repair a gun that has damascus or twist barrels. And if they will not repair one of their own guns there must be a good reason for it.

"Why, the Ithaca Gun Company will positively not knowingly furnish parts for guns that have damascus or twist barrels because they claim in selling such parts they would be encouraging the use of dangerous guns. You know Ithaca's a reliable outfit anxious to please shooters and make new friends, but not at the expense of keeping one of those damascus shotguns in operating order. Why don't I make the parts to fix the gun, you say? Not me, Mr. Breves. You know, I sort of think there is quite a bit of sense in that old saying, 'Fools rush in where angels fear to tread.' "

The Steel and Heat Treatment. With the exception of those parts which are made from cold rolled steel and case-hardened or carburized, nearly all working gun parts are made from carbon drill rod, tool steel, or, in the case of special pins, alloy steel. Selecting the correct type of steel for each part is, of course, most important, and the purpose a part serves is the deciding factor in this matter. This topic and the necessity for heat treating parts is discussed in detail in Chapter Fifteen. A thorough understanding of the subject material in that chapter is a necessary background to any sort of parts making work, and for that reason the gunsmith is urged to think of annealing, hardening, tempering and surface hardening in terms of a practical partner to the making of parts and tools, rather than an isolated, theoretical topic.

A Missing Part. Duplicating a part when there is a broken or worn one to go by is one matter, but making a part without a model or a drawing is another and, not infrequently, near impossible, task. And unfortunately this writer knows of no easy method whereby the dimensions of a missing part can be arrived at. Frequently it is possible to duplicate a missing gun part from a catalog picture of it, providing the picture is of sufficient clarity to illustrate the true shape of projections, contours, holes, et cetera. This idea of duplicating a part from a picture is recommended only as a last resort and where the part is of such a shape that the recess or hole in which it fits provides some degree of guidance in fitting the part.

A missing part which fits in a space that does not give very much clue as to its shape usually cannot be duplicated with any degree of accuracy and hence should not be attempted, (e.g., the trigger plate assembly on a Luger pistol). The same difficulty is encountered in trying to duplicate a key part (e.g., the hammer in a Spanish revolver) which connects to, meshes with, and directly or indirectly controls a number of parts.

The simplest missing parts to duplicate are, as a rule, firing pins, extractors, plungers, pins and screws. Still, the gunsmith should not automatically assume that the making of such parts, from a picture and by the cut-and-try method, is a snap job, for frequently a little radius or chamfer not cut just right can interfere with smooth functioning of the part and cause the gunsmith to grind and file everyplace but where it is needed.

Duplicating a missing part for a particular gun with which the gunsmith is familiar is a task that calls for an understanding of the principles of gun design. For example, if the gunsmith has worked on the Colt caliber .25 Pocket Automatic, the task of making a firing pin (striker) for the Fabrique Nationale 7.65mm pistol and like automatic pistols is comparatively easy because it is obvious, after field stripping, that they both have firing pins on the same order. By the same token, a familiarity with the working mechanism of American double barrel shotguns makes the job of parts making for Belgian and French double guns much less mystifying. As the gunsmith becomes more experienced he will note that there are types of hammers, firing pins, sears, cocking levers, et cetera, that are used in guns whether they are made here or abroad; he will also note that but for a slight difference in dimensions these parts are nearly interchangeable.

Although it is sometimes difficult to take the exact measurements of a duplicated part, it is a good idea for the gunsmith who does very much parts duplicating work to make a dimensional sketch of each different part he makes and file it away for future reference. It only takes a few minutes to catalog a part in this manner and it may save hours of time at a later date when the same part must be made again. Perhaps 10 years hence the gunsmiths of America will be offered a book containing the dimensions of a few hundred foreign and obsolete parts, compiled by a fellow who knows when he has a stone for killing two birds.

Pins. Except for hinge pins, crossbolt pins, and of course, firing pins, there are very few pins used in guns that cannot be made from drill rod and used as is without being hardened and tempered. However, as every lathe hand knows, drill rod is not the nicest steel in the world to machine and when it comes to cutting fifteen or twenty-thousandths off a piece of small diameter stock the resulting dimensions are not always what is expected, because of the rod's springiness. Therefore, it is economical in the long run for the gunsmith to have a length of each diameter drill rod from No. 1 to No. 75, including the intermediate fractional sizes by sixty-fourths of an inch, on hand at all times. Making a pin then is only a matter of cutting or sawing off a piece of desired size, rounding the corners and blueing, because this suggested assortment of drill rod offers differences in diameter from 0.001" to 0.004" at most.

The pin vise illustrated in Figure 24 is useful for holding small pins that have to be split, squared on an end, or drilled to take a plunger.

Screws. While it is sometimes possible to modify or alter a common fillister head screw to serve in a gun mechanism, the finished product does not always look too well. Frequently the threads are mashed up from being held in a chuck, the slot is too wide, or the head is ovoid as a result of being filed to a smaller size. Best practice, it would seem, is for the gunsmith to make needed screws from cold rolled stock, and then case-harden them. Screws so made will not only look good but also stand up very well. Because it does not thread well, drill rod should never be used for a gun screw unless the screw is actually an integral part of a plunger or plug that calls for an intermediate degree of hardness which cannot be had with cold rolled steel.

In Figure 55 there is illustrated a series of steps showing the way a screw is made on a lathe. The purpose of the adapter illustrated is to provide a means for holding the threaded stock while shaping the head and cutting the screwdriver slot. The adapter

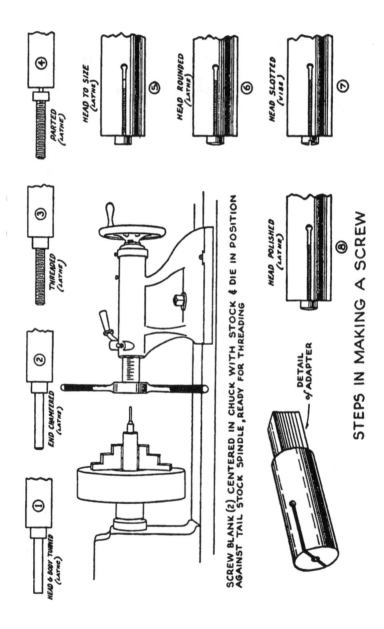

STEPS IN MAKING A SCREW

is made from drill rod or tool steel, drilled, tapped and marked as to what thread it is for. The slots, while not absolutely necessary on the larger size of adapters ($\frac{1}{4}$" screws and over) do come in handy when a small diameter screw is a little hard to get out. A thin wedge (or the end of a screwdriver blade) is pushed in the slot and the hole will spread enough so the screw can be turned out by finger nail pressure. Though it is not absolutely necessary, it is none the less handy to cut square about a 0.50" length on the opposite end of the adapter so it can be held more positively between the vise jaws when the screw head is slotted.

A screw head slot can be cut with a standard hacksaw blade. However, a much neater job can be done with the special type blade sold by the L. S. Starrett Company and others. There is also a narrow hacksaw frame which makes hand cutting of slots a good deal easier because of the rigidity it provides for the blade.

After the screw head has been slotted, it should be polished with abrasive cloth and case-hardened.

Plungers. Plungers can vary in shape from a short length of pin with one end slightly chamfered, to the more complex type having one end pointed with an interrupted flat and the other end chamfered and undercut. Generally plungers are used as a means of keeping spring tension against a part. Therefore, the end of the plunger that rests against the part is subject to an appreciable degree of wear and must be hard. Also, this hardened end must be free from tool marks, scratches or contour irregularities that would in any way retard the free movement of the part under tension.

Plungers under light spring tension are best made from cold rolled steel, or screw stock, and case-hardened.

Plungers under heavy tension should be made from drill rod, hardened and tempered to a dark straw color.

On a ball end (hemisphere) plunger the end should be gently buffed with a very fine buffing compound before and after hardening. This will make for a glass-smooth surface.

Helical (Coil) Springs. Although the evils of using coil springs that are "almost the right size" are discussed in detail in Chapter Five this writer cannot resist the opportunity at this juncture to again point out that the vital dimensions of a spring (Figure 30) are much more important than the average mechanic is prone to suppose, and to urge that special coil springs which are to be put in obsolete or foreign weapons be carefully measured and tested before being considered as acceptable.

The approximate size of firing pin springs (rebounding type) can be estimated very closely, when the original is missing, by measuring the pin diameter and also the diameter of the hole in which the pin fits. The difference between these two measurements (minus approximately 0.008″ allowance for free movement, slight kink set, et cetera; slightly less for small diameter springs, as high as 0.015″ for long heavy gun springs) divided by two, gives the maximum diameter of the spring wire that should be used (see Figure 56).

The fully compressed length of this hypothetical spring (Figure 56) is limited by the distance "C," and the number of coils

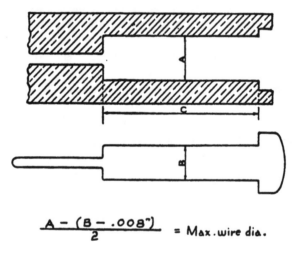

$$\frac{A - (B - .008")}{2} = Max.\ wire\ dia.$$

DETERMINING DIAMETER OF SPRING WIRE.

FIGURE 56

governs its "strength," i.e., more coils, more "strength" and vice versa. The theoretical maximum number of coils that a spring can have (in other words the strongest possible spring of correct diameter wire that can be compressed in a well of given length) is arrived at by dividing the diameter of the wire into the depth of the well, both measurements in inches and fractions thereof. Just as a matter of illustrating these little spring formulas, let the gunsmith for a moment look at Figure 56 and consider measurement "A" as 0.500"; "B" as 0.432" and "C" as 1". Thus we have

1) $\dfrac{A - B - 0.008''}{2}$ = Wire Diameter

2) $\dfrac{0.500'' - 0.432'' - 0.008''}{2}$ = Wire Diameter

3) $\dfrac{0.068'' - 0.008''}{2}$ = Wire Diameter

4) $0.034'' - 0.008''$ = Wire Diameter

5) $0.026''$ = Wire Diameter

6) $1.000'' \div 0.026''$ = 38 coils (approx.)

Of course it goes almost without saying that the gunsmith will probably not bother to get out his slide rule every time he must fit a special spring, but he should appreciate the great help a pencil and paper can be when wrestling with problems where there are more than a few variable factors.

For measuring the diameter of spring wells and similar blind holes, where rule measurement is not accurate enough, drill rod, or the shanks of number, letter and fraction size drills can be used with good success. However, the drill shanks should be free from tears and burrs or the "mike reading" is apt to be thrown off quite a bit. Depth of holes can be measured by this means also but allowance must be made if the shank end of the drill is pointed.

Winding Coil Springs. When a coil (helical) spring is of such unusual dimensions that a duplicate of it is not available either from a selection of gun springs or from a dealer in springs (look up the local springmaker in the classified section of a telephone book) then and only then should the gunsmith give some serious thought to winding a spring. Because the first few springs a novice winds are usually not good enough to be used for any purpose where positive spring actuation is a must, he should consider his initial attempts only as training time and not charge it up to a customer.

Having selected the proper diameter tempered spring wire, a mandrel must be selected (or turned down) that is smaller in diameter than the desired inside diameter of the spring. It is around this mandrel that the spring is wound, and it must be smaller than the inside diameter of the spring, for the latter will "spring out" (expand) after being wound. There is no figure that can be given as to how much allowance should be made between mandrel size and spring size because of the varying amounts of tension different individuals exert against the wire that is being wound. Also, the wire diameter and the outside diameter of the spring are factors in the amount a spring will expand. After the gunsmith winds a few dozen springs, he will no doubt be able to approximate how much should be allowed when making a spring winding mandrel, providing he uses the same method for winding all of them.

Actual winding of a spring is best done on a mandrel that has been cut (in the manner of a left-hand thread) with a definite pitch corresponding to the number of coils per inch of the spring. The depth of each "thread" in the mandrel does not have to be great, but only as deep as the diameter of the wire. By winding a spring on a mandrel of this type the gunsmith is assured that the spring will have the required number of coils and that they are correctly spaced.

Although a spring can be wound on a mandrel by hand, it should be done by this method only when a lathe is not available, for a hand wound spring (even on a "threaded" mandrel) is something that just does not come up to specifications.

When winding a spring on a lathe, the mandrel is held in the chuck and the latter turned very slowly (with the back gears in). The wire, kept taut by passing between two brass blocks held in the tool post holder (see Figure 57), is moved in a horizontal direction by having the longitudinal feed operating at the same speed it would for cutting a thread equal in pitch to the distance between the coils. In Figure 57 the tailstock center is shown in place in the end of the mandrel because this is more often than not a necessity in winding small diameter springs where the tension of the wire against the mandrel will bend it. Note also in this drawing the hole in the mandrel to hold one end of the wire. On very narrow mandrels the starting end of the wire can be soldered on, rather than placed in a hole, since the smallest of holes in a thin mandrel tends to weaken it.

From the foregoing description the gunsmith should very well be able to appreciate why the making of small coil springs is something that is best left to those manufacturers whose business is springmaking. Taking into account the time of making a mandrel, setting up the lathe and winding the spring, it is not hard to see how an hour of the gunsmith's time can be consumed in making a part that can usually be bought for much less than the cost of such time.

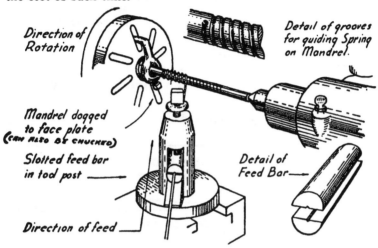

Direction of Rotation

Detail of grooves for guiding Spring on Mandrel.

Mandrel dogged to face plate (*can also be chucked*)

Slotted feed bar in tool post ——

Detail of Feed Bar——

Direction of feed——

SPRING WINDING ON LATHE

FIGURE 57

Flat or "V" Springs. Special flat and "V" springs can either be procured from one of the gun spring makers which advertise in "The American Rifleman" or made by the gunsmith himself. The instructions contained in Chapter Fifteen on making springs from flat stock should be read over very carefully—*and understood*—before attempting this sort of work. It is poor policy for the novice gunsmith—or any student mechanic for that matter—to skim over a description of how an operation is performed or a part is made and then jump to the conclusion that he is now equipped to do it himself. More often than not the person of average comprehension has to read most descriptive material over at least twice, and the important numbers a third time, before he can lay the book aside and roll up his sleeves. It is very discouraging to fail miserably at one's first attempt, whether it be springmaking, gun blueing or trigger pull adjustment, merely because of failure to remember an important temperature figure or a point of caution. Indeed, practice makes perfect, but only practice that is founded upon correct principles.

Firing Pins. In Figure 58A there is illustrated a group of firing pins used in center fire weapons. Yet, as odd and diverse as

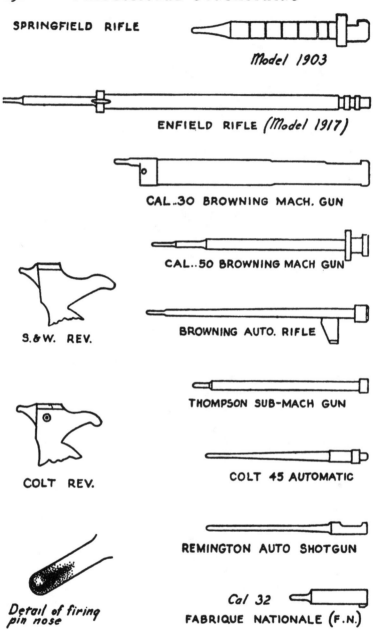

SPRINGFIELD RIFLE

Model 1903

ENFIELD RIFLE *(Model 1917)*

CAL. 30 BROWNING MACH. GUN

CAL. 50 BROWNING MACH GUN

S. & W. REV.

BROWNING AUTO. RIFLE

THOMPSON SUB-MACH GUN

COLT REV.

COLT 45 AUTOMATIC

REMINGTON AUTO SHOTGUN

Detail of firing pin nose

Cal 32
FABRIQUE NATIONALE (F.N.)

FIGURE 58A

they are in general appearance, they all have the same shape, and almost the same size of nose. From this the gunsmith who expects to make special firing pins should be able to see that there is little room for expression of personal taste when it comes to forming the nose of a center fire firing pin. The dimension of the end of a firing pin for center fire cartridges, though not exactly the same for all guns, is about 0.075″ diameter, and the gunsmith should use this figure as a minimum measurement when working on *special firing pins* for rifles and hand guns. It is permissible to vary this measurement minus to the extent of 0.002″ (to 0.073″) and plus to the extent of 0.015″ (to 0.090″). The gunsmith should, however, stay as close to 0.075″ as possible when working with firing pins for center fire rifles if he has an alternative.

Although it has been stated by various competent gunsmith-writers that the 0.075″ diameter is the *only* correct size for a center fire firing pin *for all guns,* such a statement, while technically correct, is none the less confusing to the student who mikes up some shotgun or handgun firing pins and finds that they run to 0.106″ diameter, and occasionally larger. Therefore, when the gunsmith is making a firing pin according to measurements taken from a factory firing pin he should not hesitate to machine the new firing pin according to the dimensions of the factory item. The 0.075″ dimension, while near ideal, has not been standardized for all guns, as is quite evident to the mechanic who will but spend a few minutes with an assortment of different firing pins and a micrometer.

The gunsmith will find that he must make plus and minus allowances in fitting special firing pins so they will pass freely (but not sloppily) through the hole in the bushing or bolt face. Of course, where a bushing hole is greatly oversized, the firing pin should not be made to fit freely in this enlarged hole, but rather the bushing should be removed, a new one made and installed.

On some double barrel and autoloading shotguns, it will be found that the firing pin nose is considerably larger in diameter than the 0.090″ recommended as maximum. This is not uncommon, especially in guns where the firing pin travels through the bushing at an angle so it will strike the primer on center. When the need for such a firing pin requiring an "extra large" diameter nose portion is indicated, the gunsmith should carefully check the firing pin hole in the bushing to make certain that it is not excessively worn.

The nose end of a center fire firing pin should, when installed in a gun, be hemispherical (not pointed or a parabolic) in shape and free of tool marks, scratches and burrs. This means it should have a mirror-like finish brought about by highly polishing the nose end with crocus cloth while the firing pin is rotating at high speed in a lathe or drill press. The crocus cloth polishing should not be undertaken, however, until tool and file marks have been leveled off with abrasive cloth.

It is a waste of time to use crocus cloth or any fine grit polishing cloth or compound on a piece of steel when the latter's surface has tool marks of any appreciable depth in it. Crocus cloth is for final polishing on steel; it should not be used to remove scratches because it just will not do it, at least not within a reasonable length of time.

After a firing pin has been properly fitted in a gun, it should be heat treated (see Chapter Fifteen), wiped free of excess oil and adhering grit, and installed. After being installed, it should be again tested for proper protrusion with the type of gage illustrated in Figure 10.

Firing pins which have a projection as an integral part of them (the F.N. firing pin in Figure 58A, for example) are not too difficult to make provided the gunsmith proceeds cautiously in his plan for making the part (i.e., which operation to perform first, which operation second, et cetera). The practice of thought before action when dealing with the manufacture of individual special parts (that are produced by expensive jigs and fixtures in a production setup) cannot be stressed too much because when it is ignored the gunsmith is likely to find himself in the same position as the fellow who paints his floor, only to find when the job is almost done that he has backed himself into a far corner.

For instance, in Figure 58B there is illustrated a series of steps showing one quick way in which the F.N. firing pin can be made on a lathe without running into any special obstacles. The gunsmith should note that the firing pin is turned on the piece of drill rod it is made from, and not sawed off (or cut off with a parting tool) until the nose length has been cut and the hole for the spring has been drilled. In making the firing pin by this method, the concentricity of the spring hole and nose are assured, as would not be the case if the pin were made by

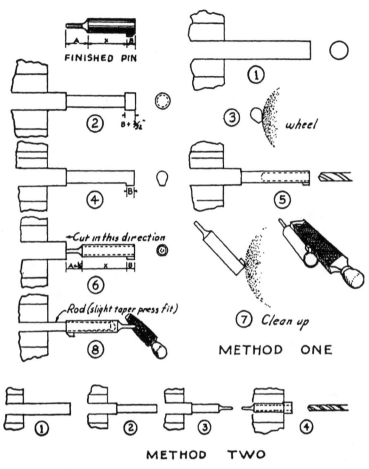

FINISHED PIN

② B+ ³⁄₃₂"

④ ⟨B⟩

Cut in this direction

⑥ A ⟨X⟩ B

Rod (slight taper press fit)

⑧

① ② ③ wheel

⑤ ⑥

⑦ Clean up

METHOD ONE

① ② ③ ④

METHOD TWO

FIGURE 58B

Method Two (Figure 58B). Also, the problem of grinding the sear lug to rough shape is easier by Method One (Figure 58B) because the operator has a length of rod to hold on to rather than just the firing pin body, as is the case with Method Two.

Of course, if the gunsmith intended to go into production on F.N. (Fabrique Nationale) firing pins, he would not do the job by Method One, but probably use an off center turning setup on the lathe and a special milling machine setup to correctly form the sear lug. However, the firing pins produced by this latter method would in no way be superior to those made with less specialized setups.

Making odd firing pins for center fire guns is something that the gunsmith should learn to do well because they are a functional part that he will be called upon to make more frequently than any other.

Firing pins for rim fire guns (the .22 caliber, primarily), like those for center fire weapons, must have a mirror-finished nose surface and be so made that they protrude only a certain maximum distance beyond the face of the breech face or bolt (see Figure 10). The nose shape of firing pins for rim fire weapons is unlike that of center fire, however, because the former can, in addition to being hemispherical in shape, be wedge shaped, circular, rectangular, and rectangular with rounded nose (Figure 58C). Though the merits of each type have been argued out

RIM FIRE FIRING PIN NOSES

FIGURE 58C

time and time again, we still have each type represented in one or another of the modern guns. Therefore, it would be incorrect to say that any particular type is no good or dangerous—except when it is not properly formed on the nose. Hence, in finishing off the nose of a rim fire firing pin, a stone (Arkansas hard stone or its equivalent) should be run across all sharp edges or corners in such a way as to eliminate any sharpness that might, under the driving force of a spring or hammer, cut the very thin metal of a rim fire case, and cause to be released gas under eight to 10 tons pressure.

Extractors. The size and shape of a missing extractor can as a rule be pretty definitely established by measuring the space in which it fits. Where the extractor is of a type that serves as an ejector also (some single shot weapons, and double barrel shotguns), the rear face of the extractor, which fits against the lower rear portion of the chamber, should be fitted by the cut-and-try method, using prussian blue to insure a perfectly true fit. An extractor of this type that is sloppily fitted can cause a great deal of trouble in opening and closing the gun and can also be instrumental in breaking a firing pin if the former is not properly grooved or chamfered to ride over the firing pin nose.

Extractors of the type commonly found in low power rifles and automatic pistols must have a correctly formed claw (Figure 59), proper backing (by virtue of the extractor plunger, and

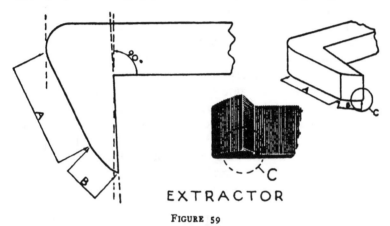

EXTRACTOR

FIGURE 59

plunger spring), and be so shaped along the forward end (Surface A, Figure 59) that they will not butt against any portion of the rear barrel and so create a condition of excessive head space.

Surface B, Figure 59, of an extractor that must snap over a chambered cartridge should be formed and highly polished so it rides over the cartridge rim with a minimum of effort.

Surface C, Figure 59, on some types of extractors should be ever so slightly rounded to permit easy passage (stripping) of the cartridge from the magazine lips to under the extractor.

Ejectors. Ejectors of the solid type that are screwed, pinned, or in some manner fastened to the receiver of a weapon, should, for low power cartridges, be made from cold rolled steel and case-hardened. An ejector so made will be sufficiently strong to withstand the pounding imposed upon it and hard enough to resist face deformation. An ejector having a soft face, that is short in length, or even slightly loose in its mooring, can be the cause of much malfunctioning, and especially in an autoloading weapon.

The spring-and-plunger type of ejector, which is found in

both the M1 rifle and the U.S. Carbine Caliber .30 M1, seems to be excellent in principle and of a design that should be more widely used on commercial autoloading weapons of medium and high power.

Layout Work. When the gunsmith undertakes to make a part of a shape more complicated than a plunger or firing pin made from round stock, he should, like a good machinist, make a layout on the blank of tool steel from which the part is to be cut. The layout is best made by tracing around a sample part that is to be duplicated.

If the sample part is broken, then the separated pieces should be sweated together (Figure 59A) with a very thin film of solder and in such a careful way as to avoid any possibility of incorrect joining. The application of too much solder or haphazard placing of the broken segments during the soldering process can cause a part to assume exaggerated dimensions and contours.

If only a portion of a sample part is available (the other section having been lost or worn off), then the shape and dimensions of the missing section can usually be estimated closely enough for layout purposes. However, all estimating as to how much of a part is missing should be conducted with a "plus-side" mind so that the want of a few thousandths will not be the cause of a finished part being unusable. As mentioned earlier in this chapter, catalog pictures are frequently of inestimable value when judging the size or shape of a part.

Some gunsmiths, instead of soldering a broken part together prior to tracing around it, prefer to sweat the broken segments right to the piece of steel from which the new part is being made. Then they machine the part out, using the old one as a guide. On some parts this modus operandi is acceptable, if not a very good practice, but its application is limited to parts that are completely flat and true on at least one side. Inside shotgun hammers adapt themselves very well to duplication by this method.

The best method, where possible, it would seem, is to sweat the broken part to the piece of steel and then trace around it with a scriber so that if one or more of the affixed segments works loose the outline of it will still remain as a guide.

When a part has a pivotal hole in it, the gunsmith would do well to drill and ream (or at least drill, if a proper size reamer is not available) this hole first and then utilize it as a means of fastening the part-to-be to a drill press table, or face plate.

After the pivotal hole has been drilled in a part, all plus allowances should be made in a radial direction from the hole rather than from the extreme ends of the part.

When a part is layed-out, it should be done on a piece of steel that is large enough to allow for any slips or mistakes the gunsmith might make during the machining process. Waste side-of-the-line metal frequently comes in handy when a part has contours that are segments of a small diameter circle. Then a center punch mark can be made and a drill used to form the contour (Figure 59A). Too, where possible a part of the type illustrated should be layed-out on a blank of steel large enough so that it can be gripped firmly for purposes of easier handling during drilling, and especially rough grinding, operations.

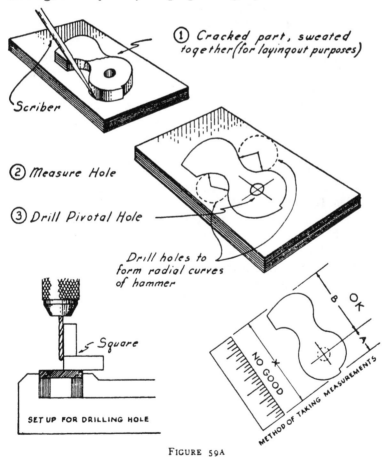

FIGURE 59A

In making a small part the gunsmith should give little consideration to the matter of wasting a square inch or two of steel if this few cents wastage will allow him to make the part faster and better. Time is the overwhelming cost factor in making individual special small parts, and the cost of the raw steel used barely enters into the consideration. Only when one undertakes to make hundreds of a particular part by jig and fixture methods does the matter of utilizing every bit of finished steel stock begin to be important. Penny wise and pound foolish aptly describes the mechanic who struggles with a piece of "scrap steel" when making a special part. This writer does not recommend that raw materials be extravagantly wasted, but he does believe that the value of *time*, of which all good mechanics seemingly have so little, should be placed paramount.

For the student gunsmith who has had little previous experience in doing machine or bench work, leisure time can be wisely invested in reading a book on layout work (e.g., "The Starrett Book," see Chapter Twenty) and doing a bit of practicing with files, cold chisels and a hammer on a block of steel. Not infrequently the beginner with a sincere desire to learn can pick up most all the needed points of partsmaking work by duplicating all the small parts in a single shot shotgun receiver. Such a gun can be bought very cheaply and the original parts used as models.

By making a complete set of parts the gunsmith can observe (and feel) the flaws in his handiwork when all the parts are assembled. It is best to tackle a project of this sort by setting apart an hour every other night and making one part at a time. Then when the hammer is finished it can be installed in place of the original, tested, and if completely satisfactory, left in the gun. In this same way all the parts should be made and installed until it is possible to use any combination of new and old parts (e.g., the original trigger and the specially made hammer) and still have a smooth working action.

CHAPTER TEN

WOODWORK, STOCK REPAIRS AND ALTERATIONS

WHILE there have in recent years been a few gun manufacturers marketing shotguns and pistols with stocks and grips of materials other than wood, indications are that walnut, the king of gun stock woods, will continue to enjoy no small popularity for many years to come.

These substitute materials, chiefly plastics of mottled brown color, have as many undesirable features for rifle and shotgun stocks as they have advantages. While possessing a certain pleasant appearance at quick glance, molded stocks do not compare in natural beauty with walnut or any of the other natural grained woods used for stocking purposes. For one thing, extreme temperatures affect the plastic stocks now in use to the extent where they are more liable to warp or break than a stock made of good walnut.

Pistol or revolver stocks made of a good plastic material are all right for certain types of target guns where thumb rests and molded grips are wanted, because they can be mass produced much less expensively than can a similar item of wood which must be extensively hand tooled.

Just what the future will bring in the way of synthetic stocks is largely a matter of conjecture, but the chances are that wood will not be displaced so long as there are shooters and gun lovers who feel that firearms are more than just mechanical contrivances which are strictly utilitarian pieces. So much for these stray thoughts, however, now let us consider the problems of stock work.

The art of stockmaking is an exacting one and goes back many hundreds of years. In the beginning stocks were made more with an eye towards ornamentation rather than practicality; yet as better and more accurate weapons were made, an increasing amount of thought was accorded the gunstock as an aid to accurate shooting.

While some rifles used by the early American pioneers and

Kentucky riflemen had queer looking stocks they were so made for a good reason. The unusually big drop of the stock enabled the user to fire the rifle from an upright position with his face and eyes well back from the flash when the priming ignited. From this innovation progress in the design and manufacture of stocks has come to the point where today a shooter gives much consideration to the stock on a target or hunting weapon before purchasing it. Even at that it is not uncommon for a gun owner to have the stock on a rifle or shotgun altered so that it will "fit" him better. Most alterations incident to this type of fitting work involve cutting away, or adding to, the exterior of the stock and require only a few common hand tools, plus sheets of sandpaper of different grits, wood filler and shellac, varnish or oil.

Fitting a Recoil Pad

One of the commonest stock alterations is the fitting of a recoil pad to a shotgun or high power rifle. And, as common as it is, far too many mechanics do not turn out a good looking job. After all, when a gun owner brings in a good looking weapon to have a recoil pad fitted, he expects, and rightfully so, that the addition of this cushion should not mar the general appearance of the piece. In short, the recoil pad should fit flush against the butt of the stock at all contacting points, blend in with general lines of the stock itself, and the old finish should not be ruined.

Selecting the Pad. When approached to do a job of this type, the gunsmith should first find out from the customer just what make of pad he desires, i.e., Jostam, Pachmayr, Red Head, et cetera. Some shooters do have very definite ideas as to what make of pad they want and as such it is advisable to satisfy these leanings rather than have them express dissatisfaction after the pad has been fitted. If, on the other hand, the customer brings in a particular pad to be fitted, make certain that it is large enough, both in length and width, to fit the gun.

Recoil pads are commercially made in three general sizes, small, medium and large. Needless to say, the pad selected should conform as nearly to finished butt size as possible, for in this way the gunsmith will be relieved of a good deal of cutting which is, among other things, a time-consuming operation.

Stock Specifications. Having decided upon the correct size of pad, the next preparatory step is to find out from the customer just how well the length of the stock, as is, suits him. In other words, is it too short or long for the type of shooting he does? If it is too long, then an extra quarter of an inch or so might have to be cut off to bring it down to proper size. If it is too short, then less than recoil pad thickness should be cut off before adding the recoil pad.

In Figure 60 is illustrated a double barrel shotgun with stock nomenclature and typical measurements indicated. The 14"

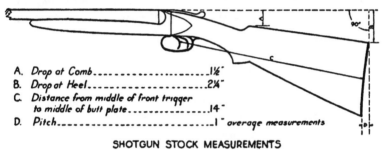

A. *Drop at Comb*............................1½"
B. *Drop at Heel*............................2¼"
C. *Distance from middle of front trigger*
   to middle of butt plate............14"
D. *Pitch*............................1" *average measurements*

SHOTGUN STOCK MEASUREMENTS

FIGURE 60

from trigger to the center of the butt plate (c), is generally considered to be suitable for the average shooter and is one of the distances which must be reckoned with when contemplating the fitting of a recoil pad. Therefore, if a customer is satisfied with the present length of his gun stock (say it is 14" for purposes of illustration), and the recoil pad selected measures 1¼" from front to back, then a little figuring must be done so that the finished length from trigger to the center of the back end of the installed recoil pad will, in this case, be 14".

To do this, take a very careful measurement from front to back of the recoil pad (at its middle section) and mark this distance off in from the end of the butt plate on both sides of the stock. Also, the distance from the trigger to the butt stock toe must be taken into account so that the proper pitch will be achieved.

After the center-line and pitch-line distances have been taken and marked off, a line should be scribed around the stock indicating where the sawing off is to be done. In this way the original pitch and general measurements of the stock will still be retained after the recoil pad is on the gun.

Pitch. Incidentally, this matter of pitch (D in Figure 60), is an important one since it can very definitely affect the shooting qualities of a gun in the hands of the individual who is accustomed to one particular pitch on his scatter gun. In the course of installing a recoil pad it is very easy, if a little thought is not resorted to, to change the pitch of a stock a great deal.

The hard rubber butt plates on many model shotguns are curved out at the butt toe and as such are very helpful to some shooters. Now, since the backs of most recoil pads are absolutely flat, the stock end to which they are fitted must also be flat. Hence, in making this section flat and true, quite a bit of wood is removed and the pitch is altered drastically. In order that the desired pitch be on the piece after the recoil pad is installed, the pitch distance should be taken into account before any drastic cutting or shaping is done.

In cases where a customer might desire to have the pitch changed as an aid towards improving his shooting, the gunsmith should bear in mind that the greater the pitch, the greater the tendency to undershoot, while a gun with little or no pitch will cause a gunner to overshoot.

Sawing the Stock Butt. When sawing off the excess end, use a very narrow bladed back saw and keep at least $\frac{1}{16}''$ to the waste wood side of the line. This is strongly recommended so that chipping of the wood, which almost always is bound to occur, will not affect the finish on the remaining portion of the stock proper. If a saw of the type recommended is not available to the gunsmith, then the next best is a hacksaw with a blade having about 14 teeth per inch. While this writer is fully aware of the somewhat uneven face that is produced on wood as a result of using a hacksaw, he is equally familiar with the effects produced on a gun stock as a result of using a wide-set cross cut hand saw on any but the best close-grained variety of walnut. The very pronounced set in a common hand cross cut saw blade often proves to be too great for the run-of-the-mill gun stock walnut and not infrequently causes a long splinter to rip off. This, of course, means that the entire stock must be refinished, or an inlay made, either of which operation takes up so much time as to do away with the normal profit realized on a recoil pad installation job.

The best setup for sawing off a piece of finished stock is a miter box and back saw. The fine pitch of the teeth on a back saw precludes much chance of wood splintering and the guide slots in the miter box keeps the saw in line. However, inasmuch as a gun stock is not flat, and consequently not parallel to the miter box base, it is necessary to build up under the narrow end of the stock so that the saw will cut at 90° to the end throughout the entire width of the butt. This method is especially desirable where a gunsmith does a great deal of woodwork on already finished stocks; too, it is within the scope of ordinary thought to believe that a practicing gunsmith with an inventive mind could devise a sort of adjustable miter box for work of this sort. Perhaps a screw arrangement must be rigged up to elevate the narrow end of a gun stock so that a 90° saw cut could be positively made on gun stocks of any size or shape. It is surprising what a little spare time experimenting will produce.

Finishing the Sawed Butt. Irrespective of what type of saw is used, it is almost always necessary to sand the butt end of a stock after sawing, and before putting on the recoil pad, in order that the latter will rest on a perfectly true and smooth surface and so no space or uneven line of demarcation will appear between the wood and pad. The best method of achieving this true surface is by means of a flat-sided wooden disc to which a piece of No. 2 sandpaper can be glued. Such a disc attached to a motor driven shaft and used in conjunction with a table arrangement, as illustrated in Figure 61, will smooth and true up the end of a stock in a couple of minutes. The stock must be fed against the sandpaper side of the wheel in such a way that it will cut at 90° to the butt. A build up arrangement similar to that suggested for the miter box would of necessity have to be employed to achieve this desired angle.

When the gunsmith does not have either the time or inclination to set up a motor driven sanding disc arrangement as suggested, then his next best choice is to place the stock vertically in between vise jaws, heavily padded with cloth or felt, and true the butt end by means of one thickness of sandpaper tacked to a flat board. The board should be made of hardwood and be about 8" long and 2½" wide. The abrasive paper should be tacked in place on the opposite side of the board from which the sanding will be done so that the tacks will not be a source of interference. For the sake of comfort and ease of handling, grooves can be cut on both edges of the board. Although simple in construction, this little block should be in the shop of every gunsmith as it is very handy for many phases of stock work (See Figure 62).

In using the hand sander on gun stock butts, it is most important that the sander be handled so that it is kept from round-

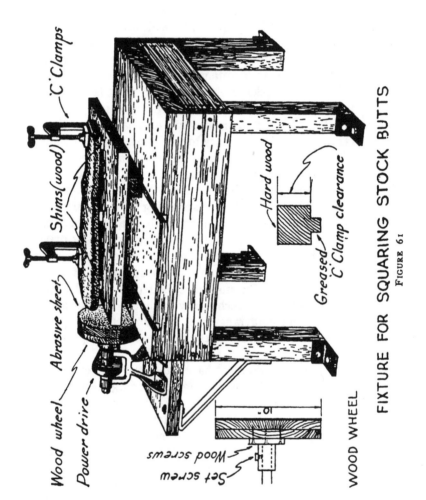

'C' Clamps

Shims (wood)

Abrasive sheet

Wood wheel

Power drive

Hard wood

Greased

'C' Clamp clearance

WOOD WHEEL

10"

Wood screws

Set screw

FIXTURE FOR SQUARING STOCK BUTTS

FIGURE 61

ing off the toe and heel during the smoothing up operation. This is best accomplished by confining each stroke of the sander to such a length that more than half of the block will be on the butt at all times. Thus the probability of the toe and heel being rounded is reduced to a minimum since little or no extra cutting pressure is applied at these points.

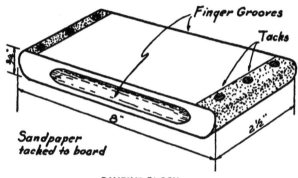

SANDING BLOCK
Can also be used for felt.

Figure 62

After the sanding operation has made the butt true and flat, then and only then is the stock ready to receive the recoil pad.

Cutting the Recoil Pad to Size. Having selected the proper size recoil pad, it should be placed against the butt stock with the heel of the pad as near as possible in line with the heel of the butt stock and the entire pad centered on the gun. So positioned, a center punch mark should be made through the top screw hole and a hole drilled to accommodate the screw. Lubricate the screw with soap and tighten it in place. With the pad thus partly in place, use a sharp thin scriber to mark the butt stock outline on the hard rubber portion of the recoil pad. Next, unscrew the pad from the stock and grind away all the excess material, being careful, however, to shape the toe of the pad at such an angle that it will blend in with the stock lines when in place (See Figure 63).

After grinding to the scribed line, the pad should again be screwed to the stock and realigned into position. At this point the toe hole should be drilled and this screw tightened in place, and if necessary a new line scribed on the recoil pad plate. This is often necessary, since the earlier mark is apt to be thrown off a bit by the locating of the second hole. From this point on the gunsmith must exert extra care in subsequent grinding since the position of the pad on the stock is now determined and there is little room for correcting mistakes other than by starting from scratch with a new pad.

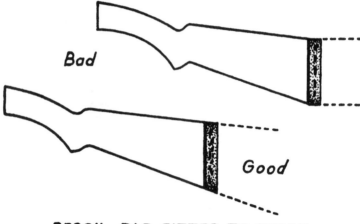

RECOIL PAD FITTED TO STOCK

FIGURE 63

The final shaping of the pad should be accomplished with a finer grit abrasive than that used for the initial cutting so that a smooth appearing surface will result. In connection with abrasives used for trimming down rubber recoil pads, it might be well to mention that the heavier grit, i.e., No. 3, is best for roughing down and No. 2 or No. 1 for finishing.

A wooden wheel, at least 6″ in diameter and 1½″ wide, with strips of the required grit abrasive paper glued or wedged in place, and running on a high speed shaft, is the best means of cutting away the unwanted material on an average recoil pad. If necessary, this task can be performed on the same wheel as used for truing up the butt stock but closer dimensions can more easily be adhered to if the abrasive paper is fixed to the periphery rather than the side of the wheel. At any rate, under no circumstances should the recoil pad be shaped while it is on the stock, for there is always that possibility that a little slip might occur and a ridge be gouged in the stock itself.

While it must be admitted that marking, cutting and fitting the recoil pad to the stock requires more time and effort than just grinding the pad down while it is on the stock, the extra time and work can be considered as well spent. There are very few, if any gunsmiths who can grind a recoil pad down while the latter is attached to the stock without scratching the stock—and a scratched stock is certainly no indication that the gunsmith is a man of great skill.

It is a good practice to rub a bit of linseed oil over the butt-end before finally putting on the recoil pad, as this will darken the edges of the wood that have been lightened in color by the sanding. However, no glue, shellac, varnish or any other adhesive agent should be applied between the recoil pad and stock, inasmuch as this would serve no practical purpose and only make difficult the removal of the pad if necessary later on to get at the stock bolt, which is a part of so many different makes and types of shotguns.

Stock Splits

Of the many types of splits that occur in gunstocks, probably the most common are those which show up behind the receiver tang. Some are very shallow and more accurately described as seasoning checks or cracks and are readily repaired by means of a brass brad or other simple means described in detail later on in this chapter. The more serious splits, which extend for some depth in the stock and allow the receiver of the gun to move perceptibly, are not only a threat to safety and good shooting, but also often place undue strain on the working parts of the shotgun. From a practical standpoint some stocks the gunsmith will encounter in this latter category will be found to be beyond repair, which means that a new stock must be installed.

Repairing a Split Stock. Where, in the opinion of the gunsmith or at the insistence of a customer, it is considered desirable to repair a stock having a split behind the tang, the following method, employed by guncraftsmen for many years, should be used:

1) Disassemble the entire receiver mechanism from the stock and drill a $5/32''$ hole through the stock at a point where a screw inserted through this hole will not interfere with the mechanism of the receiver when both are in place. Too, the hole should be so located that it will allow the reinforcing screw to exert maximum holding force around the area of the split. Counterbore the hole on both sides to a depth of $1/4''$ with a $1/2''$ counterbore.

2) Turn down in the lathe a screw having the dimensions of that in
Figure 64, the length, of course, being governed by the width

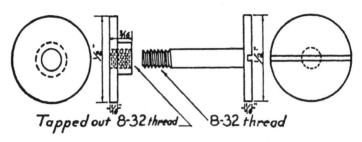

Tapped out 8-32 thread   8-32 thread

STOCK REINFORCING SCREW

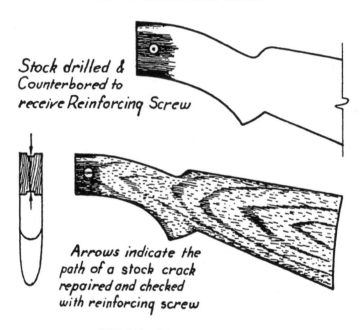

Stock drilled &
Counterbored to
receive Reinforcing Screw

Arrows indicate the
path of a stock crack
repaired and checked
with reinforcing screw

STOCK   REINFORCING

FIGURE 64

of the stock at the point where the screw will pass through it.
When finished, the screw should be approximately $\frac{1}{4}''$ shorter
than the width of the stock, where it is to be inserted, to allow
for the counterboring of the screw head and nut. Thread the
headless end with a 8–32 die and make a nut to fit it (as illustrated).

3) With a wooden wedge spread the split apart and run glue down in between this opening. Remove the wedge, after the glue has penetrated in all sections, and draw the reinforcing screw up tight, not so tight, however, as to bring any sections of the inletted portion of the stock so closely together that they will interfere with the fitting of the receiver or the movement of its parts. Probably the best way of insuring proper fit is to put the receiver and other affected parts in place in the stock before fully tightening up on the reinforcing screw.

4) Next, turn down a piece of walnut to $\frac{1}{2}''$ diameter so that two pieces can be cut off it and glued in the counterbored hole. The pieces should be cut long enough so that they will protrude about $\frac{1}{32}''$ above the surface of the stock wood, allowing this amount for finishing after the pieces have dried in place. The wood selected for making the dowels should be as near to the color of the stock as possible and turned so the direction of the grain blends in with that of the stock. Instead of using wood as a medium of filling in the counter-bored hole, a piece of plastic in any solid color, such as black, white or ivory, can be used with good results and very pleasing effect. As a matter of fact, plastic is superior to wood for this sort of work in that it looks more decorative than a wood insert, which frequently does not match the stock in grain structure. Plastic rods made in almost countless shades, colors, sizes and shapes are available from manufacturers and dealers throughout the country (See Chapter Twenty) and can be purchased in small lots.

5) Grind or file off any excess metal from the threaded end of the reinforcing screw so that it is flush with the outside face of the nut when drawn up tight; then make two or three prick punch marks around the nut where the threaded portion of the bolt comes through. This will prevent the bolt and nut from working loose as a result of recoil over a long period of time.

6) Glue in the wood or plastic dowel, set aside until the glue dries, then finish off and polish. Never use a knife or chisel to remove the excess on the inserted dowel, as there is always that chance that the wood or plastic might split or chip. Coarse sandpaper, followed by the finer grades, and finally steel wool, is the best procedure to follow in bringing the dowel flush with the surrounding stock wood.

If a stock is badly split it is often advisable to put in two reinforcing bolts, with each screw so placed as to bear a share of the strain of holding the stock together. Also, they should be spaced so that neither one of them further weakens a thin or weak section of the stock.

Minor Cracks, Chips and Dents

Cracks and splits of a minor nature, i.e., those which detract primarily from the appearance of a gun rather than its usefulness, are so varied in size, shape, location and severity that to classify and outline a corrective action for each would be neither feasible nor expedient. Yet, for all practical purposes small cracks and splits can be considered as coming under one general category and dealt with accordingly. And from the following instructions and suggestions the gunsmith should be able to find a parallel for whatever jobs come in under this heading.

At the Butt Toe. The toe of a butt stock, which has a very bad habit of breaking off at varying points, even as far up as the lower butt plate screw, is best repaired by removing the butt plate from the weapon and truing up the surface at the end of the break as in Figure 65. The steps as illustrated in this figure show successively a piece of wood held in place by glue and two brass screws, and finally as trued up with a piece of white or black plastic glued in over each of the holes drilled originally to accommodate the holding screws.

In performing the operation the gunsmith must take care to position the two brass screws so that they will not be in the way of the lower butt plate screw when the latter is put in place. The screws, which serve as supporting reinforcement to the glue, should be of the standard wood screw type, with the head turned down to a size just a few hundredths of an inch larger than the largest diameter of the screw body itself. It is recommended that these screws be made of brass so that time and climatic conditions will not affect them, as they would be if made of iron or steel. The length and diameter of the screw will vary according to the particular job, and holes should be drilled before inserting the screws, which should be coated with glue.

If the gunsmith does not choose to put in brass screws then wooden dowels, made of walnut, can be utilized. However, brass screws are recommended in conjunction with glueing the insert piece on, since a much narrower brass screw can be employed in place of a larger diameter dowel to achieve the same holding power. In some cases it might be found advisable to use one brass screw and one wooden dowel, the latter being placed nearer the butt end of the stock so that the lower butt plate screw will be able to bite into the dowel.

Colored plastic rod is recommended as a means of filling in the drilled holes since, as stated earlier in this chapter, it is of a more decorative nature and adds to the beauty of the gun without appearing as of a makeshift or cover-up nature.

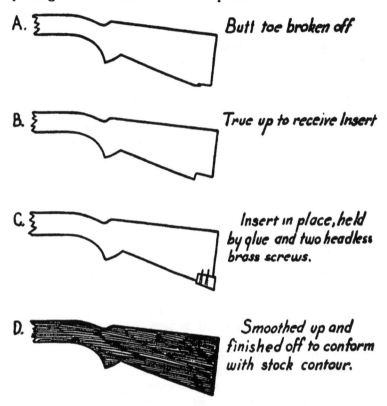

A. Butt toe broken off

B. True up to receive Insert

C. Insert in place, held by glue and two headless brass screws.

D. Smoothed up and finished off to conform with stock contour.

STEPS IN REPAIRING BROKEN STOCK TOE

FIGURE 65

The same procedure as just outlined for repairing the toe on a stock can be applied with slight changes to the heel and other portion of the stock. Where space does not permit the insertion of a brass screw the glue alone must be relied upon to hold the insert in place.

Chipped Stock. Where a small piece of wood chips off from a gunstock in one piece it is often advisable, if the piece is available, to glue it back in place, providing, of course, that it makes a perfect match. As a matter of fact, this is the very best course of action where inlaying of an insert at a thin portion of the stock is almost impossible, for example around the side plate or side lock of a shotgun where there is little room for insertion of reinforcing screws. If the chipped off piece is not available, then it behooves the gunsmith to make one from a piece of near-matching wood. For ease in fitting such a piece, it is considered permissible and advisable to scrape away a few ribbons of wood from around the chips so that a better adhering surface can be had for the glue and insert.

Dents in a Stock. Dents in shotgun or rifle stocks can often be raised by the simple process of placing a wet cloth over the dent and laying a hot soldering iron on the cloth. The steam generated by this action will raise the grain of the wood, thus lifting the fibers in the dented portion to the level of the surrounding wood. Often one or two applications of the hot iron will produce sufficient steam to achieve the desired results. However, where repeated applications do not raise the dent, then the gunsmith can feel safe in assuming that the dent cannot be raised or that it is a gouged out section and no amount of steam treatment will bring up what is not there.

The important points to follow when raising dents by steam are:

1) Have the wet cloth folded so that it is but slightly larger than the area to be raised so that the surrounding wood will not be subject to the steam.
2) See that the cloth (an old towel or wash cloth is ideal) is thick enough to resist the heat of the iron so that the latter will not burn through and sear or scar the stock.
3) Add water from a narrow mouthed bottle or spout type oil can as the cloth dries out so that steam will be in constant generation. For the same reason the iron should always be kept hot enough to keep the water at vaporization point.
4) After the dent has been raised, let the stock stand for a few hours before sanding and refinishing. This will allow for complete positioning of the wood fibers to their normal position when dry and set.

If the steaming process does not prove to be adequate for the task of raising a dent, or if a definite gouge in the stock exists, then the gunsmith has the choice of scraping and refinishing the entire stock to the level of the indentation, or making an inlay.

On expensive stocks made of imported walnut, where duplication of grain, color and pattern is very difficult, scraping and refinishing of a portion of the stock is a most practical solution to the problem. Of course, if the indent is deep, say more than ⅟₁₆″, then it can be appreciated that scraping is pretty much out of the question since the cure would produce an effect worse than the original defect.

At this point it might be advisable to clarify what is meant by a dent. A slight scratch or indent in the wood surface, which can be remedied by a few strokes of a piece of sandpaper or the application of a bit of shellac stick, does not come within the generally accepted and understood definition of a dent. Rather, those disfigurements which are the result of a gun being dropped on a rock or hard surface are more appropriately here and generally referred to as dents. Actually a practicing gunsmith soon learns to recognize stock surface imperfections and by whatever name known the important thing is that he correct them so when filled in they are barely distinguishable from the surrounding area.

For filling up pin head size knot holes and other similar imperfections in stocks, there is probably nothing better than stick shellac which is applied in a matter of seconds by heating a thin piece of steel, like a putty knife or hacksaw blade with a handle, and applying it to the stick shellac which is held against the imperfection. The shellac which readily flows into recesses under the influence of heat, is available from gunsmith supply houses, hardware stores and paint supply houses. For best results, the area in which the shellac stick is to be applied should first be cleaned with alcohol or carbon tetrachloride (carbona) to remove all traces of grease, oil and similar inhibiting substances.

Stock Scraping

In scraping a stock, the necessity for a little "engineering" before proceeding with the actual removal of wood cannot be overstressed, for as the barber always reminds a discriminating customer when he sits down for a hair cut: "Make your decisions now, Mister, because I can take it off a lot easier than I can put it back on." And likewise should the gunsmith approach the problem of wood removal. In short, decide beforehand just how much wood will have to be removed from where before the dent is obliterated, with the stock still retaining its harmonious tapered lines.

For stock scraping, or for that matter any type of scraping on wood where only a limited amount of material must be removed from a previously shaped surface, one of the finest tools for the job is a piece of common window glass. In size it need only be large enough to grasp with the fingers. A piece roughly 2″ by 4″ would seem to be ideal and it is most safely handled if the operator has a glove on his hand. Almost any glazier or hardware has a box of scrap glass which he is only too glad to dispose of. For getting around fluted sections, and small surfaces, little pieces of glass are almost indispensable, and desired shapes and forms can be had by scratching the surface of the glass with a glass cutter and then tapping it gently with a piece of wood. As the sharpness of the edge is worn, the opposite side of the piece can be utilized. After both sides are dulled, a few strokes of the glass cutter will rejuvenate them.

For scraping heavier cuts, a discarded hack saw blade, with the teeth ground off and a resultant flat surface 90° to the side of the blade is ideal, and the thicker the blade the better. The kind used in automatic hacksaws, which are better than $\frac{1}{16}$″ in width, is so desirable that investment in a new one just for purposes of conversion should not be considered as a foolish expenditure. Such a tool can be used indefinitely and requires only a few sharpenings during the course of many hours' use.

As the gunsmith learns to recognize the feel of the glass and metal scrapers he will soon become very proficient in their use. After one or two scrapes on a particular stock or piece of wood he will be able to judge the proper angle at which it should be held to achieve maximum results. Too, he will quickly recognize the direction of the surface grain and draw the scraper across it accordingly.

As it is with any type of work where material is being removed in light cuts from an already preformed surface of finished shape or dimensions, the scraper must be used with some degree of caution. The length of the cutting stroke should be governed by the general contour of the indent being worked around so that a hollow or groove will not be made. And since the wood scrapers of the aforementioned types are completely hand controlled, the gunsmith must learn to develop a "touch." This "touch" will enable him to bear lightly at one point and then very heavily at an adjacent point, both with an eye towards the expected finished product. However, nothing but practice of the right kind coupled with a knowledge of the fact that it can be done by "me," the gunsmith, will cultivate this almost indescribable faculty of "touch."

On stocks where neither the steam or scraping treatment could possibly bring about desired results, wood inlaying offers the most practical solution.

Making an Inlay. In making an inlay, the apex of achievement is to match the surrounding wood so that the inlay is scarcely discernible. To do this requires that the piece selected for inlay be as close in grain pattern and color to the stock as is obtainable; and the inlay be of such a shape as to take advantage of the natural grain lines of the stock.

Fulfilling the first of these two prerequisites is more a matter of having a good selection of small pieces of walnut available rather than skill alone. This of course does not preclude the necessity for some degree of discrimination in picking out the best matching piece.

Shaping the inlay so that it will harmonize with the stock grain lines requires that the inlay be specially formed for each individual task. Since there is no typical shape or size for an inlay it would be rather superfluous to illustrate an ideal or suggested group of them. Nevertheless, it might be well to pass along a few suggestions as to the actual forming and setting in of a wood inlay after the desired shape has been decided upon.

Before doing any cutting out on the stock, the inlay should be cut to finished dimensions and then its outline marked with a scriber on that portion of the stock where it is to be placed. The edges of the well in which it will fit should be tapered slightly from top to bottom, i.e., the smallest dimension of the taper being at the bottom. In this way the inlay can be forced into the well and when sanded to size will show very little at the lines of joining.

The depth of the well is of course governed by the depth of the stock injury but should be at least $\frac{1}{8}''$ where possible. The inlay should be made at least $\frac{1}{32}''$ greater in height than the anticipated well depth so that there will be excess wood for finishing down to stock size and contour. Both the well and the inlay should be coated with glue and the latter held in place by means of a clamp faced with a wooden block to prevent surface injury to the inlay.

In cases where a cheap stock is badly dented and the owner does not wish to invest more than a couple of dollars, the making and installing of a fitted inlay is out of the question. If the dent in one of these stocks is located in the body of the stock then it is quite frequently advisable to drill out the dent for a depth of about ¼″ and insert a piece of walnut dowel a few thousandths larger in diameter than the drilled hole. When glued in place and finished off, the dowel will be quite sturdy and well appearing enough for an inexpensive stock.

When a shooter brings his favorite rifle or shotgun to the gunsmith's shop to have a recoil pad installed or some alteration done on the stock, he expects, and rightfully so, that when his gun is returned, the stock will show evidence of having been worked over by a skilled man worthy of the too-easily assumed title of gunsmith.

Far too many gun mechanics, who do very creditable metal and general repair work, fall down badly when it comes to woodworking. True, woodworking is very much different from metalwork, but that does not excuse poor work, that merely accounts for it. In short, there is no justifiable reason why a gunsmith who accepts a recoil pad or split reinforcing job should hand back an allegedly finished stock with deep sandpaper scratches and cross grain file marks.

Refinishing a stock, after a job in which the original finish has been taken off or marred, is as much a part of a woodworking task as reblueing a receiver where filing and machining have been performed, is of a metalworking project.

There is scarcely a gunsmith, who can even pass as such, who would think of returning a customer's gun, where the blueing had been inadvertently scraped off during a sight mounting job, without at least doing a neat touch-up job. Still, the same mechanic thinks little or nothing of slapping on a recoil pad, filing it down to stock size, sanding the stock and pad to achieve harmonious (?) lines, rubbing a little oil over the splintered surface, and then considering the job finished.

Naturally this writer does not believe an entire stock refinishing job must be done each time some little bit of woodworking is done. But he does recommend that a minimum of original stock finish be "torn up" in the process of an inlay or recoil pad fitting operation, and that whatever area is marred be smoothed off and treated with oil, lacquer, varnish, or whatever substance was originally on it.

Often it is not easy to duplicate the exact color or tone of the original stock finish, but by using a little coloring matter and combining finishes it is usually possible to do a very creditable touching up.

If a large area of a stock is disfigured, as it might be where a number of dents are removed, or where a long splint has been repaired, it is frequently easier to refinish the entire stock than to attempt blending of a touch-up job.

This, however, is something that must be decided before the job is undertaken so that a fair charge can be made.

Summed up, it's a poor imitation of a gunsmith who returns a gun upon which woodwork has been done without refinishing the wood.

In addition to the work of repairing cracks, splits and dents, the gunsmith will often find himself called upon to do a little beautifying on gunstocks. This is liable to include among other things, carving on the stock, checkering the pistol grip and fore-end, and making decorative metal inlays. Technically, while all of these are phases of the gunsmithing business, they are nevertheless somewhat specialized angles of woodworking and should be attempted only if the gunsmith has the tools and skill to do the particular job in a professional manner and at a profit. The carving of ornamental designs on wood is such a specialized phase of woodwork that very few gunsmiths can profitably turn out a satisfactory job. For that reason, and also because the demand for this type of work is very slight, it is purposely being omitted from this book, which is, as stated originally, a text for the practical gunsmith. Too, the subject of wood carving is in its entirety so complex and involved that it is only properly and thoroughly covered in an entire book devoted solely to that phase of woodworking. Might as well be honest too and admit that this writer's wood carving is something which needs lots of improving.

Checkering. Checkering pistol grips and fore-ends on gunstocks for most practical purposes is a matter of patience and practice rather than just skill. This can be evidenced by the fact that people in gun factories who do the standard type of checkering on commercial guns are a long ways from being the top paid skilled workers. Women, who are noted for their patience, are not infrequently employed to do checkering and turn out very commendable work.

The sage who said, "the job well begun is half done" must

have at one time or another done some checkering work for these few words express a great truth, since after a checkering pattern has been laid out and the first cut or two made the remainder of the task is largely a matter of patience.

The simplest of all checkering layouts illustrated in Figure 66 will be used here as an example to describe a proper method

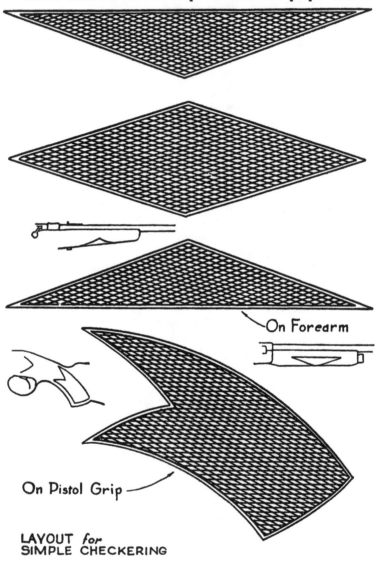

On Forearm

On Pistol Grip

LAYOUT *for* SIMPLE CHECKERING

FIGURE 66

of layout and execution of a typical checkering job on a stock. Although relatively plain compared to some of the patterns seen on expensive custom built weapons, the basic principles incident to carrying out this pattern can be extended to almost any checkering work.

Checkering Equipment. Aside from a set of checkering tools which are illustrated in detail in Figure 67 the only other tools

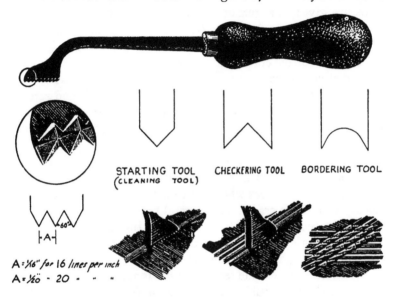

STARTING TOOL   CHECKERING TOOL   BORDERING TOOL
(CLEANING TOOL)

A = ⅟₁₆" for 16 lines per inch
A = ⅟₂₀ - 20 "   "   "

DETAILS ON CHECKERING TOOLS

Figure 67

needed are a scriber, a 12″ steel scale, a hacksaw blade for transcribing lines, a good stiff bristled tooth brush, and some other generally available odds and ends—plus a good stock holding cradle.

While dimensions for checkering tools are given in Figure 67 this writer prefers to recommend the commercially made tools which can be purchased from any gunsmith supply house at a very modest price. Checkering tools which are hand made by the average gunsmith himself are usually inferior to those which are bought from a reliable source. This does not mean that the average gunsmith is not capable of making good checkering tools but rather good ones can be bought so inexpensively that it does not pay to attempt making them. Of course, if the gunsmith finds himself with a great deal of spare time on his hands during a slow period, then there is no harm in making additional checkering tools. Even then it's nice to have a commercial tool around for a model.

The cradle illustrated in Figure 68 is only one of many styles which can be used to hold a gunstock that is being checkered, scraped, finished or what not. Although certain specific dimensions are given, the gunsmith who wishes to can ignore them since it is the basic design rather than any specific dimension which makes the particularly simple cradle so practical.

The ends for the cradle end screws can be made in almost any desired style just so long as they have a ⅜″ diameter hole, ¾″ deep, in one end, so they can be attached to the cradle end screw. These screw ends need not be threaded, pinned or in any other way rigidly affixed because the opposing pressure will hold each end in place.

Because of the many different shapes of the front end of shotgun stocks, the gunsmith must devise various means of protecting this end of the stock when it is being held up against the stationary end of the cradle. The general procedure is to use small pieces of wood to protect the inletted portion of the stock and then use a single piece to bear against these. In this way pressure will not be brought to bear on the delicate corners and sections of the inletting where the receiver and trigger guard fit.

For checkering double barrel shotgun fore-ends, one of the best type of holding fixtures is nothing more than a piece of flat steel stock with holes drilled and tapped in it to correspond with the hole or holes in the fore-end wood that are normally used to accommodate the fore-end iron screws. To this piece of steel should be attached (by brazing, welding or screwing) a piece of ½″ diameter round stock about 6″ long. The round stock section of the fixture is so made that it can be held in the vise at any angle. The same fixture can be used for many different makes and models of fore-ends by simply drilling and tapping additional holes as the occasion requires. Often it will be found that by using different combinations of already drilled and tapped holes the fixture can be employed to hold almost any type of fore-end. If the gunsmith does not care to make up a fixture of the aforementioned type, then he always has the alternative of checkering the fore-end while it is attached to the gun. However, this is a somewhat emergency procedure and sometimes proves to be very

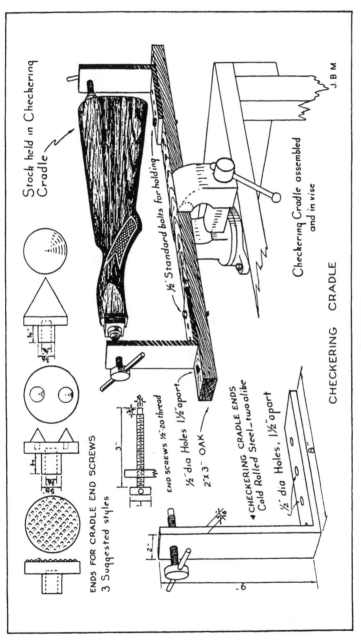

FIGURE 68

unhandy. Too, when checkering the fore-end while on the gun there is always that possibility that the tool might slip and scratch the gun barrel. Such alternatives of procedure are for the gunsmith to decide for it is he who knows, or soon learns, what is best.

Getting back to the matter of actual checkering, we shall now presume that the stock is set up in a cradle of one sort or another and the gunsmith is ready to proceed with the layout.

Pattern Layout. Start with the pistol grip of the stock and figure out just how large a complete checkering pattern can be put on it so that the pattern will appear harmonious with the lines and size of the grip. To get a general idea of how such patterns run, it is only necessary to look in any good gun catalog and note the layout on a similar commercial weapon, bearing in mind that checkering becomes more difficult to control as the cutting approaches the underside of the grip which has an extreme curvature. Therefore it behooves the beginner to design his layout so that most of the pattern falls on the side of the grip which has a fairly flat surface. After having decided upon the dimensions of the pattern, then make a good finished drawing of it on a piece of very light cardboard and cut it out along the drawn lines. This is the pistol grip template and will serve as an accurate means of laying out the pattern on both sides of the grip. Use a very sharp pointed hard pencil to trace around the template on the wood and make certain that the position of the template is the same distance from the butt of the pistol grip and trigger guard tang on each side.

Border. Although a border is not found around the checkering design on the best stocks, it is a necessity for the beginner who usually does not possess the skill to terminate each stroke of the checkering tool so as to form a full clean diamond. Therefore, it is best to make a deep cut with a single pronged tool along the previously penciled line. Make this border cut quite deep and if necessary deepen it more with the point end of a small triangular file.

With the layout and border made, there only remains the actual task of cutting the diamonds, and to insure that diamonds rather than squares will be formed at the intersection of cuts the gunsmith should, with a pencil and flexible straight edge (thin hack saw blade), mark out two intersecting lines in each direction so that the juncture of the diamond point forms an included angle of 30°. The distance between each pair of pencil marks should, of course, be the same, and as near to the pitch of the teeth on the checkering tool as is possible. Here it might be well to point out that while fine checkering (24 diamonds per inch) looks very rich and professional, the beginner should content himself with employing a tool of coarser pitch (say 16 or 18 per inch) until he has mastered the fundamentals of this phase of stock ornamentation.

Using the Checkering Tool. Having satisfied himself with the appearance of the layout, bordering and initial pencil checkering, the gunsmith should now take the checkering tool in hand and start cutting.

First cut all the lines in one direction to a depth of about one half that of the tool, then cut all the cross lines the same way. Proceed slowly and as wood dust is formed by the tool blow it away with a puff of breath. Inasmuch as the previous cut serves as a guide for the next cut, it is most important that each one be perfect. Always maintain a sufficient pressure on the checkering tool when cutting so that it cannot jump from the guiding cut if a hard section or veering grain line is encountered. This does not mean the tool must be held so tightly as to cause the gunsmith to become fatigued but rather, an even, firm pressure should be maintained at all times so that the tool is completely under control. Short back and forth strokes not only make for better control of the tool but also lessen the possibilities of having a splinter of wood chip off.

After all the checkering lines on the pistol grip have been cut to half depth, a tooth brush should be brought into play to clean away all the accumulated wood dust, thus making easier the detection of any lines which do not seem to be distinctly or properly formed. If any of the lines appear to veer or show a tendency towards irregularity, the three cornered file should be used to straighten them out. Thus satisfied, the gunsmith need only go over the original lines and cut them to full depth to complete the job on the pistol grip. Removal of wood fuzz is best accomplished by lightly rubbing a piece of very fine steel wool over the raised diamonds, followed by a vigorous brushing with a tooth brush that has been dipped in linseed oil.

In checkering the fore-end, the same procedure as just outlined for the pistol grip should be followed.

Before going on to consider the next phase of woodworking,

this writer would like to point out to the gunsmith that it is not always possible to turn out a good checkering job on the first few trys and for that reason practice on old stocks is highly recommended. Even then do not be disappointed if the diamonds do not finish up smooth and sharp, for the type and quality of the wood being worked upon have a great deal to do with the results. The finer grained woods are the easiest to checker, while some of the stocks found on inexpensive shotguns and rifles are so coarse grained that it is near impossible to cut a checkering pattern on them.

In the interest of profit and reputation, checkering should not be attempted on a commercial scale unless the gunsmith knows he can turn out a creditable job at a price commensurate with the general grade. This does not mean that checkering work need be turned down while the beginner is practicing its finer points, for the job can always be sent to the factory or specialist for checkering and a modest profit realized as middle-man in the transaction. However, in a short time the gunsmith who spends enough of his spare hours at practicing will find that he is sufficiently skilled to execute the finest checkering designs that his most discriminating customer might suggest.

Beading. Where the beginner wishes to decorate the pistol grip and fore-end of a gun but does not care to risk a checkering job, then beading offers a very desirable alternative method of providing an anti-slip surface.

The tools needed for beading are a small beading punch and a light machinist's hammer. The beading punch illustrated in Figure 69 is best made from drill rod, which can be hardened and tempered so that it will retain its impression edge for an extended period of time. The size of the beading tool end does not have to be exact but the four most practical sizes are $\frac{1}{16}''$, $\frac{3}{32}''$, $\frac{1}{8}''$, and $\frac{5}{64}''$.

To make the tools, cut lengths of $\frac{3}{8}''$ drill rod about 5'' long, face both ends, knurl, and shape as indicated in Figure 69, allowing $\frac{1}{64}''$ at the punch end diameter for finishing. Use a very small center drill to spot the center of the impressing end and then drill with desired size drill to a depth so that the cutting lips just touch the end face of the punch. Smooth out the drilled hole by using a round ended piece of steel stock covered with emery cloth or emery dust, and finish off the outside of the punch so that it conforms to the shape in the drawing.

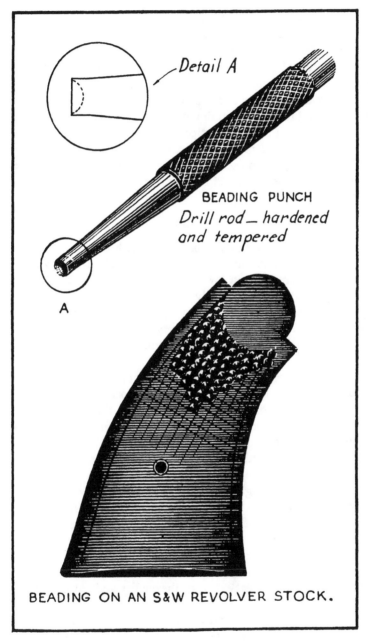

Detail A

BEADING PUNCH
Drill rod — hardened
and tempered

A

BEADING ON AN S&W REVOLVER STOCK.

FIGURE 69

After bordering the desired pattern in the same way as that used for checkering, select a beading punch and impress the entire surface within the border, being very careful to apply the same amount of force at each blow of the hammer. Do not overlap the beads but place them as near to each other as possible. Almost endless varieties of bead combinations can be used, such as four small beads surrounding one of double size, et cetera. Yet for best results it is good practice to make a few sample combinations on a piece of scrap wood. Too, try to carry out patterns that will end up evenly on each border edge. Knowing the width between borders and the size of the punch, this is very easy to figure out.

Stock Finishing

Linseed Oil Treatment. The beautiful finish on the stock of an expensive weapon has always been, and probably always will be, as long as there are gun lovers, the object of great admiration and desire. Almost invariably such a finish represents many hours of hand rubbing of linseed oil into the wood pores by an expert stock finisher. Although this type of finish is desirable on every stock, it goes almost without saying that such is well nigh impossible.

Only when a customer is willing to invest many dollars can the gunsmith profitably undertake to finish a stock by applying coat after coat of a mixture consisting of two parts linseed oil and one part turpentine to the wood until it will not absorb any more, followed by rubbing with a pumice stone-coated felt pad and final polishing done with the ball of the hand, or a piece of soft dry felt.

An oil finish is highly recommended on a newly made stock of good wood or on an old stock of high quality walnut, but it is more or less a waste of time to put an oil finish on the stock of a cheap gun. However, if a customer insists upon having an oil finished stock, do not attempt to argue him out of it so long as he agrees to pay a stipulated price and is aware that the resulting finish depends to a great extent on the quality and natural beauty of the stock wood.

Before Applying Oil. Before oil finishing a stock, the wood must be *very* smooth. This is best accomplished by using sandpaper of varying grits, starting with the coarsest that is deemed necessary, according to the depth of scratches or tool marks in the wood, and ending with the finest steel wool obtainable. When sanding a stock, or for that matter any piece of gun woodwork, do not proceed to use sandpaper of a grit less coarse than that being used until all scratches made by the piece preceding the one being used are obliterated. Extra effort is required to secure a scratch free surface around the pistol grip and the area behind the tang of the receiver, for the location of these places is such that they are very difficult to sand in the direction of the grain.

Raising the Grain. After the surface of the wood has been smoothed to the point where tool, file and all but the scarcely perceptible abrasive paper scratches have been removed, the wood should be "whiskered." This is done by rubbing the wood over with a wet cloth—not soaking wet, but moist enough so the wood surface will appear wetted after a rub over. Follow this operation with a drying process, by holding the stock over a gas flame, Bunsen burner or alcohol torch, to dry out the introduced and inherent moisture. As the wood dries out, as a result of the applied heat, the surface grain will rise and feel "whiskery" to the touch. The whiskers are best removed by rubbing over the wood with a pad of steel wool; sandpaper is not recommended because it tends to fold over the whiskers rather than cut them off at the "roots." Three or four repeats of the wetting, drying and steel wool ritual should suffice for most stock woods. However, if the whiskers are particularly easy to raise (true of the softer grades of wood) it does no harm to raise the grain five or six times.

In raising the grain on a piece of wood the gunsmith must be careful to guard against allowing the hot flame to burn or char any of the sharp edges of the butt, pistol grip, inletted portions, et al. As a matter of fact, it is good practice to have the butt plate and pistol grip cap on the stock when the grain raising is being done—providing, of course, they are of a metallic nature and not rubber or plastic.

Wood Filler. After whiskering, the pores of the stock wood should be treated with a commercial wood filler which is procurable from any hardware or paint store. When the filler has set, remove any excess by rubbing fine steel wool over the stock's surface, or better still, if available, use water-proof, silicon carbide abrasive paper, that has been slightly moistened.

When heating linseed oil and turpentine together, always use a low flame lest the whole batch catch fire and send a spray of black soot towards the ceiling. Constant stirring while the mixture is being heated helps to lower the flash point of the turpentine and also aids in producing a more uniform concoction.

Apply the oil and turpentine mixture to the stock while hot by means of an old towel.

When, after repeated applications, it appears that the wood will absorb no more oil, then wrap the oil soaked rag around the stock and let it so remain for a day or two and again repeat the soaking treatment. After the stock has absorbed all the oil it can, allow the oil to oxidize for a week and then polish the stock on a high speed muslin buffing wheel to which a pumice stone and water mixture is constantly fed (use light pressure on the stock against the wheel). If facilities for buffing are not available, the polishing can be done by hand, which, incidentally, is a very tiresome and ultra time consuming job. However, for those who must, or choose to polish a stock by hand, the following method is suggested:

Polishing an Oil Treated Stock. Dip the felt covered wood block, illustrated in Figure 62, in water. Next coat the now wet felt with pumice stone; this is best accomplished by having a small box partly filled with the powdered abrasive. With light, even pressure, rub the coated pad back and forth on the stock, always following the grain line until the oxidized oil begins to take on a polish. Cover the stock in this manner by sections until it is entirely finished and then blend all sections by rubbing with the palm of the hand which has first been moistened with a few drops of oil. Finally, allow the stock to stand for a day or two before placing it on the gun for general handling.

During the process of oil finishing a stock, the gunsmith must use a good deal of judgment. For example, some wood has a tendency to lose a great deal of its natural beauty when too much oil is applied; it starts to assume a very dark brown color which is not altogether pleasing. When such a condition arises, then the application of oil should cease and only that amount already applied should be allowed to oxidize as a basis for final polishing. On the other hand, some strains of walnut remain light in color no matter how much oil is applied. This, of course, necessitates the addition of some coloring material, such as burnt umber, to the oil so that the figure of the wood will be brought out to better advantage.

Too, great care must be exercised after the stock has been

sanded and just before the oil is applied. Foreign substances, especially perspiration, will leave marks on a freshly sanded piece of wood that will show up even after many applications of oil. Likewise be doubly careful when polishing a stock on a motor driven buff—keep a firm grasp on the stock at all times and do not allow the wheel to polish upon checkering or act on any corner or inletted point in such a way that it might throw the stock against the nut or spindle of the polishing head. Certainly nothing could be more discouraging (and costly) than to have a stock become badly scarred in the last few minutes of working on it just because of a little thoughtlessness.

On Oil and Rubbing. While it must be admitted that a beautiful finish can be produced by the foregoing method, i.e., linseed oil and rubbing, this writer is willing to stick his neck out and say that there has probably been more lip service given to the alleged benefits of linseed oil and secret methods of applying it, than there has to Billy the Kid's fast draw. Lots of gunsmiths, both professional and amateur, talk a good oil finish but when it comes down to cases they sneak out the old Japanese drier, spar varnish, duPont clear lacquer and shellac and go to work. And that's O.K., too, just so long as these various finishes are of good quality and applied with care.

Frankly, some stocks just don't radiate the beauty they should after having been doused with two quarts of linseed oil and two weeks' rubbing. Yes, linseed oil and rubbing are still a good combination but there are other finishes and combinations of finishes which are also O.K. Don't be afraid to experiment with them.

Lacquer or Varnish. If the gunsmith does not feel that it is necessary or wise to use an oil finish on a particular gunstock, then he has the alternative of employing either clear lacquer or varnish as a protective and beautifying agent. Much has been said and written against both of these coatings as stock finishing agents, yet most of our commercial guns today have stocks coated with one or the other of them, not only on the very inexpensive boys' rifles but also on autoloading shotguns selling in the neighborhood of $60.00. True, clear lacquer and varnish are used by large arms companies because of the economy of applying them but nevertheless, correctly applied, they can beautify and protect a gunstock in a manner closely approaching that of oil.

Preparatory to applying either clear lacquer or varnish, the stock should be prepared in the same way as it would be for oil except that no filler is really necessary. An extra durable finish can be produced by spraying or brushing one coat of the desired coating on the stock and, after it has dried thoroughly, rubbing it down with a piece of very fine steel wool or waterproof abrasive paper. A second and, if necessary, third coat can be applied over this. However, it is wise to steel wool each coat except the last that is put on, so that the liability of chipping or flaking off will be reduced to a minimum. Another precaution, do not attempt smoothing down of lacquer or varnish until it is absolutely dry.

Since the cost of finishing a stock is almost all labor, the gunsmith should not hesitate to use only the best oils, lacquers and varnishes obtainable and follow the manufacturer's directions, as stated on the label, to the letter.

If a gunsmith finds that he is especially interested in stock finishing, then he would do well to make contact with a cabinet maker in his locality and seek out advice on some of the tricks of the trade. It is surprising how much one can learn from some of the local craftsmen, many of whom are gun enthusiasts and more than willing to swap ideas.

The sooner the up and coming gunsmith learns that it is no disgrace or sign of being a novice to seek out advice so that he may learn newer, better and more efficient ways of performing different phases of his work, the sooner he will be on the right track towards becoming a master of his trade.

Although the average gun owner does not usually realize, when he pays a few dollars to have a special job done, that a full-fledged gunsmith must be a cabinet maker, machinist, tool and die maker, machine operator, bench hand and general mechanic first class with extraordinary patience, it is none the less the truth. And while the gunsmith cannot tell each customer that it took him as long to learn his trade as it does a lawyer to become qualified for practice before the bar, by turning out work of superior quality, the gunsmith can in time become as esteemed in the eyes of his customers as the barrister is to his clients. By the same token, the gunsmith should remember that lawyers who get ahead in their profession are constantly reading up on court decisions, both past and present, so that they might give best service to their clients. As a follower of an equally honored profession, the gunsmith should not brush aside the words of experts who write on specific subjects pertaining to his work.

About Stockmaking

Long years ago, when many of the guns in use were hand-made by individual gunsmiths and gunmakers, it was imperative that every gunsmith know how to make a gunstock from any type of wood that the customer might consider to be his favorite. In short, it was absolutely necessary that the gunsmith of 150, 100, and even 60 years ago be a first class stockmaker. Nowadays, with at least 90% of the firearms in circulation being the product of factory methods, the problem of stock replacement resolves itself into a matter of merely ordering a new one from the factory when the job requires it. The main exception to this procedure is when a customer has a military weapon, (which are noted for their poor stocks for hunting purposes), and desires a stock of better appearance and dimensions. Also, a person with a flair for having something just a little bit different on a commercial gun will occasionally feel inclined to invest a few dollars in a hand-made stock.

Nevertheless, whatever the case might be, the gunsmith should not undertake to make a gunstock unless he is very sure that he can make it to specifications, and at a profit. This writer knows well from experience that there is very little margin of profit in making custom stocks unless one is a specialist at this sort of work and has both the required skill and tools to do it efficiently. However, if the gunsmith feels he must restock a gun, then he should purchase a pre-inletted stock from one of the individuals who make a specialty of this work. Dave W. Thomas, of Vineland, New Jersey, will inlet any stock so that it is ready to fit at a very reasonable fee. By availing himself of a service of this sort, the gunsmith can more confidently undertake to do restocking work for then he will only have the work of shaping the outside of the stock to desired dimensions, a task which is child's play compared with that of inletting.

Outside shaping of the stock is best done with rasps, a spokeshave and chisels. Before any shaping is done, however, the final dimensions of the stock, such as length, drop at comb, drop at heel and pitch angle, should be known and marked out on the blank accordingly.

Even the task of exterior shaping can be greatly lessened if the gunsmith includes the dimensions covering the aforementioned distances to the person who pre-inlets his stocks, requesting that the outside shape of the stock also be roughed out. Thus, when the gunsmith receives a gunstock pre-inletted and rough-shaped, he is relieved of a burdensome and time consuming job, and can then devote his entire energies and talent to the matter of doing the final shaping and finishing of the stock.

The field of woodworking offers a very good source for revenue to the mechanic who realizes his capabilities and does not undertake jobs without first being sure that he can complete them on time, at a profit, and in a workmanlike manner.

For the embryo gunsmith who thinks he might do well at this phase of gunsmithing, this writer can think of nothing better than to recommend the three Linden Booklets on Stock Inletting, Stock Shaping and Stock Finishing. Alvin Linden, the author of these master texts, was just about tops when it came to making *good* gunstocks and he was no back number when it came to getting his time-tested ideas across to the reader. He is apt to jar a lot of the old armchair stockmakers a bit but that is to be expected—Brother Linden can back up what he says, and he says it with 100,000 words and plenty of pictures. (Note: Mr. Linden died July 4, 1946.)

CHAPTER ELEVEN

REVOLVER REPAIRS

ALTHOUGH it has been predicted many times within the last 40 years that the revolver would be replaced by the automatic pistol, there is at this time very little evidence to indicate the wisdom of those predictions. As a matter of fact, during that time improvements have been made on the revolver which have enabled it to maintain its reputation as an accurate and dependable handgun for police and target work. However, as an official military sidearm it has almost ceased to exist. One reason for this can be charged up against the fact that the revolver, as a weapon, is much more difficult to repair than an automatic pistol, in that it does not lend itself readily to field disassembly for easy replacement of parts by the individual soldier or company mechanic. Furthermore, a selection of special tools is necessary to effect the installation of such easily broken parts as firing pin, mainspring or cylinder stop.

To fix a revolver, so that when finished its action is smooth, crisp and in perfect timing, requires a thorough understanding of the particular type action being repaired, and skillful handling of small tools for the incidental hand fitting work.

In order that excess words which might possibly tend to obscure the important descriptions of repair functions can be eliminated, this chapter is presented in a direct manner. This method of presentation should also make the task of reference easier when the gunsmith desires to check on a particular phase of repair work in a hurry.

In referring to parts, the proper names, as listed in the respective manufacturers' parts list are used at all times. When the reader is in doubt, he should not hesitate to refer to the catalog listing, lest he misinterpret the meaning of the directions.

Inspection procedure in the ensuing paragraphs on Colt revolvers applies particularly to the following models: Police Positive, all calibers; Pocket Positive; Banker's Special; Detective Special; Police Positive Special, all calibers; New Service, all calibers; Shooting Master, all calibers; and Officer's Model, all calibers.

Inspection Procedure to Determine Condition of Weapon

Ejector and Ratchet. With the thumb draw back the cylinder latch and swing the cylinder out; check the ratchet for alignment with the chambers in the cylinder, and test it with the fingers to see that it does not turn on the ejector rod. Proper alignment of the ratchet, which is screwed (R.H. thread) on the ejector rod and then staked in place, is maintained by two small diameter pins placed in the cylinder itself. These pins must coincide in position with two cutouts on opposing arms of the ratchet. Spline cuts in the ejector rod, which ride in the spline cuts of the cylinder bushing, restrain the ejector rod from turning when the rod is pushed up to eject cartridges. Considerable play can be tolerated in the ejector rod spline, just so long as the ratchet returns to its proper place when allowed to snap back after actuating the ejector rod.

Ejector Rod and Spring. The ejector rod spring is held in place in the crane by means of the ejector rod bushing. This spring must be of sufficient strength to return the ratchet to its proper position after the actuation of the ejector. Failure to do so indicates a weakened or bound spring. In either case the latter must be removed from the crane to effect remedial action. A bent ejector rod can also interfere with smooth ejection action. This condition can be detected by rotating the cylinder, when in the gun, and observing the rod as it turns. It can be quickly straightened by placing a piece of flat brass between the ejector rod and barrel and tapping lightly with a hammer on the rod just forward of the bend. This usually requires a few tries and the rod should be tested after each tap so that a bend in the opposite direction will not be made.

Cylinder. When the cylinder is completely swung out of the revolver frame it should be tried for free rotation. If it does not spin around easily under power applied to the ejector rod head by thumb and forefinger, it is safe to assume that either the crane is bent; it is in need of cleaning and lubrication; or the side plate screw is loose and rubbing against the cylinder proper. Corrective measures for the latter two are obvious. Straightening of the crane is a very tricky operation and is covered in this chapter under that heading.

Chambers. Next, insert a live cartridge in each of the chambers —they should drop in by their own weight and should come out with little or no pressure on the ejector when the gun is held barrel up. If difficulty is encountered in either loading or ejecting, each chamber should be tested carefully for deformation or the presence of burrs around the edges. Burrs can be removed by rotating a dowel rod fitted with No. 2/0 emery cloth, or crocus cloth, in a breast or hand drill. In this operation, remove only so much metal as is absolutely necessary, for an enlarged chamber does not give proper support to a cartridge case, a condition which might in turn lead to split cases and dangerous gas escapement.

A chamber which is dented in to an extent that does not permit practical use of abrasive cloth as a corrective measure can often be straightened out with a hardened steel mandrel. This mandrel (Figure 70) should be $\frac{1}{100}''$ larger, at its widest point, than

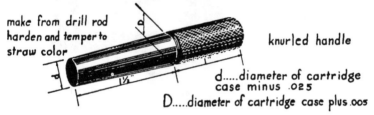

make from drill rod harden and temper to straw color

knurled handle

d.....diameter of cartridge case minus .025

D.....diameter of cartridge case plus .005

MANDREL FOR REMOVING DENTS FROM REVOLVER CYLINDER CHAMBERS

FIGURE 70

the measured diameter of the cartridge case. However, it is not recommended that this mandrel be used where the chamber deformation exceeds $\frac{1}{32}''$; otherwise the chamber might be weakened to a point where it would not stand up under firing pressure.

Crane and Cylinder. When the front face of the cylinder appears marked up, it is an indication that the cylinder is rubbing against the rear face of the barrel. This is caused by a bent crane; worn cylinder at the point where it rubs against the crane (Figure 70A); or worn crane where it contacts the cylinder. If straightening of the crane does not correct the defect, then a steel shim of a thickness anywhere from $\frac{1}{1000}''$ to $\frac{8}{1000}''$ should be installed. The proper size shim is usually determined by cut-and-try methods. Put in a shim of only that thickness which permits a clearance of from $\frac{2}{1000}''$ to $\frac{6}{1000}''$

between the cylinder and barrel—the nearer to the minimum tolerance the better. This distance should, of course, be checked with a thickness gage, while rotating the cylinder. Varying tolerance between individual chambers indicates a bent crane. However, a couple of thousandths variation is permissible providing the minimum is not under $\frac{2}{1000}''$ and the maximum not over $\frac{6}{1000}''$.

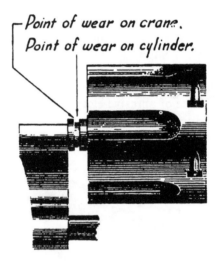

Point of wear on crane.
Point of wear on cylinder.

POINT OF WEAR ON CRANE AND CYLINDER OF REVOLVERS

FIGURE 70A

On occasions where the barrel in a gun is not the original one or a factory replacement, it is possible that it has not been trimmed down enough to allow free movement of the cylinder. This latter condition can usually be proven where there is little or no play noticeable between the cylinder and crane contact points and yet the front cylinder face continues to rub against the barrel. Thus a certain amount of metal must be removed from the rear barrel face by means of a fine file. When using the file, remove only a very little metal per cut and try the cylinder for fit after each couple of strokes. To remove any burrs left after this operation, use the same cutter (Figure 71) as used when fitting a new barrel, or use a countersink and rotate it with the fingers.

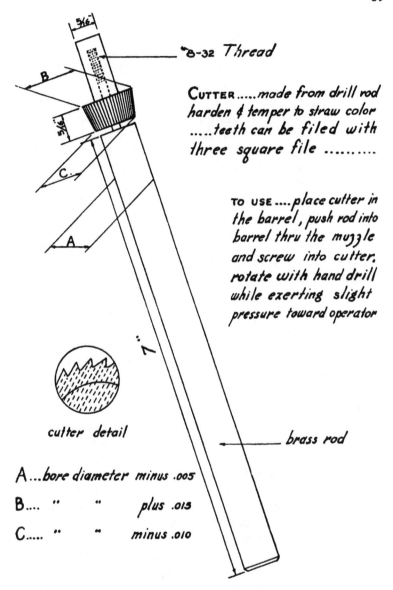

8-32 *Thread*

CUTTER......*made from drill rod harden & temper to straw color .....teeth can be filed with three square file ....*

TO USE ....*place cutter in the barrel, push rod into barrel thru the muzzle and screw into cutter, rotate with hand drill while exerting slight pressure toward operator*

cutter detail

brass rod

A ...*bore diameter minus .005*

B.... " " *plus .013*

C..... " " *minus .010*

CUTTER — WITH ROD ATTACHED FOR REMOVING BURRS FROM LEED & REVOLVER BARRELS

FIGURE 71

With the cylinder loaded with cartridges, the hammer is drawn back to a point where the cylinder bolt is clear of the locking recesses in the cylinder. Spin the cylinder by hand and note if there is any drag on the rear face of the cartridges. Marks on the primer or case head indicate insufficient clearance between cartridges and breech face of revolver, usually a loose or burred up recoil plate (firing pin bushing), causing them. A few strokes of a very fine file, followed by crocus cloth wrapped around the file will alleviate the burr interference. A loose or protruding recoil plate must be reset (See paragraph on installing recoil plates).

Bolt. Excessive play between the cylinder bolt and locking recesses in the cylinder can be checked by trying to move the cylinder in a sideways direction when the trigger is held at its extreme rearward position, in other words, simulating the position of the gun action at the instant of firing. While a perfect fit between these locking surfaces is desirable at all times, a certain amount of play can be tolerated before installation of a new cylinder bolt is necessary. Some cases of play can be corrected by peening over a slight bit of metal at the point of the cylinder recess showing the greatest amount of wear, and then scraping out any excess peened over metal with a sharp chisel ground to proper size. The chisel should be used as a scraping tool, since only a very small amount of metal will have to be removed.

If the cause of play between bolt and cylinder cannot be laid to the latter, then the bolt is either worn or the screw holding it to the frame is loose. In rare instances, sidewise cylinder movement can be traced to a distortion of the frame on the outside section of the hole where the bolt protrudes. If the metal surrounding this hole appears to be bent outward, permitting the bolt excessive freedom of lateral movement, it should be restored to proper size by means of force. A brass or copper drift should be laid against the high point and struck lightly until no high point remains. To preclude the possibility of bending in the metal to the extent where it might cause the bolt to bind, a punch of large diameter and absolutely smooth face should be used—$\frac{1}{2}$″ is about right.

Latch Pin. Failure of the cylinder to lock in place when swung into the frame (this should always be done gently—not by swinging the gun and having the cylinder snap into place) usually indicates that the latch pin is stuck or worn, or the latch spring is weak or missing. Now and then it will be found that a bent crane might be the offender, since it does not allow the cylinder to go far enough into the frame. A burred latch, or one having insufficient clearance on the surfaces where it rides in the side plate recess, can also produce the same condition. By the same token, a buckled or burred side plate at the latch recess can prevent the cylinder from being properly engaged by the latch pin. With the exception of a bent crane, corrective action on the other faults consists of either replacing the offending part or when possible stoning or filing off burred surfaces.

The recess in the cylinder ratchet that accommodates the latch pin sometimes becomes burred over to the extent that it does not allow the latch pin to enter. In such cases, and where the ratchet is otherwise serviceable, the overhanging metal is easily removed by means of a small sharp scraper, or better still, a mounted abrasive wheel held in a hand grinder or drill press. The abrasive wheel should be slightly smaller in diameter than the recess so that it will not cause the recess to be enlarged or "belled" at its mouth.

Timing. With the cylinder locked in place, the first thing to check on the revolver as a whole is its timing. A revolver is considered to be out of timing when the cylinder is not locked in place when the gun is cocked, ready for firing. When a gun is properly timed, the cylinder bolt will enter into the cylinder recess as the gun is cocked slowly by drawing back the hammer (single action). Cocking the gun slowly is stressed, since fast action cocking will often spin the cylinder into locked position by action of its rotational momentum. Revolvers which are out of timing are not uncommon and the gunsmith must learn, when dealing with Colt revolvers, to recognize this defect and localize the specific fault. Contrary to most beginners' impression, the cylinder ratchet is not the main cause of revolvers being out of timing. As a matter of fact, a bad ratchet is on the bottom of the list of parts contributing to this condition. This should be regarded as very fortunate, for replacement of a ratchet (ejector) is no "while you wait" job.

Hand. As with many other revolver faults, the timing defect can also at times be traced to a bent crane. If straightening of the crane does not correct the fault, then the next possible offender is the hand. By examining the two-fingered hand of a

Colt revolver, it will be noted that the first finger, "A" (Figure 72) engages one arm of the ratchet and in so doing rotates the cylinder until the next arm is engaged by finger "B." It is finger "B" that rotates the cylinder to the position where the bolt engages its corresponding recess and brings the chamber and barrel into alignment.

With the side plate removed from a Colt revolver, this foregoing function can be observed. If finger "B" of the hand is worn to the point where space between it and the ratchet arms it engages is noticeable, then a new hand should be installed. Precautions and kinks incident to this are described farther on in this chapter.

Where no appreciable space exists between finger "B" and the ratchet, but the hand appears to be bulged out, then it is possible the body of the hand is bent in reference to the pin by which it rotates in the trigger. Since any bend in a hand would naturally shorten its length, then to achieve full length the hand must be straightened. One of the most effective methods of doing this is to place the pin part of the hand between copper vise jaws with the body of the hand parallel to the top of the vise and bend it upwards with a screwdriver (Figure 72). Inasmuch as the hand is rather hard and brittle, care must be exercised lest the hand snap at the point where it is cut out to accommodate the rebound lever. Only the experience of performing this operation a few times will instill in the gunsmith the confidence to tackle this job, and others, without fear of doing more harm than good.

Another frequent cause of a revolver being out of timing is produced by the trigger being short at the point where it engages the hammer notch. To appreciate how a short trigger can affect timing, one has only to look at the mechanism of the Colt revolver, with the side plate removed, and note how the movement of the trigger affects the upward travel of the hand. Thus if the trigger is short, the hammer ceases to act on it before the gun is cocked. In this way the hand does not have the benefit of full travel, and consequently the cylinder is not rotated to the point where the bolt can engage the proper notch.

If the trigger is only slightly short, then a new hand (which is slightly oversize) will most likely correct the trouble. Otherwise, there is no alternative but to fit a new trigger, a job which automatically entails readjustment of trigger pull. It might be

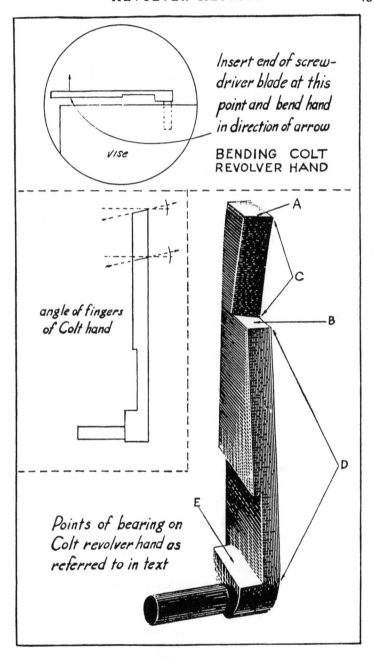

Insert end of screw-
driver blade at this
point and bend hand
in direction of arrow

BENDING COLT
REVOLVER HAND

vise

A

C

B

angle of fingers
of Colt hand

D

E

Points of bearing on
Colt revolver hand as
referred to in text

FIGURE 72

well to point out here that a revolver can be perfectly in timing before a routine trigger pull adjustment job and out of timing after the job is completed to perfection of pull. This is brought about by the gunsmith removing too much metal from the hammer engaging the end of the trigger in order to achieve a smooth, light pull. In many cases the gunsmith has no alternative but to install a new trigger when he discovers that in adjusting trigger pull he has inadvertently put the gun out of timing. However, these are the somewhat unexpected turns of events that the gunsmith must be prepared to cope with at all times. It is for this reason that paragraphs in the earlier section of the book stress the importance of not giving an exact price as to what a particular repair job costs unless it is of such a nature that no unpredictable factors can possibly enter into the estimate.

"Overtiming." Although a revolver is not generally regarded to be "overtimed" there is a condition occasionally encountered which, for want of a better definition, can be referred to as such. This fault is recognized when in cocking, the cylinder is locked by the bolt before the hammer is pulled back to the point where it engages the trigger. Continued drawing of the hammer beyond this point becomes more difficult, because finger "B" of the hand is pressing against the ratchet, while the bolt retards any further cylinder movement. Naturally this makes for a very rough action and an abnormally hard trigger pull. Removing the required amount of metal from finger "B" will correct "overtiming." This should be a cut-and-try proposition with very little cutting between tries, or excessive metal removal might produce the opposite of the desired effect.

Trigger. Another trouble which can be frequently traced to a malfitting hand is the failure of the trigger to return to its proper position after firing. This happens when a hand is too wide, or bulged out, and drags against the side plate. When this condition exists, either the hand or the side plate will show marks of rubbing. If straightening of the hand, as described earlier in this chapter, does not remedy the defect, then the outside of the hand must be filed and then stoned or rubbed on emery cloth until it presents a mirror-smooth surface that does not drag on the side plate. However, before filing any metal off the hand, it is well to make sure that it fits properly in the trigger. The pin on the hand, which fits in the trigger, sometimes is deformed to the extent where it does not fit into the hole in the trigger. By the same reasoning, the trigger hole might also be peened over and prevent proper hand seating. Corrective measures for either are simple and self-indicative.

Rebound Lever. As well as the aforementioned defects, which can make for a dragging hand, there are times when the rebound lever is bent outward or so loosely fixed that it causes the hand to be forced against the side plate. Straightening of the rebound lever, replacement of the rebound lever pin, or squeezing together that portion of the butt frame where the rebound lever is pivoted on its pin, should bring the lever back into proper alignment.

It might be well to point out here that a loose rebound lever pin, which is not held laterally in place, can cause a revolver to jam up completely. When a pin is encountered that can be pushed in and out easily, due to frame wear around the pin, then an oversized pin should be installed or a prick punch indentation made on the frame around the holes to hold the pin in place.

Cylinder "Skips." When a revolver becomes old or has been subject to a great deal of use, it frequently has the tendency to "jump shots" when being fired double action. To test for this defect, mark one of the cylinder flutes on the left hand side of the gun with a pencil or piece of chalk and snap the trigger (double action) smartly. If all is well, the marked flute will move only ⅛th of a complete turn, that is to say, the *next* chamber will come into alignment with the barrel. If a defect is present, the cylinder will skip one or two chambers before coming to a locked position.

Generally, there are four things which will cause a cylinder to skip, they are:

1) weak bolt spring;
2) bolt with oversized or deformed recess;
3) peened over or deformed cylinder recesses;
4) rebound lever projection oversized or out of position at the point where it rests against the inside end of the cylinder bolt.

Corrective action for these four faults are respectively:

1) replace with new spring;
2) hone or file bolt where it is oversized or deformed; if this does not suffice, then fit a new bolt;
3) where conditions permit, recesses should be scraped out in the manner described earlier in this chapter;

4) the projection on the rebound lever which actuates the bolt sometimes becomes burred to the extent where it prevents the bolt from dropping down at the rear end, thus precluding locking of the cylinder. Honing on this point of the rebound lever, or bending inward of the bolt so it can disengage itself when the rebound lever comes to rest at the end of its downward stroke, are two recommended correctives. Tightening of the bolt screw, which will force the bolt closer against the frame, is another indicated remedy in some cases.

When none of these suggestions bring about successful repair, then it is possible that the rebound lever is not dropping down sufficiently to allow the bolt to become disengaged. Cause of this can be traced to the rebound lever coming against the back of the hammer at a higher-than-should-be position. This in turn can be caused by the rebound lever being loosely pivoted by its pin. This latter condition can be corrected by installing an oversize pin or a new rebound lever. Where the rebound lever hits the hammer back, look for a loose hammer pin in the frame, which would permit the hammer to move erratically, or file the rebound lever at the offending point.

Safety. To check the incorporated Colt safety, which prevents accidental discharge if the hammer slips or the gun is dropped accidentally, the cylinder should be swung out of the frame and the forefinger of the left hand held flat against the recoil plate where the firing pin protrudes. Draw back the hammer almost to full cock position (the trigger should not be touched) and let it snap freely forward. The firing pin should not protrude beyond the outer face of the recoil plate. If it does, either the safety is worn; the firing pin is too long (very rare); or the safety is not properly connected to the safety lever. In the latter case, it usually is only necessary to disassemble the gun and reassemble it, making sure to connect the trigger to safety lever and safety lever to safety. In later model Colt revolvers, it is almost impossible for the safety to become disengaged because of a beveled pin connection arrangement. Older models, however, not so equipped, have a tendency to become disengaged when the side plate is loosened and the trigger is snapped.

A rebound lever having a worn bolt-engaging stud should be suspected when the bolt does not disengage itself from the cylinder recess as the gun is cocked for either single or double action. Another possible cause of the same operational defect is a hand slightly oversized at finger "A." In removing metal from finger "A," take care to remove only so much as is needed to effect a correction. Otherwise finger "B" will tend to engage the next arm on the ratchet before "A" has rotated the cylinder sufficiently. This will not only make for a very jumpy action but ultimately cause the breakage of parts being subject to the undue strain.

A trigger that does not return to its proper position after actuation might possibly be pivoted on a broken trigger pin that does not show up until the side plate is removed. A weak mainspring, a rebound lever dragging on the side plate or bolt, or, as mentioned before, a dragging hand, can also affect free movement of the trigger.

When a cylinder seems to stick as it is swung into or out of the frame for loading and it is definitely not being impeded by the barrel, then it is possible that the point of finger "A" on the hand is protruding beyond the inside face of the frame. Although in this case the immediate temptation would be to file the hand, it is better to investigate the rebound lever at the point where it rests on the hand. Examination of the hand at point "E" in contact with the rebound lever will reveal how directly the latter can affect the position of the hand. So before doing any filing on "A," always check the contact point "D."

Fitting a Hand. In fitting a new hand to a Colt revolver, there are certain precautions that must be observed lest the new fitted part be no better than the one discarded.

As a new hand comes from the factory, it is by no means ready for direct installation. Yet a few file or stone strokes on the right points can make it ready in short order.

In Figure 72 is illustrated a hand with its various points of working contact. These are the points which regulate the hand in its relation to the other parts that actuate, and are actuated by, it.

To install a new hand, place it in its proper position in the trigger hole so finger "A" rests under one of the ratchet flanges. Slowly cock the hammer, at the same time holding the hand in place with the left thumb. If the bolt does not unlock as "A" starts to rotate the cylinder, then it is too long at this point. Removal of metal from this point should be done with a fine file, a few strokes at a time, until the desired results are obtained. Replace the hand and proceed as before, observing surface "C" as the next flange rotates into alignment. If "C" has a tendency to hit against the flange and be forced outward against where the side plate would be if it were in place, then surface "C," extending from finger "A" to finger "B," should be filed slightly with cutting emphasis nearest point "B." Incidentally, the best way to see how this angle should be cut can be gained by observing the hand on a new Colt revolver. This will more than prove the old Chinese proverb that one picture is better than 5,000 words.

Presuming that surface "C" has been properly adjusted, the hand should be reinserted in place and the hammer again cocked slowly. As finger "A" rotates one ratchet flange, the next flange is brought into line to meet finger "B." If "A" does not push "B" in proper alignment with this second flange, then "B" is too long and must be filed. Filing on "B" is a tricky proposition, for if too much metal is removed, the whole purpose of the hand's being installed can be defeated by one file stroke too many.

In filing either finger "A" or "B" on Colt revolver hands, this writer has found that many minor difficulties of fitting can be eased by filing them at a slight angle as illustrated in Figure 72. This angle must be very slight or it will produce a condition which can only be corrected by starting from scratch again, with a new hand.

If a hand does not seem to position correctly even after being fitted at points "A," "B" and "C," then it is well to look at points "D" and "E" to see if these are causing trouble. "D" should have a smooth polished surface so that it will ride freely along its track. Surface "E," upon which the rebound lever rides, must occasionally be filed to a slightly different angle so that it will coincide with the angle of the rebound lever. By noting the position of the hand in relation to the rebound lever, the gunsmith can readily see the working association of their two parts and adjust the angle accordingly.

In addition to making the adjustments previously described, it is also usually necessary, when fitting a new hand, to remove metal from the surface which lays adjacent to the side plate. The proper amount is best determined by putting the hand in place and affixing the side plate with its screws. Drag between these two surfaces can be felt as the gun is cocked. After sufficient filing has been done, the hand surface should be finished to a mirror-like surface by rubbing it across a sheet of fine emery cloth fixed on a flat board and then polishing it on a buffing wheel dressed with one of the fine compounds described in Chapter Sixteen.

Crane Straightening. Frequently, in this chapter, reference has been made to remedying various defects by straightening the crane of a revolver. As it is with other phases of gun repair work, the task of crane straightening is one that requires caution, knack and an understanding of the limitations of the corrective measure. Crane straightening is neither a cure-all nor a short-cut repair method. Properly employed, when its use is indicated by looseness between crane and frame, it can correct defects which no other expenditure of parts or labor can accomplish as well.

Other than a vise, no tools are required for this operation except of course the finest pair of tools in the gunsmith's collection—his two hands.

With lead, wood or brass jaws in the vise, place the revolver cylinder between them as illustrated in Figure 73. Tighten the vise so that the cylinder is held firmly, but not to the extent where there is any possibility of bending the thin chamber walls.

With the right hand around the grips and the left hand around the barrel, exert a twisting force as indicated in Figure 73. Unfortunately, no number of words can describe the exact

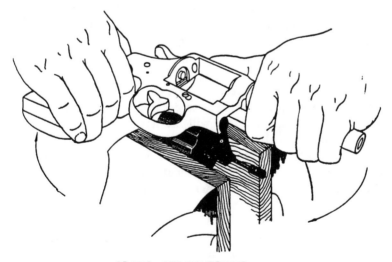

CRANE STRAIGHTENING

FIGURE 73

amount of force that should be applied to effect a straightening of the crane. However, if the force is applied gradually, the gunsmith will, at a certain point, notice that a resistance is felt. Beyond this point of resistance the bending starts to take place and, since even the loosest crane requires very little bending, only slightly increased force should be applied.

After the first try at crane bending, the revolver should be removed from the vise and the cylinder swung into place. If the cylinder goes into the frame but does not seem to lock in place, or locks tightly, then the crane has been bent excessively. To correct this, place the gun in the vise as before and apply force in the opposite direction, but more gently than done originally.

If, on the other hand, the first bending does not force the crane snugly against the frame to the point where there is no play, then the crane should be subject to additional straightening until the desired results are obtained. As a matter of precaution, it should be remembered that crane straightening is not recommended for Smith & Wesson revolvers. The method used on S&W revolvers to lock the cylinder in place precludes the employment of any but factory methods for crane straightening.

Fitting a Bolt. In fitting a bolt to a Colt revolver always make certain that the end which is designed to fit in the cylinder recess fits perfectly before removing any metal from the end that contacts the rebound lever. This latter end will usually have to be touched up, but only very slightly. Most of the adjusting will be in the nature of smoothing up or bending inward the section over which the rebound lever flange passes on its downward stroke.

Fitting a Ratchet. In fitting a ratchet (extractor) to a Colt revolver, the important thing is to get the ratchet screwed completely on the rod, so that it will lay flat against the cylinder when brought into alignment with the pins and respective chambers. If it cannot be screwed down with reasonable effort, then a countersink held in a hand drill should be used to chamfer the threaded end of the ratchet that comes in contact with the extractor rod shoulder. When screwing on or removing an extractor, the tool described and illustrated in Chapter Three should be employed—and with care. The arms on the extractor are, as is evident upon examination, quite thin at points and can be bent out of shape when any sudden or undue force is applied.

Removing and Inserting Mainspring. When removing or inserting the V type mainspring found in all Colt revolvers except the Single Action or Camp Perry Model, it is not advisable to use needle-nosed pliers, since they have a tendency to score the spring, and more so because there is a more efficient method. Proceed as follows:

To Remove the Spring: Lay the revolver flat on a bench, remove side plate and push hammer back about ¼″ with forefinger of left hand. Holding screwdriver in fist grip in right hand, press down on spring near stirrup with tip of screwdriver blade. Push hammer forward, thus disengaging stirrup from spring. Spring can then be removed from frame with the fingers.

To Insert the Spring: While the revolver is held flat on a bench with left hand, grasp spring with thumb and forefinger of right hand and slide slot of spring underneath hammer stirrup, guiding the latter into place by moving the hammer on its pin with the forefinger of the left hand. When stirrup and hammer have been engaged, then lift bottom section of spring onto rebound lever with thumb of right hand.

To those who have never tried this method of spring removal or insertion, the writer highly recommends that they try it once or twice before assuming that it is one of those things that works out better on paper than in actual practice. A few tries should convince the most skeptical of its superiority over any other method. As a matter of fact, after a little practice one can do it with the eyes closed.

Smith & Wesson Revolvers

Basically, many models of the Smith & Wesson revolver are like the Colt revolver in that there are similar main parts, even if somewhat different in shape and size, but that do serve to perform similar functions.

These models, which we shall discuss in some detail in the ensuing pages, are all the same in arrangement and function of parts. They are: Hand Ejector; .38/32; .38 Military and Police, all barrel lengths and butt styles; .357 Magnum; the K-32 Target; the .38/44 Heavy Duty; the 1917 Army Model; the 1926 Model, .44 Target & Regular; the K-22 Masterpiece; the .22/32 Target; the .22/32 Kit Gun; and the Regulation Police Model in both .32 and .38 calibers.

As can be observed by visual inspection, the chief outward differences between the Colt solid frame revolvers and the S&W solid frame revolvers are:

1) Direction of cylinder rotation: Colt to the right (inward); S&W to the left (outward).
2) Barrel: Colt has no lug on the bottom; S&W does, for the purpose of locking extractor rod at its forward end.
3) Cylinder latch: Colt is pulled rearward to release cylinder; S&W is pushed forward; the shape of the latches indicates their respective actuation motions.
4) Side plate: the Colt is on the side with the cylinder latch; the S&W is on the opposite side.

Inspection of the S&W revolver should be conducted in the same manner as that of the Colt Revolver described earlier in this chapter.

Cylinder Locking Mechanism. In the S&W revolver, the thumb piece, which is pushed forward to allow release of the cylinder, is connected to the latch, which in turn acts against the center pin to push the locking bolt forward and free of the extractor rod. This mechanism, which assures locking at both ends for the cylinder, is a very dependable arrangement and does not very often get out of order. When it does, it is usually because the gun has been dropped and the extractor and center pin bent. Generally speaking, it is very difficult and impractical to straighten an S&W extractor rod after it has been bent. However, if the gunsmith wishes to attempt straightening, he should first insert a piece of snug-fitting drill rod in the hole that passes through the center of the extractor rod, so that any force he applies will not decrease the hole diameter.

Extractor Rod. One of the best ways to straighten the extractor rod is to put it in the lathe chuck or collet, holding it on the threaded portion with the threads protected by a piece of crocus cloth wrapped around them. Even with this protection, only a very little amount of force should be applied to hold it, lest the threads be smashed or deformed. By running the lathe at its lowest direct speed, the point or points of bend can be readily observed and if slight, the tailstock center can be inserted into the opposite end of the ejector rod, and while the rod is spinning a rawhide hammer used to tap on the high point. In performing this operation the tailstock of the lathe should be left loose enough so that as the rod straightens out the former will be free to move and allow for the increasing length of the rod.

"Frozen" Cylinder. Frequently a S&W owner will bring his revolver to the gunsmith and complain that the cylinder is frozen—it just won't turn; and besides it is locked in place in the frame and can't be swung out. Invariably the cause of this ill is the extractor rod, which has become partially unscrewed by the action of the cylinder's rotation.

Corrective action involves tightening of the rod with a pair of pliers, having a piece of cloth between the jaws to prevent marring the rod.

Never attempt to force a stuck S&W cylinder out of the frame until it has positively been determined, by trying to screw the extractor rod in, that the latter has not become loose. Incidentally, this operation should be performed in the confines of the gunsmith's back room, out of the customer's sight, so that the latter will not be hesitant about paying the gunsmith for "that bit of work."

Other functions of the cylinder group, such as weak extractor spring, et cetera, should be checked in the same way as outlined for the Colt revolver. Disassembly of all the parts in this group is easily effected (after freeing the crane from the frame) by unscrewing the extractor rod.

Space between the front face of the cylinder and rear face of the barrel should be held to the same tolerance ($\frac{2}{1000}''$ to $\frac{6}{1000}''$) as for the Colt revolver.

Strain Screw. If the hammer on an S&W becomes very difficult to cock as it is drawn almost to maximum rearward position, then it is possible that the strain screw, which rests against the mainspring, is either too short or not screwed all the way in. If the mainspring is not bowed enough by the strain screw, it rests in the path of the hammer and causes the latter to be blocked, thus impeding proper and easy cocking.

Cylinder Stop. The cylinder stop on the S&W is actuated by a flange on the front end of the trigger. The trigger, in turn, is actuated forward, after being pulled, by a spring contained within a rebound slide.

Sluggish Trigger. When the trigger becomes sluggish, it can at times be traced to: a worn cylinder stop; a broken rebound slide spring; a loose trigger stud; or a loose cylinder stop stud.

Cylinder Skips. A cylinder which skips can be caused by a weak or broken cylinder stop spring, or from an accumulation of dirt under the top of the cylinder stop where it contacts the underside of the frame. The aforementioned defects can also be the cause of a cylinder not locking when it is swung into the frame. Corrective action for either defect is self-indicative.

Timing. From experience, this writer can say without fear of rebuttal that an S&W revolver out of timing is a rare thing. This is due to the fact that both hand and trigger for this make revolver are very hard, and as such do not wear readily. However, in the case of bad timing where a new hand is indicated, the process of installing one should be done in the same way as for a Colt. It should be noted, however, that the S&W hand has only one finger and therefore all the touching-up must be done on this finger. It is not usually necessary to remove any metal from the side of the hand where it contacts the side plate, since the part is finished to very close tolerance when it comes from the factory.

Hammer Block. In some of the older model S&W revolvers, the hand is not held under tension against the extractor by means of a spring in the trigger, but instead is so held by a pin and spring, which are retained in the side plate by means of the hammer block. This hammer block, in addition to its aforementioned function, also serves as an incorporated safety by preventing the hammer from going forward all the way unless the trigger is at its maximum rearward position.

The hand, in these models, can be recognized by the beveled flange on the side which contacts the side plate.

If the cylinder in these models does not rotate when the hammer is cocked, then it is most probable that the hand is not being forced against the ratchet by the spring-actuated pin. To remove these parts for inspection and subsequent cleaning, oiling, or replacement, press down on the hammer block just above the point where the pin protrudes, and the pin and spring will jump out.

Erratic Action. When either single or double action cocking is jerky, the side plate should be removed and the action studied while the gun is cocked, first by means of the hammer, (single action) and then double action. Note to see if the trigger flange brings the cylinder stop down as the hand starts to rotate the cylinder. If it does not, then check the cylinder stop stud and trigger stud for looseness. If the fault is not there, then either the cylinder stop is worn and must be replaced, or the contacting point on the trigger flange has been rounded from wear (unlikely), or has been tampered with to the extent where the case-hardening has been removed, exposing the softer core metal which has subsequently worn.

Erratic action in the Colt, as well as the S&W, can sometimes be traced to a worn sear (called hammer strut on a Colt) which does not become engaged with the cocking point of the trigger soon enough. Consequently other points on the hammer and trigger clash, instead of camming, and produce a very undesirable type action. Only by observing these parts in motion, by virtue of the side plates being removed, can the source of trouble be noted and corrective measures taken. Sometimes it involves replacement of a part or spring—other cases may require only the removal of a burr or accumulated dirt.

Rebound Slide. The rebound slide on the S&W revolver, in addition to its named purposes, also serves as an incorporated safety to prevent mechanically accidental discharge. A slightly raised portion on the top of this part is kept in the way of a corresponding portion on the hammer until the trigger is pulled back to its maximum rearward position. It is not very often that either of these parts wears at the aforementioned points, but when the firing pin projects beyond the face of the recoil plate when the trigger is in its forward position, then both the hammer and rebound slide should be inspected at their contact points.

Because of the close fit between parts in the S&W revolver, it will at times, when a gun presented for repair is clogged with dried oil and dirt, be found expeditious to clean out the action and parts as described in Chapter Six, before proceeding with a diagnosis. This cleaning process will, in the long run, make a difficult job much easier.

As a matter of good business, the gunsmith should always recommend to the customer who brings in a revolver for any type of repair or adjustment, that he have his gun thoroughly cleaned while it is in for other work. If the job is setting the customer back the best part of $10.00, then it would not be amiss for the gunsmith to discount the price for cleaning a revolver by 50% or so.

Hammer Nose (Firing Pin). Upon examination of the firing pin, that is fixed in either the S&W or Colt revolver by means of a pin, (called a rivet by the manufacturers), the gunsmith will notice that the firing pin can be moved up and down in the hammer nose. This is the way it should be, so that the firing pin, which travels in an arc, can be made to come through the recoil plate hole, which is only slightly larger in diameter than the firing pin. A firing pin of this type which does not have free movement, should be removed from the hammer and adjustment made to insure this movement. Sometimes it is just a matter of cleaning the hammer recess in which the firing pin moves. Then again it might be necessary to remove burrs from the firing pin, or even replace the rivet which holds the firing pin in the hammer. This rivet should be of such diameter that the firing pin can rotate on it freely; yet it must be large enough so that it will not tend to move sideways in the hammer and rub against the frame.

Hammer Nose Rivet. The S&W hammer nose rivet is made with a countersunk portion at each end, so that it can be staked firmly in place with a punch after being driven into place. In this way the same rivet can be used over and over again. The Colt rivet, on the other hand, must usually be replaced with a new one after it has been removed once, since its ends become marked and make for a bad appearing finished job if put back again. At any rate, the rivet should always be flush with the side of the hammer before it is put back in the gun. The best way of doing this is to take a piece of No. 3/0 emery on a flat, true board and rub the hammer across the cloth until the outline of the rivet becomes almost imperceptible. To achieve a final mirror-like finish, buff the hammer with tripoli compound on a high speed cloth buffer.

S&W Hammerless Revolvers

The S&W .32 and .38 safety hammerless revolvers, which are somewhat different in construction than their swing-out cylinder models, should be inspected for defects by the same standards as applied to the latter type. Certain of these inspection phases, such as those dealing with crane defects, and functions peculiar to single action cocking, do not, of course, apply in the case of a hammerless weapon.

Trigger Troubles. One of the most frequently encountered defects with these hammerless models is trigger trouble of one sort or another, most of which can be traced to a broken or weak trigger spring. The trigger spring, which is housed in a well in that front part of the trigger guard that fits in the frame, is easily accessible for inspection or replacement by removing the trigger guard.

Removing Trigger Guard. To remove the trigger guard, which is held in place by virtue of its own springiness, grasp the guard between the thumb and forefinger and squeeze its rear end towards the muzzle end of the gun until the projection on the guard, which fits into a slot in the frame, is sprung free. The guard can then be lifted from the gun, thus exposing the spring, which can be lifted out.

Firing Pin. The firing pin in S&W hammerless models is of the inertia type and as such does not protrude beyond the face of the bushing, except for a split second when stuck by the hammer. The most positive way to test this type firing pin is by actual firing of a cartridge from which the bullet and powder have been removed, leaving only the live primer intact. Of course, a fully loaded cartridge would be better still, since there would not be the permanent primer set-back that sometimes makes cylinder rotation hard when just the primed cartridge is used. However, since it is quite possible that not all gunsmiths have surroundings that will permit firing of live ammunition, the primer method is suggested. *After "primer testing" a firing pin, always clean the chamber and bore immediately.*

If neither of the above methods can be employed, for some reason or other, then the firing pin can be tested by holding a small piece of wood with a flat, smooth surface against the bushing and snapping the trigger. The depth of the indent in the wood will give an indication as to the protrusion and force of the firing pin blow. Don't test firing pin force with the finger tip, since this method proves nothing and only serves to put one's finger out of commission.

Occasionally, the spring that keeps the firing pin under tension will become weakened, or break and allow the firing pin to protrude beyond the face of the frame to the extent where it can block the rotation of the cylinder by dragging on the face of the cartridges.

To remove the spring and firing pin for replacement or inspection, first drive out the pin, which is located at the top of the frame, and snap the trigger until the bushing holding the aforementioned parts protrudes about far enough beyond the face of the frame to be grasped by plier jaws. At times it will not be necessary to use the pliers since the snapping of the trigger will pop the bushing and two parts free of the frame. At all times during this removal of the bushing by the snapping method, hold the left hand in readiness to catch the bushing in the event it jumps out with unexpected force.

Extractor. When the extractor on an S&W hammerless revolver does not spring back into place after the barrel is fully tipped forward for extraction, then the extractor cam should be inspected for wear or deformation on its hook. An accumulation of hardened oil or dirt can also cause operation failure of this sort. Too, an extractor post not fully screwed onto the extractor can, in addition to causing the aforementioned condition, also prevent the extractor from fully seating into the cylinder. Corrective action consists of screwing the post up tightly while the extractor is held partially away from its seated position. By not having the extractor fully seated during the tightening up operation, there is much less chance of the extractor spring becoming twisted out of shape. Incidentally, this spring is very vulnerable to deformation during assembly of extractor and extractor post, and as such the operation should be performed with great care.

Assembling and Disassembling. As a final note on S&W hammerless revolvers, the following points incident to their disassembly and assembly are suggested. Some of these suggestions are also applicable to other weapons and as such can be so utilized:

1) In removing pins which hold parts in the frame, use drift punches of near pin size and have the gun supported firmly before undertaking removal, so that there will be no chance of the gun shifting position suddenly, causing the punch to slip and mar the surrounding metal. If the ends of the pin are marred during removal, they should be refinished and reblued before putting them back in the gun. When driving the pins back, use a brass drift punch so that the ends will not be flattened or deformed.

2) After the side plate screws have been removed, do not attempt to pry the side plate loose; instead remove the stocks and tap on the stripped frame with the end of a screwdriver handle. This tapping will cause the side plate to be jarred loose to the point where it can be lifted out with the fingers.

3) To remove the hand, which must be taken out before the trigger can be removed, use a pair of needle-nosed pliers or tweezers to compress the hand spring and lift the hand out.

4) Removal of the hammer can be greatly facilitated if the trigger and cylinder stop are first taken out and the safety lever depressed when the hammer is being lifted out. In short, the hammer should be the last part removed when taking the gun apart and the first part installed when being reassembled.

5) When putting the joint pivot in place, always make sure that the little projection on it is aligned with the recess provided for it in the counterbored portion of the hole in the receiver.

Barrelling Work on Revolvers

The removal and installation of barrels on revolvers is a task which should be attempted only when the gunsmith has the tools and fixtures to perform it correctly. To better appreciate the reason for these requirements, the gunsmith has only to realize that a revolver frame can be sprung beyond the stage of practical repair when a barrel job is not handled correctly.

Barrel Threads. The threads in both the S&W and Colt revolver frames are right handed and therefore the barrels going into or being removed from them are turned in the conventional manner of standard screws. Threads in both make revolvers are of the V type. However, the S&W has a finer pitch than the Colt.

S&W Barrel Pin. The S&W also has a pin going through the barrel and frame which must be removed before any attempt to unscrew the barrel is made. After a new barrel has been installed in the S&W, a cutout must be made on the barrel to accommodate this pin. The cutout is best made (after the barrel has been drawn up to its proper position) by means of the proper size drill, held in a breast drill, utilizing the frame hole as a guide. The drill press or a powered hand drill can be used, but cutting is accomplished so rapidly with these tools that there is always the danger of the hole not being drilled straight so that it will connect on a line with the hole in the opposite side of the frame. One way of avoiding this disturbing possibility is to drill in half way from each side of the frame. In this way any angular offset will be less pronounced than at the points where it would be noticed.

As should be done with all press fit pins, whose ends become upset during the process of removal, the S&W barrel pin should be deburred and its ends rounded before being put back in the gun. The quickest way to do this is to run the pin in the drill press chuck and hold a very fine file against the end of the pin, then finishing it off with a piece of No. 3/o emery cloth. This will not only make a better appearing pin when installed, but also make easier the job of installation.

Removing the Barrel. If the barrel being removed from a revolver is worn out and of no value to either the gunsmith or customer, then no effort need be made to protect it during the process of removal. This course of action is not suggested as an encouragement for slovenly work, but rather to speed up an otherwise time-consuming job. However, when the barrel must be removed without mar or injury, then leather, or specially formed hard wood jaws, as long as the barrel and cut out to accommodate the shape of the barrel, must be used.

After the crane and cylinder, as an assembly, have been removed from the revolver frame, the barrel should be placed between the prepared vise jaws, which are then drawn up as tightly as possible, but not so much as to collapse the walls of the barrel.

A hammer handle, or a piece of wood such as oak or locust, about 12″ long and about 1½″ square, should be inserted through the cylinder opening in the frame, thus affording a means of leverage for unscrewing the frame from the held barrel. It must always be remembered that with this long piece of wood being actuated by both hands, a tremendous amount of force can be exerted. So much, that it is possible to bend the frame out of line if the force is not applied gradually and with an eye on the frame at the point where the side plate fits in. It is at this last mentioned joint that the effects of undue force are first noticed, since the side plate and frame will show signs of spreading apart. This is a danger signal—do not ignore it. Immediately stop applying force if the barrel does not start to loosen up before this spreading takes place, and apply a little heat by means of a Bunsen burner or alcohol torch to the frame of the gun where the barrel screws in.

The application of heat should be limited to short duration, and must not be allowed to produce any discoloration of the frame metal, a condition which would indicate too high a heat. The purpose of heating, which is suggested as a last resort, is not to produce an expansion of the frame metal, but rather to liquefy any oxidized oil that exists between the frame and barrel threads and tends to hold them together.

If neither of the above two suggested methods produces the desired results, then there is another which can be employed. In this method the gun is held in the vise by means of two special blocks (Figure 73A) placed around the frame at the point where the barrel screws in, and a strap wrench (or pipe wrench if the barrel is to be discarded) is used to twist the barrel from the frame.

Frame Blocks. These blocks (Figure 73A) which can be made from steel or brass, are best made on a milling machine, but they can be formed with a few drills and an assortment of files. There are no specific dimensions other than that the blocks must be

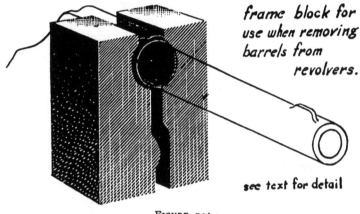

frame block for use when removing barrels from revolvers.

see text for detail

FIGURE 73A

tooled to such a size that one will fit around half of the frame, at the point where the barrel screws in, and also fill the recess normally occupied by the crane. The other block is cut to fit the contour of the other half of the frame.

Although there is quite a bit of cutting and fitting to making a set of these blocks, they are very handy if the gunsmith expects to do much revolver rebarreling work.

A set each for the Police Positive frame, the Official Police frame, and the Service frame will be found adequate to handle practically all the Colt revolver models.

For the S&W revolvers, the main frame sizes are the M&P Model, the M1917, and the Hand Ejector model.

Installing the Barrel. Before putting a new barrel in a revolver, the threads in the frame and on the barrel should be cleaned of all dirt and then oiled with a light lubricant. This done, the barrel should be screwed into the frame by hand, and notice taken of how far in it can be screwed by this method. If it screws up within a thread or two, then it is very likely that the remaining distance can be forced up by means of one of the methods used in removing the barrel. Should it be that the barrel screws in only a few threads by hand and then it becomes difficult, if not impossible, to advance it any farther by hand or by using the vise-and-stick method, then it is necessary to chase the threads in the frame by means of a special tap for the job, as described in Chapter Three. In the absence of a tap of this sort, a sharp triangular shaped file can be used on the barrel threads which must be deepened to facilitate fitting to the frame.

Although it is possible to secure an easier fit between barrel threads and frame threads by chucking the barrel in a lathe and chasing the threads with a fine cut three square file, this writer does not recommend the practice since it is only too easy for the file to slip and mess up the threads. Also, because of the exterior taper on revolver barrels it is not an easy matter to chuck them up very true.

When tightening a barrel into the frame, care should be taken to see that the front sight, and in the case of an S&W, the barrel lug, are not subject to bending as a result of being allowed to act as stops between the vise jaws.

"Drawing Up" the Barrel. At times the gunsmith will find that it is not possible to draw the barrel up far enough to achieve proper alignment of the front sight with the rear sight. In instances of this sort, the barrel must be loosened from the frame and metal removed from the shoulder flat of the barrel. The amount that must be removed to effect a proper fitting can be determined to a close degree by noting the position of the front sight, when drawn up to maximum possible tightness, in relation to where it should be, i.e. in line with the rear sight. If the barrel lacks say $\frac{1}{4}$ turn of proper alignment and the barrel thread has a pitch of 20 threads per inch, then one complete turn advances the barrel $\frac{1}{20}$ or $\frac{5}{100}$″. One quarter of a turn, then, is equal to about $1\frac{2}{1000}$″. Thus, by chucking up the barrel in a lathe and removing $1\frac{2}{1000}$″ from the shoulder flat, the barrel used as an example should draw up to alignment.

Occasionally the gunsmith will encounter a barrel which does not tighten up even when it is in position. This is caused by the barrel shoulder not resting on the frame. Usually it is only a matter of a few thousandths of an inch that must be added to the barrel shoulder to make up the deficiency in length and this can be done by any of the following three means:

1) The face of the frame that contacts the barrel shoulder can be tinned with solder and the excess filed off until a proper thickness is secured. Only a little solder at a time should be flowed on the soldering iron when performing this operation so that the solder can be run on evenly and the chances of any dropping onto other parts of the gun will be held to a minimum.

2) A steel shim of the desired thickness, cut from a piece of shim stock, will serve excellently for the purpose, providing that all side trimming is done before the barrel is screwed in place. Otherwise the shim is apt to buckle under the squeezing and leave metal protruding from between the frame and barrel.

3) While it is not recommended except for emergency cases, slack between the frame and barrel shoulder can be taken up by hammer peening the latter, so that a bit of metal is turned over. This method is best used on old barrels which come loose from longtime wear and where exterior appearance of the gun is of small consideration.

After the barrel is drawn up tightly to correct alignment, the crane and cylinder assembly should be put back in place and a determination made as to how much metal must be removed from the rear barrel face to insure proper clearance between barrel and cylinder. This done, the burrs remaining from the filing should be removed with the aid of the barrel chamfering tool illustrated in Figure 71.

Test Firing. When possible, a gun which has had a new barrel installed should be test fired, so that any discrepancy in sighting can be corrected before the owner finds it out himself and returns the weapon in indignation, claiming that the gunsmith did a second rate job.

Recoil Plate Installation

Although it is not very often that the gunsmith is called upon to replace a recoil plate in a Colt or S&W revolver, he should be equipped both with tools and knowledge to perform the job efficiently and correctly.

Preparatory to doing any work on the recoil plate, the gun must be partially disassembled. The crane and cylinder assembly, the hammer, mainspring, and stocks are first removed, and the butt section of the frame placed between brass covered vise jaws.

To remove the old recoil plate, use a drift punch having an end diameter of such a size that it will not fit through the firing pin hole, but will enter the recess behind the recoil plate without touching the frame. Lay the end of the punch against the rear face of the recoil plate and strike it with a hammer. Start off with light blows and increase the force gradually until the recoil plate breaks loose.

It will be noticed, after the recoil plate has been removed, that a thin "ribbon fringe" of metal remains around the well in which the recoil plate fits. No attempt should be made to scrape or file this metal off, since it is this that holds the recoil plate in place, when peened over the rim of the latter. When this fringe of metal is not completely turned out of the well sufficiently to permit insertion of the new recoil plate, then it is permissible to use a $\frac{1}{16}''$ diameter round-nosed drift punch to straighten it out. This latter operation is accomplished by holding the revolver in a vise, barrel pointed towards the ceiling, and tapping around the inside of the recoil plate well until all the fringe is parallel with the walls of the well.

With the gun still securely vise-held in the upright position, the recoil plate should be laid in place by hand. To seat it, a steel rod of about $\frac{1}{100}''$ less than bore diameter, having one end turned to recoil plate diameter minus $\frac{1}{32}''$, should be passed through the bore and allowed to rest on the face of the recoil plate. The length of this rod should be such that no more than one inch of it projects beyond the muzzle of a six inch barrel revolver. In this way the same rod can be used for any similar make and caliber revolver. A few light taps on this rod should suffice to seat the recoil plate fully in its well.

When the recoil plate is fully seated, the ribbon fringe surrounding it should be tapped over with the round-nosed drift punch described earlier. This done, the final locking in place of the recoil plate is accomplished with the tool described and illustrated in Figure 12. In using this tool, whose function is to crimp the ribbon fringe over the chamfered portion of the recoil plate, the gunsmith should make certain that the rim of it is in proper position before striking it with a hammer. Otherwise it tends to crimp only one part of the fringe and tip the recoil plate. This crimping tool is inserted through the barrel in the same way as the seating tool, and best results are obtained when the fingers are tightly held about that portion which projects from beyond the muzzle, so that the tendency for it to rebound will be held to a minimum.

After the recoil plate has been seated and crimped, the hammer should be put back in the gun and moved through its normal path of motion by hand. If everything is correct, the firing pin will pass through and withdraw from the recoil plate without sticking or catching. If it does not, then a small diameter round Swiss file should be used to touch up any spots in the hole which seem to be impeding the progress of the pin. Needless to say, only a little bit of filing should be necessary; otherwise the firing pin hole will be enlarged to the point where it is sloppy and might allow the primer to be struck too far off center. Where extensive filing is required to allow passage of the firing pin, it must be presumed that the recoil plate has been seated off center and therefore must be removed and a new one put in place.

In completing the recoil plate replacement, the face of it, which contacts the cartridges, should be touched up with a flat smooth file having a safe edge so that the underside corner of the top strap will not be cut. Finally, a piece of crocus cloth wrapped around the file should be used to remove all previously made tool marks and burrs.

The removal and insertion of recoil plates (firing pin bushings) on Iver Johnson and H&R revolvers is a great deal simpler than on "the other two makes" since the former two are screwed in place.

To remove these firing pin bushings, a tool as illustrated in Figure 74 should be used. When using this tool in a revolver having a solid frame, the head of the tool is laid in place in the bushing and the rod inserted from the muzzle end of the bore. The attaching pin is then inserted and the bushing can be unscrewed.

If the revolver is of the tip-up type where the bushing can be worked on without passing a rod through the bore, then a short rod, say about two inches, should be used.

The pins which fit into the holes should be turned to such a size that they can be knocked out, if they become broken or deformed, and new ones inserted.

A few different size heads used with the long and short rod should fill the bill for almost all revolvers that the gunsmith is liable to encounter. Like all other special tools, all the components for this tool, complete with heads, pins, and rods, should be kept in a special box that is marked as to its contents. It takes a long time to make most special tools, but it only takes a few careless moments to lose component parts of them.

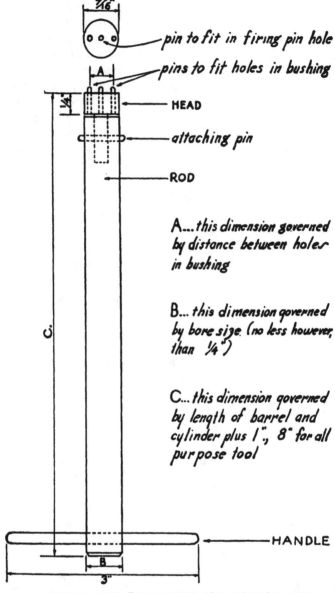

pin to fit in firing pin hole

pins to fit holes in bushing

HEAD

attaching pin

ROD

A....this dimension governed by distance between holes in bushing

B... this dimension governed by bore size. (no less however, than ¼")

C... this dimension governed by length of barrel and cylinder plus 1"., 8" for all purpose tool

HANDLE

TOOL FOR REMOVING AND INSTALLING
SCREW TYPE FIRING PIN BUSHINGS IN REVOLVERS

FIGURE 74

In the absence of such a tool, a small diameter, round-nosed, drift punch can be used to tap the bushing loose. This latter method is not to be recommended too highly, since it generally results in a burring up of the two holes in which the punch must be inserted at an angle. Even though these burrs can be filed off, the unprofessional-like appearance of the job is difficult to conceal.

Notes on the Inexpensive Revolvers

Besides the Colt and S&W revolver, the gunsmith will, depending on his geographic location, have presented to him for repair revolvers of cheaper make, such as Iver Johnson, Harrington & Richardson, U.S. Arms Co., Thames Arms Co., Forehand & Wadsworth and others. While the last three makes are no longer manufactured, there are still many of them in circulation. However, for all practical purposes, all five makes and others similar in design are subject to the same general method of inspection and repair.

In all fairness, it must be stated that the H&R Sportsman, H&R Eureka and H&R Single Shot Target Pistol, as well as the Iver Johnson .22 Target Single Action, should not be considered in a class with the cheaper made arms, since they are different in design and far superior in construction.

Inspection procedure to determine the faults of an Iver Johnson or H&R revolver should be conducted in the same way as for a Colt or S&W, inasmuch as the basic functioning of all revolvers is about the same.

The most common faults encountered on these make revolvers are broken or defective trigger spring, hand spring and mainspring (if of the flat type). Worn hands and worn ratchets, which tend to put the gun out of timing, are also frequent offenders as sources of malfunction.

Inasmuch as the construction of these weapons is such that a working action comparable to the Colt or S&W cannot be expected, the gunsmith must learn to overlook minor deficiencies in the working mechanism, trigger pull and timing in the Iver Johnson or H&R revolvers. This is not an invitation for slovenly or slipshod work, but the novice gunsmith should realize that only a certain degree of repair perfection can be achieved in any gun which, when new, is basically of second rate construction.

These remarks should not be construed as a slight against any make of gun, but rather as a statement of established fact. Surely the buyer of a $10.00 gun does not expect to get a weapon equal in quality to one that costs three times that price. By the same token, a gunsmith cannot be expected to make a proverbial silk purse from a sow's ear by the expenditure of a few parts and a few hours.

Assembling and Disassembling. Disassembly of the H&R or Iver Johnson revolver is quite simple and should not present any particularly difficult problems for the gunsmith who proceeds with the caution expected of a craftsman. On the other hand, reassembly, while basically no more difficult can, however, be slow if the few following kinks are not part of the gunsmith's repertory:

1) When reassembling parts which are held in the revolver by pins, always have these parts positively aligned before attempting to drive in the regular pin. This can be achieved by using a drift punch of proper size having a slightly tapered end for about ¼" of its length. The smaller end is employed to align the parts from one side of the hole while the regular pin is inserted from the other side. As noted earlier in this chapter, the gunsmith should, before inserting the regular pins, make certain that their ends are free from deformation, and slightly chamfered to facilitate entrance.

2) Where a pin is employed in a gun to hold a part within another part, which in turn is held by the same pin, as the sear and trigger guard are pinioned in many of the H&R and Iver Johnson revolvers, an auxiliary pin can be used to great advantage. An auxiliary pin is nothing more than a pin which is used to hold subassemblies together while they are being pinned in place by the regular pin. For example, an auxiliary pin for holding the sear in the trigger guard should be of such a diameter that it can be pushed into these parts by the pressure that can be applied by the fingers. The length of this pin should be slightly less than the width of the trigger guard at the point where the latter fits into the frame. The ends of an auxiliary pin should be much chamfered so that it will not snag on parts as the regular pin is driven in and pushes it towards the opposite side of the hole.

3) When screwing the extractor extension onto the extractor, always push in with each turn. In this way the extractor spring will have less tendency to become snarled up on the extractor. If turning becomes difficult, then it is safe to assume that the spring is becoming twisted out of shape. Do not try to twist

harder; instead, loosen up the extension, check the spring and try again.

4) Never hold a top break type revolver in a vise by means of pressure of the joint section, i.e., that part where the barrel and receiver are joined together. It only requires a very little bit of pressure to cause these parts to bend, and consequently make for a very hard job of getting them back to proper clearance and working order. When a revolver must be held in a vise, the stocks should be removed (and if necessary the stock pin) and the butt frame placed between brass or leather jaws.

Spanish Revolvers

Another type of revolver that the gunsmith will encounter occasionally are those of Spanish make. Generally speaking, all Spanish made revolvers are nothing more than very poorly made imitations of either the Colt or Smith & Wesson. They are made in models almost too numerous to classify, mostly all having one thing in common—ill fitting parts in a poorly machined cast frame.

Due to the poor quality of steel used in parts for Spanish revolvers, they get out of order quite frequently and in such condition reach the gunsmith. Inasmuch as their action is similar to that of the "big two" makes of the U.S. revolvers, diagnosis of trouble can be conducted along the lines recommended for the latter. However, the procurement of replacement parts is by no means as simple, since the maker's address is rarely, if ever, imprinted on the gun. Some large gun houses like A. F. Stoeger & Co., in New York, N.Y. generally stock certain parts for these weapons and, as can be appreciated, the prices, as compared to similar Colt or S&W parts, are rather high.

Repairs should be undertaken on Spanish revolvers only after the customer has indicated a willingness to pay whatever the gunsmith believes it will cost—plus a dollar or two if something unexpected springs up that did not show up in the original inspection or develops during the course of repair. As a matter of fact, it is a good policy to get a cash deposit amounting to at least the value of the parts before proceeding on the repair job.

In this chapter on revolver repair, one of the longest in the book, some details are included which might be obvious even to the novice. However, it is hoped that the reader will appreciate the necessity for covering these points in the interest of continuity and understanding.

CHAPTER TWELVE

Automatic Pistol Repairs

OF THE many different kinds of recoil-operated pistols in existence that will come to the gunsmith for inspection and repair, all of them can be divided into two general operating classes: straight blow-back and short recoil.

Types of Operation

Straight Blow-back. In this type mechanism, the slide of the pistol, plus resistance from the recoil, hammer and other springs, acts to keep the cartridge case as a breech seal until the bullet has left the bore of the gun. In short, the sheer weight and resistance of the moving parts affected by recoil serves as a form of breech lock. Typical of this class of pistol are the Colt calibers .25, .32 and .380 pocket pistols.

Also coming under this type of operation are pistols like the Savage Pocket Automatic in calibers .32 and .380, in which some mechanical arrangement is employed to delay somewhat the opening of the breech block. In the Savage, for example, there is a lug on the barrel which rides in an angular track that is milled in the slide. The path of this track tends to rotate the barrel through approximately 5° and so slow down the unlocking process.

Short Recoil. The short recoil type of automatic pistol, represented by the Colt caliber .45 Government Model and Luger pistol, is so made that the breech block and barrel of the weapon are locked together at the instant of firing and remain so locked until the barrel recoils a short distance, when they are unlocked by inbuilt links or cams. This system is used on guns which shoot cartridges having higher instrumental velocities and/or heavier bullets than the pocket model pistols.

Inspection Procedure

Inspection of any make of automatic pistol can be made very rapidly. Obviously, no single suggested test method could possibly include a specific test for every part of each type pistol. However, in the ensuing paragraphs is outlined a procedure of inspection on the Colt .45 Government automatic that should serve to indicate the points to be observed when inspecting any automatic pistol.

Magazine Catch Assembly. Withdraw the magazine from the gun, noting the action of the magazine catch. If the magazine catch drags when depressed, or fails to return to place, then either the magazine catch spring is broken or the lock magazine catch is burred at the head. Changing the spring or filing the burrs off the lock should correct this defect. If the lock is badly enlarged at the slot in its head, then it is best to replace it so that subsequent removal and installation of it will not be made more difficult.

Push the magazine back in the gun to make sure it locks in place when inserted all the way. If the bottom of the magazine extends beyond the butt of the weapon, but can be pushed farther in by hand, then it is possible that the catch is worn. On the other hand, it might be that the notch in the magazine which engages the catch is worn. To localize the trouble, try another (new if possible) magazine. Should this other magazine lock flush in place, the old magazine should be replaced with a new one. If the same test indicates the catch to be worn, the catch should be replaced. In either case, a corrective action must be effected since a magazine which does not seat far enough into a gun can be the cause of much cartridge feeding trouble. This is usually the direct cause of a slide's not stripping off a round as it travels forward, since not enough of the cartridge rim projects upward to be caught by the slide.

Magazine. If the magazine seems to drag as it is inserted or withdrawn, the magazine body should be checked for dents or bulges that would cause it to rub against the inside of the frame. Should the magazine prove to be free from defects, then the inside of the frame where the magazine fits is probably the offender. Long stock screw bushings (which can be filed down) or a slightly inbent section of the frame (which can be straightened out) are two prominent causes of this fault. On automatic pistols, other than the .45 Government, which have plastic or hard rubber grips that are subject to shape deformation of any sort from climatic conditions, the possibility of their warping and dragging against the magazine should not be overlooked.

Testing with Dummies. The next test on the pistol, which involves the running through the gun of a magazine full of dummy cartridges, serves as a good substitute for actually firing the gun to determine its defects. The latter, of course, is highly recommended when facilities exist for conducting such a test.

Having the magazine loaded with dummy cartridges, the gun should be held in the left hand and the slide operated with the right. The slide, when fully retracted, should be allowed to snap forward under full force from the recoil spring. If the cartridge does not strip from the magazine, then the latter should be checked as described earlier in the chapter. If the cartridge strips only part way from the magazine or jumps up vertically in the path of the slide, then it is safe to assume that the lips of the magazine are either worn or bent to the extent where replacement of the magazine is indicated. Bending, or, as a matter of fact, any repair to the lips of a magazine for an automatic pistol, cannot be recommended, except in emergency cases where a repaired magazine is better than none at all. Otherwise a defective magazine should be replaced with a new one, since this comparatively inexpensive part is the heart of the gun.

Should a cartridge strip from the magazine all right, but catch as it enters the barrel ramp, then the extractor should be checked for burrs on its claw, or lack of proper springiness. The cause of this defect might also be traced to a protruding firing pin, or a burred up breech face. Also, a rough surface on the ramp, or the latter's not blending into the frame contour properly, can cause a cartridge to stick at this point. Corrective action for each of the aforementioned defects can be accomplished by either stoning or replacing the parts involved. In some remote cases it is possible that a cartridge might stick as it approaches the chamber because of a weak recoil spring. Installing a new recoil spring will quickly show if this be the cause of the trouble.

Link and Barrel Lug. In the .45 Government Model pistol, in which the barrel and slide are locked together for about the last 1/4″ of the closing stroke, the movement of the link on its link pin and between the barrel lug should be checked when the slide does not close on a partially introduced cartridge. Constant pounding of the barrel lug against the slide stop often burrs over the lug, thus preventing full free movement of the link. Restoration of proper clearance between the two sections of the barrel lug, by filing, should make for proper freedom of movement.

Extraction Troubles. Extraction trouble, either noted during hand testing or called to the attention of the gunsmith by a complaining customer, calls for an inspection of the extractor (for broken or deformed claw); the chamber (for rings or pits in which a fired cartridge might cling); or link trouble of the sort described in the previous paragraph. A defective extractor, as well as a barrel having a badly marred chamber, should be replaced, since the time required to effect repair (even when possible) is so great as to make it impractical. A rough breech face is also detrimental to proper extraction, since the cartridge case face drags along this surface during the unlocking phase.

Sluggish Slide Action. When the slide drags as it is being retracted, or goes forward sluggishly, and the trouble cannot be traced to a defective recoil spring or link, then the working parts should be disassembled from the receiver and the slide worked back and forth by hand. In this way it can be determined whether the sluggishness is caused by excessive friction between the slide and receiver alone, or is a result of the hammer or disconnector, or both, pressing against the breech end of the slide.

If the slide does not move back and forth freely in the ways of the receiver, then contacting surfaces on both parts should be examined for high or rough spots, which might be conducive to excessive friction between them. A very smooth cut file, used cautiously, should be employed to remedy this undesirable condition, followed by stoning to remove any marks left by the file.

To determine whether the hammer or disconnector is making for sluggish slide operation, all the moving parts, with the exception of the hammer, should be assembled in the receiver and the slide actuated back and forth by hand. If the slide drags on the disconnector, to the extent where the smooth operation of the slide is impeded, then it is reasonable to assume that the disconnector is defective in some way. To localize the defect, remove the slide and depress the disconnector by hand. If it depresses readily from pressure applied either in a vertical or horizontal direction (the latter simulating the slide's method of actuation) then the hole in which the disconnector moves and the point where the disconnector contacts the sear spring are all right.

On the other hand, if the hole in the frame in which the disconnector moves is elongated to the extent that the disconnector moves in a back-and-forth direction rather than depressing as the slide passes over it, the hole must be bushed with a piece of steel. Needless to say, bushing of the disconnector hole is a very uncommon operation and is usually required on a gun that is otherwise well worn and battered. If the customer is willing to foot the bill for a job of this sort and the gunsmith is willing to tackle it, then it should be done. However, it should be attempted only with full knowledge that the old hole must be drilled and taper reamed out to accommodate the new bushing, which must be turned on the outside to fit the reamed hole, and carefully drilled and reamed in the inside hole where the disconnector fits.

Should inspection reveal the top of the disconnector to be rough or sharp so that it drags on or cuts the underside of the slide, then the disconnector should be replaced with a new one. At the same time, the offending portion of the slide should be filed and honed smooth, so that the top of the new disconnector will not be defaced.

It might be well to mention that a disconnector having a worn or battered top (Point B, Figure 75) can sometimes be salvaged,

DISCONNECTOR FOR A
COLT .45 AUTOMATIC PISTOL

FIGURE 75

provided that the amount of metal which must be removed from it does not shorten the disconnector to the point where it cannot function as it was designed to. Since it takes only a few minutes to smooth up the top of the disconnector to conform with the shape and surface of a new one, this should be tried before proceeding with the installation of a new one. To check the efficiency of a disconnector, either new or repaired, refer to the tests described in detail farther on in this chapter.

If the hammer, after being assembled to the receiver, proves to be the cause of slide drag, then there are a few underlying factors aside from actual contact between the hammer and slide that should be investigated:

1) Check the sear to see if it is worn to the extent where it allows the hammer to bear too far forward when in the cocked position. If it is so worn, it must be replaced.

2) Check the full cock engaging-notch in the hammer for excessive wear which would also allow the hammer to bear too far forward.

3) Check the mainspring to see that it is a proper factory spring and not a substitute having excessive tension that would cause the hammer to bear too heavily on the underside of the slide as the latter is actuated. Also check the spring for kinks or deformation that would tend to hinder movement of the mainspring in the housing.

4) Check the mainspring plunger for deformation or burrs that might cause it to drag inside the housing and consequently impede free movement of the hammer.

5) Check the hole in the mainspring housing and make certain that no burrs or deformation interfere with movement of the spring or plunger.

6) Check for bend in the hammer strut, which would cause it to make for difficult initial cocking and consequent easy actuation of the hammer at the end of its rearward motion.

Any one or more of the foregoing six points might easily prove to be the cause of a dragging slide, and as such should be remedied in the most direct manner, i.e., deburr those parts in need of it and replace those which cannot be repaired.

Ejector. If test functioning of the dummy cartridges discloses a defect in the manner of cartridge ejection, then the ejector should be checked for looseness in the frame and wear or deformation at the point where it contacts the cartridge case. In addition, the extractor should be checked for a broken or deformed claw that would tend to drag on the rim of the case, thus interfering with proper release of the case when it contacts the ejector. The foregoing check should also be made when a customer complains of an automatic pistol throwing the fired cases back in his face.

Slide Stop. Having run a magazine full of cartridges through the mechanism, the pistol should next be checked for function of the slide stop. To do this, insert the empty magazine in the completely assembled gun and pull the slide back briskly. The slide (remember, we are still speaking of the .45 Government) should remain locked in the rearward position. If it does not, then try a new magazine. If the new magazine actuates the slide stop, thus holding the slide back, then the lower half lip on the old magazine is defective. If upward and outward bending of this lip does not correct the defect, then a new magazine followei should be installed, inasmuch as repeated bending of the lip will only weaken it and make it so that it might break off under the strain of actual usage.

When a new magazine does not serve to push the slide stop up in the slide locking position, then it should be examined for wear at the point where it is actuated by the magazine follower lip. If it is short, then the slide stop must be replaced. However, before discarding the slide stop as worn, check the slide stop plunger to make sure that it is exerting tension against the slide stop, for if the slide stop is not held snugly against the frame, the protruding distance of its magazine follower engaging lug is decreased and consequently is not actuated. In some cases the slide stop is prevented from engaging the slide as a result of burrs on the slide stop or slide at the point of contact. Small as the possibility of this may be, it should not be overlooked as a source of trouble.

Lock Safety. To check the safety lock, cock the gun, put the safety on and apply pressure to the trigger gradually, easy at first, then with increasing pressure, until it has positively been determined that no amount of finger force which can normally be applied to the trigger would cause the safety to fail. Should the safety jump out of position, or in any way allow the hammer to fall during this test, then in all likelihood it is defective and must be replaced. When installation of a new safety does not correct this condition, it is most probable that the hammer is worn and, therefore, must be discarded in favor of a new one.

Grip Safety. The next of the safeties checked should be the grip safety. This is accomplished by cocking the gun and, without wrapping the hand around the gun, so that the grip safety is not depressed, apply finger pressure against the trigger. The hammer should not fall. If it does, the three-leaf sear spring should be removed from the receiver and a check made to see if the leaf which exerts tension against the grip safety is broken, or not bent out enough to force the grip safety against the normal weight of the grip safety itself, when the latter is in position. Of course, if the leaf spring is broken, then it must be replaced; but otherwise it should be bent backward further (by hand) so that it will bear with more tension against the grip safety. This accomplished, and the parts reassembled, another test for grip safety efficiency should be made. If spring bending has not corrected the defect, then it remains that either the trigger or grip safety is defective. To fully appreciate this last statement, the gunsmith must remember that the trigger is prevented from releasing the sear because point "A" on it contacts point "B" on the grip safety (Figure 76) when the latter is

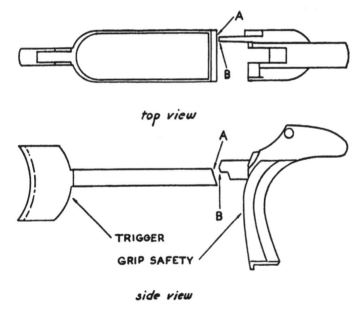

top view

side view

TRIGGER AND GRIP SAFETY OF 45 COLT AUTOMATIC
SHOWING POINTS OF WEAR

Figure 76

not depressed. However, when the grip safety is depressed, as it is when the web of the hand contacts it for normal shooting hold, it pivots around the pin which holds it in place, thus elevating the projection on it, which otherwise blocks movement of the trigger. Generally it will be found that it is the grip safety rather than the trigger which is worn and must be replaced. Nevertheless, this should not deter the gunsmith from trying an old trigger with a new grip safety, and vice versa, to determine the true cause of the trouble.

Half Cock Notch. The half cock notch on the hammer, which is provided to arrest full movement of the hammer should it slip from the thumb while being cocked, can and does break off or wear, so that it no longer functions as it was designed to. Checking of this point consists of first allowing the hammer to slip from under the thumb, and then pulling the trigger when it is at the half cock position. If it does not stand up under either or both of these tests, then the old hammer must be discarded and a new one installed.

Disconnector Tests. To test the disconnector, grasp the gun in the right hand, cock it, push the slide back $\frac{1}{4}''$, and pull the trigger. The hammer should not fall; if it does, the disconnector is defective and must be repaired or replaced. Repair, when possible, involves filing (at most $\frac{1}{100}''$) from both points marked "A" in Figure 75.

Another required test for disconnector function involves locking the slide in its rearward position by means of the slide stop and then releasing it, at the same time squeezing the trigger as the slide goes forward. If the hammer falls, the disconnector is faulty. In connection with this last test, perhaps it might be well to point out that a gun that "follows through" also acts in the same way, i.e., the hammer follows the slide as the latter goes forward. Therefore, before drawing any positive conclusion as a result of this test, it is well to also make this test for "following through":

Grasp the gun in the left hand, but do not apply any pressure to the trigger, and retract the slide smartly with the right hand. When it reaches the end of its rearward stroke, let it snap forward under full momentum. If the hammer follows the slide forward and the cause of this defect cannot be ascribed to a faulty disconnector, then it is most probable that the trigger pull is below the safe minimum—$4\frac{1}{2}$ pounds, for this pistol. Correction of this fault can be accomplished by increasing the trigger pull to the minimum by any of the following means, singly or in combination:

1) Bend inward the leaf of the sear spring which lays on the sear. Doing this will raise the trigger pull anywhere from ¼ to ¾ of a pound. By the same token, a slight reduction in trigger pull, when needed, can be effected in the same manner, except the spring leaf must be bent away from the sear.

2) Increase the trigger pull by honing the sear, hammer, or both. (See Chapter Seven).

3) Replace the sear spring if the sear leaf is broken or has lost its resilience.

4) Replace the hammer, sear, or both, if they are so badly worn as to preclude their serving in proper fashion after being honed.

Comments and Notes on Disassembly of Pistols Other than .45 Government

Aside from the foregoing tests outlined for the .45 Government pistol, but applicable in general to many automatic pistols, there are others, such as barrel inspection, grip inspection and inspection for metal finishing, that are covered in other chapters, or are of such an obvious nature that additional comment would serve no purpose.

Even apart from the numerous make and caliber automatic pistols of Spanish manufacture, which are of poor construction and in the same category as Spanish revolvers, the gunsmith will encounter many automatic pistols which at first glance not only appear strange but also difficult to disassemble.

Some of these weapons might include the German-made Luger, Ortgies, Mauser, Schmeisser, Walther, and Dreyse; the Belgian-made Bayard, Clement, Pieper, and Browning; or the American-made Remington, Savage, Harrington & Richardson, and Smith & Wesson.

Disassembling Pistols. Almost all automatic pistols can be broken down very easily and quickly if the proper sequence of disassembly is known. However, because of the great number of different type and make pistols, only a gunsmith who has been in business for some time, and has been fortunate enough to have these weapons brought to his attention, knows the correct method of disassembly. For the novice who is confronted with a type of automatic pistol foreign to his talents and knowledge, the temptation to loosen all screws and drive out pins is very great. Almost needless to say, this course of action usually leads only to a point where all the parts eventually become jammed together and resist the best efforts at dislodgment. This sort of practice is scarcely to be recommended or condoned under any circumstances, since the damage done to both gun and parts not infrequently is much greater than that which prompted the customer to bring the gun in for repair.

When a strange pistol is brought in for repair that necessitates its being taken apart, the gunsmith should always study its action and mechanism carefully before attempting to take it apart.

Bearing in mind the theoretical aspects of all guns, as covered in Chapter Five, any and all disassembly should be performed cautiously and with an eye toward the ever-necessary reassembly job.

Removing the Slide. Before removing any of the parts housed within the receiver of an automatic pistol, the slide and attached components should be removed so that the receiver mechanism may be better observed and the chances of receiver parts becoming jammed greatly reduced. In many pistols it will be found that the barrel either helps to hold the slide in place (like the Colt Pocket Automatic pistols or Spanish pistols), or can be removed only after the slide has been taken off (like the Ortgies pistol). Almost invariably the slide can be released by removing some sort of pin or catch that passes through the receiver or barrel. Sometimes, as in the case of the Ortgies pistol, a catch is pressed in and the slide can be lifted from the frame. On some pistols, like the Walther PP and the S&W, the trigger guard must be pulled down.

Removing the Grips. After the slide has been stripped from the pistol, the grips should be removed from the receiver, which usually involves only the removal of anywhere from one to four screws. Occasionally, some manufacturers employ a tricky system of holding the grips to the frame. For example, the Ortgies, in which a two-pronged catch, accessible only through the opening where the magazine fits, engages a cutout in the back of each grip. By pressing a rod against the catch, both are released simultaneously. Although this is somewhat of an unusual method of grip attachment, it should serve to indicate to the novice gunsmith some of the odd construction features he will have to figure out from time to time.

With both grips and the slide removed, it is easier to visualize the position of the parts in the receiver. In possession of such knowledge, the job of diagnosing trouble and taking the gun apart will be greatly simplified.

Making Special Parts. Often the gunsmith will find it necessary to make a part for a foreign automatic pistol, when the part cannot be procured commercially. In undertaking a job of this sort, there are a few factors which should be taken into account. Briefly, they are:

1) The type and amount of stress that the part will be subject to; this is necessary so that the correct steel can be used and the proper heat treatment applied to the new part.

2) The exact dimensions of the part to be duplicated; generally speaking, the only way to obtain this information is to have the old part and make allowances for its wear by measuring the places where the new part must function within the gun.

3) Approximately how many hours will be required to make the part; by knowing about how long it will take to make a special part, the gun owner can be given a close idea of how much it will cost to repair the weapon. If the estimated cost of repair seems to be too high, the customer can decline having it fixed, thus saving the gunsmith a needless expenditure of time and effort which might be the case if the job is completed first and the customer informed of the cost afterwards.

In certain cases where it is either not practical or possible to duplicate a needed part, the gunsmith should inform the customer of this fact as soon as possible, so the latter will not wait a long time believing that the gun is being fixed, only to be disappointed many days or weeks later by the truth of the matter. The practice of keeping customers informed at all times as to the status of their guns not only applies in cases where special work is being done, but at all times. No gunsmith should or can expect to prosper if he indulges in the poor business practice of "putting the customer off" or "kidding him along." No matter how disappointed a customer might feel after being told that his favorite gun is beyond the stage of practical repair, he will be far less disturbed if he is told the truth as soon as possible.

Gunsmith's Reference System. After completing a successful inspection and repair for the first time on a strange pistol, it is a good practice to make a few comments on a card that can be filed away for future reference. These comments should include a listing of the make, model, caliber and serial number, together with a brief description of the gun's appearance and functioning.

In addition, abbreviated reference should be noted as to the best method of disassembly and assembly of the gun, plus any tricky or unique mechanical features. In this way, a record will be available for the gunsmith's use, should he be called upon to fix the same type of pistol long after he has forgotten about its features.

Such a practice as this should not be regarded as one reserved for amateurs or beginners, for it is certainly "anything but" as even the most experienced craftsmen in all fields of mechanical endeavor find it necessary to refer to books or notes when they are dealing with machines about whose working they are somewhat doubtful. It is far better to do a job correctly and efficiently by referring to notes than to mess it up because needed information cannot be summoned from the very unpredictable human memory.

The Luger Pistol. The German Luger, a very popular pistol, is one of the few automatic handguns which has a screwed-in-tight barrel. Removal of this barrel is not an easy job, due especially to the fact that the receiver in which it fits seems to act somewhat on the delicate side when subject to the torsional stress of the barrel being unscrewed. No attempt to remove a Luger barrel should be made unless some sort of inside support for the receiver is inserted, and the outside portion is firmly supported between the vise jaws. In Chapter Four a suggested form of block is described. Due to a slight variation in the size of the space between the sides of the Luger receiver, it will be found necessary to shim this block up to size on certain individual guns. With this block in place, the chances of the receiver being twisted out of line are greatly minimized.

Screwing up of the barrel, so that the rear sight will be aligned with the front sight, should be done in the same manner as recommended for revolvers in Chapter Eleven.

Factors Affecting Accuracy in the .45 Government Pistol

Accuracy, which is a much-discussed feature of automatic pistols, is affected adversely in the .45 Government automatic by the following factors:

1) Excessive play between the barrel and barrel bushing; to correct this condition, either the old barrel bushing must be replaced by a new one, or the barrel changed.

2) Excessive wear in the two holes of the link; corrective action for this defect involves substitution of a new link, and, if this

does not prove sufficient, the link pin and slide stop should be changed.

3) Excessive wear in the barrel lug hole; this can be remedied by inserting a slightly oversized link pin made from drill rod, usually entailing the reaming of a few thousandths of an inch from the link pin hole in the link.

4) Excessive wear between the locking ribs on the barrel and the corresponding recesses of the slide; generally, the installation of a new barrel will correct this deficiency, but if it does not, and inaccuracy cannot be traced to any of the aforementioned causes, then the installation of a new slide is indicated. This latter recourse is very rare, but when necessary no alternate method of repair will accomplish the desired results as well.

5) Excessive play between the barrel bushing and the slide; this necessitates either changing the barrel bushing or the slide.

As can be seen from the description of the foregoing five points of wear on the .45 Government automatic pistol, all are concerned with parts which, when worn, affect the rigidity of the barrel. This importance of a barrel being firmly set in the frame of a gun during the time when the bullet is leaving the gun, and its ability to return to that position for each succeeding shot, cannot be overestimated. Therefore, the gunsmith should bear this fact in mind when dealing with inaccuracy trouble in any make, model or caliber of automatic pistol which is of the semi-fixed barrel type. Although the position of the parts might be somewhat different from the .45 Government Model, the aforementioned factors affecting accuracy should be checked.

As a final note to this chapter, the writer strongly recommends to the gunsmith who prides himself on knowing that each and every gun that leaves his shop is mechanically perfect to the extent where the user, be he bank guard or peace officer, can depend on his weapon, the practice of test firing the weapon with its own magazine. By this small expenditure of a few pennies and minutes, the gunsmith can return each pistol so tested with the personal satisfaction of knowing that he would depend on it as a means of personal protection if he were the customer.

An excellent book on the theory of operation and particular features of almost all popular automatic pistols is "Textbook of Automatic Pistols," by R. K. Wilson. From this work, which is profusely illustrated, the gunsmith or inventor can learn a great deal about specific peculiarities common to virtually every type of pistol that he will ever have occasion to repair.

CHAPTER THIRTEEN

RIFLE REPAIRS

WHILE there is a great variety in the makes, models and calibers of modern rifles that can logically reach the gunsmith's shop, from the standpoint of repair they can all be pretty much classified under five general headings (See Figure 77). And although there are variations as to the shape and size of parts in different makes of the same type of gun, the gunsmith who is familiar with the principles of operation as outlined in Chapter Five should not find it beyond his capacities to diagnose troubles and effect corrective action on any rifles presented to him for repair. This does not mean that the mechanic can approach any weapon, no matter how strange to his talents, breeze through an analysis, disassemble it, repair it and reassemble it without a hitch. It does mean, however, that the gunsmith with a good theoretical background and good sense of logic can accomplish any repair job on any strange gun in an efficient and profitable manner.

Headspace and Headspace Gages

Aside from the general repairs, such as trigger pull adjustment, stock work, sight mounting, action smoothing up, and blueing performed on rifles, which are covered in detail in other chapters of this book, there are certain phases of rifle repair which warrant specific discussion, and prime among these is the matter of barreling work.

Before attempting a barrelling job, the gunsmith should thoroughly understand the matter of headspace as outlined in Chapter Five for headspace not only affects the accuracy of a rifle but, more important, it has a direct bearing on the safety of the weapon. And, since turning out a safe gun should be the first consideration of any gunsmith, no halfway processes in the matter of securing correct headspace can be condoned.

Actually, since it would be financially prohibitive for the small shop gunsmith to have a set of headspace gages suitable

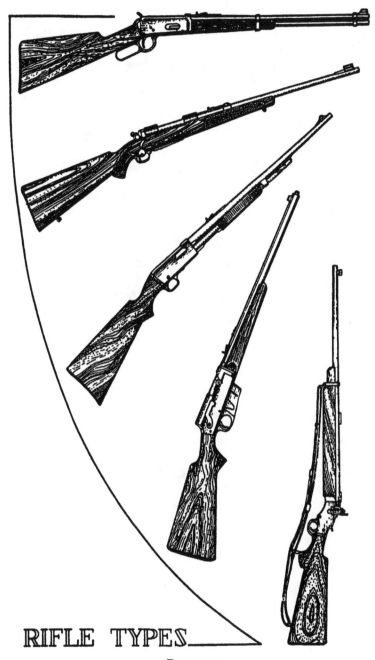

RIFLE TYPES

FIGURE 77

for all caliber rifles, the following alternative method of gaging headspace is suggested for those mechanics who do rebarrelling of rifles, but who do not have regular gages.

On rifles chambered for rimmed cartridges, such as the .22 rim fire, the .22 Hornet, the .303 British, et al, headspace measurement is computed as that distance from the rear face of the barrel (or rim counterbore) to the face of the bolt when the latter is fully closed and locked (See Figure 78). Thus when a rimmed

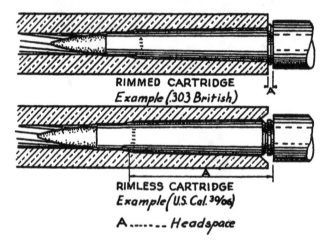

RIMMED CARTRIDGE
Example (.303 British)

RIMLESS CARTRIDGE
Example (U.S. Cal. 30/06)

A .... Headspace

MEASUREMENT of HEADSPACE

Figure 78

cartridge is fully seated in the chamber, the rim, under ideal conditions, should occupy all of distance "A" (Figure 78). If it does not, then the rear end of the cartridge case has some degree of latitude to move against the rear face of the bolt. Up to a certain extent, this rearward movement can be tolerated; beyond that point it is dangerous.

When a new barrel is installed in a rifle chambered for a center fire rimmed cartridge, the maximum allowable headspace should be average rim thickness plus $6/1000''$.

Average Rim Thickness. Average rim thickness is obtained by measuring the rims of at least three new cartridges, from two or three different brands and averaging out the results. For example, say that the rims of three Remington cartridges of a particular caliber measure $59/1000''$, $60/1000''$, and $58/1000''$; rims on cartridges of Western manufacture measure $59/1000''$,

$59/1000''$ and $61/1000''$; while those of foreign manufacture in the same caliber measure $59/1000''$, $62/1000''$ and $58/1000''$. By adding these nine figures together we get $535/1000''$, then after dividing nine into it, we find the average rim size of the particular cartridge to be approximately $59/1000''$. Thus, the rim on the "no-go" gage should measure $65/1000''$; that is, average rim size $59/1000''$, plus maximum allowable tolerance of $6/1000''$.

To make headspace gages for the above rimmed cartridge (or for any other rimmed type cartridge using, of course, different measurements) select two new cartridges and fire them, being careful not to mar or dent the cases when they are introduced into or ejected from the rifle. Knock out the fired primer by means of a drift punch inserted in the vent hole which is accessible from the inside of the case.

The "Go" Gage. Next, turn down the rim of one case until it measures $58/1000''$ ($1/1000''$ less than average rim size); this will be the minimum, or "go" gage. In other words, the bolt of a gun must close and lock with ordinary operating pressure on the minimum gage.

The "No Go" Gage. The maximum, or "no-go" gage, is made by sweating a piece of steel stock, the same diameter as the rim, to the base of the cartridge. This piece should be about $1/100''$ thick so that a few thousandths can be turned off it to desired size after it has been sweated in place. In this way the face which comes to bear on the bolt face will be true and smooth.

As a final step, a $1/8''$ hole should be drilled through the steel shim so that it meets the primer pocket. Then if the firing pin is accidentally snapped when the cartridge gage is in the chamber no harm will be done to either firing pin or gage.

In affixing the steel shim to the cartridge case, coat both the base of the cartridge case and one side of the shim with a very light film of solder, then place both tinned sides together and apply enough heat to melt the solder. At that point press them together until the solder cools to point of hardening. Any excess solder that oozes out between the joint can be trimmed off when the shim face is being turned. Incidentally, one of the best ways of holding the cartridge case in either chuck or collet is to press a short length of steel, about $1''$ long, into the neck of the case so that its end does not protrude beyond the mouth of the case. When this piece, which should be of such a diameter as to require pressing in place, is seated, it precludes the possibility of the cartridge neck being crushed or deformed when chucked up or being used as a gage.

In using these alternative headspace gages or, for that matter, any headspace gage, the bolt of the rifle should not be forced, rather only a "feel" amount of pressure need be applied. Too, the extractor should be removed from a bolt when a headspace gage is being used. This not only prevents damage to the gage but also to the usually brittle extractor.

On rifles chambered for rimless cartridges, such as the .30/06, the .257 Remington Roberts and the .270, headspace is measured from the face of the bolt to a point approximately half-way down on the forward taper of the shoulder (Point A, Figure 78).

To take this measurement with instruments ordinarily available at the small gunsmithing shop is near impossible. Therefore, the gunsmith who proposes to do rebarrelling work on rifles chambered for rimless cartridges should, if he does not choose to purchase regular hardened and tempered steel gages, convert *unfired* cases, with the bullets pulled and the primers fired, into gages.

With two cases so prepared, one should be used as a minimum gage. The other, with a $\frac{4}{1000}''$ steel shim sweated to its base, can serve as maximum, or "no-go" gage. Including the one or two thousandths that will be taken up by the solder, the shimmed case should measure about $\frac{6}{1000}''$ longer than the "no-go" gage. The best way to check this measurement is to mike the "rims" of both cases. To do this it might at times be necessary to grind a slight flat on the body of the case just forward of the extractor groove so the micrometer can be brought into place.

It will be noted that in the instructions for making rimless case gages the cartridge case should be disassembled from the bullet rather than fired. This is suggested so that the gunsmith will not be using an expanded case as a gage. Such a case would give an altogether false reading and would be worthless.

In outlining the procedure for making headspace gages from cartridge cases, this writer is not trying to convey the impression that such gages are as good as a standard steel gage. However, when correctly made and used, they do serve very well to indicate relative headspace on any given caliber of rifle. At best, these cartridge case gages, which are made from soft brass capped with non-hardened steel, are good only for two or three barrelling jobs where they have to be used three or four times on each job. For safety's sake, gages so made should be checked with a micrometer before and after each job and immediately discarded when they are more than $\frac{1}{1000}''$ off from desired measurement. This might sound like a very small variation but since these gages are not held to the tolerance of, or made as well as factory ones, such precautions are imperative.

After the barrel has been fitted to a rifle and screwed fully into place, the headspace gages are then used to determine if the headspace is all right. They can also be used in making a routine headspace check on a rifle that is suspected of having insufficient or excessive headspace.

Using the Headspace Gage. With the extractor removed from the bolt, slide the minimum, or "go" gage into the chamber of the gun, first having made sure that the chamber and bolt face are free from oil and any other foreign matter. Gently apply force to the bolt handle, lever, or whatever closing mechanism it might be, depending upon the type of rifle—the bolt should close freely and lock readily on this gage. If it does not, then the rifle has insufficient headspace. This means that the chamber must be reamed out a trifle more so that the cartridge case will seat a bit more deeply. And, unless the gunsmith has a chambering and throating reamer for this particular caliber, it means that the barrel must be sent to the factory or sub-contracted to another gunsmith who has this tool.

Although the condition of insufficient headspace is mentioned here as a possibility in rebarrelling work, it does not very often occur. However, it is well for the gunsmith to know just what significance it has if it does crop up.

Excessive Headspace. If the "go" gage gives a favorable reading, then the maximum, or "no-go" gage, should be inserted in the chamber and the bolt or other breech mechanism gently eased into the closing position. With this gage in the chamber, the bolt should *not* close and lock. If it does, then the gun has excessive headspace and means that a ruptured cartridge case might be the result if the rifle is fired in that condition.

If the barrel is of such a design that there is no extractor groove in it and it does have a fixed front sight or dovetail bases, then it is possible, when excessive headspace is encountered, to remove the barrel from the gun and turn a few thousandths of an inch from the shoulder that contacts the receiver. In this way the barrel can be screwed a bit further into the receiver, thus decreasing the tolerance between the bolt face and the rear face of the barrel.

This same operation can also be performed on any barrel which has an extractor groove cut in it or with a fixed sight, but since these points must again be brought into proper alignment with the extractor and rear sight respectively, it means that enough metal must be removed from the shoulder so that another complete turn of the barrel can be made. On top of this, the chamber must also be deepened to compensate for the amount of metal that of necessity would have to be removed from the rear barrel face so that minimum headspace could be achieved, because when a normal rifle barrel's screwed-in length is increased by the pitch of one thread, it is usually so much that a condition of insufficient headspace occurs.

Again, if the gunsmith does not have chambering tools, he must send the barrel to someone who has the proper tools to complete the job.

Selective Assembly. It might be of interest here to point out that the condition of excessive headspace can often be overcome by means of selective assembly, i.e., trying different bolts in a gun until one is found that fits within the limits of safe headspace. This system is used very extensively in ordnance repair shops at military installations on such guns as the Springfield 1903 and the Garand (M1 Rifle). However, when a rifle which is listed as having excessive headspace is brought in for repair, the inspector or armorer uses a field test bolt (master bolt held to very exact measurements) with his "no-go" headspace gage. If the test bolt closes on the gage, then indications are that replacement with a new bolt will not correct the deficiency and a new barrel must be installed. If, on the other hand, the test bolt does not close and lock on the "no-go" gage, then various new bolts (which, because of allowable manufacturing tolerance, vary in size) are tried until correct headspace is achieved.

For the small shop gunsmith a practice of this sort is somewhat out of the question since the cost of having a few dozen bolts on hand for each different weapon would be very expensive. Too, it would scarcely be worthwhile inasmuch as rifles having excessive headspace are hardly an everyday occurrence in the neighborhood gunsmith shop.

Headspace on the .22 Rim Fire. In the precautions just outlined, no mention was made of the universally popular .22 caliber rim fire rifle. However, this does not mean that this caliber gun, because of its small appearing cartridge and generally underestimated power, is exempt from considerations and precautions in the matter of headspace. As a matter of fact, headspace is considered so important in the famous Springfield .22 caliber rifle, which was sold through the director of Civilian Marksmanship to National Rifle Association members, that a mechanical arrangement is provided on the bolts of the M2 models so that the headspace adjustment can be made by qualified ordnance personnel. As a matter of standard operating procedure during the inspection of any Army owned .22 caliber rifle, the ordnance inspector checks the headspace of all such weapons, be they of Springfield or commercial manufacture.

If a commercial .22 is found to have excessive headspace then the rifle is withdrawn from service and sent to an arsenal or base shop for correction. If a Springfield .22 is found which allows the bolt to close on the "no-go" gage or does not close and lock on a "go" gage, then it is deemed to be in need of adjustment.

Headspace on the Springfield .22 Caliber. In Figure 79 there is illustrated the mechanism by which headspace is adjusted on the M1922, M2 Springfield .22 caliber rifle. From time to time the gunsmith is apt to be confronted with one of these rifles for

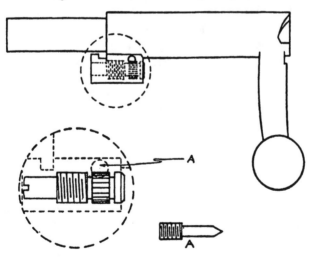

HEADSPACE ADJUSTING MECHANISM

FIGURE 79

repair and it is well that he should know how to make headspace adjustment on them.

On some of the earlier model Springfield .22's the headspace adjusting screw was of the conventional type, i.e., standard screw with milled slot in head. However, it was found that persons who were not qualified often tampered with this screw and changed the adjustment. Therefore, on later models the Ordnance Department substituted an "Allen Type" screw so that a special hexagonal wrench would be required to make an adjustment. However, on either type, headspace is adjusted in the same way.

If a Springfield .22 is found, after examination, to have excessive headspace, then the bolt handle should be disassembled from the bolt assembly and the headspace adjusting screw locking plug (B) knocked out with a drift punch. The headspace adjusting screw can then be tightened up a fraction of a turn, which advances the front portion of the screw so that it will bear more against the receiver and thus force the entire bolt nearer to the rear face of the barrel. After the first adjustment, the bolt should be reassembled and tried again with the headspace gage. If it proves to be satisfactory, then the headspace adjusting screw locking plug must be put back in place, thus insuring that the screw will not jar loose. If the first turn of the screw does not correct the condition, repeated adjustments must be made until proper headspace, as indicated by the gage, is achieved.

The same procedure as just outlined also applies on this type of rifle when the condition of insufficient headspace is encountered, except that the adjusting screw must be turned to the left so that the bolt will be moved farther away from the rear barrel face.

On commercially made .22's, there is no provision for making headspace adjustment other than by changing the barrel or bolt of the gun. Therefore, if a gunsmith is presented with a rifle of this class and the customer complains of ruptured cartridge cases or gas spitting back around the bolt when the gun is fired, the gunsmith should put his "no-go" gage to work. If excessive headspace proves to be the fault, then the customer should have the entire situation explained to him. If the explanation is presented in the correct manner, the customer will generally be quite willing to spend a few dollars for a new bolt, unless, of course, the rifle is of the $6.00 variety and hardly worth repairing. In any case however, the matter should not be passed off as insignificant, nor should any makeshift or compromise repair be made.

Making .22 Headspace Gages. Headspace gages for the .22 rim fire rifle are illustrated in Figure 9, and can be made by any gunsmith who owns a lathe. Needless to say, the indicated dimensions must be followed to the letter in order that the gages may give accurate readings. If a grinding attachment for the lathe is available the gage should be made from tool steel, then turned slightly oversize, hardened, tempered and ground to size. However, if the gunsmith does not have a grinding attachment, the gage should be turned from mild steel, highly polished and then case-hardened. After case-hardening, all vital dimensions should be rechecked to make certain that warpage or scale has not affected them. Usually slight variations in size can be rectified by a bit of hand honing with a fine stone.

When using the .22 caliber headspace gage, always remember to remove the extractor and cartridge guide from the bolt or insert the gage from under the bolt in such a way as to prevent having to snap the extractor or guide over the brittle rim of the gage.

Also remember that the trigger of a gun should never be snapped when a headspace gage is in the chamber.

This is doubly important on .22 caliber rim fire weapons since no provision can be made on gages for this gun to make a recess or hole where the firing pin is apt to strike.

Installing and Removing Barrels

Gun owners do not always desire to change the barrels in their rifles simply because they are worn or badly pitted. Often they prefer a rifled tube which is heavier, or of greater length, or even of a different caliber, which can be adapted to the action under consideration. Nevertheless, no matter what reason prompts a gun owner to ask for a rebarrelling job, the gunsmith must know beforehand just what is wanted and just what the owner expects in the way of a finished job.

Special Considerations. True enough, on some jobs, such as fitting a new barrel to an inexpensive .22 rifle, there exists little or no need for lengthy discussion, but where a customer expects better grouping or almost impossible new weapon life from a new barrel, there are points which must be discussed and understood by both customer and gunsmith before any actual mechanical work takes place.

First and foremost is the matter of barrel selection. This must cover the exact length, type (straight, round, tapered, heavy weight, standard weight, octagonal, et cetera), desired by the customer. It is important that this be known since the barrel the customer might have in mind might not be of factory standard and would therefore have to be custom-built by a barrel specialist. Such a selection would naturally influence the price of the finished job and the length of time required to complete the work.

Secondly, agreement must be concluded as to what type sighting equipment will be required on the newly barrelled gun. If a standard factory barrel is being installed, this will be a small matter but if a special type barrel is to be fitted, then provisions as to cost and type of sights must be made beforehand.

Lastly, and of equal importance, is the matter of secondary alterations—those repairs and work which become necessary after a main job has been performed. For example, if a customer wants a heavy barrel put on a rifle which formerly had a standard barrel on it, then it is usually necessary to enlarge certain portions of the forearm to accommodate the new and larger diameter barrel. Also, a new barrel band, handguard, extractor or magazine modification might be required. All this must be anticipated and settled by the gunsmith before he can agree to rebarrel a rifle to a customer's satisfaction.

Thus, when all factors are considered, the novice gunsmith should easily understand why it is not only desirable but imperative to know what he is up against before he glibly agrees to rebarrel a gun for barrel cost plus a few hours labor time. As mentioned earlier in this book, it is much easier to reduce the price on a job when the customer comes to call for it than it is to hem and haw and beg for a few dollars above the original estimate just in order to come out somewhere near even on the transaction.

Pinned in Barrels. On some of the inexpensive .22 caliber rim fire rifles, barrels are retained in the receiver by means of a snug fit between contacting surfaces, augmented by a pin driven through both receiver and barrel. Removal of a barrel from a rifle of this type necessitates only drifting out of the pin; then the barrel can be freed from the receiver by simply pulling it loose. Installation of a new barrel is just as easily accomplished, though occasionally it might be found necessary to turn a few thousandths off the shoulder or periphery of the barrel where it fits into the receiver. Headspace adjustment can quickly be made on threadless barrels since it is only a matter of turning down or shimming up the shoulder to secure the proper tolerance between bolt face and rear face of the barrel.

Screwed in Barrels. If all rifle barrels were held in the receiver or frame by means of a pin the problem of their removal and installation would indeed be a simple one. However, since the majority of them are tightly screwed in place, the gunsmith must be equipped and qualified to cope with the most obstinate combinations that he might possibly encounter on any job. And as a fair warning it should be stated that some barrels, especially those on old foreign military rifles, often are so tightly screwed in place that it seems to the gunsmith who attempts removal that the barrel and receiver are welded together. This fact is here mentioned because this writer has read numerous articles in which the author, all too frequently an amateur, covers the subject of barrel removal in a sentence or two, leaving the novice with the impression that barrels can be screwed out and in with little or no effort or special tools. Such statements are either the figment of someone's imagination or a cover-up of the true difficulty of such a job. At gun factories, government arsenals and military base shops the matter of barrel changing on rifles is regarded as a major operation and only skilled personnel and the best of special tools and equipment are used to insure a first class job being turned out. Therefore, the gunsmith who is faced with his first barrelling job should not be inclined to underestimate the work involved or possible hitches that can crop up.

Barrel Vise. For barrel changing work of most any type the first requirement in the matter of tools is a good barrel vise sturdily affixed to a solid bench or table. There is no substitute for this tool and the Pacific Barrel Vice retailing in the neighborhood of $15.00 has been a standby of gunsmiths for years. No doubt a barrel vise can be constructed by an enterprising mechanic but chances are that it would cost twice as much in the long run and not be superior to this commercial model.

Receiver Wrenches. All reports to the contrary notwithstanding, there is no single wrench made to date which can be used for unscrewing all receivers from barrels. Actually the Stilson type wrench can be fitted around most any size or shape of receiver but the slightest amount of pressure on this type of wrench and whatever it bears upon is immediately engraved by some marks which can scarcely be considered of a beautifying nature. Unquestionably the Stilson wrench was a great invention but it definitely has no place in the gunsmith's tool collection for barrelling work.

The size and shape of the wrench to be used on a rifle receiver depends entirely upon the shape of the receiver at the point where the wrench is to be used and the wrench must be made to order by the gunsmith, or, if he does not have facilities, by a blacksmith or machinist. This may seem to be an expensive proposition at first glance but in reality it is not, for a barrelling job can be done in a fraction of the time by using the proper wrench and barrel vise, rather than a Stilson wrench and a light bench vise. Also, with improper tools there is always the chance of marring the barrel and receiver so that cover-up work must be done—at the gunsmith's expense.

The receiver wrench shown in Figure 28 is for a Springfield rifle and should serve to illustrate how simply such an efficient tool can be made. Wrenches for the Enfield and Mauser rifles and various other commercially made bolt action weapons can be made in the same way. Knowing the basic style and principle of receiver wrenches the gunsmith should be able to fashion a receiver wrench for almost any type of rifle. However, in designing and making a receiver wrench there are a few points which must be remembered:

1) Always make the wrench to fit around the strongest portion of the receiver and as close to the rear of the barrel as possible.

2) On high-side walled receivers, such as a lever action rifle, steel blocks should be employed if the wrench is so made that it will bear on an unsupported wall section. Such blocks should have smooth surfaces and be held to close dimensions.

3) Avoid the occurrence of knife edged corners on the inside of the wrench where it comes against finished surfaces of the receiver. Put a very slight chamfer on such corners so they will not have a tendency to cut into the receiver when pressure is applied.

4) Hold the dimensions of the wrench to as close tolerance as possible so that there will be no tendency for it to slip and bind on the receiver or spring the wrench.

5) From the drawing of the Springfield Receiver Wrench it can be seen that cut-outs must be made in the wrench so that it can pass over projections on the receiver in order that the wrench

can be brought to bear at the proper position. These cut-outs should be made only as large as need be and their dimensions held to close tolerance lest there be weak spots in the wrench.

6) The handle on a receiver wrench should be both strong and so made that it can be handled comfortably. Wooden grips, made from walnut scrap, and finished to a smooth splinterless surface, should be affixed to the last six or eight inches on the metal handle, which, incidentally, should be about 18″ long for maximum efficiency. This will afford ample leverage and when a receiver does not budge under influence of such force, then the gunsmith should proceed slowly so that no damage to the receiver will occur. Hammering or jerking on the receiver wrench should be avoided since such a procedure might easily result in springing or cracking the receiver. For the same reason additional leverage in the form of a pipe attached to the handle cannot be recommended except for the most obstinate cases where all other means fail.

Before Removing a Barrel. Before removing the barrel from a rifle the entire weapon should be disassembled. Subassemblies of the gun need not be taken apart but all mechanism in the receiver, the stock and other wood components and magazine tubes must be removed so that they will not be subject to torque, stress or accidental injury. These same precautions likewise are in order when a barrel is being put into a rifle since the same possibility of injury to parts exists.

While removal of a barrel is essentially a simple operation when the proper tools are available, the possibilities of some little hitch cropping up cannot be totally ruled out. As mentioned previously, a stubborn barrel, i.e. one that resists all normal effort at dislodgment, can cause the gunsmith many anxious moments when things do not proceed according to preconceived notion. During such moments the gunsmith should not be tempted to resort to drastic sledge hammer tactics. Almost invariably this latter course of action culminates more in disappointments than in results. In barrelling work, as well as almost any phase of gunsmithing, there is no substitute for carefully engineered procedure based on preliminary analysis of the job at hand.

When the barrel of a rifle is firmly held in the barrel vise, and the correct receiver wrench is being used, and still the barrel cannot be loosened, then it is permissible to apply a bit of heat to the receiver threads with a Bunsen burner or alcohol torch. The amount of heat applied depends upon the weight of the metal which must be affected. All in all, the receiver should not be heated to a red or blue heat, but rather to a point where smoke starts to issue from between the barrel and receiver. This will indicate that any oil or similar compound existing between the threads is now in a very fluid state and not acting as a binding agent. Generally, the application of limited heat will aid in dislodging any barrel, no matter how firmly it is in place. Also, it might be well to remind the gunsmith that he should first check to see that no pins or screws are in place that might possibly hinder the loosening of the barrel.

While it is a well known fact that few, if any, manufacturers use any such devices to hold a rifle barrel in place, it is always possible that some gunsmith or erstwhile gun mechanic might have installed the barrel in the gun and, being unable to achieve a tight fit, resorted to pinning or screwing it in place. This writer has even encountered rifles in which the barrel and receiver had been soldered in place. Though such methods of holding barrel to receiver are uncommon, and almost unheard of among high grade manufacturers, the possibilities of their existence cannot be entirely ruled out since the rifle may have been in the hands of a half dozen would-be gunsmiths before it reaches the bench of a competent workman. Therefore it behooves the gunsmith who encounters a tough combination to explore every possible avenue of resistance.

Using the Receiver Wrench. In using the receiver wrench, apply force in a gradual manner rather than by a sudden jerk so that neither wrench nor receiver will be sprung or broken. Also, make sure that the barrel is held as tightly as possible in the vise. This does not mean that the vise must be tightened to the extent where it will bend the barrel but it must be tight enough so the barrel will not be scarred as a result of its being too loose.

After Removal. After the barrel has been removed the threads in the receiver should be checked for deformation. If deformed in any way a specially formed scraper can be ground from an old file and the threads restored to correct shape and dimensions. Then a solvent such as carbon tetrachloride or gasoline can be used on a toothbrush to clean away all accumulated foreign matter such as dried oil, dirt and metal chips. Similarly, any burrs on the shoulder of the receiver should be removed with a fine file or small honing stone, exercising care, so as not to remove any more than is absolutely necessary from this vital point.

Installing a Barrel. When putting a new barrel into the receiver, the threads of the barrel should be cleaned with a solvent of some sort and then chased with a file or stone where burrs or flats exist. Too, a film of light oil should be applied to the threads on both barrel and receiver.

Before attempting to screw the barrel into the receiver by means of barrel vise and receiver wrench the barrel should be turned in by hand to see how far it will go. If it screws up easily by hand to, say within a turn or two of the receiver, then the vise and wrench setup can be brought into play to complete the job. However, if it is very difficult to screw the barrel up even a few turns, then indications are that the barrel will be very tight going in all the way. Frequently it will be found necessary to chase the threads lightly with a fine file so that the barrel can be started into the receiver. However, under no circumstances should chasing, filing or cutting be done on the threads of the receiver unless they are definitely deformed in some way. In short, all cutting and honing should be performed on the barrel.

As a matter of fact, this admonition applies to any type of part fitting where the receiver is involved. For example, if a bolt or ejector is being fitted to the receiver, then all filing and cutting should be done on the parts being fitted unless, of course, some portion of the receiver is banged up to the extent where it would normally require fixing or adjustment.

Drawing up a Barrel. If a barrel, when drawn up fully to the receiver shoulder, is at such a position that the fixed sight or extractor grooves are not in correct position, then adjustment must be effected to achieve proper alignment.

Where the barrel overshoots its draw mark a shim must be placed between the barrel shoulder and receiver. The shim should preferably be made from stainless steel so that it will not rust and bind between the barrel and receiver. If it is not possible to secure stainless steel then brass shim stock should be used. Only as a last resort should mild steel be used for shim stock.

In some writings it is often recommended that the shoulder of the barrel be peened over instead of using a shim. This prac-tice can only be recommended where the gunsmith is willing to turn down, polish off and blue the shoulder of the barrel after he has peened it over. This will at least insure a workmanlike job showing no series of hammer dents around the barrel shoulder periphery.

In cases where the barrel is of such dimensions that it does not even come up to the draw mark on the receiver then some metal must be removed from the rear face of the barrel shoulder so that full draw up can be achieved. A good idea of how much metal must be removed to insure proper draw up can be very closely calculated by a simple means. For example, let us presume that a barrel having 16 threads per inch draws up to within $\frac{1}{4}$ turn of the draw mark. By simple figuring, we can see that one complete turn of the barrel advances it $\frac{1}{16}''$. One quarter of this amount is $\frac{1}{64}''$. Therefore if $\frac{1}{64}''$ is removed from the barrel shoulder rear face, the barrel should draw up to correct position.

Often the gunsmith will find it helpful, when fitting a new barrel to a receiver of the Mauser type, to measure the distance from the shoulder to the rear face of the chamber on the old barrel and use these dimensions as somewhat of a guide in bringing the new barrel up to correct size.

After Installing a Barrel. Immediately after the barrel has been fitted, the bolt, with extractor in place, should be put in the gun and slowly pushed towards the rear barrel face. If the extractor fits nicely into its corresponding groove in the barrel, then the "go" and "no-go" headspace gages should be tried. If they do not reveal any deficiencies, then the barrelling job can be considered as being complete except for the setting in place of the sights.

On the other hand, should the extractor not fit properly in place, then the barrel must be moved in the indicated direction, i.e., forward or backward, to effect a proper fit.

If the headspace is not up to requirements then the instructions and methods outlined earlier in this chapter should be followed.

Final check on the new barrel should include running of a clip of dummy cartridges through the magazine so as to make sure that abutments on the new barrel do not interfere with the feeding process. This is especially true of certain autoloading weapons which have a ramp on the barrel that serves to guide the cartridges from the magazine into the chamber. It is imperative that this ramp be in proper alignment with the magazine follower and also be very highly polished so that bullets will not catch on its surface and interfere with the normal process of feeding.

Another point to be observed, especially on bolt action rifles of the Springfield or Mauser design, is that of marks on the rear barrel face caused by the front of the extractor riding against this area. This is not infrequently caused by a burr on the face of the extractor or rear barrel face. In either case it is cured by stoning or filing the burrs from the offending surface.

When a new barrel is put in a rim fire rifle, the firing pin should not be snapped until test or measurements indicate that the nose of the firing pin does not contact the rear face of the barrel. If it does, then a few thousandths of an inch must be turned off the barrel face until such a condition no longer exists. Few things can ruin a rim fire barrel faster than an oversized firing pin or barrel which allows a gash to be made around the chamber that invariably interferes with feeding, ignition and extraction and if permitted to exist it will also cause inaccuracy. The proper care of this "anvil" is of first importance.

Ailments Common to Each Type Rifle

Although it would require many volumes to list all the possible malfunctions that might occur on every make and type of rifle, none of them should be beyond the diagnosing and repair ability of the gunsmith who fully understands their theory of functioning as outlined in Chapter Five. Yet there are some particular points concerning malfunctioning and disassembly on various types of rifles that occur more frequently than others, and these warrant more extended and specific consideration.

For purposes of easier delineation and understanding, each general type of weapon will be considered individually, i.e., Bolt, Lever, Autoloading and Pump.

Bolt Action Rifles. With bolt action rifles of the military style, i.e., Springfield or Mauser, it is most important that the trigger guard be always screwed tightly in place. A loose trigger guard can result in very poor accuracy since the barrel under such circumstances is free to wobble around under the influence of loading and firing. Also, a loose trigger guard can be the cause of malfunctions in magazine feeding as a result of the bullet point catching between the underside of the receiver ramp and top of the trigger guard body. Even when the trigger guard screws are tightly screwed up and feeding troubles are encountered, it is not beyond the realm of possibility that the trigger guard is in at an angle.

Corrective action involves removal of both the trigger guard and the guard screws. Then the guard should be replaced and carefully tapped into full seating position with a rawhide or wooden mallet. The screws should both be put in place at the same time and each tightened alternately. In this way there will be no tendency for the guard to be tightened up at an angle.

Occasionally it will be found necessary to use a wood chisel or scraper to cut away a little wood that interferes with the proper seating of the trigger guard. This should be done slowly and carefully so as not to remove any more wood than is absolutely essential to insure a perfect fit.

For best results on any metal-in-wood fitting of this sort some coloring agent such as prussian blue in oil should be coated on the metal surfaces which contact the wood. Thus, when the coated metal surface is moved into the place where it fits, some of the color will be transferred to the points on the wood which are rubbing against the metal. This operation is known as "spotting in" and the points which become coated as a result of contact are referred to as "high spots." The prussian blue, which is obtainable at almost any hardware or paint store, should be of very thin consistency so that it can be applied easily as a coating of microscopic thickness.

When a bolt action of the type having a fixed magazine throws cartridges up from the magazine two at a time, then either the follower is worn, the magazine spring is defective, or that portion of the receiver opening where the cartridges pass through is badly worn. The first two can be quickly corrected by changing the offending part. The worn receiver poses a bit more of a problem, however, since it is nearly impossible to add metal to this portion of the gun successfully, though often it will be found that a new or slightly oversize follower will remedy the defect. When it does not, then there is little that can be done other than to use the rifle as a single loader or take a chance with it as is. This condition of worn receiver above the magazine well does not occur very frequently, but when a gunsmith is confronted with a gun having such an ailment, he should recognize it quickly and not waste a great deal of time trying to get it to work right.

On a Springfield .30/06 rifle if the front of the bolt is very difficult, if not near impossible, to introduce into the receiver, then either the ejector is broken or burred on its rear portion or the locking lug on the bolt which has a slot in it that passes between the ejector is badly burred. To correct the first fault, just remove the stock from the rifle, knock out the ejector pin and put in a new ejector. If the slot is burred or turned over from pounding against the cut-off, then file away the peened over metal with a thin file but do not enlarge the slot any more than is necessary.

A sluggish moving bolt on a Springfield rifle can often be traced to the presence of what is known as a bolt stop. A bolt stop is a part that was inserted up from under the receiver, through the bolt slide near the ejector, on early Springfield .30/06's, but eliminated on those of later manufacture. When the projecting part of this bolt stop becomes worn or deformed, it often interferes with free bolt movement and should be removed, and since it actually serves no important purpose, the gunsmith should never hesitate to remove it when he suspects it to be a source of trouble.

Sometimes when the bolt on a Mauser type rifle is difficult to lift up or close, the trouble can be traced to a tight extractor collar. Corrective action for a deficiency of this type is simple and involves: first, removal of the extractor; second, placing the bolt between two blocks of wood in a vise with the wood pressing against the collar; third, forcing graphite grease between the collar and bolt body; fourth, insertion of a dowel rod, which has previously been chucked in a hand drill, into the deep hole in the bolt which normally houses the firing pin mechanism, and then rotating the drill (and bolt), thus loosening up the extractor collar (See Figure 80).

Rough bolt action can also be caused by the presence of burrs or scars on either the camming surfaces of the bolt or cocking piece. In either case stoning of the parts with a fine oilstone should produce satisfactory results. However, in some cases where the damage is extensive, it might be necessary to replace either one or both of the offending parts. Files should never be used on the working cocking surfaces of either of these parts, for the resulting surface (if the file even cuts them) would be so rough as to preclude a smooth working surface.

As to general disassembly, there is probably no class of weapons easier to take apart than bolt action rifles. Most of them, with the exception of the .22 rim fire variety, are of military design and as such are of necessity simple and rugged. Removal of the bolt is usually accomplished by either pulling back on the trigger, or releasing a catch located on the left side of the receiver, or both.

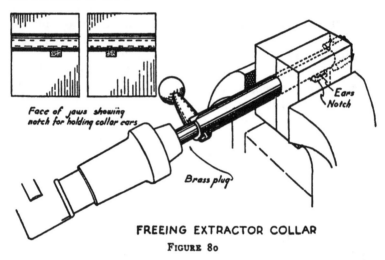

Face of jaws showing notch for holding collar ears

Brass plug

Ears
Notch

FREEING EXTRACTOR COLLAR
FIGURE 80

The bolt in turn can best be disassembled by cocking the gun, throwing the safety to the "on" position, and then unscrewing the cocking piece. This will free the firing pin, and firing pin spring, which in turn is completely disassembled by drawing back the firing pin sleeve and lifting off the striker (in the case of the Springfield .30/06) or by turning the cocking piece one quarter of a turn (in the case of an Enfield or Mauser rifle).

The extractor on most all military rifles is removed by turning the extractor around on the bolt until it can be disengaged and slid forward and off. When putting the extractor on, it will often be found necessary to squeeze the extractor collar "T" together so the extractor can be put on easily and without damaging either collar or extractor.

On .22 caliber rim fire bolt action rifles, the bolt is generally disassembled by knocking out various straight pins which hold the extractor, cartridge guide, firing pin and cocking piece in place, and these present no particular problems.

Lever Action Rifles. When taking apart a lever action, the first part removed should be the stock. In this way, part of the receiver mechanism will be exposed, so the sequence of the succeeding steps can be more easily figured out if any doubt exists as to what part or assembly should be removed next.

Most trigger guard assemblies are held in place by a screw or pin, either of which must be taken out before the guard can be removed. Some guards can be lifted directly from the receiver, while others must be slid out towards the back of the gun. In either case it should be positively determined which way the guard comes off before resorting to any degree of force to dislodge it. The trigger guard on old guns, as a result of being in place for a number of years, is very difficult to remove because of the oil and dirt that have collected between it and the receiver. Nothing but a light rawhide or wooden mallet should be used to force the guard from its seating. Even then caution should be the watchword, for damage can be done to the trigger guard itself, which is generally of light construction and readily subject to bending.

To remove the breech bolt from most models of lever action rifles, it is first necessary to drive out the pin that connects the lever to the bolt. This pin is accessible for drifting out by means of a hole that is drilled through both sides of the receiver at the same relative position on either side. However, before the pin can be driven out, the lever must be actuated until the pin in the bolt can be lined up with the holes in the receiver. Once aligned, the pin can be pushed out with a drift punch.

Autoloading Rifles. Virtually all of the autoloading rifles on the legitimate commercial market nowadays are recoil operated, represented by the .22 rim fire of the straight blow-back type, and the long recoil type as represented by the Remington Model 8. From the gunsmith's standpoint neither type of autoloading rifle is any more difficult to repair than the bolt action, lever action or any of the other shoulder weapons. However, it might be well to point out that autoloading weapons, as a rule, must be kept cleaner and better lubricated than manually operated rifles.

Too, when a customer brings an autoloading weapon in for repair and claims that it will not feed, extract or eject, and preliminary visual examination reveals no defects, the next step is test firing with live ammunition. There is no substitute for this sort of testing in cases where diagnosis by other means does not bring to light the offending part or parts. Frequently, as pointed out elsewhere in the book, many malfunctions of an autoloading weapon can be traced to a rough or scarred chamber.

Also, and this is especially, though not alone true of foreign autoloading rifles and pistols, the ammunition can be the offending component. For not infrequently weapons of the autoloading type will be found to work best, and occasionally only, with a certain brand of cartridges. And while all otherwise unsolvable autoloading rifle troubles cannot always be blamed on the ammunition brand peculiarity, this factor should always be kept in mind when all other avenues of repair have been tried and proven to be fruitless.

Extractors on autoloading rifles must have the benefit of extra careful examination for they are subject to great strain and stress, and must be free from burrs, cracks and other sorts of deformation that might conceivably contribute to a malfunction in the weapon's operation.

Pump Action. Most pump action rifles have tubular magazines which can be a great source of provocation to the gunsmith when they get out of order. A very slight dent in the magazine tube can bring about a complete failure to feed, or in some cases cause sporadic feeding, i.e., the first one or two cartridges will come to the carrier and then the gun must be jarred to bring the next cartridge to the receiver feeding point.

Some magazine tubes are so constructed that slight dents can be pounded out in the same manner as on a shotgun barrel. Others, however, are too frail to endure very much pounding or stretching, and must be replaced. Nevertheless, no matter how the tube is made, an attempt should be made to pound out the dent for there is always the possibility that it can be repaired without ruining the tube. A point of caution: when a customer complains of poor feeding in a tubular magazine rifle, always check it with new cartridges to be sure that battered cartridge heads (from reloaded ammunition) that the customer might be using are not at the root of the trouble.

Another fault common to pump action rifles is that of the breech bolt not being locked when the gun is ready to fire. This can be caused by worn parts or, in rare cases, a collection of dirt and oxidized oil between the locking lug on the bolt and the locking recess in the receiver. To test for this fault, put a dummy cartridge into the magazine and feed it into the chamber of the gun. When the hammer is cocked, try hard to pull back on the forearm cocking piece. The breech bolt should not retract. If it does, explore the possibilities of collected dirt and foreign matter as mentioned above. Repeat the same testing operation and if the bolt retracts, then some vital part is either worn or broken and must be repaired or replaced. After taking corrective action, make the same test again to be sure that the work performed has been done correctly and thoroughly.

A worn sear or hammer notch can also cause trouble on a pump action rifle, if either is so far gone as to allow the hammer to fall when the breech bolt is actuated vigorously. To test for this, fill the magazine with dummy cartridges and actuate the pump mechanism very rapidly and with more than usual force. The hammer should not fall, even to half cock, so long as the finger is kept off the trigger. If the hammer falls to either half cock or full fire position during this test, then chances are that either the hammer or sear is worn and must be adjusted or replaced. Sometimes just a bit of honing on the sear or hammer (this will usually increase the trigger pull somewhat) will correct the fault. In rare cases a weak trigger spring or sear spring can cause the hammer to fall prematurely.

Safeties. On any rifle that comes in for repair the gunsmith should always test the safety. If it works, all well and good, but if it does not a note should be made and the customer informed when he returns so that the gunsmith will not be liable to censure if an accident occurs as a result of the defective safety. Most gun owners have a great deal of confidence in the safety on their rifle or, for that matter, any gun, and with the safety at the "on" position do not hesitate to apply pressure against the trigger and subject the weapon to jars that they would not risk if the safety was in the "off" position. Wrong as this sort of practice may be, there is very little the gunsmith can do about it other than to see that the safeties on all guns he repairs are in first class shape.

Unfortunately, not all gun safeties are of the best basic design and worse yet, are too often made of soft stamped out parts which become reduced in size at vital contact points. When these parts wear they should be replaced, even though the temptation to elongate or reshape them by pounding is very tempting. As a matter of fact, certain component parts of safeties of the cheaper variety can often be greatly improved by case-hardening them, for when so treated the parts are much less affected by normal wear and consequently last longer and serve their purpose more reliably. Very thin parts, that is, those which are less than $\frac{1}{16}''$ thick, cannot always be case-hardened successfully because of the high temperature required for this heat treating operation.

There is no room for improvisation or makeshift work on gun safeties and the sooner the gunsmith becomes aware of this fact, the sooner he will have taken a greater step nearer the goal of being a reliable craftsman.

Bedding. On inexpensive rifles the matter of bedding is of little or no concern since target group accuracy is almost out of the question. On target rifles and high power bolt action weapons, however, bedding is a matter of great consequence, for the accuracy of the piece is affected in no small way by it.

Broadly speaking, bedding concerns the matter of seating a barrel and receiver in the stock of a rifle. When a receiver and barrel are properly bedded, maximum accuracy, from a machine rest standpoint, is obtained. On the other hand, almost no good groups can be consistently expected if the bedding job is poorly done. Thus, when the gunsmith appreciates that bedding is largely a matter of hand fitting a barrel and receiver to a stock, he can fully realize why bedding cannot be taken into consideration on guns selling in the low price category, and also why these rifles cannot be expected to compare in group shooting qualities with more expensive weapons that are properly bedded.

Good bedding requires, among other things:

1) That those portions of the barrel and receiver which contact the stock lay properly in their place, i.e., not be forced into undersized recesses or be permitted to float around in oversized recesses.

2) That a bushing be provided for the trigger guard screws in bolt action rifles. Also, that the trigger guard screws or any other means of fastening the stock to the barrel and receiver be kept tight at all times.

3) That only the fore-end tip of the stock be permitted to bear against the barrel throughout its entire length of proximity to the stock, and the barrel so stationed that it can be pushed away from its resting point with a force of about five pounds. This will assure that the rifle is not barrel bound.

4) That no inletted portion of the stock be so cut as to force the barrel and receiver to a canted or off-center position when the screws are tightened up.

5) That the main bearing or bedding be against the recoil shoulder, which is there for that purpose.

6) That no accessories, such as sight bases, be so positioned that they tend to cant the barrel and receiver in the stock.

7) That the barrel band does not bear on the barrel in such a manner as to constrict its free movement. Actually, the barrel band should not bear on the top half of the barrel at all.

From the foregoing facts the gunsmith should be able to diagnose and make appropriate repairs to correct most causes of inaccuracy which stem from improper fitting between the wooden and metallic components. Often the gunsmith will find that sloppy inletting on a stock can cause the rifle to place shots all over a target, and that by shimming up here and cutting away a bit of wood there the better shooting qualities of the rifle can be brought to the fore.

All factors considered, though, it is safe to say that such matters as improper or defective sights, poor trigger pull, bad barrel, badly dimensioned stock and the human element should be investigated before the possibility of bad bedding is entertained too seriously.

Personal Safety

When anyone works with tools on any sort of mechanical equipment there is always the lurking danger of injury from improper handling of either the tools or equipment. Such incidents are usually referred to as "accidents." Actually, however, the word accident is somewhat of a misnomer, for an accident is defined by the dictionary as something happening by chance, and it is more often carelessness or thoughtlessness than chance that causes a person to be injured by a screwdriver, chisel, hammer or other tool. Tools that are kept in good condition not only make any job easier and mark the mechanic as a man of good training, but also greatly reduce the possibility of an accident. For example, a correctly ground screwdriver is far less liable to slip from a screw head slot than is one which has a malformed point, and in the same way a sharp chisel is much less likely to slip than is one having a dull edge or incorrectly ground bevel angle. These, of course, are only a few specific illustrations. Nevertheless, none of the others are any less potent as a means of causing injury to the person using them. Also, it should be borne in mind that tools in good condition will not alone prevent accidents unless these tools are properly handled.

Any screwdriver can cause a nasty gash if it slips and the mechanic's hand is in the tool's path of travel.

Around machinery personal dress can be an accident provoking factor. For example, loose clothing or a necktie can catch in running machinery and put a man out of work for days.

Under any circumstances an accident which causes injury to a person and causes him to lose time from his work is most regrettable, and when it occurs to a person who runs a one man business it is worse yet. Since the possibility of an accident occuring to anyone, in spite of all their good intentions and carefulness, is always present, the gunsmith who operates a business should investigate the matter of accident and health insurance so that he will receive some sort of income when forced to close his shop temporarily as the result of an accident. Any insurance agent of reputable standing in the community can provide all the necessary details as to the procurement and benefits realized from policy coverage of this type. The cost for such a policy can often be realized by charging as little as 5¢ extra on each repair job and setting aside this money to meet the policy premium when it comes due.

"What has all this to do with rifle repairs?", the reader might be tempted to ask at this point. Well, this writer will never forget a very serious finger slash he once suffered when hastily fitting the trigger guard assembly to the receiver of a Remington Model 8 autoloading rifle. Result—had to stay away from the shop for six days but learned that there are very few guns which do not have corners or edges capable of inflicting a very bad cut to the gunsmith's two really necessary tools, those hands of his.

CHAPTER FOURTEEN

Shotgun Repairs

DURING the course of a year there is probably no other type of weapon that will cross the gunsmith's counter in such quantity and variety as the shotgun—from the engraved, expensive British and German double barrel custom made jobs to the single shot eight dollar pride of a boy, to say nothing of the standard pump, lever, bolt and autoloading type in representative numbers. And like a mother chick with her brood the gunsmith must learn to know and love them all. Love yes, for woe betide the guncraftsman who publicly refers to some customer's pet type of scatter gun as being inferior to another type. While it is sensible practice to tell a customer that his damascus barrel job was not designed to handle modern loads and might blow the family heirloom apart if they are used, it is poor business practice to condemn a shotgun as being of an inferior type.

Although some hunters or skeet-shooters might take criticism about their weapons very lightly, there are others who are so sensitive that they might challenge the gunsmith to a shooting contest. So in the interest of customer relationship and continued prosperity, the gunsmith's best course of action is to be like a doctor who always agrees that each new baby he delivers is the acme of something or other.

Knowing these various shotguns is another thing, however, and though this phase is somewhat more difficult to master than the loving aspect, when mastered it is easier to carry on.

Irrespective of what type shotgun is presented for inspection and repair, the gunsmith can be sure that diagnosis of trouble will be a great deal easier if he is familiar with the general procedure of all gun operators as outlined in Chapter Five.

Such fundamental functional operations as extraction, ejection, firing pin action, hammer fall and sear contact can readily and positively be determined by the visual inspection-and-try method on all types but the autoloading shotgun. For this latter type, actual firing is recommended when possible because of the many small quirks that show up only under firing stresses. When this is neither possible nor practical, then reliance must be placed on the customer's diagnosis, coupled, of course, with the findings of the routine inspection.

Notes on Disassembly and Assembly

Double barrel shotguns (and double rifles, which are similar in construction) are so designed that a good deal of mechanism is fitted into a very small space. Usually this mechanism is accessible for inspection and repair only after the side plates and/or bottom plate and stock are removed.

Side Plates. The two side plates are usually held in place by one long screw passing through both. Sometimes a smaller screw is also used near the forward end of each plate to hold in that end. If there is no small screw, then the forward end of the plate generally has a tongue on it that fits into a groove in the frame.

Bottom Plate. If a shotgun has only a bottom plate, or side plates and a bottom plate, this latter piece is usually held in the frame by means of two or three screws. In addition to a short screw at the forward end of the plate, there are two others, of which one usually comes down from the top of the frame from under the top lever and fastens to the inside of the plate. The third is generally placed behind the safety and has its head either on the topside of the tang or, if put in from the underside of the gun, its head is to the rear or under the trigger guard tang.

Due to the thinness of side plates and bottom plates, the screws holding them in place usually have a head of abbreviated thickness. Consequently, the slot in which the screwdriver fits is often not as deep as it is in a conventional screw. This is especially true of foreign made shotguns. Thus it is of prime importance that screwdrivers which are used to loosen these screws be sharpened correctly and fit the screw head perfectly. The threads on these screws are usually of fine pitch and therefore hold tightly in place. When applying screwdriver force, always remember to bear down on the screwdriver with goodly pressure while turning it so as to minimize the possibility of the screwdriver jumping out and cutting the screw head if resistance to the turning force is encountered.

To remove either side plates or bottom plates, after the screws have been taken out, use the same method as suggested for side plate removal on revolvers, i.e., tap the frame surrounding the plate with a rawhide hammer or top of wooden handle screwdriver. Never attempt to pry plates loose, since this is not only an inefficient way to do the job but also results in burring up both the frame and plate.

Sears. After the plates have been removed, most of the remaining working mechanism can be studied. If the side plates do not serve as a housing for the sear, hammer, and mainspring mechanism, then such parts will be in the frame proper. When the sears are not included in the side plate, it is usually necessary to remove them before the stock can be taken off, since they are so placed that they lie in the path of the stock's travel when attempting to slide the latter off. The sears are removed by driving out the pin that passes through them and then lifting them from the mechanism. It is then possible to take off the stock by loosening the bolt that holds it to the frame. This bolt, which fits in a deep hole within the stock, is made accessible for working by removing the butt plate.

To get at the head of this bolt it is necessary to use a long screwdriver as shown in Figure 13. The particular type handle on this screwdriver enables the gunsmith to exert enough force to loosen the most stubborn of stock bolts, provided, of course, that the gun is held firmly in a vise and the screwdriver is used properly. As a matter of fact, the stocks of many other type shotguns besides double barrel are frequently held in place by a bolt. This fact should be borne in mind when any shotgun stock does not seem to come off even though the smaller screws passing through the frame have been removed.

Butt Stock. Occasionally it will be found that even after all screws holding a stock in place are taken out the stock will resist removal. This is especially true of guns having a very close-fitting stock in which wood shrinkage has taken place. While it is all right to attempt removal of the stock by hand with a straight line pulling motion, the gunsmith is cautioned against employing any appreciable up-and-down motion lest the edges of the stock which fit against the metal parts of the frame or trigger guard break off. When no normal amount of force which can be applied by hand alone avails to loosen a stubborn stock then the only recourse is to increase effort. To do this, wrap a towel or heavy soft cloth around the stock at the forward end of the comb. Strike this cloth-protected section with an entire newspaper which has been rolled around a short section of broom stick or dowel rod until the stock comes loose. By proceeding in this way, the chances of the stock being marred by the blows delivered are reduced to a minimum. One or two sharp blows are better than a series of light taps, since it is generally a sudden blow that will break any adhesion existing between the wood and metal components.

Sluggish Safety and Hammer. Sometimes, after the mechanism of a double barrel is cleaned and the stock is replaced, the hammer and safety of the gun will have a tendency to operate quite sluggishly. This is due largely to the holding screws being tightened up more than they were originally; thus some of the normally moving parts are pressed against the inletted portions of the stock and excessive inter-surface friction results.

To remedy such a condition, a non-ferrous metallic shim (brass, copper, aluminum) or washer should be so placed that it will limit the extent to which the screws passing from trigger guard to upper tang, and vice versa, can be tightened. In this way the necessary minimum working clearance between the wood and moving metal parts will be maintained at all times.

This trouble will not be encountered in every gun that is reassembled but it is well for the gunsmith to know that such an unexpected factor can enter into the picture when a shotgun is merely disassembled, cleaned and reassembled. Too, there is always the possibility that the same condition may arise when a new stock is put on a double barrel shotgun, or, for that matter, any type of shoulder weapon in which the inletted portions of the stock are held to very close tolerance in the immediate region of moving parts.

Before going any more deeply into the specific considerations of shotgun repairs, it might be well to devote a few paragraphs to some special thoughts on the business aspect of shotgun repair work.

The Business Aspect

Time and Parts Cost. On many of the double barrel type scatter guns, the replacement of a 25¢ pin or spring not infrequently requires an expenditure of two hours' labor time, because the gun must be completely disassembled to remove the defective part and put a new one in place. Or, as is sometimes the case, a very expensive imported shotgun will be presented to the gunsmith for cleaning or minor adjustment. In either case the gunsmith must of necessity make a charge which is apt to startle the gun owner when he hears it pronounced in dollars and cents. Nevertheless, the charge must be made and in either instance it is absolutely justified. In the former it is a question of straight labor brought about by the mechanical complexity of the gun. In the latter, where the gunsmith has in his custody for a time a very valuable item upon which he must work with the care and skill of a surgeon, there is much added responsibility in just having the gun around the shop, subject to theft, fire or damage, which, if it occurred, would require indemnification of the customer.

In short, then, the gunsmith must not, when working on double barrel shotguns, be tempted into making hasty repair charge estimates unless he is very familiar with every extenuating factor that might possibly crop up. This familiarity generally, but not necessarily, comes only after long experience in dealing with guns of every sort.

Hurry-up Job. Another time when a gunsmith can make what might be called a premium charge is when someone wants a job done in a hurry. This sometimes involves the making of a special part or parts which, under ordinary circumstances, could be procured from the factory at a fraction of the cost required to make it by hand and ordinary shop machinery. Such a job should be computed entirely on the basis of labor, plus a special service charge for doing it completely at the customer's convenience.

Making Special Parts

For Foreign Guns. On German made shotguns, or, for that matter, German weapons of any type, the gunsmith is at the present time faced with a special problem since the arms business of the Germans will no doubt be at somewhat of a standstill for at least a few years while the Allied Control Commission decides whether or not the Germans should be allowed to make anything that might in any way aid them in planning or waging war. All of which means that parts for German manufactured guns must be made by hand. Some of these parts can be so made in the gunsmith's shop—others cannot. Each gunsmith should, as a matter of policy, be able to look at a part and know whether or not he can reproduce it with the tools, machines and skill he has at his disposal. If he is prone to overestimate these capacities, then only too often will he find himself losing money or customers as a result of not being able to live up to a promise.

Two in One. On some special parts that the gunsmith must make by hand, he will often find that it is possible to make two of the same required parts in almost the time he can make one, e.g., some shotgun hammers (internal type) which are simply formed pieces of flat stock with a drilled hole and two cuts added for full and half-cock notches. When the gunsmith has occasion to make a part of this sort, it should be made from stock of slightly larger than double the finished thickness of the part so that in fact two parts will be fabricated at one time. When completely machined, the part can be split with a hacksaw or milling cutter, and the width of each half ground or filed to desired finished size. After the one part to be used has been installed in the gun, the other should be cleaned in a solvent, heavily greased, tagged as to what make, model and caliber of gun it is for, and put in stock.

Chances are that if it is a very odd part, it might not be needed for many months, but when it is required, the gunsmith will appreciate the wisdom of this course of action. Even if the gunsmith does not have occasion to use the extra part in connection with his own repair work, he may be able to sell it to another gunsmith or dealer who needs it badly and is willing to pay a good price. Also, it might be well to include on the identification tag the amount of time required to make the part (so that a price can be put on it) and any pertinent details of its manufacture, such as heat treating temperature and size of drills or reamers used.

Simple straight holding pins and odd size coil springs for certain types of obsolete guns also lend themselves well to double duplication, and over a period of time more than repay the gunsmith for the little extra effort required to make two of the same part instead of one.

The True Defect. Diagnosis of trouble on a double barrel shotgun is, from a financial standpoint, more important than on any other type of gun because of the time required to disassemble and reassemble the breech mechanism. Therefore, it is imperative that every possibility of a simple fault being present be thoroughly explored before concluding that one of a more complicated nature exists. This warning should not be construed as advice to go ahead and presume that every trouble is always of a minor nature, but rather to encourage thorough analysis of each repair problem to the exclusion of all other questionable causes.

Limit of Reassembly. Another point to remember—when a new or repaired part is installed in the receiver of a double barrel gun, do not put the entire gun together to make a functional test unless it is absolutely necessary, for it is often quite possible that the repaired part might need further adjustment before it can be regarded as O.K. For example, if a new hammer is fitted in a shotgun, only those parts necessary to test how the hammer works should first be put back. This would normally include the hammer, the mainspring and the sear. Thus it can be seen that there is no need for putting back the top lever stop, the bottom plate or the trigger guard; and if the sear spring is on the bottom plate, its place can be taken for purposes of test by pushing the sear into place against the hammer with the end of a screwdriver. If the hammer works, all well and good—then the entire gun can be fully reassembled. On the other hand, should it not work, then only a few parts will have to be removed each time until proper fit and adjustment are finally achieved.

Considering that it often requires as many as four or five tries to fit some parts in a gun, it should not be difficult for the gunsmith to see how as much as an hour can be saved on a single job by adhering to the foregoing method of procedure.

For Old Guns. Although there are not many of the old type side hammer shotguns being made nowadays, there are still no few of them in existence. Their appearance in a gunsmith's shop is not uncommon and in some rural localities they are very popular. Certain parts for these weapons, such as firing pins, can be made with comparative ease, while others, such as hammers, sears and flat springs, require much time and no little skill in the matter of heat treating them correctly. For the gunsmith to attempt manufacture of these more complicated parts is not recommended unless he has first assured himself of the following:

1) That the parts cannot be procured in a rough-forged, or better yet, finished condition, from a parts supply house such as A. F. Stoeger & Co. in New York, N.Y.

2) That no parts from a similar type of gun, that can be used, are stuck away in some part of the shop.

3) That the defective part cannot in some way be reworked

(brazed, welded or metal insert made) so that it will adequately and safely perform the function that it is intended to.

4) That he can by measurement fully reconstruct the exact size of a missing part, or obtain the measurements from a major section of a broken part.

5) That he has the proper type of steel for the part and knows what amount and kind of heat treatment is required to make the part stand up under the wear and abuse it will be subject to.

6) That the customer will pay the price for having such a special job done. This may sound like a too oft-repeated phrase in this book, but it is again reiterated at this point in connection with old shotguns because the majority of these guns, it would seem from the writer's experience, are owned by people who believe them to be very valuable until they are told that a new part will cost in the neighborhood of $10.00. Upon hearing such a figure, the owner then does a bit of sputtering and attempts to bargain for a lower repair price on the grounds that the entire gun is hardly worth the price quoted for repair. To all this the businessman-gunsmith, who sooner or later becomes hardened to such verbal bric-a-brac, must turn a deaf ear and, while smiling, flatter the customer into agreeing to the repair charge or going away with another shotgun from the gunsmith's selection of renovated used guns.

Working with Springs

A long time ago a very wise fellow said that one does not appreciate the water until the well runs dry, or words to that effect. A more modern gunsmith's version along the same line might read that one does not appreciate the power of a double barrel shotgun hammer spring until he tries to get one into its proper place.

Coil Type Mainspring. Of the two types of hammer springs, (mainsprings) the most difficult to install is the coil spring, for the reason that there is no place to keep a grip on it when it is forced into its well or recess. Usually the whole secret of putting an obstinate coil spring into place hinges on holding the receiver of the gun so tightly between padded vise jaws that absolutely no sudden shift of the receiver is possible. In this way all effort can be concentrated on getting the spring and hammer pinned in place without having to be concerned about the receiver jumping around—with its attendant danger to the hands. The use of a special pin having a slight taper will aid greatly in getting the hammer hole aligned with its corresponding hole in the receiver once the spring has been at least partially compressed. By using the taper pin, the necessity for having perfect alignment of holes can be avoided. However, the taper pin should not be wiggled around carelessly or the edge around the receiver hole will be burred up and made ovoid in shape.

Using a "C" Clamp. Often, by using an ordinary ten cent store "C" clamp, with its universal head ground to special shape and placed around the receiver with the head against the hammer, the spring can be compressed gradually by turning the screw of the clamp. As a matter of fact, this method can be employed to great advantage on many types of parts which must be compressed into place against the tension of a stiff spring. All these possibilities cannot very well be listed, but the gunsmith with an alert mind will not take long to discover that a good deal of somewhat dangerous and patience-trying work can be accomplished with ease by the use of special tools improvised from odd bits of metal and screws that too often are regarded as being just so much scrap.

Making the Job Easier. Just pushing against a stiff spring with a screwdriver or similar hand tool can quite frequently be avoided if the gunsmith will, when confronted with this or any other operation that has always been distasteful and accomplished by hit-and-miss methods, take a few minutes out and ask himself if there should not logically be an easier and more efficient way of accomplishing the task at hand.

Such an analysis can be conducted by asking one's self a few questions. First, why is this particular operation so distasteful and difficult to me? Second, is there any other similar job which I do on other guns that seems far easier and more routine? If there is, then what tools or methods do I use on those guns that I am not using on this seemingly more difficult job? Third, what factor or combination of factors prevents me from using those tools or methods? Fourth, if I cannot use those tools or methods because of basic differences in part or receiver construction, then isn't there some other easily made special tool that I can use? And finally, would the expenditure of time and materials in making this tool be justified? In other words, do I have occasion to perform this particular operation frequently enough to warrant making a special tool, and will the resultant saving in time, wear and tear on my nerves, and less exposure to accidents, be of appreciable consideration?

The "V" Type Spring. The "V" type hammer spring, which is most often encountered in shotguns having side plate locks, can best be handled by a pair of pliers as illustrated in Figure 81. Essentially, this tool is nothing more than a pair of flat nose pliers modified so that the spring can be grasped between the recessed jaw faces and then compressed to desired size by means of the wing nut attached to the screw passing through both handles. Once compressed to desired size, the spring can be put where it fits and the wing nut slowly loosened until all tensions of the spring are brought to bear on the parts to which it is connected.

The advantages of the tool in Figure 81 should be quite obvious to the gunsmith for it will enable him to hold a very stiff spring under any desired degree of compression while fitting it into any recess or position.

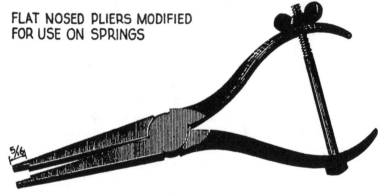

FLAT NOSED PLIERS MODIFIED
FOR USE ON SPRINGS

FIGURE 81

Common Double Gun Ailments

As a double barrel shotgun becomes old, not from the standpoint of age, but from continued use and abuse, it often develops certain ailments which, while not always of an incapacitating nature, do nevertheless cause the shooter many moments of annoyance, inconvenience and anxiety. All of these troubles can be directly attributed to wear between engaging or moving parts of one sort or another. We shall consider them in their order of frequency, as ordinarily encountered during the course of an extended period of general gun repair work.

Loose or Jumping Off Forearm. On the inexpensive variety of double gun, where the forearm is locked against the barrel by means of a bent flat spring rotating eccentrically on a pin, the forearm will become loose and rattle or jump off as a result of one or both of the following defects: short spring as a result of wear on its engaging end, or excessive bending near the fixed end.

In an emergency it is often possible to effect a temporary repair for the first mentioned defect by peening the engaging end of the spring, or, in the case of the latter, by hitting the apex of the bend with a hammer. In either case the repair is a makeshift at best, and the original trouble will crop up again after a short period of use. If a temporary repair of this sort is accomplished, the customer should be told that it is only so done to satisfy his present demand and that a new part should be installed as soon as his immediate need for the gun no longer exists.

In some cases the lug on the barrel where the fore-end catch or spring engages will be found to be the offending member. However, this possibility should not be accorded any too much attention until the gunsmith has fully convinced himself, by inserting a new catch or spring in the fore-end, that the fore-end locking mechanism is not at fault.

If the fore-end barrel lug is badly worn, it must be built up at the point where the locking spring engages it by means of a hardened steel insert. The insert, which can be a flat piece pinned or dovetailed in place, or just a small screw tightened in place and ground to dimensions, should be so placed that it adds in size only to the area where the catch, or spring, engages it. In order to satisfy this condition, it will at times be necessary to file or cut away a portion of the lug itself so that the shim will have sufficient area to be retained solidly. If part of this lug must be filed, then care should be taken to see that its general contour is not changed in any way that will make rebuilding of the lug a major, if not near impossible, task.

While it would be very easy to solder or braze a shim on the lug, this procedure cannot very well be recommended in as much as the application of heat above 350° F. might very definitely affect the solder which is used so extensively to hold the rib on a double barrel shotgun in place.

After the shim has been fitted in place, the fore-end should be put in place slowly and without resort to banging or pounding, which would only result in bending of the spring or deforming of the catch. If it does not go in place and lock readily, then the built up lug should be filed or stoned a little at a time until a proper fit is achieved.

The use of prussian blue during a fitting operation of this sort is highly recommended since it will remove virtually all of the guesswork as to where the filing must be done.

If preliminary diagnosis and some degree of repair of the sort just outlined does not completely effect a proper repair, then a detailed examination of the fore-end iron is in order. The points where the iron contacts the receiver should be examined for burrs and protruding pins, screws, or sections of overhanging wood. If the fore-end iron is cut out to accommodate the cocking lever or extractor mechanism, these recesses should be carefully examined for the presence of foreign matter or deformation. Likewise the engaging ends of the parts actuated by the fore-end iron should be thoroughly inspected and deburring performed where necessary.

Cocking Trouble. Generally the hammers of double barrel guns are brought to the full cock position by virtue of the barrels being tipped downward. This is accomplished mechanically by means of a lever, connected to each hammer, which in turn engages a lug or recess on the breech end of the barrels. Each hammer is retained at full cock position by the sear, which is constantly under light spring tension, tending to push the sear into the engaging notch on the hammer.

As wear or deformation occurs on the cocking lever, hammer notch, or a sear's engaging end, the gun will very often develop a tendency to either cock very hard or not cock at all. In some instances only one hammer will cock.

To determine which of the parts is at fault, the bottom plate, side plates, or all three, depending on the type of gun, should be removed to permit observation of the mechanism in motion as the barrels are slowly tipped downward to accomplish cocking of the piece.

At this point in the inspection, look closely to see if the hammers are far enough retracted to cock when the barrels are tipped all the way forward, i.e., are the hammers back sufficiently to permit the sears' ends to engage the hammer notches? If they are not, then either the cocking levers are bent or worn, the point where the cocking levers engage the barrel lug fore-end iron is worn, or some obstruction is preventing the barrels from being tipped fully forward. To find out which of the above is the direct offender, detailed examination and testing should be conducted to eliminate each part from suspicion.

Often a bent cocking lever can be straightened out or an obstruction can be removed from between clashing parts. However, worn parts must, of obvious necessity, be replaced. Wear on the barrel lug or barrel lug pin, where the end of the cocking lever rests, is almost never encountered and when it is, sufficient buildup on the parts can be made by using the methods suggested for repairing worn fore-end barrel lugs.

If the cocking lever and cocking lever barrel lug are in good mechanical shape, then the hammer notches and sear end should be inspected for deformation in the form of improper engaging angles and rounded or worn contacting surfaces.

Stoning of engaging surfaces when they are worn round or at negative engaging angle, will frequently correct the situation, but only if the parts being stoned are made of hardened steel or still retain their case-hardened surface after adjustment. Chances are, though, that once a sear end or hammer notch is worn, the part that was originally case-hardened has worn off. Otherwise the contacting points would not have worn so badly. Therefore, to play safe in such cases, the parts should be recase-hardened after honing, or the first few snaps of the trigger, and the sear and hammer notch will again be the cause of cocking troubles.

Almost needless to say, there is only a very limited amount of metal that can be removed from either sear or hammer. And while this amount cannot be laid down in terms of thousandths of an inch, because of the almost infinite possible number of cases, it can be safely predicted that if just a little too much is honed away, a short hammer fall, with its subsequent light firing pin blow and faulty ignition, can only too easily result.

In this little discussion on the problems of faulty double gun cocking, the matter of weak or defective sear springs has been held until last, not because it should be the last possibility of trouble to be explored, but rather because it is not very often that a weak sear spring will be found to be the source of trouble. As a matter of fact, the sear springs should be the first to be inspected when making diagnosis on a gun represented as having a defective cocking mechanism. For when testing the hammers, sears and cocking lever, the sear springs will not be brought into play if the bottom plate of the gun, to which they are attached or held in place, is removed, as recommended, in order that the mechanism might be visually studied. Therefore, during the testing of the sears and hammers, the gunsmith will find it necessary to actuate the sears by gravity (hold the gun with the top of the receiver parallel to the floor), or by means of a screwdriver pressed against the sear as the engaging notch of the hammer comes into position.

Loose Barrels. In old shotguns, that is, double guns designed and built when modern high velocity loads were unknown, and in some of the more modern inexpensive ones, the barrels will sometimes rattle when the gun is held with both hands around the stock and then shaken. This, as can be appreciated, indicates that excessive wear has taken place between the parts which, when functioning properly, hold the barrel assembly tightly in place to the receiver when the gun is closed and fully locked.

For all practical purposes, the base trouble contributing to loose barrels can be laid to one or more of the defects listed below, these defects acting singly or in combination:

1) Worn or bent hinge pin;
2) Worn barrel lug, which engages the hinge pin;
3) Worn or bent locking pin;
4) Worn hole or recess where the locking pin engages.

If the hinge pin is bent, there is no other alternative than to replace it with a new factory pin or one that has been turned by the gunsmith from alloy steel which will stand up under the constant pounding strain imposed every time the gun is fired. Here it might be well to point out that removal and installation of a hinge pin that was pressed in at the factory when the gun was made, is a very difficult operation and not ordinarily within the small shop gunsmith's capabilities unless he has an arbor press with which to press out the old pin and press in the new one. Also needed for this job are specially made blocks to place in the receiver so that the pressure imposed upon it by the force required to dislodge the hinge pin will not bend or crack the receiver. These are the factors which must be taken into account if the gunsmith must or elects to do a hinge pin job himself rather than send it to the factory.

If the hinge pin is of the type that screws into the receiver, then it is entirely practical for the gunsmith to make and install a new one, providing he has or can obtain a high grade of alloy steel, turn it to size, and heat treat it correctly. A properly ground and long shank screwdriver must be used when unscrewing a hinge pin, and close examination made to make sure that all locking screws or traversing locking pins have been removed.

A worn barrel lug, or lump, as it is often called, can in some cases be peened over to make up for a few thousandths wear. However, if the wear is considerable, then it is usually advisable to make a steel shim insert, or, if possible and more practical, put in an oversized hinge pin.

On expensive shotguns peening should not be resorted to since the owner of such a gun will generally be more inclined and willing to invest a few extra dollars for the more lasting insert type job.

Where the locking pin is worn, bent, or in any other manner defective, it should be replaced, since it is neither practicable nor profitable to do otherwise, and if the part is procurable from commercial sources, it should be bought rather than made, because of the nature of its function, which is so closely connected with the basic safety of the weapon..

When the hole or recess where the locking pin engages is worn, the gunsmith will very often find that he is faced with a condition that quite nearly defies practical repair, unless there is enough metal surrounding the hole or recess to allow for the inlay of shims or bushings. If space does permit making such an inlay, then very careful measurements of all affected parts must be taken before any cutting or reaming is done, so that no unexpected hitch will rear its ugly head and possibly spoil the gun altogether. Also, the gunsmith should assure himself, by testing with a file or center punch, that the receiver on which he expects to work is machinable, that is to say, if it is case-hardened or pack-hardened will he be able to grind away enough metal to bring the hand and machine tools into play? If indications are that the metal cannot be successfully prepared for a bushing or inlay without incurring undue risk, then the entire project should be abandoned without hesitancy and the customer advised of the situation. Surely it is better to justifiably pass up a five dollar job than to ruin a thirty dollar shotgun that is apt to be worth fifty dollars when the customer finds out he is to be indemnified for his "great" loss.

If, on the other hand, the gunsmith feels that the job can be done, then he should not hesitate to proceed but being nonetheless careful to use only tool steel for the inlay or bushing, and not hesitate to spend an extra hour on hand fitting to insure that the finished job compares very favorably with the locking action on a new gun. To achieve this, the insert or bushing must be positively and permanently seated in its place; the locking pin or top lever crosspiece must fit into the newly built up section with little or no play; and the top lever must open and close with no drag or binding. Such fitting necessarily requires that spotting-in with prussian blue be relied upon so that only high spots will be filed and stoned.

As a closing note on this matter, it should be pointed out that some loose barrelled guns will come to the gunsmith which are, for all practical purposes, beyond possibility of redemption in spite of the fact that they are, from a mechanical standpoint, repairable. This may sound like double talk but it is not. Rather, it is meant to convey to the practical gunsmith that some old shotguns and some of the more modern twenty dollar double barrel versions are not worth repairing because basically they are either of such poor design or made of such soft steel that insertion of a hardened locking pin or hardened bushing will only throw the shock stress incident to each cartridge discharge on to other parts of the gun, which in due time will break or become deformed. While it would be convenient to have a listing of all double barrel shotguns that fall in this category, such is not possible. Therefore, the individual gunsmith must learn to evaluate each of this type weapon that comes to him for repair, and on the basis of his general mechanical knowledge, good common sense and capabilities to do a particular job, accept or reject them accordingly.

Sweating on Barrel Ribs

It is not very often that a gunsmith is called upon to sweat a new rib on a shotgun unless it be for a single barrel pump or automatic which is to be used for skeet or trap-shooting, in which case one can be procured from the factory and installed by the same general method as that for sweating a loose rib on a double barrel gun.

Sweating on a loose rib, whether it be the top or bottom one, can be either a difficult or easy job, depending entirely upon the preparatory work the gunsmith performs before applying heat to the parts being joined.

Precaution. First remove the barrels from the gun proper and, if at all possible, take off the sights and any other accessories that might in any way be adversely affected by the application of heat, or interfere with the affixing of clamps to the ribs.

Holding the Barrel. If it is the top rib which is to be worked upon, the barrel should be held by its breech lug between padded vise jaws. The muzzle end of the barrels should also be supported by means of a board cut to a length that will allow one end to rest on the floor while the other rests against the bottom of the barrel.

A more permanent type of muzzle support (Figure 82) that

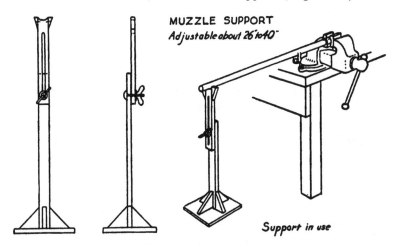

MUZZLE SUPPORT
Adjustable about 26"to40"

Support in use

FIGURE 82

can be used for any type of shoulder weapon can be fashioned from a few pieces of wood and a screw and wing nut. Simple as it is to make and use this fixture will always come in handy when long objects of any sort are held between the vise jaws.

If the bottom rib is to be worked upon, then the breech end of the barrel itself must be held in the vise, in which case the pin should be removed from the stationary jaw so that the latter will swivel at an angle to bear evenly on the tapered length of the barrel. Here again the muzzle support should be employed as an auxiliary holding medium.

Raising the Rib. With the barrels set up in the vise the loose rib should be lifted up so that a small wooden wedge can be placed at the extreme end of the break between rib and barrel. If the rib is parted at two or three places along a given length, but holding on between these breaks, then the rib should be parted from the barrel up to the point of the last break. In this way the sweating can be done much easier and the completed job will be far more lasting. Sometimes where the rib is loose at many points throughout its entire length, or hanging on only at its last few inches, it is advisable to remove the entire section rather than try to work around a few points that are holding.

Scraping the Rib. If the entire rib is removed from the gun, the job of scraping the old solder from it and the barrels can be done very quickly and efficiently with any sort of edged scraper made from hardened drill rod or tool steel. As a matter of fact, a scraper made from a discarded triangular file with the serrations ground off makes a very fine tool not only for this particular job, but any place where a scraper is needed. (The edge of a converted file scraper can be made to last longer by heating it to a cherry red and quenching it in water; then polish with fine emery cloth until the metal surface is bright, reheat over a torch until a light straw color appears and again quench in water.) Scraping the solder off the barrels and rib when the latter is only partially lifted from the gun requires special effort and the use of small odd-shaped scrapers fashioned from bits of a hacksaw blade.

Cleaning the Rib. After scraping, the surfaces to be tinned should be further cleaned by means of emery cloth glued to a very thin piece of wood or metal. Finally, alcohol or carbon tetrachloride, applied by means of cotton on a stick to the scraped surface, will insure removal of any remaining tinning-inhibiting matter.

Cleaning of metal surfaces prior to tinning cannot be overstressed, for the success of any soldering or sweating job depends almost entirely on how well the surfaces to be joined are tinned, and a good tinning job requires that a surface be as chemically and mechanically clean as possible.

Tinning. Where an entire rib and barrels are to be tinned, a conventional gas or electrically heated soldering iron can be used very efficiently. However, where only a short length of rib and barrels are to be tinned, a soldering iron having a very thin copper with a long tapering point must be employed so that it can be inserted between rib and barrels without fear of having the solder flow on to portions of the barrel where it is not needed.

If such an iron is not available, then the gunsmith can make one for the job from a thin sheet of copper riveted to a steel rod having a wooden handle. Due to its thinness, such an iron will not hold the heat as well as a heavier iron, but it will be far more suitable for work of this sort. On the other hand, if a gunsmith so chooses, he can grind a long slender end on a conventional soldering iron and retain this iron for work where one having such a shape is either necessary or desirable.

Irrespective of what type of soldering iron is used, it should be filed or polished to a copper-bright surface, after being heated, and its end dipped quickly into some sort of flux such as No-Kor-Ode soldering paste; then a bit of the same flux should be applied to the surfaces to be tinned, by means of a wood sliver. Next, coat two opposing surfaces of the iron with solder. Not a big blob that will form a ball at the top of the iron, but rather a smooth, uniform coating that can be transferred to the rib and barrels. After the rib and barrels have been thoroughly tinned, clean the iron again, dip it into the flux, and go over the tinned surfaces until a thin, uniform coating is achieved throughout. Any excess that cannot be removed by this method should be scraped off so that no solder will collect into little droplets and fall between the barrels when the rib is sweated on. This may sound like an insignificant point as here discussed, but any gunsmith who has had to remove a freshly sweated on rib and then resweated it in place just to extract a few small balls of solder that rattle around and give the impression that loose parts are running around between the barrels, can readily testify to the importance of this factor.

Sweating It On. With all preparatory work done, any wooden wedges remaining should be removed and the rib brought to bear against the barrels by means of "C" clamps placed about six inches apart along the length of the entire rib (Figure 83). If it is the bottom rib which is being sweated in place, then a steel rod about ⅜" in diameter, and as long as the entire rib, should be placed between the clamp and the rib itself. In this way the radius of the rod will bear more evenly on the convex surface of the rib than would the flat end of a "C" clamp.

Tighten up the clamps until the rib is positively against the barrels and properly in the center; then with a Bunsen burner or alcohol torch apply heat, but no more than is necessary to make the solder flow freely for solder that is overheated tends to become grainy when it hardens. Work from breech towards muzzle over a length of six inches at a time. As the solder melts and begins to flow freely (this will be obvious, for the solder will seep out between rib and barrels) the appropriate clamp screw should be tightened until the rib is fully against the barrel. Any excess solder which flows out from between the joint should be wiped off with a cloth before it has a chance to harden and set on a portion of either the barrels or rib where it is not wanted. Repeat this same operation all along the rib until the entire loose unit is fully and positively joined to the barrels.

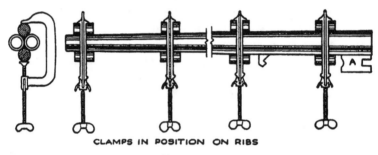

CLAMPS IN POSITION ON RIBS

FIGURE 83

Finally, look at the muzzle of the barrels and see if any solder is needed at that point; such a need will be quite evident by the presence of an opening between the top and bottom ribs. This opening should be filled in by flowing solder from the iron into the opening and then trimming off the excess with a piece of emery cloth laid against a flat stick or file.

After sufficient time has elapsed to allow for normal cooling by the surrounding air (do not pour water on the barrels to induce rapid cooling as it might seep into some minute crack existing between the rib and barrels and form a steam pocket), remove the clamps, and with a very narrow chisel gnaw away any traces of solder that show between the joined surfaces, being careful not to cut below the solder and so scratch the barrels. To forestall any possible rusting that might occur as a result of using the solder or flux, the barrels should be wiped over with a solvent-soaked rag, dried off, and coated with light oil. The insides of the barrels should be similarly treated.

Occasionally, in spite of his best efforts, the gunsmith will discover, after the sweating job is done, that some balls of solder have found their way between the barrels, and chase each other around every time the gun is elevated or depressed. Although it is necessary more often than not to heat up and remove the front section of the lower rib in order to extract the pesky pellets, there is an alternative method which can be resorted to on inexpensive shotguns. This method works very well if the pellets are small, that is, no larger than $\frac{3}{16}''$ at their widest part. However, since there is no positive way of determining how large the pellets are, the gunsmith must be content to take a chance and hope they are small. At any rate, this is the method: make a light center punch indent in the center of the lower rib, approximately eight inches distant from the breech end of the barrels, and drill a $\frac{1}{8}''$ hole through the rib, being careful not to allow the drill to go in any deeper than is absolutely necessary to completely pierce the rib.

Next, clean out the hole with a tapered reamer. This will cut away any ring of metal remaining at the bottom of the hole, and allow the pellets to roll along on the inside of the rib, and drop out through the hole as the barrels are slowly tilted from end to end à la see-saw fashion. If all the pellets can be removed through this size opening, all well and good; if they cannot, then successively enlarge the hole $\frac{1}{64}''$ between tries with a drill or reamer, until the maximum allowable size of $\frac{3}{16}''$ has been reached. If there are any solder pellets that will not come out through a hole of this size, then there is no other alternative except to loosen up (by heat) a section of the rib and get them out that way.

Under any circumstances the drilled hole should be tapped out with a very fine pitch thread and a short screw inserted to fill it up. The screw should be cut to proper size, polished, and blued before it is inserted, so that it will not look like a patch job against the finished appearance of the rib.

Removing Dents from Barrels. If all the dented shotgun barrels in any given locality were brought on the same day to the local gunsmith's shop for fixing, he would be a mighty busy man for very many days.

In spite of the constant admonitions sounded by gun manufacturers, gun editors and firearms authorities against the practice of shooting shotguns that have dented barrels, many, too many in fact, shooters continue to fire their pet scatter guns just as long as the worst dent does not prevent the shot charge from somehow squeezing through the bore.

Just why so many otherwise gun-conscious shooters choose to ignore the presence of dents in their shotgun barrels has always been something of a mystery to all those who have campaigned for safer and better-shooting guns. Perhaps it is because they do not realize that a dented tube cannot be shot out and that every charge fired through such a barrel has the makings of a blow-up that might injure innocent bystanders as well as themselves. Too, a dented barrel can conceivably affect the patterning qualities of a gun, for in passing through the tube some of the pellets in the shot charge do become deformed by the dents. Add this to the fact that ballistics experts have demonstrated that deformed pellets, by virtue of their unsymmetrical shape, fly off in unpredictable directions, and the gunsmith can better appreciate the necessity for urging his customers to have dents removed from the barrels of their shotguns.

As a means of promoting this sort of repair work, the gunsmith, without resorting to high pressure salesmanship, should, if he can, scout around and try to locate a shotgun that has a blown up barrel which occurred because of a dent, dents or obstruction that was present when the gun was fired. Usually such a memento can be picked up for a few dollars and then placed in the showcase, store-front window, or some similarly conspicuous place, with a nicely lettered sign in red ink briefly pointing out the dangers and disadvantages of a shotgun with a dented barrel.

Further promotion of work along this line can be achieved by bringing to the attention of a customer the presence of dents in the barrel of his shotgun, whether the gun is in for cleaning or a major repair job. Here a word of caution might be in order: the gunsmith should always come to an agreement as to price, delivery date, et cetera, on the primary repair (i.e., the defect that motivated the customer to bring the weapon in for repair) before broaching the subject of dent removal, or, for that matter, any sort of additional repair work suggested by the gunsmith.

When bringing up the subject of dent removal to a potential customer, the gunsmith should, before he launches into a tirade describing how unsafe a shotgun with a dented barrel is, sound out the man on the other side of the counter very diplomatically. For example, casually mention how unsafe such a gun can be and note his reaction. If he does not warm up to this thought too well, then say a few words on how a dented barrel affects the patterning qualities of a shotgun and note the reaction to this. He may be more inclined to favor this latter reasoning as a basis for having the dent removed, rather than the safety angle.

The method of approach as just outlined might sound odd to some gunsmiths who believe, and rightly so, that the mere mention of a potentially unsafe gun should bring any customer in his right mind around to having a necessary repair job done. Yet for some not fully understandable reason such is not always the case. Therefore, the gunsmith must sound out a customer, so to speak, and find out just what avenue of approach is best to use on him as a particular individual.

Perhaps this thought can be more clearly conveyed by citing a little story that a friend of this writer, an insurance salesman, (who are noted for their ability to contact and get results from the most obstinate people) used to relate:

"When proposing life insurance to a customer," he said, "I always try to sound him out first and find out whom, of all the people that might possibly suffer financially from his passing, does he think the most of. When I find this out I play up that point for all it is worth. After all, in the long run the insurance money will benefit his children just as well as it will his wife; but," he confided, "occasionally I do find a husband who intimates that he does not give a hoot whether his wife is taken care of or not after he dies, but by the same token can not even bear to think that his favorite young son or daughter would have to go without higher education if he passed on and left no money to take care of them."

In the same way, many shooters will scoff at having dents removed from the barrel of their scatter gun just because it might blow up. But tell them the same dents might very well raise hell with their shot pattern and they will immediately agree to have the job done pronto and with no expense spared. It goes almost without saying that this same method of customer approach applies to more phases of gunsmithing work than just dent removal. It is business angles of this sort that often cause the beginner gunsmith to shake his head and wonder if gunsmithing is not just a bit more than having a few tools and the ability to use them on all types of weapons.

As it is with many classes of gun repair work, the process of dent removal has its limitations. By this is meant that not every dent can always be removed. True, though by far and large the majority can be straightened out, deep indentations which are located in the thicker section of the barrel, i.e., within five or six inches of the breech end, are often very difficult, if not practically impossible, to iron out correctly. In the same category are very deep dents present in the muzzle section of the barrel, which can be knocked out but require so much pounding to accomplish it that the tube develops an almost imperceptible, but no less dangerous, crack.

From a very technical standpoint, there cannot be put down a set of hard-and-fast rules which would serve to guide the gunsmith as to whether or not he should undertake to perform a particular dent removal job. Nevertheless, the beginner would do well to bear in mind the above two classes of dents to steer clear of until he has done a few dozen run-of-the-mill jobs and is fully aware how stubborn a very shallow dent can be. Equipped with such experience, he will be more familiar with his own capabilities and have a working knowledge of the metal used in the various makes of shotguns.

In Figure 21 there are illustrated two of the most efficient and practical tools for removing shotgun barrel dents. The diametrical dimensions are, of course, governed by the gauge of the tube either type of remover is to be used in, and to that end the true bore diameter used by American shotgun manufacturers for each gauge is listed in the same figure.

Although there are no complicated machine operations necessary to fabricate either of the dent removers illustrated, they must be made from tool steel, properly hardened and tempered, and ground to a mirror finish. There are no substitute dent remover specifications for the simple reason that one not meeting the above listed specifications would, if soft, become scarred by the dent rather than remove it. And if the surface which contacts the walls of the bore is not absolutely scratch-free, the dent might be well removed but only at the expense of scarring the bore, which is certainly no more desirable than a dented barrel.

If the gunsmith has the facilities (lathe and tool post grinder), there is certainly no objection to his making his own dent removers. However, if he does not have the needed machine tools or does not feel qualified to make the removers, then he should not hesitate to procure them from a commercial source or have them made by a competent machinist. Incidentally, if the gunsmith chooses to have them made by a machinist, he should have it clearly understood that the dent removers will not be accepted and paid for unless they meet the specifications, as to dimensions and finish, according to a drawing or sketch furnished by the gunsmith. This is one of the few instances where the gunsmith will be able to demand as good work from a fellow craftsman as his own customers expect of him.

To be fully prepared to handle most types of dent removal work, the gunsmith should have at least one remover of each type for the 12, 16 and 20 gauge shotgun. If there are, by any odd combination of circumstances, a number of 28 gauge and 410 bore shotguns in the gunsmith's locality, then, and only then, should he consider investing in dent removers for guns of these bore sizes. It might be well to point out here that shotguns having a bore smaller than 20 gauge do not as a rule dent very easily, for the tubes of these guns are generally quite heavy and resist the force of banging around that would normally dent the barrel of a shotgun with a larger bore. Furthermore, small bore shotguns are nowhere near as popular as are the 12 and 16 gauge weapons.

As it is with every other special tool there are many wrong ways but few correct ways to use and care for a dent remover. In the first place, the gunsmith should have a special cloth or felt-lined wooden box in which to keep the dent removers when they are not being used. Also, after each usage they should be cleaned and oiled before being put away in this box. As a double precaution against possible rusting, the lining of the box should be impregnated thoroughly (not dripping) with oil; otherwise an oiled dent remover might rust after extended storage as a result of a dry lining absorbing all the preservative from the surface of the tool.

Before the dent remover is inserted in the bore, it should be wiped free of any foreign matter clinging to it; similarly, the bore of the gun should be made perfectly clean. In this way the chances of either the bore or tool getting scratched, as a result of some fine abrasive particles being interposed between them, is reduced to a minimum.

After disassembling the barrels from the receiver and removing the forearm or any parts that might interfere with holding the barrel between padded vise jaws, the dent remover should be wiped over with an oil-dampened cloth, inserted into the gun tube from the breech end, and pushed forward by means of a steel rod until the dent halts it. This steel rod should be of drill rod, about 24″ long, ⅟₃₂″ less than bore diameter, and have a pronounced chamfer at both ends. Like the dent removers, the rod should also be well cared for and stored with a coat of oil on it. Next, tap the rod with light blows until the dent remover body is under the dent. This action should raise the dent. If it does not appear, from the outside, to be level with the surrounding surface of the exterior of the barrel, then knock out the dent remover by inserting the rod from the muzzle and tapping on it. Run a clean patch through the bore and examine the latter under a strong light. If only a very slight shadow appears where the dent was originally, then reinsert the dent remover until it is again under the dent, and gently tap around the dent with a fiber, rawhide or plastic hammer. This tapping, when done properly, will generally fully raise and round out the indentation to conform with the normal internal and external radii of the barrel.

Sometimes, in spite of his best efforts, the gunsmith will find that although the dent appears from the outside of the barrel to have been removed, the inside of the tube will still show evidence of its having been there. In such cases it is permissible and wise to lap out the bore at this point by means of No. 6/0 abrasive cloth attached to a power rotated dowel rod, followed by a similar treatment with crocus cloth. Although very little actual metal is removed by this method, it will enhance the appearance of the bore no small bit. The same precautions as outlined in Chapter Six (when polishing a shotgun tube after the removal of a bore obstruction) should be observed when lapping a bore after dent removal.

As a final word on dent removal procedure, the gunsmith would do well to remember that the muzzle section of a shotgun barrel, because of its choke, is smaller in diameter than the bore proper, and therefore no attempt should ever be made to force the dent remover out of the muzzle end of the gun. In rare cases where the gun is a true cylinder bore, i.e., no choke, it might be possible to ignore this warning. However, since the gunsmith is not very liable to encounter many guns of this type, he might play safe and presume that all shotguns he works upon have some degree of choke.

Dents or deformations present at the muzzle of a shotgun barrel are best removed by using the tapered tool illustrated in

Figure 21. When possible, this tool should be inserted from the breech end of the barrel and tapped into the muzzle until it is straightened out. On some shotguns, where the muzzle is badly battered, it is often better to turn or file off $\frac{1}{16}''$ from the muzzle and recrown it rather than incur belling it by using the muzzle dent remover. No more than $\frac{1}{8}''$ should be removed, however, since this will alter the choke of the barrel, and consequently affect the patterning of the gun.

On some of the inexpensive single shot and double barrel scatter guns, choke is achieved at the factory by swaging about $\frac{1}{2}''$ of the barrel muzzle. Therefore, very little can be removed from the barrel of one of these guns without drastically reducing the choke. Fortunately, it is easy to recognize a barrel which is swage-choked by its bent-in appearance around its periphery at the muzzle.

Sawing 3" off the muzzle end of any shotgun barrel will remove all choke and convert the gun to a true cylinder bore. Reducing the length of a shotgun barrel by this amount is, however, necessary when that much of the barrel is blown apart as a result of snow, dirt or some obstruction's being in the barrel when the gun is fired. Some slight bit of choke can be put back into barrels that have been so shortened by cutting a $\frac{6}{1000}''$ to $\frac{9}{1000}''$ deep recess, about 2" long, starting $1\frac{1}{2}''$ back of the muzzle. Such a recess is best cut by wrapping a few thicknesses of No. 2/o emery cloth around a near bore diameter dowel rod and rotating the rod by motor power. If a portable drill is not available for the purpose, the tailstock can be removed from the lathe and the rod put in the chuck. Some sort of stop must be put on the rod so that the cutting will be done the same distance from the muzzle around the bore. The actual undercutting is achieved by moving the barrel around the abrasive cloth as the rod is spinning. The progress of the cutting should be checked with inside calipers each time the barrel is withdrawn to permit attachment of a new piece of emery cloth to the rod. This will be every few minutes, for the abrasive will wear out very quickly when subject to this sort of usage. After the desired depth has been reached, a finer grit of abrasive should be used to bring about a scratch-free surface.

The choke put into a barrel by the above method will not always produce a pattern that is too much better than that given by a cylinder bore. Nevertheless, it is worth the try when a customer insists that he wants some sort of choke in his cut-down shotgun.

Incidentally, the gunsmith should never cut the barrel of a shotgun below the legal length of 18″ or he is apt to find himself running afoul of the law. Even common gun sense should convince him that a shotgun having a barrel of less than 18″ in length would not be of much use to any legitimate customer who considers himself to be a sportsman of any respectable proportions. This same admonition applies, for the same reasons, to the minimum length of cut-down rifle barrels.

A good way to improve the patterning qualities of a single barrel cut-down gun is to have a Poly Choke, Cutts Compensator, Weaver Choke, or Limon Adjustable Choke fitted to it. The manufacturers of these chokes will supply any interested gunsmith with a schedule of prices and time required to make an installation, upon receipt of a letter containing all the necessary information as to make, model and gauge of gun. This procedure of contacting the manufacturer is suggested because the installation of any patented variable choke is a job requiring special tools not commercially available to the gunsmith, and not a paying investment even if they were available, unless he intended to specialize in work of this sort.

About These Last Four Chapters

Within these last four chapters this writer has tried to cover the most frequently encountered specific problems of diagnosis and repair common to each type of gun. Yet in each of these chapters there are references to certain precautions and methods which apply equally to weapons of the type covered in the other three chapters. For example, in the chapter on Rifle Repairs, the matter of manually operated safeties is discussed in some detail, with special accent on wear between soft engaging surfaces, but in the chapter on Shotgun Repairs the topic of safeties is discussed more in reference to their contact with the stock of the gun. This does not mean that the safety on a shotgun is any less subject to wear or consideration than one on a rifle, but that repeating the same information in two chapters, besides being repetitious, would be to somewhat underestimate the level of intelligence possessed by so highly skilled a mechanic as a gunsmith. In the same way, such topics as trigger pull adjustment and sight work are covered in special chapters since these phases of gunsmithing work apply in a general way to all types of guns.

To get the most out of the information contained in chapters

on Revolver Repair, Pistol Repair, Rifle Repair and Shotgun
Repair, the gunsmith should analyze all parts of each chapter,
and with an open mind see if the precautions, diagnosis and repair applicable to a part of one type gun cannot logically be
applied to the same part of another type gun. A thorough understanding of Chapter Five should make this analysis and application more easily appreciated and understood.

CHAPTER FIFTEEN

Heat Treatment of Small Parts and Springs

BEFORE going into the practical why and how of heat treating, perhaps it might be well to cover a few general thoughts on the subject—general in the sense that the man who has never before done any heat treating work will appreciate what he is up against, and not delude himself into believing that any old piece of steel can be fabricated into a part, heat treated, and presto! it will be ready to stand up under pounding, bending, stretching, and pressure contact with another piece of metal, without showing a sign of wear.

Nor should the gunsmith believe on the other hand that because he does not have the money, space or specialized knowledge to equip, harbor and operate an extensive laboratory, simple heat treating operations are beyond his undertaking.

All that is known today about the ways and means of producing steel parts for a million and one mechanical contrivances that serve their purpose better than they did at an earlier date, because of better heat treatment, was not learned in a short time. For many years fabricators of steel and parts made from steel, have experimented endlessly towards improvement. Yet today, in spite of the great strides that have been made, there is still much to be desired along this line.

In spite of the extensively financed best efforts of metallurgists and chemists we still encounter steel parts in automobiles, airplanes and boats, as well as guns, that break under the strains and stresses imposed by normal operating conditions. Selfishly we might well be thankful for this state of affairs or there would be little need for repairmen. Too, indications are that the guaranteed unbreakable steel part for a firearm will be a long time in coming and should not cause the most youthful aspirant to gunsmithing to worry about the decline of future business on this account.

Aside from knowledge, which it is hoped will be augmented by perusing this chapter, the man who intends to do even a limited amount of heat treating work must have certain equipment and supplies. While it must be admitted that some of the old swordmakers and knifemakers, whose reputations are still perpetuated in story, poem and legend, might have used other since-forgotten equipment and means to produce their wares, the 20th Century gunsmith may rest assured that he will be far better off if he procures the most modern items available within the reach of his pocketbook, and should not concern himself with the allegedly "lost secrets" of ancient masters.

Required Equipment

Furnaces. The number one requirement is, of course, a furnace, and preferably one that is gas fired and equipped with a pyrometer. Such a setup will not only remove the guesswork from almost all phases of hardening and tempering, but will also allow the gunsmith much extra time that would ordinarily be required if the torch-and-plier method of heating is used.

An electric furnace is no less desirable than a gas fired one. However, this writer would not suggest that electricity be used as a heating medium unless the gunsmith is located in a territory where electric current is very cheap, and such is not usually the situation unless the current is supplied by a company that has access to water power. In most of the larger cities where steam turbines are used by generating companies, the electric furnace would cost so much to operate that the per job profit, especially on the small items which a gun repairman has occasion to deal with, would be too low.

For all practical purposes, the heating furnace does not have to be very large because it will be used chiefly for small parts, unless the gunsmith chooses to work on other mechanical devices, in which case the size of these parts will necessarily determine the size of the furnace. To this writer's way of thinking, a furnace which would accommodate metal or metal parts up to 8" in length and 6" across would be quite adequate. In this connection it should be borne in mind that the smaller the furnace is, the quicker it will heat up and, consequently, the cheaper it will be to operate. However, the economy factor alone should not unduly influence the gunsmith in his selection of a furnace for heat treating work.

Although there are quite a few furnaces available commercially (See Chapter Twenty), these are as a rule a bit more elaborate and, consequently, a little more expensive than one made locally by a plumbing contractor or heating engineer. Either of these two latter types of establishments generally has the necessary fire brick, pipes, steel plates, connections, heating units—as well as the know-how and facilities to fabricate a small furnace that will satisfy the gun repairman's needs. The same person who makes the furnace can also purchase and install the very necessary pyrometer so that it will be positioned correctly to give true readings.

Where it is not possible to have a furnace made locally by a competent mechanic the gunsmith should give serious thought to purchasing one of the types pictured in this book. A letter to the Chicago Flexible Shaft Company, of Chicago, Ill. (Stewart Industrial Furnace Division) will bring a copy of their catalog and very informative handbook. In the letter to this company the gunsmith should state his requirements and type of fuel (gas, oil, et cetera) normally used. With this information, the company will be able to recommend the best furnace for use under the stated conditions.

If one does not choose to purchase or have made a furnace just for heat treatment work, then a conventional forge, designed to burn soft coal, and equipped with a motor or hand-driven bellows, can be used. A heating unit such as this can also be used for forging work of any operations where very high temperatures are required.

A coal forge is not without disadvantages, however, for it must be equipped with an exhaust cover of some type to carry off the noxious gases and dust that are evolved when it is in use. Also, a supply of coal must be kept on hand at all times and a new fire built each time it is desired to use the forge. Consequently, it cannot be recommended very highly for use in a city gunsmith's shop, although it might well be considered ideal for the man who does his work in a barn or isolated building in a suburban region.

Tongs. For removing parts or pipes containing parts, tongs are considered to be must equipment. Eventually the beginner will find that he has made a great error if he has not supplied himself with at least one pair of tongs for holding and moving hot pieces of metal. As can be seen from Figure 84, tongs for heat treating and forging work are equipped with long handles and specially shaped jaws that lend themselves well to the type of work for which they are designed. They provide a means of

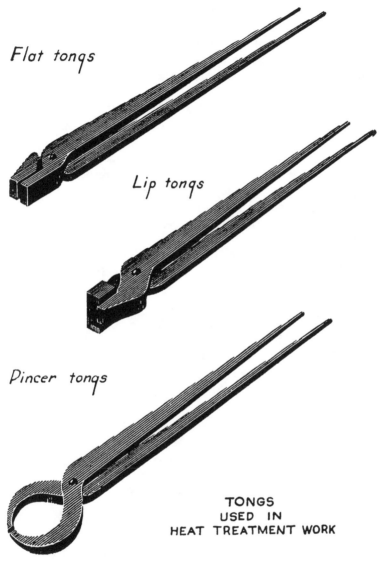

Flat tongs

Lip tongs

Pincer tongs

TONGS
USED IN
HEAT TREATMENT WORK

FIGURE 84

insuring a positive grip upon shaped objects and permit the user
to exert leverage from such a distance whereby his hands will not
be affected by the heat of the object being held. All of which is a
very subtle but positive lead-up to the time-worn admonition that
pliers should not be used in place of tongs. When used for the

purposes for which they are intended pliers will give good service for many years, but when employed to handle hot objects, they will quickly lose their temper and consequently their usefulness, to say nothing of helping the gunsmith to some surprisingly hot times of a definitely undesirable nature.

Pipes. Next in importance to a furnace and tongs is another essential item of the heat treating "laboratory" and that is pipes —not special pipes, but just a half dozen lengths threaded at both ends and provided with caps to screw on these threads.

Three pieces of pipe about 3″ long and about 1″ inside diameter; two pieces of pipe about 6″ long and about 1½″ inside diameter; and one piece about 7″ long with an inside diameter of 3″ will provide the gunsmith with a very useful set of containers for holding parts to be annealed, normalized and case-hardened.

One of the caps on each pipe should be provided with a pair of lugs as illustrated in Figure 85. These lugs, which will stand up

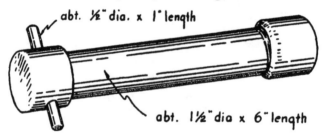

abt. ½″ dia. x 1″ length

abt. 1½″ dia x 6″ length

DEVICE FOR HEAT TREATMENT WORK— MADE FROM COMMON IRON PIPE

FIGURE 85

well if made from ½″ diameter cold rolled steel, should be about ¾″ long and screwed or welded to the cap. Their purpose is to provide a quick means for loosening the cap when the contents of the pipe have to be emptied into a pail of oil or water for quenching after heating.

Molten Bath Containers. Containers made of ⅛″ black iron, welded together, must also be made for holding molten lead (for hardening springs); potassium nitrate (for tempering springs and small parts); and cyanide compounds (for case-hardening work).

For most purposes these containers should be about 10" long, 6" wide and 6" deep. There is no particular objection to these containers being any larger than the suggested size except that the larger they are the more chemical will be required to fill them to a desired height, which is at safe maximum within two inches of the top of the tank.

Although any of these containers can be placed directly over an open flame to be heated, a more ideal setup is indicated in Figure 86. In this arrangement the container is placed within a fire brick unit that is provided with a heating appliance, thereby eliminating the possibility of the container being upset while it is being heated. Also, the container will heat up much faster and far less heat will be wasted.

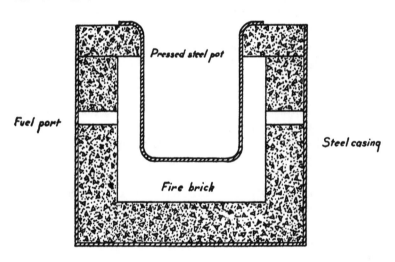

HEATING UNIT FOR HOLDING LEAD & SALT CONTAINER

FIGURE 86

If an arrangement of this order is wanted by the gunsmith, he must make or have each container made with a 1" overlap all around the top so they will rest on the fire brick. A set of handles should also be welded to the overlap at each end of the container so it can be lowered and removed from the fire brick unit as the occasion requires. A light weight sheet iron (not galvanized) cover should also be provided for each of these containers so that the solution will not be a receptacle for old cigarette butts and foreign matter when not in use. And as a first line safety measure, a trunk style box placed in some out-of-the-way corner of the shop should be used as a place to store these small containers as well as the spare ingredients to fill them. In short, a place for everything and everything in its place; a trite saying, perhaps, but nonetheless an excellent practice.

One type of container which is manufactured and sold by the Chicago Flexible Shaft Company is especially made for molten bath solutions, and because of its scientific construction is ideally suited for holding small gun parts. The rim around the edge of this container acts as a stop when the container is placed in a heating unit designed to hold it. For the man who would rather buy his molten bath containers ready made than go to the trouble of forming and welding them, these commercial containers are highly recommended.

Needed also in connection with heat treatment operations are the following listed items and a brief reason for their necessity:

Miscellaneous Equipment, Chemicals and Oils

A Bunsen Burner. With about 8' of hose connection for use in applying heat to gun parts and sections of a gun that must be heated locally; for example, sweating on shotgun ribs, and sight ramps and removing soldered-on rear sight bases from foreign military weapons.

A Container for Holding Water. To be used for quenching purposes; a galvanized iron garbage pail equipped with a cover is ideal.

A Container for Holding Tempering Oil. Same specifications as for water container.

Sodium Cyanide (CaCn) or Potassium Cyanide (KCN). For use in connection with case-hardening work. In as much as these chemicals are deadly poison and react to give off very noxious odors when heated or brought in contact with an acid, they should be used with care and stored away in a closed and clearly marked container when not being used.

Slaked Lime, which is a very finely powdered chemical, is a poor conductor of heat, and, therefore, should be available for use in connection with the annealing of small parts.

Bone Dust, which is sold at florist shops or any other establishments dealing in fertilizers, is a necessity for pack-hardening operations since it is a compound that is very rich in carbon.

Finely Ground Charred Leather. Also for the same general purpose as bone dust and should be made from scrap pieces of leather that are pretty much free of oil. To char the leather cut it up in pieces and heat it in a pan until it crumbles and can be ground into a powdered state. Most shoe repair men have scrap pieces of leather around their shop and will usually part with them for the asking.

Oil for Quenching Purposes. Can be procured commercially from any of the widely known oil companies, or it can be made by mixing equal parts of paraffin oil, linseed oil and lard oil. In the long run it is cheaper and less troublesome to buy at least ten gallons of commercially made tempering oil. A letter to the industrial oil division of any of the well known gasoline or oil companies will bring information as to the specifications, price and minimum quantity of tempering oil they will ship.

Also, especially desirable are: asbestos or similar heat resistant gloves; a pair of properly fitted eye goggles; and a plastic face mask for the gunsmith's protection against eye and skin injuries, which are all too potentially present in this phase of his work.

Terms and Definitions

Having equipped himself with the tools and accessories required for heat treatment work, the mechanic who wishes to turn out good work in this line of endeavor must also be familiar with some special terms, or nomenclature as they call it in the Army, each of which conveys something very definite when he knows what they mean. In the following paragraphs these terms are defined primarily in such a way as they apply to the gunsmith for practical working purposes, and, though technically correct, they are not delineated in such great detail as to obscure their meaning with technicalities.

A knowledge of these terms will not only enable the gunsmith to better understand this chapter but also make it easier for him to delve into other writings on the subject with a better basic understanding. Too, as a means of expression in connection with correspondence and talking with persons similarly versed on the subject, their correct usage is an absolute necessity:

Heat Treatment. A series of operations involving the heating and cooling of a metal in its solid state for the purpose of obtaining certain desirable characteristics. It is the rate of heating and cooling that determines the crystalline structure of the metal.

Heating. Raising the temperature of the metal to a desired point.

Cooling. Returning metal to room temperature by quenching it in water, oil, or some similar liquid substance.

Soaking. Keeping a piece of metal at an elevated temperature for a definite time, in order that it may become thoroughly and uniformly saturated with heat, and permit the desired changes in grain structure to take place.

Critical Temperature, as often mentioned in the ensuing pages, means that point where chemical changes in the carbon (which is the chief hardening element in steel) alters the structure of the metal. For all practical purposes, when dealing with the steel that a gunsmith generally uses, it is between 1350° and 1450° Fahrenheit. In terms of color it is when the metal under ordinary room light appears to be between medium cherry and full red.

From a very technical standpoint, the critical temperature varies with different types of steel, that is to say, for steels having different carbon content. However, it is safe to presume that for purposes of small shop gunsmithing work where the mechanic's biggest heat treating job is that of hardening and tempering firing pins, holding pins, sears and similar small parts, he will be working mostly with drill rod with a carbon content between .90 and 1.00 and tool steel having a carbon range from 1.00 to 1.20. Spring steel comes under a separate classification and must be worked at a different temperature range. This matter is discussed in detail farther on in this chapter.

The importance of knowing the critical temperature of a piece of steel cannot be overestimated, for upon this figure the success of any heat treating operation depends. It is for that reason the mechanic should order steel from a reliable company and tag or mark each length in such a way that it can be identified. Catalogs and handbooks are available from steel mills which tell the carbon and alloy content of each type of steel they sell. With this knowledge, the matter of guesswork, which has no place in any phase of gun repair work, least of all heat treatment, is eliminated.

In large shops the ends and sections along each piece of steel in stock are painted a color that can be checked against a color chart for identification purposes. For example, carbon drill rod might be marked with green paint and the color chart would indicate this.

Annealing. Resorted to for the purpose of reducing internal stresses, refining the grain structure and, most of all from the gunsmith's standpoint, rendering a piece of steel soft enough to be machined with conventional hand and machine tools.

Spot Annealing. A means of softening a small area of a hardened piece of metal that cannot, or should not for safety reasons, be annealed as a unit. For example, spot annealing is called for when it is necessary to drill and tap sight screw holes in a hardened receiver such as are on some of the old Springfield Model 1903 rifles.

Normalizing. A form of annealing in which internal strains set up during machining, forming, forging and welding are removed. To properly normalize a part, it must be placed in a furnace where the temperature can be regulated and held at a stipulated point for any desired length of time. The part or parts to be normalized are placed in the furnace and heated to a point about 100° F. above the critical temperature of the metal being treated, and then kept at that temperature for a sufficient time to allow soaking of the pieces. After they are properly soaked, the parts must then be removed from the furnace and allowed to cool in room air.

The temperature to which the parts must be raised for normalizing depends entirely upon the make-up (presence of carbon and alloys) of the steel, and the time it must be kept at the proper temperature depends upon the mass of the piece being treated.

Although the operation of normalizing is not ordinarily carried out on small gun parts, it is often necessary to normalize arbors and shafts that the gunsmith might have occasion to make in connection with special tools and machines for gun repair work.

Carburizing. A phase of heat treating work in which the carbon content of the metal's surface (it must be an iron base alloy) is brought in contact, when at a definite temperature, with a carbon-rich solid, liquid or gas. The absorption of the carbon by the metal tends to make the surface so treated much harder than the core metal of the piece. The longer a piece of metal being carburized is held under influence of the carbonaceous substance at a required given heat, the greater will be the depth of hardness. The surface hard layer resulting from a treatment of this type is known as a case. Thus we have the expression "depth of the case."

Cyaniding. A method of case-hardening steel in which either commercial hardening salts, sodium cyanide, or potassium cyanide is employed as the carbonaceous substance. This process does not impart as deep a case to the metal as do other methods of case-hardening. However, for some parts that are used in guns it is quite satisfactory.

At this point it might be well to mention that some sort of hood should be provided over the tank in which the cyanide is being heated so that the poisonous vapors evolved will be deflected away from the nose and mouth of the operator. An exhaust fan used in conjunction with hooded lead-heating and cyanide-heating tanks is the ideal safety first setup.

Hardening. The heating of an iron base alloy a little above its critical temperature and then quenching it in water, oil, or some similar cooling medium to produce a uniform degree of hardness throughout its structure.

In raising the temperature of a piece of metal to, or slightly above, its critical point, the matter of overheating must be given serious consideration. For to overheat a piece of metal (in the case of gunsmithing work it is usually a part on which much time has been spent to make it) is often to render it so that it will not longer be of correct size or shape, due to even a very slight amount of oxidation on some of the close tolerance points. Here again we can appreciate the necessity for a small furnace and some type of accurate temperature indicator (pyrometer).

In using pipe or box as a holding medium for work that is heated for purposes of hardening or tempering, it is most advisable to pack around the part with borax or common sand. This action will prevent almost any sort of carburization or oxidation that might ordinarily occur if the piece were heated in air or rested against some portion of the heating container. Common table salt (sodium chloride) can be used for the same purpose as sand or borax in carrying out an operation of this order.

When heating for hardening purposes the heat should be applied gradually and held at the critical plus temperature just long enough to insure complete heating of the part.

After a piece of metal has been heated it must be cooled quickly for purposes of hardening or tempering. The quenching bath, as mentioned before, is generally some liquid substance, i.e., water, water with salt in it, or oil.

When quenching a piece of metal the receptacle holding the

cooling medium should be large enough so as to allow room for agitating the piece as it is being immersed. Also, a spacious receptacle will accommodate a large quantity of the cooling medium which will not rise in temperature as much as would a smaller amount.

The ideal setup for a quenching bath is one in which the liquid can be kept in a state of agitation. In this way there is no need to move the work around and, consequently, there is little or no chance of uneven hardening, all other conditions being ideal, of course. Such an arrangement as this requires a small electric motor to be hitched up to a shaft having a propeller-like attachment. A mesh or screen would have to be rigged up around the propeller so that the work would not be struck by the rotating shaft or blades. A constant flow of water into and out of the quenching bath, by means of a pipe and overflow arrangement, is also a satisfactory means of securing agitation.

Nevertheless, no matter what type of quenching bath is employed, the part being cooled should not be carelessly dropped or thrown into it, for if this method of operation is carried on, the best results cannot be expected, due to the fact that uneven cooling is quite apt to take place when the part being quenched comes in contact with, or comes to rest on, the metallic surface of the cooling tank. This thought applies especially to parts which have considerable mass and do not become cool by the time they sink to the bottom of the container. On the other hand, very small parts such as pins and the like can be plunged into the quenching medium, agitated a little, and then dropped to the bottom of the container, since, because of their small mass, they cool very rapidly.

Tempering. After a part has been hardened properly it is, for all practical purposes, entirely too hard and brittle. Therefore, some additional heat treatment is required to make the part so that it possesses the correct degree of hardness for the purpose it is to serve. Bringing a piece of metal to this degree of hardness is known as tempering.

Tempering Colors and Their Application

Tempering, like all other phases of heat treatment of metals, is in itself a science and at large manufacturing installations there is a separate department where this type of work is carried on under the direction of qualified metallurgists. Most of the equipment used in these shops is far beyond the financial reach of the average neighborhood mechanic, though this does not make it any less desirable. Yet, as she does so often, old Mother Nature, with a little help from some very observing individual, has provided us with a fairly accurate and workable means of judging the approximate temperature of a piece of steel. This is the color method of temperature determination and can be used to great advantage by the gunsmith who does not have a pyrometer.

Figure 87 gives a list of these nine colors which are distinctly discernible when they appear on the oxidized surface of a piece of heated steel.

In using these colors to determine the point at which a piece must be quenched to achieve a desired degree of hardness, the gunsmith should understand that shop illumination plays a part. For example, under an intense light coming from one direction, dark blue might appear as light blue, while the same color might appear to be purple under another condition of illumination. Therefore, it behooves the mechanic who would like to achieve near perfection and uniformity in matters of heat treatment to place his lighting equipment in such a way as to bring about shadowless and subdued illumination. This same type of illumination will also be of immeasurable value in judging the various degrees of the heat colors, i.e., dark red, cherry red, full red, et cetera.

Pale yellow, which is the first distinct tempering color to be observed after heating a piece of metal, indicates a temperature of about 430° F. If a piece of drill rod or carbon tool steel is quenched at this point it will come out of the bath very hard. So hard, in fact, that it will hardly be suitable for any moving gun part.

A straw colored surface also indicates a hardness that does not lend itself to gun parts. However, such tools as reamers or hammers will stand up very well if drawn at this temperature.

Golden yellow or bright straw also produces a very hard piece of steel when the latter is quenched at this point. Scribers, engraving tools, prick punches and scrapers should be drawn when this color appears at the working edge of the tool.

Sears, hammers and similar working parts in gun mechanisms, excluding springs, should be drawn when the surface shows brown with light purple spots. To achieve uniform coloration

OXIDE COLOR

Pale Yellow	430
Straw	445
Golden Yellow	470
Brown	490
Brown with purple spots	510
Purple	530
Dark Blue	550
Bright Blue	565
Pale Blue	610

Temperature(approximate) Deg. F.

TEMPERING COLORS
for carbon steels

HEAT COLORS
for carbon steels

Faint Red	900
Blood Red	1050
Dark Cherry	1075
Medium Cherry	1250
Cherry (full) Red	1375
Bright Red	1550
Salmon	1650
Orange	1725
Lemon	1825
Light Yellow	1975
White	2200
Dazzling or Sparkling White	2350

Temperature
(approximate).
Deg. F.

J. B. m.

FIGURE 87

(indicating uniform temperature) such metal parts as mentioned above should be placed on a block of steel and flame heat applied to the block. In this way it will be easier to observe the change of colors as they occur. And also there will be less risk of some engaging point such as a sear end or hammer notch being burned as a result of the flame coming in direct contact with it.

Drift punches drawn when the working end of the punch is purple color will retain their shape very well under constant use and yet will possess enough flexibility to resist snapping off.

Bottoming chisels, gouges, and similar woodworking tools, with the exception of saws, should also be drawn when the cutting area of the tool registers purple.

Dark blue is the color which indicates the proper temperature for firing pins to be drawn or tempered. Here again, as with sears and hammers, the part must be heated uniformly if it is to stand up under the constant stresses it is subject to.

Tempering Firing Pins. Actually, the best method for tempering firing pins is to immerse them in a bath which can be heated to a temperature of 550–570° F. In this way the entire pin can be heated to a uniform degree throughout. Such baths, which will withstand heating to a temperature of this degree, can be of special tempering oil which is commercially procurable (See Chapter Twenty), or potassium nitrate, which can be heated to about 700° F. without danger of toxic effects or fire hazard. However, in using a tempering oil or potassium nitrate as a tempering bath, a pyrometer of some sort must be employed. There is no easy or short cut to determine the temperature of the bath otherwise. And if the gunsmith intends to do much work of this order, then a pyrometer is a must. All things considered, the amount of money invested in a good temperature taking instrument of this sort is well spent and can hardly be considered as superfluous or luxury equipment.

Preheating. When tempering a part in a heated oil or chemical bath, it is necessary that the part either be preheated by flame or placed in the bath when the latter is far below the desired temperature. By doing this the chance of the part cracking or warping as a result of its being thrust into the hot bath when the former is at room temperature is precluded.

Preheating can be done in boiling water provided all traces of aqua remaining on the part are shaken off or allowed to dry by heat or evaporation before it is dropped into the tempering bath.

because if a water wetted object is dropped into hot oil or potassium nitrate, there is apt to be a bit of action on the part of these quenching media which would cause the gunsmith to wonder if he had done the right thing.

The oil bath can be advantageously employed in tempering any parts, while the potassium nitrate bath, because of its comparatively limited temperature range at molten state, can be used only from the brown to pale blue color range. Irrespective of which is used, however, the necessity for a pyrometer is in no way lessened.

A piece of steel which is quenched at pale blue, indicating a temperature in the neighborhood of 600° F., is hard, yet springy enough to stand the shocks imposed on hand saw blades for cutting wood.

Having covered the list of necessary equipment and pertinent definitions, now let us consider the actual work and preparation incident to the practical side of annealing, carburizing, cyaniding, hardening and tempering, as each applies to gun repair work.

Annealing Procedure

For purposes of modification or adjustment, the gunsmith often finds that he must soften a hard gun part before it can be machined or filed. For example, let us presume that a shotgun sear requires extensive filing that cannot be accomplished while the part is in its hardened condition. Therefore, it must be annealed or softened.

To do this, select one of the short pipe lengths with one end closed, and half fill it with slaked lime; then place the part in the pipe in such a way that it does not rest against any portion of the pipe. Completely fill the pipe with more slaked lime and screw on the other pipe end. Place the pipe in a furnace or heating forge and turn on the heat. Allow the pipe to remain at slightly above the critical temperature for about a half-hour in the case of this, a small part; longer if the part has considerable mass, and then shut the furnace off and allow the pipe and its contents to cool to room temperature.

If work conditions are such that the furnace is needed for other work, then remove the pipe and bury it in a pail of sand or lime so the cooling action will be slow.

Incidentally, this writer does not recommend that any major

assembly, such as a receiver, bolt or barrel, be annealed unless the gunsmith has the *knowledge, skill* and *facilities* to restore the proper temper of the piece. *And it is so seldom that anyone but the factory or a firm doing only heat treatment work can restore the correct temper to these vital gun parts, that the gunsmith would do well to steer clear of annealing these parts.*

Thus annealed, the sear of our example can now be worked on with file, drill or scraper. However, before it is put back in the gun to serve a useful purpose, it must be rehardened and tempered, for in its softened condition it is worthless as a sear.

Spot Annealing. Where softening of a small area on a receiver is required to drill and tap for sight screws, spot annealing is permissible. The section to be annealed should be surrounded with a paste made of ground asbestos and water, and heat applied inside this blocked off area. After the critical temperature plus has been reached, the receiver should be quickly thrust into a pail of lime and allowed to cool slowly. Due to the small area heated, this cooling will generally be complete in 10 or 15 minutes, after which time the spot should be tried with a file or prick punch to see if it is soft enough to allow machining. If it is not, then the heating operation must be performed until the desired degree of metal softness has been achieved.

The most efficient way to raise a spot that must be heated to red color is to use a torch with a very fine tip so that the hot cone can be concentrated on a very small area. An oxy-acetylene setup is ideal for this type of work except that renting the oxygen and acetylene gas tanks entails prohibitive costs unless the mechanic does other welding aside from his gun repair work.

Often spot annealing on receivers or other parts can be avoided by using a mounted abrasive wheel in a Handee Grinder, or similar high speed tool, to cut through the hard steel shell that often protects an otherwise soft core piece of steel. When practicable, this possibility should be explored for it is best to avoid annealing on any part when a desired mechanical operation can be performed by the use of abrasives or tools that can cut through hard steel without being ruined in the process.

Surface Hardening Processes

In discussing the merits of a case-hardened part, gunsmiths often ignore one of the most salient points of case-hardening and that is the case depth. Some mechanics, in condemning surface-hardening, too often have in mind the parts of cheap Spanish guns or inexpensive shotguns in which the case is scarcely skin deep and does not stand up under even normal usage.

Actually, a good case-hardening job is an object of beauty and utility when correctly performed on such parts as shotgun hammers, sears and trigger guards, to mention but a few. The hammer and trigger on any of the Smith & Wesson swing-out cylinder revolvers, and the receivers of some of the better made double barrel shotguns, are outstanding examples of this fact.

Case-hardening, carburizing, or pack-carburizing, which are but three different names applied to very similar operations, often provides the only practical shop means of treating a piece of metal, such as a hinge pin made of S.A.E. 2315 nickel alloy steel, so that it will have a highly resistant surface to wear, and yet be able to stand up under the shock of pounding, because of its tough flexible core.

Carburizing Procedure

To case-harden a part for utility purposes alone, i.e., without regard for producing the mottled color tints, select a short length of pipe and fill it half way with bone dust, place the part in the pipe, and fill completely with more bone dust in such a way that the part is completely surrounded with at least ½" thickness of the carburizing substance. Screw on the other end of the pipe and place in a forge or furnace at a temperature of 1700° F. Allow the pipe and its contents to remain at this temperature for the desired length of time (See Figure 88). Then remove it with a pair of tongs, unscrew the cap, and dump the contents of the pipe into a pail of water held at room temperature. After the part has cooled, check it for hardness with a smooth cut file. If the part has been treated properly it will resist the file. If it does not, then the facts must be faced—the part has not been case-hardened properly and must be processed again. Before proceeding with a second operation, however, check the furnace, the pyrometer and the hardening compound to make certain that no detail has been overlooked.

Producing Colors. Where colors are desired on a case-hardened part, the charred leather dust mentioned earlier in the chapter should be used in place of bone dust. Also, the part should have a highly polished scratch-free surface and be chemically cleaned with gasoline or carbon tetrachloride before it is placed in the

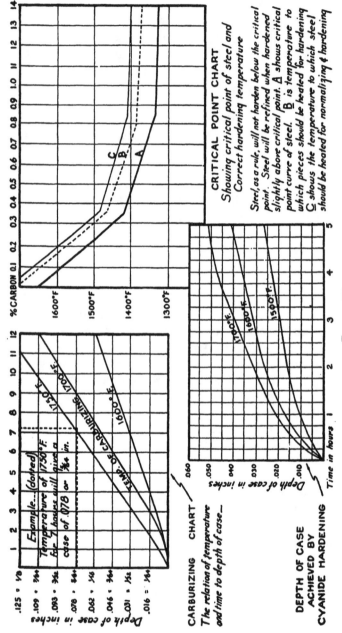

CRITICAL POINT CHART
Showing critical point of steel and
Correct hardening temperature

Steel, as a rule, will not harden below the critical point. Steel will be refined when hardened slightly above critical point. A shows critical point curve of steel. B is temperature to which pieces should be heated for hardening C shows the temperature to which steel should be heated for normalizing & hardening

CARBURIZING CHART
The relation of temperature and time to depth of case—

DEPTH OF CASE
ACHIEVED BY
CYANIDE HARDENING

FIGURE 88

pipe. The purpose of the cleaning is to remove any traces of polishing compound or perspiration stains that might show up after the part has been hardened.

When case-hardening very small parts, the gunsmith can often effect an economy in the expenditure of leather carbon (considering the time required to prepare this substance) by using the very smallest pipe or other similarly constructed container that will accommodate the part and the necessary minimum of surrounding carbonaceous material. This sort of economy is very important when a comparatively inexpensive part is to be case-hardened and the old profit factor rears its ever-present head.

Where an exceptionally deep case is required on a hammer or similar part that has quite some degree of mass and is subject to a great deal of wear, the pipe and contents can be left in the furnace for two or three hours. For shotgun receivers a heating period of five or six hours is not unusual.

On very thin parts, or parts that are long but have very little mass, such as cocking levers on some foreign guns and trigger guards, an allowance for shrinkage or warpage should be anticipated and allowed for in machining the part. A film of oil spread over the top of the quenching water also helps to minimize this possibility of warpage by slowing down the sudden cooling action on the part.

Cyaniding Procedure

Cyanide, which produces at best a shallower case than pack-carburizing (See Figure 88) has, nevertheless, a definite place in the program of the gunsmith's heat treatment work, for such parts as small pins, screws and the like.

Cyanide hardening follows along the same general rule as carburizing, i.e., the rate of penetration, and the concentration of the carbon in the case depends upon the temperature and the length of time the steel is heated.

For most cyanide work, twenty minutes' immersion in molten cyanide is considered the proper time for temperatures of 1500° to 1600° F. The carbon will penetrate $6/1000''$ in the first 15 minutes and only $3/1000''$ in the next 40 mintues. Therefore, 20 minutes seems to be a good time limit for most cyanide work.

Before placing the part to be hardened in the molten bath, preheat the part to about 700° F. by means of a Bunsen burner or similar hot flame. When this procedure is not practicable, then preheat the part in boiling water.

The cyanide process has many advantages to counterbalance some of its shortcomings; a very hard case is obtained, finished pieces come out nice and clean, and have a smooth appearance.

As a matter of fact, cyanide seems to be the only practical method of hardening small pins and screws, and other similar parts that must retain their accurate dimensions during the hardening operation. Due to the uniformity of the bath, the parts are heated uniformly and, as a result, evaporation is reduced to the minimum. Oxidation is almost completely eliminated, and the finished product is clean, smooth and hard.

A cyanide container should be of the pot type and the furnace fitted with a hood to take away the poisonous fumes. For very small work a wire basket is recommended. While some parts might require oil quenching, cyanided parts, as a rule, are best quenched in cold water, and if a mechanical or air agitator is used in the quenching bath, mottled surfaces can often be produced on the hardened parts.

Hardening Procedure

Steel, as a rule, will not harden when heated below the critical temperature and then quenched. Therefore, it is most important that the critical temperature of the steel being used be known. In this connection the chart in Figure 88 should be of help to the gunsmith who knows the carbon content of the steel he is using, or at least knows the S.A.E. number of the steel, in which case he can find out the carbon content by looking up the S.A.E. number in Chapter Nineteen and noting the carbon range.

In as much as the grain structure of steel will be somewhat refined if heated to just a few degrees above the critical point and then quenched, it is recommended that such practice be followed.

As in other operations, uniform heating is essential to good hardening. Overheating a piece of steel does not give it increased hardness but, instead, increases brittleness. Therefore, if a piece is overheated by mistake it should not be allowed to drop to the hardening temperature and then quenched, but should be removed from the furnace, allowed to cool, and then reheated to the proper temperature for hardening.

The formation of scale on a piece of steel is especially undesirable on finished parts and thus must be precluded so that the dimensions of a part will not be changed from the time of being finished machined until it is placed in the gun.

Preventing Scale Formation. To prevent scale formation, the part being hardened should be coated with a mixture of bone charcoal and oil, or a coating of melted boracic acid, or enclosed in a pipe as suggested earlier in this chapter. The gas and air coming into the heating furnace must also be so regulated that an excess of air is not permitted to flow into the heating chamber. The correct furnace atmosphere, as indicated by the manufacturer's catalog, should be adhered to.

The quenching pail should be as near as possible to the furnace or forge so that the part can be moved from the heating chamber and immediately immersed. In this way there is little chance of air attacking the heated part and promoting the formation of scale.

Although the temptation to heat a small part, like a sear, by means of a Bunsen burner or acetylene torch is great, the gunsmith should always bear in mind that there is little to be gained by short cut heat treatment work. More often than not, such methods result in turning out a finished product which is but little better than an untreated piece of metal. When a mechanic asks to be paid for time spent in doing a job, he is expected to utilize the time in a manner which produces a finished job that is of a professional standard. True, some parts which are heat treated by the torch-and-plier method do possess some degree of hardness, but they all too frequently go to pieces when subjected to any continued usage. For example, a torch-heated firing pin might well be able to stand up under a few demonstration blows, only to break as a result of being too hard, or upset as a result of being too soft, after a short period of actual service.

Tempering Procedure

Under the definition of tempering covered earlier in this chapter, the various distinctly discernible colors are listed and the qualities a piece of carbon tool steel or drill rod will possess if quenched at any desired one of them. This color method of tempering is not suggested as the best temperature guide but is included because this writer realizes that the color method has long been used by mechanics who believe it to be very satisfactory for much of the heat treatment work done in a small gun shop.

These colors appear only on the surface and are due to a thin film of oxide which forms on the metal after the temperature reaches about 430° F. In order to see these colors, the surface must be highly polished on a soft-back abrasive wheel or with a piece of fine grit emery cloth. When tempering by the coloring method, an open flame cannot be used because on very small parts the heat colors travel so rapidly along the metal's surface that the part is too often quenched at a higher temperature than it should be. A better method is to lay the part to be tempered on a block of steel and apply heat to the block. In this way the absorption of heat by the part is achieved more slowly and uniformly. Consequently, the change of colors does not occur so rapidly and the part can be scooped into the quenching pail just as the desired shade appears on the surface.

Tempering Salts and Oils. The use of tempering salts or tempering oil is without doubt a better and more positive method of bringing about a desired degree of hardness in a working gun part. Although potassium nitrate is satisfactory where the temperature range does not exceed 750° F., there are commercial salts available which have a working range of as high as 1000° F. (See Chapter Twenty). Thus, by using these commercial salts in conjunction with a pyrometer, there is almost no reason why a gunsmith should have to resort to guesswork or temper a part with crossed fingers in hopes that it will be satisfactorily tempered.

Preheating, prior to tempering, can, in dealing with most of the small parts the gunsmith has occasion to work with, be done in boiling water. Preheating a piece before dropping it into the tempering bath lessens the possibility of the part cracking or warping as a result of going from one temperature to another that is much higher.

The quenching media listed earlier in this chapter are, for all practical purposes, the only kinds with which the gunsmith need concern himself, although it might be of interest to point out that for certain special work such substances as milk, mercury, sea water, soapy water, lime water, beeswax and compressed air are employed.

The addition of a small amount of sulphuric or hydrochloric acid (a few ounces to 5 gallons of water) to a water quench will have a tendency to clean the work off. The same results can be obtained by adding a few tablespoonfuls of lye or trisodium phosphate to a water quenching bath.

The addition of salt to water (enough salt to make a 10% solution) is often recommended where the maximum degree of hardness is desired of a piece of hardened steel.

Fabrication and Heat Treatment of Springs

Before going into the ways and means of heat treating springs, perhaps it might be well to cover the important points in the making of a spring. Incidentally, in referring to springs in the course of this chapter, we are considering only springs made from flat stock and not helical or "coil" springs, which are wound from "piano" wire.

Helical springs are too easily and cheaply purchased for the gunsmith to spend much time in their making. Most of the small helical springs in small arms list at less than 25¢ each and this means the gunsmith could not profitably spend much more than ten minutes in making one and still come out on the black side of the ledger.

In practice it is not very often that one encounters a broken coil spring in an obsolete model gun, or weapon of foreign make, that cannot be replaced by one of the same vital dimensions (diameter of wire, diameter of spring and number of coils per inch) available from American gun manufacturers' selections or from a company that makes helical springs as a specialty.

Spring Steel. Almost needless to say, the first prerequisite of spring-making is steel, or more correctly, spring steel. According to old time gunsmiths, the best spring steel is made in Sweden and England. However, at this writing it is possible that spring steel stock from these sources might be some time in arriving in this country and so the American produced steel must be used. To this writer's way of thinking, the temporary loss of imported spring steel should not prove to be a great blow to the gunsmith, for actually the domestic stock, if properly forged, formed and heat treated, will make an excellent and lasting spring. America's industrial contribution to World War II has, I am sure, served well to dispel much of the "old country" superiority bunk that has been given extensive lip service during the past 50 years. Too often a mechanic trained in some of the European apprentice ways (Continental sweat shop) migrates to this country and, because he cannot perform his job properly, blames it on the lack of good raw materials which were available in the old country. Thus, when a gunsmith turns out a spring that breaks or "sets" after a few compressions, he should not attribute the failure to the steel. Rather, he should examine the spring for tool marks, high spots, unsymmetrical taper, and evidences of poor heat treatment.

Preparatory Work. In most cases where the gunsmith has occasion to make a flat or V type spring, he will have the advantage of having as a guide the worn out or broken spring he is duplicating. As a matter of fact, it is almost imperative that at least a major portion of the spring being duplicated be on hand for comparison, so that the finished product will have the proper shape, dimensions and tension.

Before proceeding with fabrication of a spring, measurements of the old spring should be taken and a rough sketch drawn indicating these dimensions. By doing this it will not be necessary to check and recheck the dimensions of the old spring each time a doubt arises as to a particular measurement while the gunsmith is in the process of forging, grinding or filing. Also, and this may sound like so much trivia to a novice, the paper with the sketch and dimensions should be tacked up where it can be seen so that a pile of tools and the usual miscellany that accumulates on a work bench need not be tossed about each time reference to the paper is necessary. To one who is experienced in the tremendous trifles of gunsmithing, however, the simple suggestions just outlined will not sound unusual, for there is nothing more disconcerting when forging a part than to forget a dimension and have to put the metal back in the furnace and go scouting around the shop for the drawing or look up and remeasure the old spring.

Making a Spring. Having done this much, the next step is to select a piece of spring steel having dimensions as near to the width and thickness of the finished product as is available. Saw off a length of it, allowing about ⅛" for wastage. (Step 1, Figure 89.)

Next, grind, file or mill the required taper on that flat which is to be the inside surface of the spring (Step 2), and polish this surface with a canvas or felt-back wheel that has been dressed with No. 200 grit abrasive. In performing this operation, grind the spring in the grain direction (i.e., lengthwise) and constantly dip it in water during the process, so the spring does not heat up to the point where the surface oxide colors appear. After this grinding operation has removed all traces of

STEPS IN DUPLICATION OF A SPRING

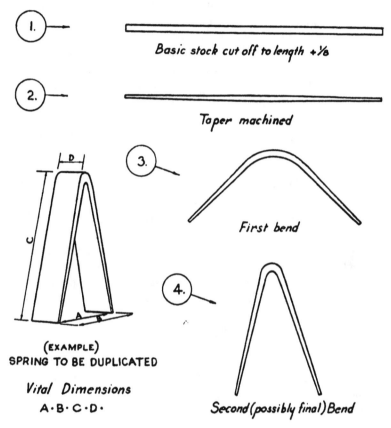

1. *Basic stock cut off to length +⅛*

2. *Taper machined*

3. *First bend*

4. *Second (possibly final) Bend*

(EXAMPLE)
SPRING TO BE DUPLICATED

Vital Dimensions
A·B·C·D·

FIGURE 89

tool marks and scratches, use a buffing wheel coated with Lea Compound for final polishing on the machined taper surface.

Steps 3 and 4 in Figure 89 show the first and second bends. Sometimes a third bend might be necessary, but on small V springs two bends will generally be sufficient to bring it to finished shape.

The bending of the spring, if it is of thin stock, can be done with two pairs of inexpensive pliers, each having the outside of one jaw ground quite flat, so that when the pliers are used for bending purposes, the width of the jaws placed against the inside of the spring will not prevent bringing the leaves of the spring close together.

The number of bends required to bring a spring to finished shape depends to a great extent upon the mass of the spring. A very thin spring, because of its little mass, does not hold heat very well, and therefore must be worked very quickly or, if this is not possible, it must be put back in the heating furnace and brought up to the working heat again.

Working Heat. The working heat of spring steel is about 1500° F., with an allowable plus and minus deviation of about 25° F. from this figure. This is the temperature to which spring steel should be heated for purposes of forging and bending. In working this type of steel, do not continue bending or forging after the heat color has gone below full red, which is about 1375° F. To do otherwise is to invite trouble in the long run, for when spring steel is worked below this point, internal strains and potential weak spots are set up which might easily render the completed spring near worthless.

Overheating. If, in the course of heating up a spring, the temperature for some reason or other rises to a point where the steel takes on a very bright color, such as orange or light yellow, then it is best to cool the steel off and consign it to the scrap pile because in all probability it has lost much of its potential quality of resilience, and further working on it would only be an additional waste of time and effort.

Having bent the spring to required size, as guided and checked by calipers which were originally set to the sizes of the vital dimensions, the outside surfaces of the spring should be ground and polished in the same way as prescribed for the inside surfaces.

Naturally, the forging and forming of all springs is not quite as simple or easy as the one used, for example, in Figure 89. Nevertheless, the basic principles for all are the same.

When making springs which have a stud or projection on them, as have most of the type which are used in connection with shotgun top levers, allowance must be made for these projections when selecting the basic stock and grinding it to shape.

Springs which have a slot and recess for a stirrup should not present any special problem because the slot can be milled or filed in the proper place and the recess can be made by forming it over a piece of round stock of appropriate size while the steel is at correct working temperature.

When possible, all machining work should be done on a V

type spring before any heat is applied to the stock. In this way the gunsmith will have the advantage of working on steel that is easily toolable, i.e., soft. If filing must be done on a spring after it has been formed, then after the last working heat the steel should be placed in sand or lime so that it will cool slowly and, consequently, be in an annealed state when it cools.

As recommended earlier in this section, filing and polishing on surfaces which constitute the inside surfaces of a V type spring should be performed before the bend is put in it. For, as can be appreciated, it is very difficult to remove tool marks and impart a polish to the area of a spring near its bend. The restricted space at this section makes the use of files and small abrasive stones difficult to the point where the mechanic might conceivably be inclined to intentionally forget the importance of removing deep scratches and tool marks, and so turn out a spring that is far from being good.

Prior to heat treating a spring, the last step in its fabrication, the gunsmith should very carefully check all its dimensions and make alterations where such are indicated. The tapered surfaces should be tested for uniformity and any high spots present blended to shape. The ends of the spring should be checked for presence of burrs or rough edges and, if there is supposed to be a chamfer or radius on either or both ends of the spring, they must have the proper contour and a mirror-like finish.

Heat Treating a Spring. The spring now ready for heat treatment should be coated with a paste, made by mixing alcohol and powdered chalk together. This mixture acts as an inhibiting agent between the hardening bath and the spring steel by preventing the lead from clinging to the steel surface and interfering with uniform hardening.

Lead Bath. While the lead hardening bath is heating up, place the spring in the furnace and preheat it to about 800° F. When the lead bath has reached the desired temperature (1400° F.), immerse the preheated spring in it. Allow the spring to remain for from five to ten minutes in the lead bath; then remove it with a pair of tongs and quench it in oil. Do not drop the spring in the oil at first, but rather swish it around so that uniform cooling will take place. During this period the temperature of the bath should not be allowed to rise above 1450° F.

Because steel will float on molten lead, there must be some means provided to keep the spring submerged in the bath during the process, and the general method is for the mechanic to hold the spring down with a length of steel rod or pair of tongs. If this old reliable method is used, then the gunsmith would do well to put on a pair of asbestos or heavy gloves so that his hands will be protected from the heat that rises from the bath. Another safety measure—a must—is to sprinkle a good heavy coating of finely powdered charcoal over the top of the lead. In as much as the charcoal acts to absorb much of the poisonous vapor generated by the heated lead, it should be put on the surface before the bath has reached its molten state.

Salt Bath. Before putting the spring in the salt tempering bath, clean off any scale or particles of lead adhering to it. This will keep the bath from becoming filled with foreign matter and eliminate possible occurrence of hard spots on the springs.

The tempering bath, which can be either potassium nitrate or a commercial tempering salt, should be heated to 700° F. before the spring, which has been preheated in boiling water, is immersed in it. Allow the spring to remain from 7 to 15 minutes in the tempering bath and then quench in a light-bodied oil.

Except for a final polishing operation, which is done on a tripoli treated buff, the spring, after being forged, formed, hardened and tempered, is finished.

Testing a Finished Spring. The first step in testing a finished spring is to measure the distance "B" with a micrometer and note the figure. Next, place the spring between the smooth jaws of a vise that have been coated with a film of grease or heavy oil, and gradually bring the jaws together until the ends of the spring are compressed as they would be when in actual use. Repeat this test five or six times and remeasure point "B" again. If the spring has been made and heat treated correctly, then there will not be a variation of more than $15/1000''$ from the originally noted measurement. Should there be a greater set than $15/1000''$, chances are that some phase of the springmaking operation was not carried out right, in which case there is no other alternative than to make another spring. If the spring is of an especially complicated type, it might be worth repeating the heat treatment operation. However, this practice cannot be very enthusiastically recommended for the results are not often fruitful.

Within these pages on the subject of heat treatment, this writer has tried to present the practical side of a subject which, even in its most elementary phase, is very technical, and abounds with particular conditions for various types of steel. A thorough understanding of the subject cannot be realized alone from reading and memorizing figures.

In order to turn out good heat treated parts that will serve the purpose which is expected, the gunsmith must augment his theoretical knowledge with occasional experimenting and experience he has garnered from practice. There is also the matter of progress, which in this age is not infrequently quite rapid. As new types of tool and spring steel are offered commercially, the alert gunsmith should not hesitate to write the manufacturers and request descriptive literature which might very conceivably make his work a great deal easier and more profitable.

So that this chapter would not take on the appearance of a commercially written handbook, this writer has in most cases listed the hardening and tempering temperatures for a particular make of steel. While these figures are very close to the overall average for all makes of a specific type of steel, i.e., drill rod, spring steel, et cetera, it should be remembered that for best results the exact carbon and alloy content for each type of steel should be known. To that end the gunsmith should, as a matter of practice, always learn the S.A.E. rating of the steel he buys from the source of supply.

CHAPTER SIXTEEN

GRINDING, POLISHING AND BLUEING

BLUEING a gun, in the true analysis, takes into account much more than rubbing a bit of solution on a piece of metal or dipping a piece of metal in oil and holding it over a gas stove. Yes, it is possible to blue a gun by these methods and by almost countless others, but that does not mean a good coloring job will be the result. Blueing a gun, or refinishing it, as it can also be called, requires a great deal more experience and equipment than the amateur or novice generally has at his disposal. Therefore, the gunsmith who knows his guns and knows the different types of blueing and how and on what kinds of guns to use them has a potentially good source of work lined up if he goes about it correctly.

Frequently many of the fly-by-night "blueing specialists" that set up shop are only interested in soaking big prices for putting a high-luster blue on a barrel and calling it a super deluxe job. Some of these outfits ask prices for reblueing that are as high or higher than the factory that makes the particular gun would charge; and this writer has yet to see a blueing job done by a gunsmith shop, big or small, that is superior to, if as good as, the overall refinishing work done by Smith & Wesson, Colt, Winchester, Remington, Ithaca or Marlin.

No genuinely interested student of gunsmithing should give serious thought to merely specializing in reblueing work unless he is located in a large city where there are many dealers who will want to have only refinishing work done. Even at that, blueing as a full time proposition is a very monotonous and dirty job and one soon loses a great deal of his interest in gunsmithing by doing this sort of work day after day.

This writer's advice to the student gunsmith is that he learn blueing and know all the ways by which it can be done well and in an efficient manner, so that repaired and modified metal work, on which the blueing of necessity must be removed, can be refinished in a manner befitting the quality of the work itself.

370

Further, the student should at all times be on the alert for new, easier and better ways to do blueing. The best way he can do this is to subscribe to one of the metal working trade journals or to the magazine "Metal Finishing," 11 West 42nd Street, New York City.

In this chapter various types and kinds of refinishing equipment are listed and their usefulness described. Only the individual gunsmith, knowing his neighborhood, his customers, his financial condition and his aptitude can decide what equipment is best for him. The writer has gone into detail describing some equipment, supplies and processes because he believes from his experience that they are superior to others. In some matters the reader might be in complete disagreement with the writer, preferring another method or product; that is understandable and to be expected. However, nothing in the way of equipment, materials or methods is suggested or recommended that this writer does not have first hand knowledge of; any commercial product recommended is so recognized because it has been found to be more than satisfactory for the purpose intended.

In Chapter Twenty under various headings are listed suppliers who deal in materials and supplies used in connection with metal refinishing.

Deoxidizing Equipment and Its Use

The first thing that must be done after a gun to be reblued has been disassembled is to remove any traces of old blueing from the parts. When this removal of blueing is done by chemical means it is known as deoxidizing.

The Tank. Deoxidizing, so far as the gunsmith is concerned, is best accomplished by immersing the work in a glass or crockery tank that is filled to a depth of 2" with hydrochloric acid (muriatic acid) and water in equal proportions.

The dimensions of an all-purpose crockery deoxidizing tank should run about 44" long, 6" wide and 6" deep. However, a smaller size tank (as short as 31") is satisfactory for a majority of work ordinarily handled.

If even a small glass or crockery tank is not obtainable, a wooden tank lined with sheet lead and soldered at the joints will serve as well, provided it is carefully made and sharp objects such as front sights (attached to a rifle) are not allowed to drop on the bottom lead sheet and cut a hole in it.

No matter what type of tank is used, a tight fitting lead or rubber lined wooden cover must be provided so that the fumes which rise from the acid can be kept down at all times. The cover is a *must*, for acid fumes of any sort will permeate the atmosphere of a small shop in no time and cause a film of rust to form on guns, tools, machines or any and all iron or steel parts. Therefore, when possible the acid tank and the bottle of acid should be kept in a room or enclosure apart from the shop proper and, weather and other conditions permitting, the de-oxidizing work should be done in this room or in the open air.

Tank Stand. A sturdy stand made of heavy wood or light angle iron should be provided to hold the tank about two feet off the ground.

Safety First. When using the acid dip tank, the gunsmith should wear a rubber apron, elbow length rubber gloves and a transparent face mask or goggles. Rubber guards for protecting shoes can be fashioned from pieces of rubber cut from an old inner tube. While this equipment on the operator might make him look like a man from Mars, it will keep him from being burned and ruining a lot of serviceable clothes and shoes.

When opening a bottle or carboy, or working around hydro-chloric acid, one should avoid inhaling the fumes. Not that they are deadly poisonous like those from sodium cyanide, but they do have a decidedly unpleasant odor and often induce coughing or sneezing, and with some people jades the appetite. An exhaust fan or blower arrangement in the room where the acid is used is ideal, and if much of this work is to be done, then it is imperative.

Rinse Tank. In addition to the acid tank, another tank made of black sheet iron about ⅛" thick, having the same dimensions as the other, and with a pet cock, faucet, or drain plug fitted at the bottom is necessary. This tank is filled with water, to which is added a few ounces of lye or alkaline cleaner. When the guns or parts are removed from the acid tank, they are placed in this water filled tank which checks the action of the acid and dissolves any loose scale or oxide adhering to the metal surface. The purpose of the pet cock is to provide a quick and easy means of emptying the tank after each usage. If a great quantity of work is processed at one time, say six or seven complete guns, then fresh water must be kept flowing into the tank as the old water runs off.

Like the acid tank, the water tank should also be kept away from the shop proper, and should be wiped dry after being emptied.

Pre-Oxidizing Step. Work going into the hydrochloric acid for deoxidizing should be chemically clean (pre-clean in alkaline cleaner and rinse in warm water) and suspended on a wire or, in the case of small parts, in a basket made of Monel metal wire.

The bore of a gun being put into acid should be plugged at both ends (See Figure 90) and the plugs should not be removed until the gun has gone through the after-acid water rinse.

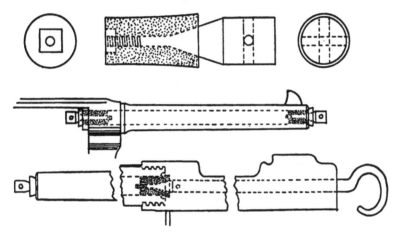

RUBBER BORE PLUG

FIGURE 90

Immersion Period. The time that work should be left in the acid bath varies with each unit being deoxidized, since some types of blueing require longer immersion than do others. If the work is clean and warm when immersed it usually takes only a minute or two for all traces of the old blue to be done away with. Some blueing leaves a brown film on metal no matter how long it is left in the acid. However, since this film can be wiped off with a cloth in the rinse water, work should not be left in the acid solution just for the purpose of removing the film.

Acid Pitting. Hydrochloric acid in any strength will pit iron or steel. Therefore, work should not be left in the acid any longer than is absolutely necessary. A large size piece of work, a barrel and receiver assembly for example, should not be left in the acid tank for an extended period of time just because one or two spots of blueing do not seem to be coming off. In most cases this sort of localized "not taking" is due to the presence of a splotch of lacquer or grease that was not removed in the cleaning solution. Or it might be a splotch of blue paint which the gun owner had put on to cover up a bare spot on the metal. In that connection, it might be well for the gunsmith to remember that hydrochloric acid will remove (deoxidize) only chemical blues. It is not intended to, and will not in a short period remove paint blues like New Method Gun Bluer. A gun which is covered with this paint-type blueing must be cleaned with paint and varnish remover or with a heavy wire wheel before the under chemical blue (if there is any present) can be removed.

There is absolutely nothing wrong with using a hydrochloric acid dip to remove chemical blueing from a gun or its component parts just so long as a little caution is observed. If the gunsmith does not do enough blueing to warrant having a separate tank for acid and another for an after-rinse, then he can still take advantage of the quickness and efficiency of acid as a blueing remover by applying the acid with a cloth, and rinsing the parts under the faucet. Rubber gloves must be worn during such an operation and any rags used should be thrown away outside the shop as soon as possible. After water-rinsing, the deoxidized parts should, if possible, be again rinsed, but this time with water to which a little alkaline cleaner, or lye, has been added. This will neutralize all traces of acid.

Etching with Acid. The ability of hydrochloric acid to etch iron or steel can be employed to advantage if the gunsmith chooses to put a dull finish on a sight, sight blade, or peep disc. The unit to be dulled should be cleaned thoroughly, rinsed in boiling water, and while very hot immersed in undiluted acid. Under favorable conditions the metal will etch quite rapidly and uniformly in less than five minutes. At any rate, after two minutes' immersion the part should be taken from the acid, rinsed in water, and examined. If the etching is deep enough the surface of the metal will appear a very dull gray and noticeably pock-marked; if it is not sufficiently etched, then it should again be cleaned, rinsed and acid-dipped as many times as is necessary to produce the desired depth of etch.

Nitric acid one part and water three parts mixed together also makes a good etching solution. It should not, however, be used for removing blueing, as it pits metal more quickly than hydrochloric acid.

Grinding and Polishing Equipment

Irrespective of what type blueing is used, the matter of grinding and polishing remains essentially the same, for a blueing job can never look any better than the surface to which it is applied. As a matter of fact, the coloring of the metal has a tendency to show up in a more pronounced manner any scratches, waves or pits that are present on the metal's surface. Therefore, a blemish-free surface must be produced before the gun or part is blued or oxidized.

To achieve a good finish on metal, certain basic equipment and skill is necessary. Without the proper equipment, it is almost impossible to acquire the necessary skill, for skill comes from constant practice of the right kind with a good polishing head or polishing lathe and suitable wheels and polishing compounds.

Polishing Head. A good polishing head can either be made or bought. In either case it must meet certain basic specifications. In the first place, the shaft should be at least $\frac{3}{4}''$ in diameter and threaded for a length of $2\frac{1}{2}''$ at each end. The shaft should be set in a heavy iron or steel unit equipped with roller bearings. Yes, bronze or babbit bearings are passable but they will not stand up under the continuous high speed beating that a grinding and polishing head is subject to, without constant maintenance. Therefore, tapered roller bearings are the most economical and efficient, all factors considered.

The motor should be at least one-half horsepower and equipped with a two place step cone pulley to match a similar pulley affixed to the shaft. The pulley should be placed in such a way as to achieve a 1 to 1 and 2 to 1 ratio, thus giving a shaft speed of approximately 1,750 and 3,500 r.p.m. when turned by a motor having a speed of 1,750 r.p.m. The low speed is for grinding operations and the high speed for buffing and polishing work. This provides an all purpose setup suitable for all phases of gun work.

The shaft unit and motor must be bolted or welded to a very sturdy and heavy stand, which in turn should be bolted to the floor. Pieces of hard rubber, of the type used for automobile engine mountings, when placed between the feet of the grinding stand and the floor, will serve to keep vibration of the entire unit at a very minimum.

The height of the polishing head cannot very well be laid down in feet and inches, for not all gunsmiths are the same height, nor do all choose to work at the same level. Generally ideal height, however, is when the shaft is at the same level as the operator's waistline.

A good arrangement for the motor switch is one so wired that is can be controlled either by hand or foot. This is especially handy when polishing rifle or shotgun barrels that require two hands to hold. In an emergency the foot can be actuated to shut off the motor, or if "dead man" control is employed the motor will be deprived of power the instant the operator lifts his foot from the switch.

Sheet metal guards placed around the ends of the shaft where the wheel rotates, and hooked up to a suction blower arrangement, are a health department must in most localities if the gunsmith employs a man in his shop to do grinding and polishing work. Even when not required by law, guards and an exhaust blower are good, because they prevent the abrasive and lint of the wheel from settling on tools and machines in the shop. If the small shop owner cannot afford this addition to his polishing head at the outset, he should not hesitate to buy it when he has a few extra dollars to invest in shop equipment for it is an eye saver and lung protector of the first magnitude.

In describing the practical polishing head, or polishing lathe as it is sometimes called, this writer has not attempted to put down any close specification hard and fast rules, because the selection of such machines is more often governed by what is available locally at a reasonable price rather than the ideal unit. Nevertheless, the writer does suggest that the gunsmith is wasting his money if he invests a few dollars in the small polishing heads, with a $\frac{1}{2}''$ shaft and powered by a $\frac{1}{4}$ horsepower motor, that are sold by some of the mail order houses. For all commercial purposes these units are worthless since they heat up very rapidly and vibrate so badly after a little usage that the grinding and polishing wheels run out of true and produce hollows in the surface of the metal being worked on. These light units might be all right for polishing jewelry or similar small objects but they are absolutely useless for gunwork.

A common but poor arrangement for a polishing unit is to

attach grinding wheels directly to the shaft of a light general purpose motor. Nothing ruins a motor as completely and quickly as this practice. While it must be admitted that some commercially marketed polishing units do utilize this means of wheel driving, it should be remembered that these are expensive units and have specially designed heavy duty enclosed motors equipped with special devices that protect the motor against injury from overloading and contact with abrasive fragments. The general run of little motors having a small-diameter, short-length shaft, however, are not made for heavy duty work imposed by polishing and grinding, and will break down in a short time if used for this type of work.

Polishing and Buffing Wheel. To remove pits, scratches and scale, and put a high finish on the surface of a barrel, receiver, part or tool, various wheels must be used. For practical purposes the main wheels that the gunsmith needs are:

2 canvas wheels	8″ dia. x 1″ wide
2 " "	8″ dia. x 2″ wide
2 " "	8″ dia. x ½″ wide
2 " "	6″ dia. x ½″ wide
1 walrus leather wheel	8″ dia. x ½″ wide
1 " " "	8″ dia. x 1″ wide
1 felt wheel	6″ dia. x 1″ wide
1 " "	8″ dia. x 2″ wide
12 cloth buffs (sewed)	10″ dia. x ⅜″ wide or ½″ wide
12 " " "	10″ dia. x 1″ wide
6 " " "	10″ dia. x 2″ wide
6 " " (Loose muslin)	10″ dia. x 2″ wide

The quantity and size of these wheels are based on the assumption that the gunsmith wants a general assortment that will enable him to take care of pre-blueing work on rifles, pistols, revolvers, shotguns, and for grinding and polishing of working parts after being overhauled, fabricated or heat treated. Although the same amount and type of work could be done with fewer wheels, it would often entail delay and inconvenience.

Abrasives and Abrasive Compound. Some of the compositions used in conjunction with these wheels are abrasive powders, Brushing NuGlu, Polishers' Bricks, cake lime, emery paste, Lea Polishing Compound, and, of course, glue to bind the powdered abrasives to the wheels.

The abrasive powders used to dress wheels are obtainable as crushed natural (emery) ores, or man-made abrasives (aluminum oxide) in various grits from 10 to 220. A good selection for a gun shop is:

> 5 pounds of 90 grit
> 5   "   of 120 grit
> 5   "   of 150 grit
> 5   "   of 180 grit
> 5   "   of 200 grit
> 5   "   of 220 grit

Mixed Glue and Abrasive. Comparatively new in the field of wheel dressing material is Brushing NuGlu. This item, which is made and marketed by the makers of NuGlu adhesive, is a mixture of a cold setting glue which is combined with aluminum oxide of definite grading. The grain sizes are #40, which is the coarsest, to #600, which is the finest. This material is marketed in one quart and one gallon containers and weighs approximately 17 pounds per gallon. It is made in various viscosities from "0" to "10." The "0" viscosity contains the least portion of grain to the glue and is quite thin; the "10" viscosity contains the most grain and is actually a very heavy paste.

Brushing NuGlu may be applied to a polishing wheel by brushing on a thin coat after the wheel has been cleaned of all the old grain and glue. One thin coat is sufficient for most work. However, two coats may be brushed onto the wheel if more production per wheel is required.

Special equipment is available (from the company) for spraying Brushing NuGlu on a polishing wheel while it is being used. This arrangement, however, is strictly for production work and not within the scope or consideration of the small shop gunsmith.

The drying of wheels which are set up with Brushing NuGlu is, like the drying of any such wheels which have been set up with cold glue and abrasive, quite important. While these wheels will drip if left at room temperature overnight, the drying can be speeded up by oven drying. An ordinary kitchen oven can be used or one can be fashioned from sheet metal. At any rate, after the wheels have been set up they should be placed in an oven which has been heated to between 150° to 160° F. Wheels can be dried and made ready for use by keeping them at this temperature for two or three hours. Though it is not often that the gunsmith will have to resort to oven-drying of wheels, it is good to know that such a heat treatment can be utilized when an emergency requires it.

Wheels which are set up with Brushing NuGlu, as well as wheels set up by the glue and abrasive method, may be used dry or with grease stick to produce a finer finish. When grease or tallow is used on the face of a set up wheel, however, the grease must be absorbed by pumice stone or Polishers' Brick before the succeeding recoat is applied.

Polishers' Brick (distributed by the makers of NuGlu) is recommended for removing oil or grease from polishing wheels before they are set up again with abrasives. It is supplied in the shape of a brick and has greater absorption than lump pumice.

Polishers' Brick, lump pumice and similar preparations need not be used on every wheel that is set up but only on those wheels which have become coated with grease, tallow or oil, which would, as can be appreciated, act to prevent good bonding between the wheel face and glue and abrasive. The cost of using Polishers' Brick is so slight that it is hardly a factor of consideration under any circumstances.

Brushing NuGlu may be used on any type of wheel, whether it is muslin, canvas, bullneck, sheepskin or felt. The only modifying factor is the matter of grease. On muslin, canvas or felt wheels no special attention is necessary, except to be sure that they are free of grease. On bullneck or sheepskin wheels, it is advisable to rough the face of the wheel by using a very coarse abrasive cloth in a back-and-forth motion so that a very slight nap is set up on the leather. Brushing NuGlu will adhere very well to a surface so prepared.

All polishing wheels, no matter what method of setup is used on them, should be "broken up" by striking a blow to the face of the wheel with a round bar at a 45° angle to the side of the wheel. By striking a blow every ¾" completely around the periphery at this angle, and then by striking another blow every inch at 90° to the first blow, a diamond pattern will be formed, which is the ideal pattern for good polishing.

As can be visualized, the "breaking up" of a polishing wheel, after it has dried and just prior to its use, also serves to localize any tendency the bonded abrasive might have to rip off if a sharp corner of the piece being worked is thrust against it too quickly.

The cake lime which comes molded in containers is excellent for putting a high polish on rubber butt plates, fore-end caps, plastics and non-ferrous metals.

Emery paste is used as a lubricant and cutting agent on wheels coated with abrasive. Emery paste comes in a molded paper container and is made in grit sizes from 90 to 180 inclusive.

Lea Compound, which is a patented buffing composition made by the Lea Manufacturing Company, of Waterbury, Connecticut is, in this writer's humble opinion, one of the finest single items that ever came to his attention during the time he blued and supervised the blueing of some 10,000 guns and countless small gun parts. It is a greaseless composition that comes in a round solid bar about 10″ long and 2″ in diameter, and enclosed in a hermetically-sealed metal foil container. And although it comes in various grits and grades, the grade "C" (200 grit) is best for all around polishing on guns and gun parts.

When applied to a revolving wheel, the frictional heat causes the compound to melt at the point of contact with the wheel and to transfer. It immediately sets up and dries on the wheel, forming a dry, grease-free, abrasive-coated wheel. After a gun has been Lea-buffed it need not be cleaned with a volatile solvent such as benzine, gasoline or carbon tetrachloride, for Lea does not leave a greasy film on the metal surface. Another advantage of Lea Compound is the ease with which it cuts. With Lea it is not necessary to apply much pressure to the work on the wheel. The artificial abrasives in it have sharp, fast cutting qualities and little or no lubrication to drag against the work.

Learok, a companion product to Lea Compound, is a clean, fast working composition used for the production of a high lustre, or mirror finish. Having no free grease to transfer back on the work, the use of Learok, of the grade made for use on carbon steel, eliminates the necessity of scrubbing or excessive cleaning.

Lea Compound can be used directly after the part to be blued has been deoxidized or, if deep pits are present, after they have been ground out by means of a canvas abrasive wheel.

Learok is used to impart a final high polish after grinding and Lea buffing operations have been finished.

After the gunsmith has used Lea Compound a few times he will no doubt appreciate what a useful addition it is to his polishing equipment. In addition to its usefulness for pre-blueing work, it also does well as a deburring abrasive on small parts and springs that resist filing.

The directions that come with Lea Compound must be followed to the letter, for when exposed to air it hardens to the point where it will not flow onto the buffing wheel. Here are the directions for using Lea Compound as recommended by the manufacturer:

1) Use a knife to cut the container close to the tapered end.
2) Remove the end.
3) Tear away a narrow strip of the container, exposing about ¼" of Compound.
4) Do not remove entire container.
5) Hold the Compound against the revolving wheel until a uniform coating is produced.
6) Allow to dry a few seconds, after which polishing may be commenced.
7) Use mild pressure of gun parts against the wheel while polishing.
8) Place Humidicap over exposed end of the tube immediately after using. Never leave the Compound exposed to the air, as it will become dry and hard.
9) On hot days place sealed bars in cold water for a few minutes before using.
10) Also store unopened bars of Compound in a cool place to prevent softening and deterioration.

Types of Wheels to Use

For removing pits—Felt wheels or stitched buffs
For over-all polishing—Loose muslin buffs

Size of Wheels to Use

6" diameter at 3,450 r.p.m.
—or—
10" diameter at 1,750 r.p.m.

The Humidicap, mentioned in the directions for use, is a cap sold by distributors of Lea Compound to keep moisture and air from affecting the compound.

Glue. Although ordinary flake glue, fish glue, hide glue, or whatever you call it (the kind that must be heated in a double boiler) can be used as an abrasive medium for setting up polishing wheels, this writer does not recommend it.

Soaking, heating, watering and messing with hot glue to set up wheels for abrasive dressing is not necessary and should not be undertaken unless no other cold glue especially made for the purpose is available.

When a person has done certain kinds of work over a period of years he comes across different products which seem, to him, to fill a very definite gap in existing supply, or to be something that is better than other similar products that have been tried. Such is the case with this writer and many products, particularly in the field of grinding, polishing and blueing, as the reader may easily note.

In the case of glue for setting up polishing wheels, this writer has found NuGlu to be as satisfactory an adhesive for the purpose as is obtainable. Now this is not an ad for the NuGlu people but just a statement of fact based on personal observation. There are other cold adhesives for setting up polishing wheels and without doubt many of them are as good as NuGlu. However, since this writer cannot vouch for the others, he does, and freely so, on the basis of extensive comparison, recommend NuGlu for use in connection with setting up dressing wheels. It is "tops" in his opinion.

If the gunsmith is using some particular prepared adhesive (cold type) with which he is satisfied, then this writer can only recommend continued usage. However, if the reader is fussing around with double boilers, soaking and hot solutions, the best advice seems to be—try NuGlu.

From the practical standpoint it might be of interest to point out that cold glues (silicate of soda base) are considered superior to the hot hide glues, in the matter of standing up under actual usage.

Rubber Wheels. There has been on the market for a number of years a type of abrasive wheel known as a rubber wheel. As the name implies, it is a wheel in which rubber is used to bond and back a powdered abrasive. It is in a class by itself for some types of grinding and polishing (for example, on flat springs, hammers, rebound levers and blocks), where it is desired to finish a small area surface to close tolerance and a high polish. For general grinding and polishing on major gun parts, however, rubber wheels are not as good as dressed canvas or felt wheels because they do not retain a flat face very long. Also, they tear easily at the corners when a sharp edge is brought against them.

Wire Wheels (Circular Scratch Brushes)

Circular steel wire scratch brushes, or wire wheels, as they are more often called, are necessary items in the gunsmith's mechanical polishing equipment department.

All Purpose Type. For removing paint and scale from steel and for putting a matted finish on sighting ramps and surfaces, a wheel 8" in diameter with 0.007" diameter or coarser wire in it is required. Keep at least two of this type on hand, because as one gets worn it gets very rough and thus a new one has to be brought into play.

Carding Type. For carding off rust in connection with the rusting process of blueing, a 6" diameter wheel with 0.0025" or 0.0035" diameter wire is ideal. Such a wheel, hand-made and with a lead-filled wooden center (this type of wheel is known as N.Y. style in the trade) is procurable from the Hanson–Van Winkle Munning Co. through any one of their distributors located all over the United States (see Chapter Twenty). A scratch brush of this specification is recommended for carding work because the wire is less dense at the circumference than it is nearer the hub. Therefore, even when this style wheel wears down it is still not too rough for carding work as are most run-of-the-mill wheels.

Wire wheels used for carding should be kept covered and away from all the grit, grease, dirt and what-not that floats around a shop when not in use. A soiled carding wheel can ruin a blueing job in nothing flat—need more be said on that score?

Carding Wheel on Motor. For powering a carding wheel a ¼ h.p., 1,750 r.p.m. motor, of the standard type, is quite satisfactory even though the speed is a little high for a 6" wheel. Nevertheless, since this specification motor is popular and readily available, nothing better need be sought. And because very little pressure is ever placed against a carding wheel, it can be attached directly to the motor shaft by means of an adapter and flanges.

In Figure 91 is illustrated a motor and carding wheel setup similar to the one which this writer has used with great success. The advantage of this rig lies in the fact that the motor and wheel can be used either horizontally or vertically, as the operator desires. As can be appreciated, the horizontal position is best for long barrels, while revolvers and similar small units are more easily handled with the wheel in the vertical position.

HORIZONTAL POSITION

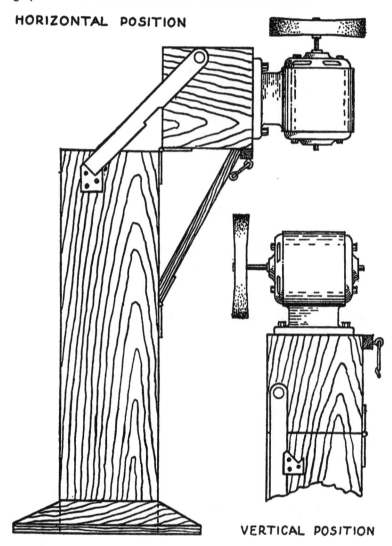

VERTICAL POSITION

MOTOR & CARDING WHEEL SET-UP

FIGURE 91

No matter how the gunsmith sets up his carding wheel motor he should always remember that it is advisable to have room around all sides of the wheel. A bench-mounted carding wheel motor is most undesirable because it restricts the space in which a long barrel can be maneuvered when being carded. All factors taken into account, it is best to have a rig on the general pattern of the one illustrated because it can be moved where needed (carding should be done near the blueing tank), when needed, and put out of the way when not in use.

A motor used for carding wheel purposes should be oiled—yes, but not so it will turn loose a spray as it rotates. A little oil goes a long way—and longer still if it gets on a part being blued.

Burrs and Wire Wheels. Although a wire wheel can be used advantageously for many metal brushing and cleaning operations, it can, if work is brought hard against its sharp, rotating wires, raise a sort of smooth burr which will interfere with the movement of closely fitted moving parts. The unusual thing about a burr (or welt might be a more descriptive term) raised by a wire wheel is that it frequently goes unnoticed until it cannot be rectified without considerable filing or stoning, which, of course, does not add to the beauty of a reblued surface.

Wire wheel burrs are caused by holding work too hard against the wheel as the wheel passes over corners, edges and rims of holes, wells or surface cutouts.

As wheels wear down they become very offensive in the way of burr raising and for that reason should be discarded or used for extremely rough work. Wheels having wire greater than 0.008" must be brought very lightly against any but the hardest steel because the large diameter wire rotating at high speed seems to "flow" metal from the center of a surface towards the edge.

The life of any wire wheel can be extended by changing its rotational direction when the wires become noticeably "bent."

In addition to the aforementioned equipment and supplies, the polishing shop supplies should also include: a few lengths of maple dowel rod for dressing wheels; a drying stand (Figure 92) for holding wheels after they have been dressed; a flat smooth board, for smoothing the surface of dressed wheels; a paint brush for applying glue; and a supply of old newspaper sheets for holding the abrasive while it is being rolled onto the wheels.

Setting Up ("Dressing") Wheels for Grinding and Polishing

The dressing of canvas, hide, cloth and the various other so-called backed wheels is a very easy task requiring little or no special skill and in order that the description of this task may be simplified, the writer prefers to present the operations and sequence in the somewhat dry but explicit Army Technical Manual style:

Step (1) On a flat table or work bench lay out the necessary items—the wheel to be dressed, an 8″ length of dowel rod (di-

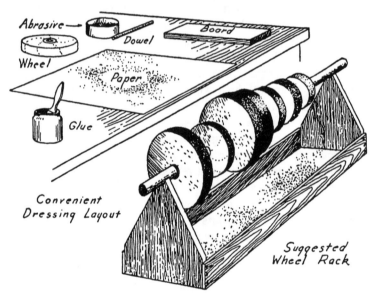

SETTING UP (DRESSING) POLISHING WHEEL

FIGURE 92

ameter to fit the hole in the wheel), the glue, a paint brush for applying the glue to the wheel, the desired cut of abrasive, the rolling board and a single sheet of newspaper (see Figure 92 for typical setup).

Step (2) Pour out about a half pound of the abrasive on the sheet of newspaper so that it covers about a foot long and two inches wide.

Step (3) Insert the dowel rod through the shaft hole in the wheel, allowing about the same length to protrude from either side of the wheel.

Step (4) While supporting the wheel in the hand by means of one end of the dowel rod, apply a thin coat of glue around the periphery of the wheel, making sure to cover every spot. If the glue collects at one section of the wheel or has a tendency to flow around and settle at the "bottom" of the wheel when it stands for a moment, then this is an indication that too much glue has been applied. If this happens, squeeze all excess glue from the brush and redistribute that which is on the wheel with the "dry" brush.

Step (5) Using the dowel as an axle, roll the wheel through the abrasive until the glue-treated surface is completely and uniformly coated. Often it will be found necessary to roll the wheel through the abrasive five or six times before a good dressing is achieved. If, after this many tries, there are still some spots or sections that are not covered with abrasive, this should be taken as an indication that more glue is needed on the bare spots.

Step (6) While still holding the wheel on the dowel rod, roll it across the flat smooth board until the abrasive forms a smooth coating over the wheel. If bumps or irregularities are present, they should be leveled off by further rolling on the board. If a ball of glue has collected to form an "unsmoothable" defect, then it should be picked off the surface, a drop of glue put in place, and new abrasive sprinkled on.

Step (7) With a knife or hacksaw blade, trim off any excess glue and abrasive, in combination, that hangs over the face width of the wheel.

Step (8) Remove the dowel rod and put the wheel on the drying rack for at least eight hours. If faster drying is required, the wheel can be placed in an oven held at a temperature of 165° F. for three or four hours.

The procedure for redressing wheels, that is, putting a coating or abrasive on wheels which have already been used and need another dressing, is essentially the same as the original operation except that most of the old grit and glue remaining on the wheel should be removed. This is best accomplished by holding a piece of hardened steel having a chisel-shaped edge against the wheel while it is rotating. Another, but less acceptable way of performing the same job involves soaking of the wheel in hot water until the old "setup" falls off. After being soaked in water, however, the wheel must be dried at room temperature before being dressed again.

The grade or grit of abrasive glued on a wheel is, of course, governed by the purpose for which the gunsmith expects to use it. For example, if a batch of guns to be ground are all deeply pitted, a coarse abrasive, such as 120 or 150, must be used to accomplish their removal in short order. The surface left as a result of using coarse grit wheels is, as can be appreciated, anything but scratch-free. Therefore, wheels coated with the finer grades of abrasive must be used before Lea or Learok buffing is resorted to.

There is no positive set of rules that can be outlined to cover the size and number of wheels a gunsmith should have dressed with each grade of abrasive. From experience, however, this writer has learned that it is not very often necessary to use a wheel dressed with anything coarser than 120 grit, wheels dressed with 200 grit being the most generally used type.

Although dressed canvas and leather wheels are most often used for general grinding work, the gunsmith will find it to his advantage to dress a couple of sewed buffs with 200 grit abrasive. These buffs so dressed are the only wheels that can be used to grind irregular shaped receivers and the like. In addition, they are excellent for use on rifle and shotgun barrels where a less flexible wheel might cut a series of wheel width marks along the length of the barrel.

For use on flat work, such as the sides of rifle, shotgun, pistol and revolver receivers, the dressed buff should not be used for it has a tendency to round off corners that should be sharp.

Internal working parts, such as sears, hammers and rebound levers, which have surfaces that must be flat, should be ground on dressed leather wheels and polished with felt wheels which are coated with Lea, emery paste, tripoli, et cetera.

Using Polishing Wheels

The most important thing to remember when working with abrasive dressed wheels is that these wheels cut, and in cutting remove metal. Unlike hard-stone grinding wheels, the soft-back dressed wheels do not give off a great volume of sparks, which often lulls the operator into believing that practically no metal is being removed. The falseness of this impression has not infrequently caused many a novice to almost ruin his first few guns to be blued by grinding hollows into the surface of a barrel.

Practicing on a Gun. Unless the gunsmith has had some experience working with this type of wheel, he would do well to engage in a bit of experimenting. For purposes of experiment, it is wise to select an old gun or receiver that is lying in the shop junk pile (preferably one with deep pits) and go to work on it. If the experiment turns out to be somewhat of a failure, then the gunsmith will not have to lay awake nights thinking up a proper excuse to tell the customer why his favorite shotgun is not quite what it used to be. After grinding the subject gun, polish it and blue it. Blueing, as mentioned earlier in this chapter, will serve to show up any hollows, deep scratches, and round corners occasioned by the grinding and polishing operations.

If this first try produces what the gunsmith thinks is a good job, then he should compliment himself, but at the same time realize that there is much room for improvement. A good ego deflator for self-satisfaction along these lines is to compare the finish on the experimental model alongside of the finish on a peacetime Smith & Wesson revolver, which about represents the acme in firearms refinishing. If a Smith & Wesson is not available, a Colt, Winchester, Remington, or any other good commercial gun with most of its original blueing intact will serve almost as well for purposes of comparison. Note the sharp corners on a factory-finished weapon; also note that the flats are free of waves, ripples and surface irregularities.

Naturally, the beginner cannot expect to turn out as good a job as the factory-trained polishers do but he can learn, and learning, as far as gun polishing and buffing is concerned, consists mainly of practice. The practicing, however, must be conducted in such a manner as to show up the operator's faults. Haphazard grinding of everything in sight without noting results and figuring out methods for improvement is a worthless sort of practice that is better off not done.

Practicing on Steel Stock. A suggested form of practice for the beginner, if an old gun is not available, consists in taking pieces of flat cold rolled steel (about 4" long, 2" wide and ¼" thick) and using various sizes and grits of dressed canvas wheels to grind the pieces. After they are ground to the satisfaction of the individual doing the job, the pieces should then be buffed, cleaned and reblued. The same sort of exercise can be carried out on round, square, and octagon-shaped pieces until the beginner has gotten the feel of the wheels, so to speak.

When the gunsmith knows how each type (canvas, felt, leather, cloth, etc.) of wheel will cut when dressed with any of the various abrasives, in different grades, he has pretty well mastered the fundamentals of grinding (or polishing, if you are using the very fine compounds) with so-called dressed wheels.

The Right Grit. Using too coarse a wheel to grind pits from a surface is poor practice because deep scratches are made which must in turn be obliterated by successively using finer grit wheels. On the other hand, using too fine a wheel makes for a slow job in which the metal gets very hot and breaks down the glue, which tends to clog the normal space between the abrasive grains.

As a rule of thumb, the gunsmith should remember to always use the widest wheel possible for the job being done. With a wide wheel the chances of waves on a flat surface are greatly minimized and the job can be done faster.

Unless a barrel is badly pitted there is really no need to use anything except a muslin buff dressed with a fine grit abrasive. If the barrel is not pitted at all, and there are no deep scratches or tool marks in it that must be removed, then more often than not a buffing wheel headed with Lea compound will cut away all the metal that is necessary to produce a surface ready for high speed buffing.

While barrels can be ground lengthwise on a formed wheel (made by cutting a concave radius in a canvas wheel in the lathe, and then dressing it) this writer does not believe lengthwise grinding is necessary on anything but a set of double barrels or a single barrel that has a full length rib on it. Standard single barrels can be ground and polished the same way they are at the factory, i.e., around their periphery, and then given a high speed buffing in any direction that will eliminate the "cross grain" grinding marks.

Working on Double Barrels. Double barrels, and barrels with a full length rib, require special treatment when it comes to using dressed abrasive wheels on them. Grinding should be held to a minimum and every stroke against a dressed, hard (felt, canvas, leather, but not cloth) wheel must be a full one running from breech to muzzle. This full length grinding on a barrel is very difficult and for that reason not recommended as a pastime or experiment for beginners, at least not until they have fully mastered the art of working on shorter objects.

Deep pits are best removed from a set of double barrels by draw filing, especially when they are near the top rib, which would take quite a beating if it was brought in contact with a revolving abrasive wheel. After draw filing and preliminary hand polish-

ing by abrasive cloth held against a file has removed all the pits
and flats, a sewn buff headed with a coarse grit emery paste can
then be used to polish and shape the barrels. A final polishing
with Lea compound and a buffing with Learok will produce a job
far superior to any that the same operator could do entirely by
hand using emery cloth and formed wooden blocks.

Polishing Spindles. Where dressed wheels cannot be used, e.g.,
inside trigger guards, cylinder flutes, bent lower tangs, underneath bolt handles, to mention a few of the most obvious places,
little gadgets like the ones illustrated in Figure 93 can be helpful. There is almost no limit to the shape and size in which these
polishing spindles can be made and when made from maple dowel
rod they will last a long time.

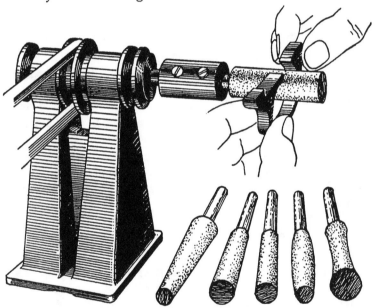

POLISHING SPINDLES

Figure 93

One way of making polishing rods is to turn the rod down to
desired size and shape on the lathe and glue a piece of felt (about
the thickness of the felt that is used in men's hats) to that part
of the rod which is to be used for the polishing. After the felt
has dried fast on the wood, coat it with glue and roll it in abrasive. When it dries it is ready for use.

The secret in making a good polishing end that will hold its shape and cut evenly lies in cutting the felt so that the two ends meet perfectly, and in using a good glue or cement to affix the felt to the dowel rod.

The dowel rod is hooked up to the grinding head by means of a little adapter which is illustrated in Figure 93. There is nothing special about this adapter other than that it should be made of cold rolled steel, and the set screws of such a length that they do not protrude above the body of it.

Polishing by Hand. Operating abrasive cloth by hand to remove scratches, scars and pits might have been the way to do an efficient job many years ago, but nowadays it is nothing but a waste of time except where absolutely required, as for example, by a beginner working on a set of double barrels, or better, the supports on a ventilated rib.

The possibilities of mechanical polishing with the various types of wheels, abrasives, abrasive compounds and buffing compounds available are unlimited and open to countless methods of application in the gunsmith shop.

Every time the gunsmith uses a fine cut file or abrasive cloth to remove a bit of metal from, or achieve a polish on, a piece of steel he should ask himself if it is not possible to do the same operations faster and better by mechanical means. There are still too many things a gunsmith has to do by hand to overlook or cast aside the thought of using power for grinding and polishing.

Blueing Tank Materials and Construction

Although the average small shop gunsmith who does only a limited amount of blueing by either the rusting or hot-dip process usually will find that sheet iron (black iron) tanks are quite satisfactory, it might be well to mention that there are other materials from which tanks can be made. Some of these materials are suited to only one class of chemical, e.g., acids, while others are more versatile.

Wood Tanks. Tanks made of Cypress, Douglas Fir or Long Leaf Pine can be used to hold room temperature water, mild sulphuric acid solution, and mild hydrochloric acid solution. Do not use a wood tank for holding lye, any similar caustic solution or nitric acid.

In the gunsmith shop a wood tank can be used to good advantage as a rinsing tank after parts have been deoxidized with hydrochloric acid. A well-constructed wood tank will last for years if it is not abused by parts and baskets being dragged across its sides as they are taken from the tank.

Lead Lined Tanks. For holding diluted hydrochloric acid a wooden tank with a lead lining is very good. In a small tank heavy gauge sheet lead should be chosen as a lining medium since there is not the danger of sag present as with the larger tanks. A wood cover with a lead lining can be used on a glass or stoneware tank as well as a wood tank.

Stoneware Tanks. Back in the days of home brew-making stoneware tanks could be bought from any malt and hops dealer. Today, however, stoneware tanks are more easily obtained from a dealer in plating and polishing supplies (see Chapter Twenty). Stoneware tanks, which are excellent for holding any acid but hydrofluoric, can be purchased with a tight-fitting cover. As such they are good for holding hydrochloric acid.

Glass Pans. Rather than go into details on the subject of glass lined tanks, which are used only for very special production plating work, this writer would rather say that the Pyrex and Fire King baking dishes, which can be purchased inexpensively at a hardware store or mail order house, are excellent containers for acids and metallic corrosives. Their only disadvantage lies in the fact that they must be handled with more than ordinary care. Heavy parts, such as receivers, rifle bolts, et cetera should not be dropped into a glass pan under any circumstances, for either the pan is apt to break or the acid will splatter—or both.

Stainless Steel Tanks. Stainless steel, although much more expensive than sheet iron, should be given serious consideration by the gunsmith just starting up in business as the material for his blueing tanks.

A basic tank of sheet iron can be covered with sheets of stainless steel (by electric welding) and converted into a sturdy lifetime tank that will give off a minimum of unwanted rust (see Chapter Twenty for suppliers of stainless steel and fabricators of tanks).

Iron Tanks. For use with either the rusting process or the hot-dip process a tank made of 12 gauge black iron, welded inside and outside, at the corners, and with the top edges turned over (about 1½" wide) to form a 90° angle, is considered to be near perfect for any capacity up to 80 gallons. A cover made of the same material, and equipped with a handle, is essential to protect the tank from becoming filled with grit, dirt, oil, et cetera when not in use.

Galvanized iron, tin plated iron, or very thin sheet iron that is soldered, brazed, wired or riveted together does not make a good tank.

Galvanized iron (zinc covered) in any thickness for use in connection with the hot-dip process is frowned upon because the presence of zinc will contaminate the blueing solution. Brazed joints are unsatisfactory for the same reason.

Soldered joints are worthless because of their low melting point and because the lead in solder will react unfavorably where a mercury base rust blueing solution is used.

This writer can see no advantage in using a tank that is just passable when it is so easy and inexpensive to have a 12 gauge black iron tank formed and welded by a blacksmith or sheet metal worker.

The tank illustrated in Figure 94 shows the main points of construction in an all-around blueing tank. While the size or shape of this tank can be altered to suit individual requirements, it does represent a more or less ideal size.

If a gunsmith expects to go in for production refinishing on pistols or rifles, then he would do well to have insulated tanks constructed so that heating costs (a big factor in production work) can be kept to a minimum.

On the other hand, the gunsmith who does little or no blueing work might choose to have a smaller tank that will require less solution, heat, space, et cetera.

These are special considerations, however, and the illustrated tank should serve as a good practical working guide.

Baskets for Holding Small Parts

In the hot-dip or niter process of blueing, very small parts, such as pins, safeties, plungers, screws, et cetera are best suspended in the blueing tanks by means of a small basket.

The mesh of these baskets should be no coarser than that found on common window screening. But copper screening should not be used to make an immersion basket since the copper will contaminate the solution.

Galvanized screening can be used but it must first be stripped of its zinc coating by immersing it in a container (an old tin can

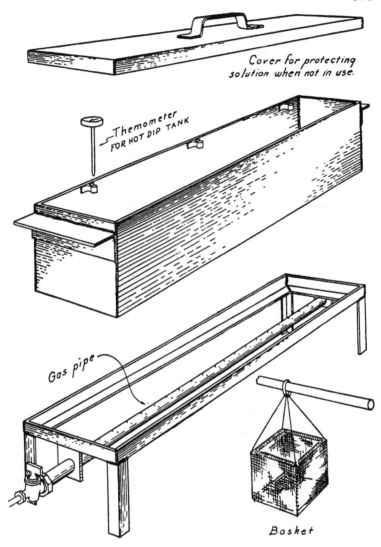

Cover for protecting
solution when not in use.

Thermometer
FOR HOT DIP TANK

Gas pipe

Basket

HOT DIP TANK
FIGURE 94

will do) in which three or four ounces of the caustic blueing salts
and a quantity of boiling water have been mixed. Allow the
basket to remain in this concoction for about 10 minutes; then
remove and rinse it in running water, which will flush away all
adhering zinc particles.

Never put a galvanized wire basket into a hot-dip blueing solution as it will contaminate the latter to the extent where regular work processed will come out with rust or grease streaks on it.

Baskets made from Monel metal or from black iron wire need no pre-cleaning since they do not contain any chemicals which are harmful to a prepared solution.

The basket illustrated in Figure 94 is of a style and size that seems to be well suited for blueing work.

Solder should never be used to fasten the corners of a basket together; instead use iron wire and tie them together.

For dipping exceptionally small parts, a basket made of two or three thicknesses of mesh will preclude almost any possibility of a pin slipping through and sinking to the bottom of the blueing tank.

The cover on a mesh basket is important and it should be fastened in place by means of a piece of wire before the basket is lowered into a solution. Light parts, of the kind usually put in a basket, do, upon being suddenly immersed tend to rise; and if the basket does not have a cover on it the parts may rise over the top and out of the basket and eventually sink to the bottom of the tank.

Replating a Gun

Every now and then a gunsmith is asked to nickel-plate a handgun, rifle, bolt, or perhaps even an entire rifle that is to be used for display or show purposes. The mere fact that a gunsmith does not have plating facilities should not deter him from taking the job, inasmuch as there are platers in or within reasonable distance of almost every large community to whom the work can be sent. In this latter connection, it is a good policy, if the gunsmith gets much plating work, to make the acquaintance of a plater (preferably local) and assure him that he will get all work just so long as he turns out nice jobs. Of course, if the plater is a big operator who does a great deal of contract work he will not be interested in any little business the average small gunsmith might give him; hence it is desirable, where possible, to make contact with a small firm where the factor of personal attention is a consideration. Often it is possible for the gunsmith to build up a business friendship with a plater so that mutual technical problems incidental to grinding and polishing can be discussed to each other's advantage. Also, under this arrangement the gunsmith can suggest to the plater that firearms are very exact pieces of mechanical equipment and as such require delicate buffing and handling not ordinarily accorded the run-of-the-mill plating work.

If a gun that is to be plated is received with blueing on it the gunsmith should go through all the operations of disassembly, cleaning, deoxidizing, polishing and buffing, and give it to the plater ready for plating. In this way the plater will not be required to do any polishing and buffing (except an after-plating buffing) and that is just perfect, because general plating establishments as a rule either do not know or do not care enough about small arms to turn out an even passable job.

By presenting the plater with a gun that does not require any special pre-treatment the gunsmith can often save himself a few cents, but most important of all he can pretty well rest assured that when he does get the gun back all the pins will not be flattened out and the corners rounded beyond recognition.

All parts of a gun that are to be plated should be wired together and a tag attached to the wire stating how many parts there are (see paragraph on Denickeling for more about this).

When possible, small pins (under $\frac{1}{8}''$ diameter) should be push-fitted into a block of cold rolled steel that has been drilled to receive them. If this is not possible or practical then push the pins into their normal location in the gun. This latter method is not too strongly recommended, however, since it is sometimes very difficult to remove pins so positioned without appreciably marring the plating.

A gun received for replating (i.e., one on which the original plating has worn off to some degree) should be forwarded to the plater after it has been disassembled. Deep pits can be ground out, and slight burrs filed off, but no extensive polishing and buffing need be attempted because the plater will probably have to do his own polishing, et cetera in order to remove what remains of the old plating.

Special Notes. If a moving part is to be plated, make certain that no hole, detent, or vital dimension will be affected. Plating, unlike blueing, has thickness; sometimes as much as 0.002" deposit will be encountered.

Do not have a part plated that is not supposed to be plated, e.g. the hammer and trigger on most models of Smith & Wesson revolvers. Trigger guards on S & W Hammerless revolvers are not plated either, because the plating will flake off each time the guard is "sprung" for insertion or removal.

The interior recesses of a pistol receiver or revolver frame are usually quite rough and so do not take a plate that will "flake" or peel off. However, if any strips of nickel or copper (copper is often used as a base on steel, for nickel-plating) are noticed on the inside of a frame after it has been plated, remove them. Peeling on moving parts should also be checked.

Little pieces of plating which strip off can foul up the works of any gun; hence the reason for such close scrutiny of this seemingly insignificant factor.

Parts in need of filing, deburring, stoning, machining or any type of working should be operated on before they are plated. Cutting or stoning on a plated part not only spoils its appearance but also tends to start peeling of the plate.

Although not an inevitable aftermath of plating, difficulty in fitting plated parts is an occurrence with which the gunsmith should be prepared to cope. The plating of two contacting surfaces, such as the crane and frame of a revolver, often requires that the plating be scraped from one of the surfaces so that normal movement between them can be achieved.

Plating build-up can be a help in some instances; for example, a heavy chrome plate will take out a good deal of sloppiness in fit between the slide and receiver of old automatic pistols and similar assemblies. Gun legend has it that a once-famous rifle overhauling firm filled the terms of a contract to salvage some condemned military rifles with excessive head space by using a plating build-up.

Black-Nickeling. Black-nickel, which is in theory the ideal finish for a pocket weapon, is something that one hears a great deal about but does not often see. Without a doubt any finish that combines the dark color of blueing and the rust protection of nickel is good. But, and this is the big factor, black-nickel is not a true plating in that a piece of steel so finished is white nickel-plated first and then black-nickeled. The black of a black-nickeling job will wear off a gun much quicker than the color of a good blueing job.

The day should not be too far off when a good durable black-nickel will be a common commercial finish for steel. Until that time, though, the gunsmith should not take too seriously all that he hears about the mystic nickel.

Denickeling (Stripping)

No matter how much he tries to avoid it, every gunsmith, at some time or another in the course of his career, is called upon to blue a weapon that is nickel-plated. More often than not it is some old broken down revolver that a good customer has fallen heir to and insists that he wants it "fixed up and blued."

Naturally, in the interest of customer harmony it is wise to undertake to do the job unless a price agreement cannot be reached or if some special individual chemical or mechanical problem is known to exist. Hence, we shall presume the gunsmith is stuck with the job, and as a matter of pride and reputation wants to make the best of it.

Broadly speaking, any conventional gun that is plated can be blued, provided, of course, that the parts are made of iron or steel. This qualification is made because this writer has seen a few foreign guns equipped with die cast material butt plates and trigger guards. Parts made of metals adapted to die casting cannot be blued with the solutions the gunsmith has at his disposal for coloring iron base parts.

Before a nickel-plated gun can be blued the plating must be thoroughly and completely removed so that the base metal (iron) will be in direct chemical contact with the coloring solution. Removing the plating from a gun is generally spoken of as stripping.

Denickeling by a Plater. Stripping can be accomplished in two ways. The first method, while not directly within the sphere of the small shop gunsmith's facilities, is to this writer's mind the most efficient and easiest way. In detail, it is this: take the gun apart completely and turn over to a plating firm those parts which must be blued and are in need of stripping. If the gunsmith is not acquainted with or does not have too much confidence in the plater he does business with, a tag should be attached to the pieces warning against prolonged immersion in the stripping bath.

When sub-contracting work to another mechanic, the gunsmith should not rely on a telephone conversation or a face-to-face verbal exchange to convey directions. Play safe and attach a tag to sub-contracted work stating in few but explicit words what is desired. Then the individual charged with handling the work will have no grounds to plead ignorance if he ruins a gun or part by just doing a routine job. Let us illustrate the point in this manner:

The gunsmith takes in a plated gun which must be stripped before it can be blued as the customer desires. He calls up his plater and says in essence, "Hey, Joe, I'm sending a gun over to you for stripping. Please be careful with it won't you?" Joe says, "O.K. Express it over—I'll take care of it."

Beaming with a smile that bespeaks great confidence in his fellow mechanic, the gunsmith packs up the weapon and sends it over to the plater's shop. When the gun arrives at Joe's shop it is opened by Joe's chief assistant who, not used to handling items so fine as a disassembled revolver, tosses it and the parts he managed to pick up from the sawdust-laden floor, into a cigar box. The cigar box is in turn tossed into a bin marked "To Be Stripped." You see, Joe's assistant knows that the gun is to be stripped because before Joe went away on the unexpected trip he said, "I'm expecting a 'pistol' from that gunsmith over in Centerville. It has to be stripped so take good care of it."

Now the man who runs the plating tanks (an assistant to Joe's assistant) gets around to stripping about every fourth day and when he does he most likely has forgotten any specific directions he has gotten relative to giving special attention to "the gun."

If luck is with the gunsmith he stands a fair chance of getting his stripped gun back in reasonably good condition. If, on the other hand, the gun was thrown in for stripping with a lot of heavily plated parts, well . . . This writer once got a stripped revolver back from a usually reliable plater with the base metal so badly etched that it had to be scrapped and a new replacement secured for the customer. And needless to say, this sort of replacement entails more than just an inconvenience in matters financial. It is surprising how the value of a customer's gun goes up when he finds out that it is ruined beyond redemption.

Wiring Parts Together. Thus, when the gunsmith sends a gun out to be denickeled he would do well not to rely on someone "remembering." Instead, wire together all the parts that are to be stripped and attach a card to the major assembly on the wire stating that the attached item is a gun, and as such must be handled carefully and watched closely during the stripping process. Also, on the same tag print in large characters the number of individual parts that are to be stripped. Count each pin, part and large unit as one and list the total so arrived at. This procedure will make it easier for the plater and his helpers to keep track of the number of parts being handled.

Having wired and tagged the parts, they should then be placed in a box and a tag attached on the outside of the box with the name and address of the gunsmith on it and the number of parts included.

Sounds like a lot of work and unnecessary precaution just to get a gun stripped, doesn't it? Actually it is not, though. It is just a systematic way of doing a particular job which happens to be a source of great discouragement if not handled correctly.

After Stripping. The chemical after-effects of stripping are of a rust-promoting nature and therefore gun components will corrode if not cleaned and oiled as soon as possible after being worked on by the plater. While it is hardly expected that a plater can be prevailed upon to run an oil-soaked brush or rag through the bore of the gun as it emerges from the stripping tank, it is worth the effort of writing on the tag: *"Please Oil Parts After Stripping."* Who knows, maybe some platers are gun lovers?

At any rate, no matter what oiling the plater does, the gunsmith should, upon receiving a stripped gun, vigorously scrub out the bore and then use the solvent-soaked bristle brush in corners and crevices where, so to speak, rust breeds. The piece can then be lightly oiled and laid aside to await grinding and blueing.

Denickeling by the Gunsmith. The second method of denickeling, which can be carried out by a gunsmith with limited equipment, seems to work fairly well on guns which are nickel-plated but does not pan out successfully on chrome-plated weapons. Though the gunsmith is not apt to come across too many chrome-plated revolvers or pistols, he should, when the following suggested method does not appear to loosen plating, suspect the presence of a chrome-plate. Needless to say, a plater can strip chrome almost as easily as he can nickel so it might be well for the gunsmith to keep his plater on the Christmas card list.

In the following formula the amount of ingredients suggested will make adequate solution to cover a pistol or revolver that is laid in a glass pan of the type used for baking. The pan need not be very deep (3″ is adequate) and only long and wide enough to accommodate the largest revolver that might be presented. A Pyrex pan is recommended inasmuch as it will stand up under jars and shocks better than an ordinary glass dish.

If the pan does not come equipped with a glass top, then a tight fitting one should be made from a piece of plate glass, or a scrap piece of shatter-proof glass. If such a cover is constructed by the gunsmith he should allow about 1″ overhang at each end to serve as handles.

Any cover, be it home-made or store bought, must fit the pan in which the solution is put in as airtight a manner as possible. If necessary to secure a tight joint between cover and pan, glue a piece of soft rubber around the cover where it contacts the top edges of the pan. The rubber also serves to lessen the chance of the cover breaking as it is laid in place each time.

Greater or lesser amounts of the solution can be made just so long as the basic proportions are observed. However, since light and heat tend to adversely affect the efficacy of such a solution, it is best to make only an amount that is needed for each particular job.

All three chemicals are fairly common and therefore should be easily procurable from a local pharmacist or chemical supply house.

Solution for Removing Nickel or Copper-Plating from Steel or Iron

Ammonium Persulphate ...... 7 oz.
Ammonium Carbonate .... 3½ oz.
Ammonia (Liquid) 28% ...... 2 qts.

To Use. Lay all the parts (frame, cylinder, latch, trigger, et cetera) in the glass pan and slowly pour solution into the pan until all parts are completely covered with at least ⅛″ to spare. Put the cover on and let the solution act until all parts show dull gray. This will indicate that all the nickel has been dissolved and that the base metal is exposed. As the parts are removed from the solution they should be rinsed in hot water, dried and oiled. Examine all parts carefully for traces of rust and also for shiny spots that indicate the presence of nickel.

If the first immersion does not strip all the nickel from any particular part or all of the parts, then they should be put back in the solution and allowed to soak until all traces have been removed.

Inasmuch as one little adhering spot of nickel can ruin the whole appearance of a blueing job, the gunsmith should make certain that the gun is thoroughly stripped before he puts away the solution and readies the blueing equipment. It is usually quite easy to detect the presence of nickel against the gray appearance of a partly stripped component so the gunsmith has nothing to blame but his own carelessness if he notes half-way through a blueing job one small but very conspicuous spot that will not "take."

Half the success in a good stripping job, by this method, lies in the cleanliness of the parts before they are placed in the solution. In a word, they must be clean. Grease or oil, no matter how slight, can act as an inhibiting agent between the ammonium compounds and the plating. Therefore, best operating procedure prior to immersion consists of first cleaning the parts in an Oakite solution and then rinsing them in clean boiling water. After cleaning, allow the parts to cool before putting them into the denickeling solution, inasmuch as hot or even warm parts laid in the solution tend to promote rapid evaporation of the liquid ammonia, leaving a residue which, when in contact with the base metal, produces rapid pitting.

Bore Plugging. Safety first gunsmithing practice dictates that the bore of a gun be plugged when it is immersed in any solution that promotes rapid etching, pitting or rusting. Any denickeling solution is one of these.

While there are many methods by which the bore of a gun can be plugged, not all of them are practical. Generally if a good tight seal is effected by some means, such as sealing wax or stop-off compound, it is often a time-consuming job to remove the plug. Wooden plugs are not too satisfactory for protection against chemicals since the wood will absorb and transmit some solution if immersed for any appreciable length of time. To this writer's way of thinking, the type of rubber plugs illustrated in Figure 90, while requiring some time to make, are in the long run without peer for many phases of work where bore plugging is a must.

Special Bore Plugs. There is no special way in which a bore plug must be made just so long as the finished product is a few thousandths less than bore size in diameter, about 1½" long and equipped with a nut and screw device so that one end of the plug will be expanded as the screw is tightened. Where the plug must be placed in a chamber that is several inches from the end of the receiver, a hook-equipped plug is desirable, with the hook being an extension of the tightening screw. Many variations, improvements and perhaps simplifications of these expanding plugs are possible and the writer knows that some gunsmiths will see the possibilities at a glance. Some might even find it handy to arrange small rubber washers on a length of threaded rod and make an expanding plug from them.

Since it takes good time to make sets of rubber plugs for all of the popular caliber guns, the plugs should be disassembled when not in use and the metal parts cleaned, dried and oiled. Rinse the plug itself in clean water and then put all the components away where they will be handy when needed. Oil will rot all but certain types of synthetic rubber, so dry off the metal parts before assembling them to the plug.

It is often difficult for the novice to realize the value of a practical set of bore plugs until he is forced to spend half a day trying to loosen a too-tightly-placed wooden plug, only to find after burning out the last remnants that a piece of wood can act like a wick in introducing a liquid from a pan to the bore.

The other alternative, of not plugging the bore in some way (i.e., when the gun is immersed in those solutions which have a rapid deleterious action), should not even be considered by a gunsmith who has respect for his customers' guns. One prolonged immersion in denickeling solution or hydrochloric acid can do more damage to an unprotected bore than days of exposure to the elements.

Nitric Acid Stripping. Another method the gunsmith can use to strip nickel-plating is to immerse the desired parts in a glass pan that is filled with acid (specific gravity 1.50). In using this chemical make sure that the parts are completely covered, the bore and chambers plugged, and that no water gets into the acid. Since this solution will dissolve a 0.001″ thick nickel-plate (and that is thick as some gun platings go) in 15 to 20 minutes, the gunsmith must watch the stripping operation constantly and remove the parts as soon as they are stripped. As the parts are taken from the fuming nitric acid they must be dipped into a chromic acid solution for a minute and then completely rinsed in water. Under no circumstances should a part go from the fuming nitric acid directly into water as the water will cause the fuming nitric acid adhering to the surface to etch the steel.

While it is possible to strip nickel from steel with ordinary nitric acid, the time required (6 to 8 hours) is so long and the possibility of etching so great that its use must be discouraged.

Like hydrochloric acid, fuming nitric acid gives off fumes which settle on and rust everything within many feet of origin. Fuming nitric acid should be stored, poured and used either outdoors or in an unused room where nothing but the door handle and light switch will rust, and rest assured they will do just that.

Rags that are used to dry off denickeled parts, no matter what chemical was used on them, should be put in a refuse pail that is kept outside of the shop proper. As a matter of fact, rags, pans, containers, swabs or, in short, anything that is used in connection with acids or rust promoting compounds should be thoroughly cleaned and stored far away from the machines, tools and guns that are in the shop. While it may appear that this writer is a bit fussy about the location of deoxidizing chemicals, it is for the reason that many dollars' worth of tools and machines can be rusted overnight by a carelessly placed rag that has been soaked in any one of the more common acids.

Stripping Copper. Though it is not very often that a gunsmith has occasion to strip anything other than nickel-plating from steel, the following formula might come in handy when an undercoat of copper (under nickel, that is) is not completely removed by the regular nickel-stripping solution:

Stripping Copper from Steel

Sulphuric Acid .... 7 oz.
Chromic Acid .... 4 lbs.
Water .... 1 gal.

Used cold this solution will dissolve a 0.001″ thick coating of copper in less than one-half hour. When heated to 200° F. it will do the same job in less than five minutes. Note: When mixing water and acid, always pour acid into water; do not pour the water into the acid or the latter is apt to splatter.

Cleaning and Cleaners

Importance. In every book, chapter, article and paragraph ever written on metal coloring the emphasis is always upon the importance of having work clean before it is put into the blueing tank or swabbed with blueing solution. To which this writer says amen and to put emphasis on the emphasis offers the following thoughts:

In the overall operation of refinishing a weapon, the cleaning phase is the most important and the easiest. Yet, for some reason or other, improper cleaning is the basic cause of more aggravation during blueing than any other factor.

A gunsmith can spend two hours filing, grinding, polishing and buffing a set of double barrels, and use the finest blueing solution and utmost care in applying it, only to discover after a couple of swabbings and cardings that the matting on the top rib refuses to color. When this sort of condition arises the first thought is to rub the matting over vigorously with steel wool, or hold it against the carding wheel. This failing, the desperate gunsmith not infrequently plunges the partly blued barrels back into the cleaning solution as a last chance.

Sometimes one of these mid-process emergency cleanings produces results; more often, though, it is necessary to deoxidize and rebuff the part that will not "take," and then give it the kind of cleaning that it should have gotten in the first place.

Work Prior to Rust Blueing. Parts to be blued by the rusting process (quick method or 10-day method) require a more scrupulous cleaning than those which are to be colored in a hot dip bath because the blueing salts of a hot dip bath have a cleaning agent in them. This, coupled with the vigorous boiling of the hot dip bath, tends to make parts oxidized in it less likely to resist coloring. Now this does not mean that the gunsmith can afford to be less thorough or careful in cleaning parts slated for hot dip blueing than with those for a rusting blueing; rather, it means that work to be colored by the later process must have a double cleaning.

Solvent Cleaning. The first cleaning should be done with a volatile solvent (benzine, gasoline, carbon tetrachloride) to remove all heavy deposits of buffing compound, wax, etc. that have been forced into the crevices and cracks of checkering, matting, knurling, and where plates join the receiver or frame proper of a gun. This cleaning should include a vigorous scrubbing with a stiff bristle brush (soaked in solvent) of all surfaces (as mentioned above) where foreign matter might likely adhere. During this scrubbing all screws should be loosened, all side or bottom plates taken off, and the solvent allowed to soak into deep holes and crevices. On double barrel guns a sharp pointed stick, on the style of a pencil, should be run down the crevice formed where the rib and barrel meet, because this is a favorite lodging place for polishing compounds, et cetera, as is the extractor hole and front sight hole.

Water Cleaning. The second cleaning should be done in a tank of boiling water to which has been added a few ounces per gallon of a commercial detergent. And although lye (caustic soda) is usually recommended as a good cleaner for pre-blueing purposes and general metal parts cleaning, this writer does not think lye should be used when a product like Oakite can be bought in any grocery or hardware store. Four ounces of Oakite added to each gallon of water makes as fine a water cleaner as the gunsmith could ask for. Oakite is superior to lye because it does a better job of dissolving grease, oil, et cetera and also contains a wetting agent which helps immeasurably when a part is to be blued by the rusting process.

Although the Oakite that is sold for household use is quite inexpensive (less than 1¢ per ounce) the gunsmith who uses a great deal of it would get a better price by purchasing any one of the special formula industrial Oakites made by Oakite Products Inc., 22 Thames Street, New York, N.Y.

This writer has yet to speak to the gunsmith (and other people who formerly used lye for metal cleaning purposes) who did not praise Oakite's superiority when he switched to it from lye.

Storing, Mixing and Experimenting with Chemicals

The chemistry of metal coloring, like all branches of chemistry, is a very fascinating subject. However, a genuine interest in the subject, or even ownership of all sorts of acids, salts and apparatus, does not help the gunsmith to any appreciable degree in concocting blueing solutions, unless he has a good knowledge of chemistry and knows how to apply it to the problems at hand.

Mixing chemicals often requires more than the basic ingredients, a scale, and a container in which to compound them. The matter of compatability, reaction and order of introduction are a few of the considerations which the average gunsmith knows little about but which are almost second nature to the chemist.

The danger of being seriously injured or suffering painful skin burns is always present when an inexperienced hand engages in chemical experiments. The trained chemist, on the other hand, knows, for example, that grinding of potassium chlorate or indiscriminate handling of bichloride of mercury are things that just should not be done.

When the gunsmith undertakes to mix his own blueing solutions and compounds he must have quite an assortment of chemicals, plus certain containers, scales, weights, et cetera. To attempt compounding without the proper equipment is foolhardy; to do it with the proper equipment is expensive. Alternative? Let your local druggist, or chemist if you live in or near a big city, compound your "special solutions." In the long run you will save money, avoid the mess and danger that attend the process and, above all, know that ingredients and proportions are correct.

As to formulas for rusting process blueing solutions, this writer is of the opinion that the professional, as well as the amateur, gunsmith is far better off if he buys prepared solutions from any one of the reliable supply sources rather than try every Tom, Dick and Harry formula that is suggested. In the long run these commercially prepared solutions are the gunsmith's best bet because of their uniformity and stability. True, they probably cost a few cents more than a similar solution that might be compounded by the gunsmith himself, but since the cost of the blueing solution in any process is insignificant and dwarfed by the labor, heating, cleaning and grinding cost, the matter of spending a few cents extra for a reliably prepared solution should not even be accorded a serious thought.

If the gunsmith uses a ready-mixed solution he is assured that the work turned out will be of uniform color and tone.

There are enough different commercial blueing solutions available so that the gunsmith need not feel his urge to try something new, different and possibly better, must be stifled. It is a good policy to try different brands of each type (quick rusting and slow rusting) in the beginning and after due and fair trial adopt the one or ones that are best suited. Perhaps the gunsmith will discover during this trial period that one particular solution turns out a pleasant tone for handguns, while another is almost perfect for shotgun tubes.

For those who must make their own solutions (because they like to) the book "Firearms Blueing and Browning" by Angier is highly recommended. The chemistry of blueing is covered in this book in a very thorough and professional manner. As a reference book on the subject it is without a peer.

Types and Methods of Blueing

For purposes of classification and orderly description this writer prefers to divide the ways by which guns and component parts can be blued into six groups. They are:

1) Cold Rusting Process (Natural Method Rusting)
2) Hot Rusting Process (Quick Method Rusting)
3) Phosphatizing Processes
4) Bone and Oil Process (Furnace Blueing)
5) Miscellaneous Processes (Niter Blueing, etc.)
6) Hot Dip Process

Because not all of these types are adaptable to modern small shop needs, only those which are practical will be dealt with in detail. However, before describing the ways guns may be colored by the cold rusting process or hot rusting process it might be well to explain what the term carding means as it applies to them; and also cover a few of the preparatory operations common only to these two processes.

Carding. After a piece of iron or steel is coated with certain types of solutions, as are employed in both hot and cold rusting processes, the surface of the metal becomes covered with a rust deposit as a result of chemical action between the steel and the applied solution. In order to remove the loose part of the rust deposit, a piece of fine steel wool, a small hand scratch brush, or a wire wheel attached to a motor is employed. The operation of removing the rust by any of these means is known as carding.

If steel wool (or a hand brush) is used, it is gripped between the fingers of one hand while the other hand is used to hold or support the part from which the rust is to be carded. Hand carding is much slower than the same operation done with the powered circular brush. Nevertheless, hand carding must be employed on some parts that are so shaped as to preclude using the power brush.

When carding by hand, the gunsmith must develop a "touch" that will enable him to rub lightly but vigorously on the rusted surface and so remove only the loose rust and not the dark undertone on the metal which is the newly produced blueing. Different types of blueing solutions used on different steels result in rust formations of varying colors and densities. As the gunsmith learns to recognize these different rusts he will know those which card off easily and those which often necessitate hard rubbing with a medium rather than fine grade of steel wool. Fine steel wool, incidentally, should always be used for the final carding, irrespective of what degree of coarseness might have to be resorted to during the preliminary cardings.

Like the circular carding brush, steel wool and hand brushes used for carding must always be kept clean and free from foreign matter. If a piece of steel wool inadvertently becomes wet or soiled with water or blueing solution during carding, it should be discarded immediately and a new piece or brush substituted.

There are no special precautions to be observed when using the power-driven carding wheel other than to hold the work against it lightly and keep it in motion at all times. If a rotating carding wheel is allowed to play on one spot it will scratch off the base color as well as the rust.

To the observing mechanic, carding should present no problem since it is chiefly a matter of knowing how much or how little pressure and rubbing is required to clear off the accumulated loose rust.

For Holding the Work. So that certain parts can be correctly held while blueing solution is being applied and carding is done, it is usually necessary that they be wired up or attached to a piece of dowel or metal in some way. The variety and shape of parts, such as hammers, triggers, bolts, et cetera precludes the issuance of any specific directions as to how such small parts should be rigged up for convenient handling, other than to caution against the use of any device that might cover up an area that has to be swabbed or carded. Although being suspended from a length of black iron wire is the commonest method of keeping track of and affording a holding medium on small parts, it is far from being ideal since the wire not infrequently gets in the way when the part is being carded. That is one of the trivial annoyances that a gunsmith has to put up with though, and one must learn to accept such annoyances until he can devise a better way of doing the job.

Large units, such as receivers, bolts and frames, can usually be held by a piece of dowel rod tapped into a hole or well, that does not have to be covered with solution.

When the make-up of any part or unit permits it, a dowel should be inserted in two places so that it can be carded all over without being touched directly with the hand. Barrels of all types come under this arrangement because one dowel can be inserted in the muzzle and the other dowel in the chamber or inside of the receiver. In effect this amounts to a plugging of the bore and if the muzzle and chamber plugs are of a proper size, slightly tapered, and tapped into respective ends of the barrel, they will serve to keep the bore pretty well protected but not completely dry. However, the purpose of bore plugs in connection with rust blueing is not so much to keep the bore bone dry but rather to aid in keeping water from dripping out of the bore, as would be the case if no plugs at all were used. Important too are the plugs, as handles, for lifting the hot barrels from the boiling water.

As can be readily seen, wooden plugs do, after a short period of immersion, become water-soaked and swell up, thus occasionally making their removal difficult. This writer does not recommend greasing the bore or greasing the plugs to forestall such an occasional occurrence because too often the grease becomes dissolved in the water in which the blueing is being done and settles on the parts as they are removed.

If the gunsmith finds that he has trouble in removing wooden bore plugs he should try drilling a hole lengthwise from one end of the plug to the other and insert a tight fitting rubber cork in the end of the hole that remains outside the barrel. This should be done before the wooden plug is wet. Then if, after being immersed, it resists removal, the rubber cork can be removed with a pick or corkscrew and the hollow plug crushed in two for easy removal. This might sound like a lot of work but actually it is only a few minutes' job on a lathe and will save lots of wasted time and aggravation that a stuck wooden plug can cause. The size of the hole in the plug depends, of course, on the bore size of the gun in which it is to be used, but hole size about one-half bore diameter is a good rule-of-thumb.

All dowel lengths used for bore plugs should be cut up in convenient lengths, boiled in water for a few minutes, and allowed to dry thoroughly for days before being turned to size. This processing tends to minimize subsequent swelling.

Hooks. For moving large units in and out of a tank filled with hot water, hooks of the style illustrated in Figure 95 are necessary. Some gunsmiths prefer to make hooks of such a length that they keep work from resting on the bottom of the tank when the hooks are suspended from the side. This is a good practice because it makes the task of lifting the work out easier and does away with "fishing" around to get the hooks under a barrel or similarly shaped unit.

Stainless steel welding rod, $\frac{1}{8}''$ diameter, with the flux knocked off and then bent to shape, makes the best hooks as they are strong and are not subject to easy rusting.

Gloves. Once a piece of work has been ground, buffed and cleaned preparatory to being coated with blueing solution, its surface must be kept free of foreign matter that might inhibit the "taking" of the blue. And one of the threats to this cleanliness is perspiration.

Some gunsmiths, after considerable experience of course, learn to resist any and all temptations to touch the surface of the metal being blued with their fingers or back of their hand. Now this is not as easy as might be imagined, especially during those instances when a part being coated or carded starts to slip from the grasp. Therefore, all but experts in the art of rust blueing would do well to have available at all times a few pairs of clean cotton gloves and to wear them from the time the gun is cleaned until it is oiled. Tight fitting gloves are best since they do not interfere with the normal dexterity of the hand as do loose fitting, long fingered gloves which catch in everything and must constantly be adjusted to keep them from falling off.

If gloves become wet during a period of blueing they should be laid aside and a clean, dry pair put on.

Swabs. For applying blueing solution to work a swab of the kind illustrated in Figure 95 is generally used. The gauze (2″ width) should be tightly wrapped around an 8″ length of dowel rod, and kept from sliding down by means of a small carpet tack inserted near the top. To keep the gauze from twisting around, the dowel rod should be slit for a length of 2″ and the starting end of the gauze placed in this slit.

Briefing. In explaining the hot rusting process and the cold rusting process this writer will deal only with steps or incidentals not already covered. For example, it is to be presumed that by the time a gun is ready to be blued it has been disassembled, ground, polished, buffed, wired up for handling, and wooden plugs inserted where necessary. Also, it is further presumed the gunsmith has assembled the necessary equipment and has read carefully the paragraphs entitled Tank Materials and Construction, Denickeling, Cleaners and Cleaning, Storing, Mixing and Experimenting with Chemicals, Baskets for Holding Small Parts, and Wire Wheels.

The Cold Rusting Process

General. Although the cold rusting process is a method by which very few gunsmiths today blue guns, it is well for the newcomer to know that such a way exists because it often can be relied upon to do a high class job when other means fail. The cold rusting process is probably the oldest means known for coloring the metal portions of firearms and, according to Angier, was used in England as far back as 1720.

It is quite simple to blue a gun by the cold rusting process and because a desired shade can be achieved and then all further action killed, it is well adapted to very expensive shotguns, or weapons which are part of a displayed collection. The slow rusting which is the basis of this method of blueing helps to produce some fine deep satin blues.

Even if he does not intend to use it as a regular reblueing method, the gunsmith who has never blued a gun by the cold rusting process should try his hand at it by doing a gun that he intends to put up for sale. He will not only be adding to the value of the gun but also getting a bit of experience in doing something he should know how to do.

How It Is Done. In the cold rusting process work which has been thoroughly cleaned, rinsed in boiling water, and wiped dry with a clean piece of cotton or flannel cloth is coated with blueing solution and hung up out of the way to dry and rust.

The time that a part should be allowed to rust depends upon the type of solution used and the type of metal being treated. However, 12 hours is a long enough period for most any solution applied cold, unless otherwise stated by the manufacturer of the solution.

After the first rusting, the part is then carded, boiled in clean water for five to 10 minutes, dried, coated with blueing solution and again put away to rust. This same series of operation, i.e., carding, boiling in water, drying, coating, and putting away to rust, is repeated as many times as is necessary to produce the desired depth of color. On some steels three or four passes (as a complete series of operations is called) will produce a beautiful color, while on harder or tougher steels as many as 10 passes might be required.

Although rusting can be speeded up by placing the coated work in a steam cabinet, this is not necessary for the small shop gunsmith as the production and piping of steam is, when done correctly, a time-consuming project. This writer can see no reason for the gunsmith to use the cold rusting process and then speed it up with steam. If one is in a hurry, then he should use the hot rusting process and leave the cold type for another time.

After the desired color has been reached, the work should receive a very careful rubbing with fine steel wool. This treatment imparts a uniform tone to the entire finished surface. Finally, a piece of cotton, soaked in finishing oil, should be rubbed all over the work to kill any further rusting action. After the work has cooled it may then be assembled, wiped off and re-oiled.

Solutions for Cold Rusting Process

No. 1.—

Bismuth Chloride	10 grams
Mercuric Chloride	20 grams
Copper Chloride	10 grams
Hydrochloric Acid	60 grams
Alcohol (grain, 95°)	50 ccm
Water (distilled)	500 ccm

Note: Add acid before salts to prevent precipitation of bismuth salt.

No. 2.—

Mercuric Chloride	25 grams
Ammonium Chloride	25 grams
Water (distilled)	500 ccm

No. 3.—(Light Blue):

Iron Chloride	100 grams
Antimony Chloride	100 grams
Gallic Acid	50 grams
Water	250 ccm

*No. 4.—*Stoeger's Gunsmith's Bluer.

No. 5.—(For Browning Damascus or Twist Steel Barrels):

Alcohol	45 ccm
Iron Chloride Solution (29%)	45 ccm
Mercuric Chloride	45 grams
Sweet Spirits of Niter	45 ccm

No. 6.—(For Browning Damascus Barrels):
Stoeger's Damascus Browner.

Hot Rusting Process

Versatility of This Method. Prior to the introduction of the hot dip process the hot rusting process (quick method rusting) was the professional and home gunsmith's method of blueing a gun. And still today, in spite of the comparatively easy method that the hot dip process affords, the barrels of double barrel shotguns and other soldered-together parts that cannot safely be put in an immersion blueing bath must be blued by the rusting process, and the quick method is the usual choice.

The quick method rusting process is very similar to the cold method except that intermittent immersion in boiling water is relied upon to promote rapid rusting, that can be dried by heat of evaporation and carded off.

Advantages. Although the quick method rusting process is actually much slower (takes about one hour average to blue a gun from start to finish; two guns take twice as long; three guns three times as long, and so on, while in the hot dip process five guns can be colored as quickly as one, just so long as the tank is large enough) than the hot dip process, it can be used to color certain types of steel and iron that the latter will not always color. Also, the subtle satin blue produced by the rusting method is often more suited to some of the better grade weapons than is the somewhat menacing black tone produced by the hot dip method.

Quick Rusting and Hot Dip. Often the quick rusting process and the hot dip process can be used in conjunction to the help of the gunsmith and the financial benefit of the customer. For example, on a double barrel shotgun or high grade rifle, where the receiver and barrel are blued by the rusting process, the small parts (pins, screws, plungers) can be immersed in a small hot dip bath and colored at the same time. In this way the gunsmith is relieved of the extremely annoying and sometimes very difficult task of blueing small parts (which do not hold heat well) by the rusting process and can devote his energies and attention to doing a faultless job on the major parts.

By the same token, the quick rusting process can often be used to advantage in blueing a part of a gun that cannot be colored by the immersion process. For example, the bolt stop lever spring on the Mauser rifle generally comes out a maroon color when blued by the hot dip method. However, it can be colored blue-black with most any of the hot rusting solutions in six or seven passes.

Although using two different processes to blue a gun is apt to result in a two-tone job, color matching can be improved by:

1) not putting a high finish on small parts to be blued by hot dip method if the main units of the gun are to be rust-blued;

2) putting an extremely high finish on a part that must be rust-blued, yet is to be part of a gun that is hot dip-blued.

Fortunate is the gunsmith who has had experience with the different blueing processes and realizes the good and bad points of each. To him gun blueing is not a matter of knowing one or two "secret" formulas and how to use them, but rather a means by which he can put a suitable finish on any type of gun from a single shot Hamilton rifle to the finest Ithaca trap gun.

Setting Up for the Job. In Figure 95 is illustrated a basic layout for doing quick rust-blueing with a minimum of running around and inconvenience. Some of the gadgets and attachments illustrated, while not absolutely necessary, are very handy when the gunsmith is up to his neck in work and running into difficulties. The difference between a good blueing job and one that is not even passable for a novice when blueing by the quick method often lies in having a clean piece of steel wool, or an extra clean swab within arm's length. That is the idea behind Figure 95.

Blueing. Though a gun can be blued by the hot rusting method using only one or two tanks, this writer believes that three tanks are necessary and that by using fewer the gunsmith automatically starts out at a disadvantage. If the gunsmith thinks (or knows from his own experience) that he can do the job with less equipment and fewer conveniences, that is to his credit. However, the student will have to bear with this writer as the various steps incident to this method of blueing are delineated and then judge for himself (after a few trial runs) what impediments, if any, can be dispensed with.

A Typical Job. Because barrels from a double barrel shotgun are the item most frequently blued by this method, their blueing will be used as a means of illustrating a typical quick method blueing job from start to finish.

After the barrels have been solvent-cleaned and plugged, they are lowered into Tank 1 (Figure 95) by means of the stainless steel hooks, for at least five minutes of a vigorous boiling, cleaning action. Next, remove the barrels from the cleaner and as swiftly as possible immerse them in Tank 2, where any adhering cleaner or previously loosened bits of foreign matter will be floated away. Allow the barrels to remain in Tank 2 for only a couple of minutes and then transfer them into Tank 3, which should be about ⅔ full of clean water, kept at a rolling boil. Also, in the corner of Tank 2 (see Figure 95) held in a somewhat stationary position with wire, is a glass container (a small mayonnaise jar is all right, but it should be cleaned in hot water and

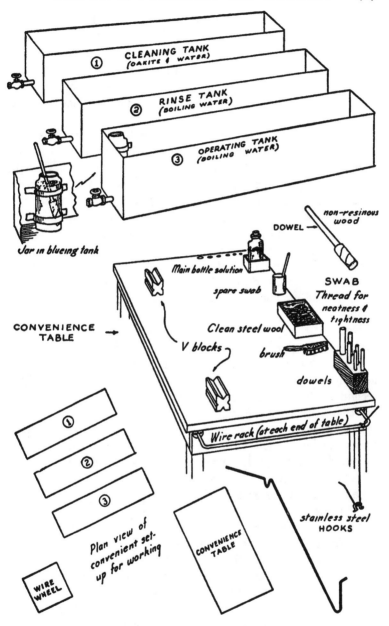

BLUEING BY THE RUSTING PROCESS

FIGURE 95

dried before it is considered acceptable) in which a couple of ounces of blueing solution (quick method) was poured when this tank was just starting to heat up. Thus, by the time the water in the tank is boiling the blueing solution is hot—and that is just what is wanted. This type of solution must be hot before it is applied to work; otherwise the finished product will not turn out the way it should.

When the gunsmith is sure that everything is ready at this point (gloves on, swab in the solution, carding equipment set, et cetera) he removes the barrels from Tank 3 (tilt them so that all the excess water runs off) and with the swab, that has been squeezed free of excess solution by pressing it against the side of the container, *rapidly* coats the barrels with solution. And "rapidly" in this operation *means to work fast,* but not at the expense of missing any corners or hard-to-get-at places. Almost instantly the solution will dry on the barrel and form a coating that is apt to appear dull silver, flat blue-black, blue-gray, or flat blue, depending upon the steel, solution, and atmospheric conditions.

Note: If the applied solution produces a definite red coating, that is a sign that trouble might be in the offing, in which case it is advisable to add about a half ounce of fresh solution to the hot solution in the container. If the same red appears after the second coating, add half an ounce of distilled water; should this dilution not correct the fault by the third coating, then another type of solution should be used. Though it is not very often that this sort of condition will arise, it is best that the gunsmith be prepared by having a spare container and some other type, or at least fresh solution, ready when a strange (in the sense that the type of steel has never before been worked with) gun is readied for blueing.

Just as soon as the coated barrels dry (blow gently on any little spots that are wet to hasten drying) put them back in Tank 3 and let them boil for about two minutes. Lift them out and just as soon as they dry (a matter of a few seconds) card off the formed rust. Use a brush, a wire wheel, or steel wool (or, if necessary, all three) but above all remove the rust from every place. When the coating of rust has been removed, it should reveal the steel as having a slightly dark tone. Do not rub this off, though—it is the first "coat" of blue.

Having completed the first carding, the barrels should be inspected for spots or corners that did not take. The location of bare areas should be remembered and examined after the second carding to make certain they are not spots which must be rubbed with a bit of abrasive cloth or steel wool before the blueing will take.

After this, place the barrels back in Tank 3 for two minutes. Then repeat the original steps, i.e., coating, boiling, carding, inspection and boiling. When this series has been carried out three or four times, the barrels should have a definite blue color to them. If they have not, then fresh solution should be brought into play and the carding operations carried out more gently. If these reforms do not give indications of bearing fruit after another two passes, then the gunsmith should call a halt to the entire operation and again start from scratch.

The possible causes of a piece of steel not taking color can, as a rule, be laid to at least one of the following factors:

1) *Cause.* Foreign matter on the work.

Remedy. Go over every direction in this chapter in regards to cleaning and check against the methods employed in practice. Check the carding equipment, swab, solution, container, tanks, et cetera. Also check to see that no shop equipment (grinding head, motor-driven machinery) is throwing off particles of dirt or oil that could be settling on the work or in the tanks.

2) *Cause.* Nature of the metal (i.e., stainless steel, hard steel).

Remedy. Learn to recognize different metals, by their appearance, trade marks, manufacturers' catalogs, et cetera and act accordingly.

Rust resistant steel, such as stainless steel or Bohler Antinit (not very often encountered) should be etched, after rinsing and before immersion in Tank 3, with a solution of jewelers' etchant (Spencer acid).

Jewelers' etching acid is applied while the metal is hot, by means of a piece of cloth saturated with the solution. Application of this etchant does not guarantee that subsequent applications of blueing solution will produce the desired color. At best the blueing of stainless steel is a difficult proposition and the gunsmith should not expect too much in the way of good results when dealing with steels having a high percentage of chromium and nickel in them.

Some hard steels, and surface-hardened steels, will "take"

blueing better if they are liberally coated with a solution consisting of one ounce nitric acid and 10 ounces of water, just after being rinsed in boiling water. The solution should be applied while the metal is hot and the part, after being coated and allowed to dry in air, should be put back in Tank 2 to boil for a minute or two. Then after this short interval the part can be transferred to Tank 3 and the blueing process carried out on top of the etched surface.

Putting the etched part in Tank 2 is recommended so that Tank 3 will not be unduly contaminated.

3) *Cause.* The blueing solution (weak).

Remedy. Often in the later stages of blueing a gun by the quick method, the gunsmith will notice that the rust coatings produced are very light and not conducive to deepening the color of the metal. This is usually due to a change in the blueing solution brought about by loss of alcohol, or precipitation of salts due to prolonged heating. Addition of a small quantity (teaspoonful) of spirits of niter or grain alcohol (if the solution originally had either of these chemicals in it) will often make for improved rusting. If a commercial preparation is being used, then addition of a little fresh solution is suggested.

Although the average set of barrels takes about seven passes to be colored by the hot rusting process, this writer prefers to recommend that the gunsmith be the judge of when a part is blued sufficiently, by observing its color and not by counting the number of passes. For some unfathomable reason a set of barrels or a revolver frame can be colored in four passes at one blueing, while at another time it will take six coatings before the color makes up its mind whether it wants to stay on or not.

After the gunsmith has blued a few hundred different types and makes of guns by the hot rusting process, he will probably be quite a master at juggling hot parts and holding a glove in his mouth while he adjusts the gas burner with his elbow; but he will be very reluctant about betting that the next gun he blues will be completed without at least one moment (extra long) of anxiety.

After Blueing. When the last carding is done and the gunsmith is satisfied with the color on the set of barrels (remember that is what we started with a few pages ago) they should be rubbed over with cotton soaked in oil and laid aside to cool. After cooling they should be again wiped dry and re-oiled with clean oil.

Thin Parts. Very thin parts (magazine tubes for repeating shotguns) made of light metal are almost impossible to blue by the quick method unless they are "backed up" with a heavier piece of metal to aid in holding heat. A magazine tube is best "backed up" by insertion of a piece of cold rolled steel or drill rod in the full length of the tube. If a snug fit is not possible, then a few feet of wire will do to hold the tube and steel together.

Small parts like pins, screws, etc., which cannot be "backed up," should be heated over an alcohol torch for a few seconds before the solution is applied. Also, it is often better to dip such parts directly into the blueing solution rather than to swab it on. In fact, the practice of applying blueing solution while the parts are hot enough to insure subsequent rapid drying of the swabbed-on solution is very important. So much so that the gunsmith should never apply solution to a part that is not as hot as boiling water can make it. Solution applied to a part that is not hot enough will often run before it dries and the finished job will be covered with streaks. Thus the gunsmith should fully appreciate the necessity for working fast when swabbing on solution.

On some thin parts that do not seem to color very well even after a few coats, it is often advisable to coat the part with solution, let it dry and put it into boiling water for a couple of minutes. Then, instead of carding the accumulated rust off, the part should be coated again, allowed to dry, and put back in the water. If this sequence is carried out three or four times between carding, then usually the most difficult-to-color parts can be blued.

Solutions for Hot Rusting Process

No. 1. Baker's Basic Solution:

Note: In his valuable book "Modern Gunsmithing," the late Clyde Baker included a formula which he used with gratifying results on many guns. There are few gunsmiths of this writer's acquaintance who have not used Baker's Basic Solution, either as originally published, or with slight changes to suit a particular whim or condition. It is reprinted here primarily because it is good and also because it does not call for microscopic quantities of hard-to-get chemicals of very dubious value.

Sodium Nitrate	¼ oz.
Potassium Nitrate	¼ oz.

Bichloride of Mercury	
(Mercuric chloride)	½ oz.
Potassium Chlorate	½ oz.
Distilled Water	10 oz.
Spirits of Niter	½ oz.

Mix the first four ingredients in a clean, wide-mouth jar. *Do not grind them* together with a mortar and pestle. Potassium chlorate when rubbed hard is apt to explode. Add the water, which is warm but not boiling. Stir the concoction with a glass rod until the solids dissolve. When this mixture has cooled add the niter and pour the whole works into a dark brown or blue bottle. Put a cork, not a metal cap, on the bottle and label it: "Blueing Solution, Hot, *Poison*." Shake before using to mix up any salts that might have settled.

No. 2. Modified Basic Solution (for soft steel):

Sodium Nitrate	100 grains
Potassium Nitrate	100 grains
Bichloride of Mercury	220 grains
Potassium Chlorate	200 grains
Distilled Water	12 oz.
Spirits of Niter	⅓ oz.

Mix same as No. 1.

No. 3. For Hard Steels:

Sodium Nitrate	110 grains
Potassium Nitrate	110 grains
Bichloride of Mercury	200 grains
Potassium Chlorate	200 grains
Distilled Water	9 oz.
Spirits of Niter	1 oz.
Nitric Acid	⅓ oz.
Tincture Ferric	
Chloride (29%)	⅓ oz.

Mix same as No. 1. Add the ingredients in the order listed.

No. 4. Works Well on Screws, Pins, et cetera:

Potassium Nitrate	110 grains
Sodium Nitrate	110 grains
Bichloride of Mercury	230 grains
Potassium Chlorate	200 grains
Distilled Water	10 oz.
Spirits of Niter	⅓ oz.
Alcohol (grain) 90°	½ oz.

No. 5. Jewelers' Etchant (Spencer Acid) Angier Formula:

Silver Nitrate	3 grams
Mercurous Nitrate	3 grams
Nitric Acid (Density 1.42)	3 ccm
Water—enough to make	100 ccm

Have this mixture made up by a druggist or chemist if it cannot be procured from a plater's supply source. Either a druggist or chemist knows the order in which the chemicals should be mixed and how to keep the silver nitrate from staining his skin.

Phosphatizing Processes

While the small shop gunsmith will probably never have occasion to need any of the phosphatizing finishes that are in use today in military installations and large industrial plants (not necessarily gun manufacturers) it is well for him to know that such processes exist.

Registered under such names as Parkerizing, Bonderizing, Parko-Lubrizing (products of the Parker Rust Proof Co., Detroit 11, Michigan) ; Coslettising, and Fermanganising (British processes) ; the finish produced by any of these processes is equal or superior to any of the commonly used oxidized blueing finishes. However, since any of the phosphatizing processes requires rather elaborate equipment and constant large volume work to justify their installation, that sort of eliminates the average gunsmith.

Although phosphatized surfaces have a tendency to be rough (microscopically pitted) and generally unsuited for the slow-moving parts in sporting weapons, many of the moving internal parts of some machine guns were so treated during the later stages of World War II.

Phosphatizing of sights on sporting arms is something that might prove to be very beneficial if the shooting public could be sold on the color and tone of the finish.

Bone and Oil Process

That very enviable finish one sees on a Smith & Wesson or Colt handgun is put on by a bone and oil process. However, it is not just a matter of mixing up some bone dust and oil and thrusting a gun into the mixture. Rather, after grinding and polishing of the highest order is done on the parts to be blued, they are scrupulously cleaned, mounted on special racks, and hung inside a specially built furnace where the bone dust and oil, or Carbonia (made by the American Gas Furnace Company, of Elizabeth, N.J.), under the influence of controlled heat and an absence of moisture, brings about the almost perfect temper blueing.

For the gunsmith who does specialty manufacturing or modification work on a production basis on handguns or small parts this process has tremendous possibilities. The American Gas Furnace Company can supply details to those gunsmiths who have a genuine interest in their type of heat blueing.

Miscellaneous Formulas for Coloring Metal

To Color Copper or Brass Black. Mix:

Potassium Sulfide	1 oz.
Ammonium Hydrosulphide	2¼ oz.
Water	1 gal.

Dip polished parts in the solution until a uniform deep black color is obtained. Wearing qualities of this finish can be greatly improved by lacquering parts which have been treated with it. Use a glass container to hold solution for dipping.

To Color Brass Green (Antique Effect). Mix:

Iron Nitrate	2 ounces
Sodium Hyposulphite	8 ounces
Water	1 gallon

Bring solution to a boil and dip brass parts (wire strung) until the desired pattern and color effects are achieved. Wearing qualities improved by lacquering.

To Color Brass Blue-Black. Mix thoroughly:

Copper Carbonate	1 pound
Ammonium Hydrozide	1 quart
Then Add Water	3 quarts

This solution should be heated to about 180° F. before the work is immersed. Coloring takes place usually within less than a minute.

To Color Aluminum Black. Mix:

Potassium Permanganate	1½ ounces
Nitric Acid (S.G.20 Be)	⅓ ounce
Copper Nitrate	4 ounces
Water	1 gallon

Heat solution to 170°–180° F. and immerse work. Coloring time runs about 30 minutes.

To Color Cadmium Black. Mix:

Copper sulphate	2 ounces
Potassium Chlorate	3 ounces
Common Table Salt	3 ounces
Water	1 gallon

Heat solution to 180° F. and immerse work for coloring.

To Color Iron or Steel Black. Mix:

2 parts by weight Lye (Caustic Soda)
1 part by weight Potassium Nitrate
6 parts Water

Heat solution to 300° F. and immerse work for coloring.

To Color Iron or Steel Blue (*Niter Bath*). Mix equal parts of sodium nitrate and potassium nitrate in a heavy iron or steel pot. When the nitrates are thoroughly melted add a bit of manganese dioxide, about ⅛ ounce to each pound of nitrate.

Parts to be colored in this bath must be buffed to a mirror finish, cleaned scrupulously, covered with a film of light oil (dipping in an oil bath is the most satisfactory way of accomplishing this) and then lowered into the bath.

Immersion time for a dark blue color varies with the type of steel and its mass.

Since the working temperature of this type bath runs around 800–900° F. soldered parts (lead or silver) or springs should not be put in it. Actually it should only be used for blueing pins, screws and similar small, nonoperating parts.

After the desired color has been achieved, the blued articles should be dunked in room temperature water, then in boiling water (to rinse away any adhering salt) and finally in oil.

The container used for niter bath should be large enough to accommodate the types of parts the gunsmith believes he will blue by this method. A pot made of ¼″ sheet iron welded all around and measuring 10″ long, 5″ wide and 3″ deep will handle almost anything that should be blued at so high a temperature. However, it takes a lot of heat to bring a bath of this size to working temperature. Therefore it is thrifty to have a little container made of the same stock but measuring about 2½″ on all sides. This size is big enough for most work and heats up in a fraction of the time required for the larger unit.

No matter what size the container is, though, there are a few cautions that apply all around:

1) Clean the container before charging it the first time and keep it covered when not in use.

2) Wear gloves and goggles at all times when using the niter bath set-up; splattering goes on no matter how carefully one transfers the parts from cleaner to bath and vice versa.

3) Do not drop articles to be blued in the molten bath; lower them in by means of iron wire.

"Flame" Blueing

From the masters to the apprentices there are very few gun mechanics who have not blued a small pin or screw by dipping it in oil and heating it over a torch or burner until it turns blue, or at least dark. It is strictly a torch-and-plier method but admittedly has a definite place in the scheme of gunsmithing.

Every gunsmith, home mechanic and tinkerer of any standing has his pet oil mixture and method of applying it. This writer favors a mixture of linseed oil and light motor oil. A polished part heated to dark red and dipped in this concoction will emerge with a passable color on it. If one heating and dunking does not produce a deep enough color, then a second and even third treatment can be undertaken with usually better results.

The Hot Dip Process

A little over a decade ago there were very few gunsmiths who thought gun blueing so easy a job that they should go out of their way to solicit work of that type. Today, however, it would appear that all the advertising gunsmiths are only too glad to take on blueing work in any volume. The answer to this rather sudden turn of events (sudden because for a couple of centuries prior to that time, blueing was definitely one of the least choice phases of gunsmithing) did and still does lie in the popularization of the hot-dip blueing process. And in this connection (so far as gunsmithing is concerned) credit goes to Stoeger Arms Corporation and their Black Diamond Blueing Salts for being the pioneers.

Advantages. To fully understand why the hot dip process has changed the gun blueing (both home and professional) picture so radically one need only realize that 10, 20, or even more U.S. .45 Government Automatic pistols can be blued by one man by the hot dip process in less time than it takes to blue one pistol by the misnamed quick method rusting process. One thing necessary in the hot dip process is to have a tank large enough to hold all the items that one would normally blue at any given blueing period. Therefore, from a time factor standpoint (and that is *the* main consideration of a gunsmith who operates a shop) the hot dip process is so superior to even the quick method rusting process that written or spoken comparison hardly does it full justice.

In addition to this, the hot dip process has an advantage over any other type rusting process in that no bore plugging is necessary and that the entire unit, inside and out, is blued a uniform color, the latter factor depending of course on the type of steel being treated.

Too, another point in favor of the hot dip process is that little or no skill is needed by the operator other than to watch a thermometer. Hence, a busy gunsmith can hire an unskilled person to assist in the blueing process while he himself goes about the more important task of repair and remodeling work.

The finish produced by hot dipping is, as a rule, darker and of greater luster than that evolved by either of the rusting methods. However, the necessity for good preparatory polishing is as great for one as it is for the other.

Disadvantages. As might be expected, the hot dip process has its disadvantages and one of these has been realized the hard way by many a novice, and no doubt a few professionals, who have tried blueing double barrel shotguns by this method. The barrels of double guns as well as any other soldered (lead-tin) parts will be adversely affected, often to the extent where they will separate while being blued, if they are immersed in a hot dip blueing solution tank. Therefore, it is foolhardy to blue such parts by this process. Some gunsmiths who have managed to blue a set of double gun tubes by the hot dip process and have them come out in one piece are often surprised three, four, six months, or even a year later to be shown the same barrels with the top and bottom rib bent out at rakish angles and hear the customer say, "I just got around to firing this gun you blued last July and when I did the ribs snapped out like this."

Soldered Parts Should Not Be Hot Dip Blued. Yet there are still some adventurers who are not too ethical and do not make it as plain as they could that soldered parts should not be blued by the hot dip process. Again, in all fairness, it must be stated that Stoeger advertises their salts as "recommended for all guns but those having soldered together barrels."

Another disadvantage of the hot dip process is that it can, if not watched closely and kept within the recommended boiling range, cover all the work that is immersed in it with the most horrible red-green rust which often proves so difficult to remove that the parts covered with it must be deoxidized in the hydrochloric acid bath and rebuffed before they can be again put back into the blueing tank. More about temperature control later.

Although the hot dip, or immersion process (salts), as it is sometimes called, is advertised in some of the gun magazines as if it were something of an esoteric nature or exclusive to the gunsmithing business, it is in the true analysis just a chemical process for oxidizing steel, whose advantages and limitations are well known to the metal finishing trade.

Commercial Processes. There are at this writing three commerial hot dip processes which are widely used for blacking ("blueing," oxidizing) articles made from iron or steel. These processes are Jetal, Ebonol, and Pentrate.

The Jetal process is a patented process of the Alrose Chemical Company, Providence, Rhode Island.

The Ebonol process is owned by The Enthone Company, New Haven, Connecticut.

The Pentrate process is patented by The Heatbath Company, Springfield, Massachusetts.

For the gunsmith who does a great deal of blueing, working with any one of these processes is more economical than buying blueing salts from a gunsmith supply house in small quantity. For the amateur, novice, or professional who does a few guns a week there is no great advantage in using any of the abovementioned processes unless a particular claim the owners of one of these processes makes appeals to him.

Though this writer has had considerable experience with the Jetal process and the Pentrate process, and has seen thousands of gun components which were blued by the Ebonol process, he can truthfully say that he never noted any particular superiority of one finish over the other two in respect to color, tone or wearing qualities. And the same can be said for Stoeger's Black Diamond Bluer, of which the writer has used many a pound.

While this writer does not care to set forth a detailed comparative evaluation of Jetal, Ebonol, Pentrate or Black Diamond, on the basis of considerable personal observation there exists so much a similarity between the chemical make-up and the finish produced by these processes that the following remarks can be construed as applying to all of them and any other immersion or hot dip process, irrespective of its trade name. The gunsmith should have no difficulty in identifying any of these processes inasmuch as they all have a working boiling point of from 270° to 315° F.—occasionally as high as 350° F.

Effect on Dimensions. Inasmuch as penetration achieved by the hot dip process is generally less than 0.0002" the gunsmith need not worry about dimensional changes of parts, bore, chamber, et cetera.

Blueing Over Old Blue. Although a hot dip finish can be applied directly over a previously oxidized surface, the resulting finish will do little more than temporarily color spots that were worn bright. Therefore, every gun or part that is to be refinished by this process should be deoxidized, polished, buffed and cleaned.

Corrosion Resistance. Though the finish produced by the hot dip process does offer a certain amount of protection against corrosion, its principal benefit is that it provides an excellent base for holding oil, wax or similar rust inhibiting agents.

Blueing Cold Worked Parts. Certain parts that are cold worked (stamped, punched) often prove very difficult to color unless they are polished with a fine grit abrasive or, when this is not practicable because of close tolerance, dipped in diluted hydrochloric acid for a minute or two.

Blueing High Carbon Steel. Though a high carbon content of the metal being processed does not appreciably affect its being colored, some cheap revolver frames and not a few double barrel shotgun receivers (that is, if the gunsmith wants to blue a double barrel shotgun receiver, which is usually case-hardened) fall in the cast iron range. As such they often emerge from the hot dip blueing tank coated with a red film which, when rubbed off with an oily rag, reveals a beautiful black finish.

Blueing Alloy Steels. While steel containing a small percentage of chromium can be successfully colored by the hot dip process, the presence of a little nickel in steel will often interfere with successful coloration. Sometimes a prolonged immersion (one hour or more) will bring about darkening of an alloy that cannot be colored in the normal dip time. A dark brown undertone, even after extended immersion, on some hot dip blued gun parts (some S&W cylinders) indicates that the alloy is high in nickel content.

Presence of Non-Ferrous Metals in the Blueing Solution. The presence of non-ferrous metals is so injurious to a hot dip blueing solution that copper wires should not even be used to suspend work in the blueing tank, nor should the baskets for holding small parts be held together in any other way except by iron welding. The presence of copper in this type of blueing solution will evidence itself at first in the form of a light red rust adhering to the finished work. This film can usually be wiped off in the final oil bath. Later on, however, as the copper concentration builds up, the rust streaks on the work will be heavy and quite difficult to remove by rubbing.

Danger from Skin Contact. While non-poisonous, the vapors which arise from a boiling hot dip blueing solution can be irritating to the skin. For that reason, and to be protected against any splattering or splashing, the gunsmith should always be so clothed that a minimum of skin is exposed, i.e., have a shirt on that can be buttoned around the neck and that has long sleeves. Wear rubber gloves, a hat, and keep a pair of goggles on the forehead at least, so they can be dropped over the eyes when putting in or taking out work from the blueing tank.

Adding Water. Because the boiling point of a hot dip process blueing tank must always be kept within a specified working range, the gunsmith will find that he has to keep adding water to the main bath in order to compensate for evaporation loss. Unless a standard processing tank, equipped with a shielded low level water spigot, is part of the gunsmith's blueing equipment, he must rig up some sort of water feed to keep the blueing tank supplied with water. A suggested method is illustrated in Figure 96 but the gunsmith should not hesitate to fashion one of another sort from material on hand just so long as he remembers that the pipe suspended into the tank must be a ferrous metal and not galvanized or tin-plated. A piece of stainless steel tubing is tops. Goggles should be over the eyes, and hands and wrists covered with rubber gloves when water is added to a hot blueing tank. And most important of all—the water should be added slowly so that splattering will be reduced to a minimum and temperature drop registered more accurately. A sudden gush of cold water into a blueing tank can not only cause a miniature tidal wave, resulting in a mess, loss of solution, and possible injury to the operator, but also it will not be assimilated into the entire solution readily enough to cause the thermometer to drop as it should. Thus, more water will actually be introduced than is needed and time and heat will be wasted while the solution is raised again to working range.

Making the Bath. When mixing the hot dip blueing bath, always follow the manufacturer's directions as to how many pounds of blueing salts should be added to how much water. Do not guess at the quantities. Weigh or measure them and stir the mixture with a length of iron rod as the salts are slowly added to the *cold* water.

Seven pounds of salts to six pounds of water is the average concentration for a solution that has a 290° F. boiling point. Each particular brand of salts is a little different but the working boiling range for nearly all hot dip solutions lies between 280° and 290° F.

The tank in which a hot dip blueing solution is to be mixed should be free from rust, oil, grease, dust, or any other foreign matter. Good practice is to rub the tank surfaces (inside) with emery cloth, then clean with carbon tetrachloride before preparing the initial mixture in it.

Inasmuch as rust in a dip blueing tank will be deposited, as a film, on work that is immersed in it, the necessity for maintenance of a clean tank cannot be overemphasized.

Temperature Control. The working temperature or boiling range of any hot dip blueing solution is so important that all three of the commercial processes can be equipped with an automatic temperature regulator or concentration control regulator. Financially, the small shop gunsmith cannot very well consider the installation of automatic controls unless he does a great deal of blueing work (at least three hours every day of actual operation). However, this does not make the ownership of such automatic controls any less desirable or decrease the necessity for watchful and careful manual operation.

When the manufacturer of blueing salts states that the boiling temperature range of the solution should be, let us say, for example, 285°–290°, he means that when the bath is boiling (a steady roll on the surface) the thermometer should read between 285°–290°. Usually the optimum temperature is stated as being nearer to the higher figure. However, just so long as the bath is *kept at proper level* and *kept at a steady boil* at the recommended temperature range, the work should come out of the bath nicely colored.

Red Stains on Work. If the work comes from the bath, after the prescribed immersion period, with a red stain on it, then the bath is being operated at too high a boiling point. In other words, there is too much salts and not enough water. This means that water must be added—but slowly, until the thermometer drops to the low boiling point figure (in the example we are using, that would be 285° F.). If, when the temperature is dropped to this point, the boiling ceases, a few moments' wait is in order to allow the thermometer to register accurately the change. If the thermometer starts to rise, even slightly, after the addition of water, but the solution does not boil, then more water must be added. Water should always be added slowly in spite of the temptation to "flood the solution" when it goes haywire and colors the work red instead of blue.

Removing Rust Stains. Sometimes, but not always, it is possible to get the red stain off a piece of processed metal by putting it back into the blueing tank after the proper operating boiling range has been restored. If this does not work, then the stained parts should be put in the alkali cleaner for a few minutes and again put in the blueing tank. Failure to respond to this second treatment is a pretty sure indication that the stained part must go through the preparatory process (acid dip, rinse, buffing, et cetera) again before a successful blueing can be done.

Although it is often possible, after considerable wiping, scrubbing, and swearing, to rub off the rust stain that comes from high temperature operation, this writer does not condone nor recommend such a course of action because it makes for an inferior job. Furthermore, the rust stain that forms on the outside of a part or receiver also forms in holes, crevices, undercuts and other inaccessible places. There is no successful mechanical means of removing the rust from these hard-to-get-at places without rubbing away the blueing or scratching the metal.

It is well known to those who have handled many guns or parts that have been blued by the hot dip process that the finish will not stand too much rubbing on a sharp corner, or even rounded edge, before the bare light metal starts to show through. Therefore, rubbing off strongly adherent rust stains to expose the blueing just is not the ethical way of doing a job. Furthermore, in the long run it is just as quick to reprocess a gun (exclusive of grinding, which, of course, is not necessary in a "second run") that is rust-stained during blueing, as it is to try and wipe the stain off each part and surface.

Types of Rust Stain. At this juncture it might be well to point out that there are two separate types of red stains or rust deposits the gunsmith is apt to encounter in operating a hot dip blueing solution.

The most common type is that which is produced by operating at too high boiling point. This deposit can be recognized by its density of covering and because it will adhere to the metal surface after being dipped in the rinse tank. Occasionally it will turn sea-weed green after it has been cooled in the rinse tank.

The other type of rust which precipitates on the immersed work is caused by copper or any of its alloys being introduced into the blueing solution. It differs from the high temperature stain in that it does not appear as dark or cling as tenaciously as that one does.

Either type of rust is objectionable since all the work in a processing tank is ruined when the boiling point gets out of hand or when non-ferrous metals precipitate.

While there is little or no excuse for the gunsmith to allow anything in his blueing tank that is non-ferrous metal, this writer must admit that it is not too easy to keep 100% away from high boiling point red stains. Even the most carefully watched baths sometimes get a bit out of hand. This fact should not be the gunsmith's excuse, though, every time the thermometer is neglected; it is just mentioned in passing so the novice will not be discouraged if he runs into quite a bit of difficulty before mastering the fundamentals of the hot dip blueing process.

Cyanide Solution. When work always comes from the hot dip tank with a light red film on it, the gunsmith can mix up 1½ ounces of potassium cyanide, for every gallon of blueing solution, in a small quantity of water and pour this solution slowly into the bath. Almost needless to say, *this cyanide and water mixture is deadly,* deadly stuff internally, in an open cut, or any place but in the tank. Therefore, pour it into the bath slowly and keep the face from over the top of the tank in case of splatters. Best time to add this mixture is just before the bath is started up. Make a few holes in the bath (if it is semi-solid, as it often is) and pour the cyanide mixture into the holes. Once the cyanide is mixed up in the bath, i.e., goes into solution, it becomes harmless since it does not retain its composition.

Take care to see that none of the cyanide solution is spilled in a tank containing acid. When cyanide comes in contact with hydrochloric acid, sulphuric acid, et al., a very deadly gas is generated. As a matter of fact, it is the same gas that is used by exterminators for mass scale rat killing and also by one of our states as a legal method of execution.

While on this topic of cyanide and what can happen when it is not used carefully, this writer would like to point out that two chemicals which are usually in every gunsmith shop, cyanide and bichloride of mercury, are, as mentioned more than once in this book, very deadly poisons.

People who read this book, or, for that matter, any text in which certain chemicals which are extra potent when mishandled are mentioned as a matter of necessity, are usually old enough to understand the meaning and significance of the words "poison" and "careless." Any time these two words are combined in action, there is always the possibility that someone might get hurt or killed.

This writer wants it clearly understood that any suggestions he makes in regard to the use of chemicals are presented because they are necessary to the text—but only as suggested. He wants to see no one maimed or sent to an early grave as a result of sniffing some air that is filled with cyanide gas or fumes, or eating a sandwich upon which some bichloride of mercury has fallen. So he cannot refrain from being repetitious and saying: be careful—be careful always.

High Rate of Evaporation. Perhaps the gunsmith who is new at the business of operating a hot dip blueing tank will do well to remember that, because of the normally high operating temperature, water is evaporating at a rather rapid rate and must be replaced if the bath is to be maintained within the desired boiling range. And as can be appreciated, the most desirable way of maintaining the proper temperature is to have a stream of water constantly flowing into the tank all during the period of boiling operation. Experience, and experience alone, teaches the operator how much water must be kept flowing into a particular tank in order to maintain a constant rolling boil. Small tanks, because of their sensitiveness to the introduction of cold work into the solution, are most difficult to control, and for that reason it is recommended that the gunsmith use as large a tank as is practicable (bearing in mind, however, that the larger the tank the more salt required, and the more initial heat to bring about boiling of the bath) commensurate with anticipated work load.

Insulated Tank. In connection with tanks and temperature control, it might be well to mention that an insulated tank is easier to maintain at the proper temperature than one that is directly subject to room temperature. Sheets of asbestos or magnesia placed around a tank and then held in place by light gauge sheet iron joined at the corners with angle iron provides a good heat retaining medium. This method of applying insulation is for tanks that are heated from the outside bottom. Tanks that are electrically heated (immersion or internal strip heaters) should be insulated on the bottom as well as around the four sides. Incidentally, electrical immersion or strip heaters should not be considered as heating units unless a 440-volt line can be tapped.

Results of Too Much Water. When work that has been immersed for the required time comes from the blueing bath uncolored, even though the bath is boiling, it is pretty safe to assume that the boiling point is too low. To correct this condition (which will ultimately correct itself if the tank is allowed to boil vigorously and evaporate a great deal of water, thus bringing about greater salts concentration), add a small quantity of blueing salts, slowly, until the intensity of the boil subsides somewhat. Actually, the only time it is necessary to add salts to a blueing bath *during the coloring operation* is when too much water has been allowed to run into the tank and force the temperature way down, possibly as low as 270° F.

As mentioned before, it is possible to wait around while the excess boils off. However, when one is in a great hurry to finish a particular batch of work that is all polished up and already too long in the cleaner, the prospect of waiting 15 or 20 minutes is usually second choice to adding a small quantity of blueing salts.

Working Level. So that a working level can be maintained at all times, a mark or marker of some permanent nature should be made or placed along the back side of the blueing tank. A piece of angle iron arc welded in one corner, or a short length of square rod welded to the back are two suggested methods.

The height of a marker is predetermined before being set in place and is based on two factors:

1) Should be placed at least 2″ below the top edge of the tank (having a capacity of 10 gallons or less; should be 4″ for any tank of greater capacity).

2) Should be placed so as to be 2″ above any work that is likely to be processed in the tank.

Now, figuring 2″ as the height of any gun part that would be immersed for coloring, it is quite obvious that the minimum depth of a blueing tank should be 6″, and that is what it should be. For hot dip blueing work on some items, a 4″ height tank is O.K. but not for the shop of a professional gunsmith. In any tank less than 6″ high, the problem of maintaining solution level is made more difficult than need be (since it is just as easy to have the higher tank made), and boiling over, with its consequences, is a very frequent occurrence.

Of course, if a gunsmith should have a very deep tank, then the marker can be placed 6″ or 8″ from the top edge just so long as the minimum requirements are fulfilled.

When the blueing tank is filled (or charged, as it is sometimes referred to) with water and salts for the first time, the cold solution level should be held right to the bottom of the marker, and every time the bath is shut off for the day (after the boiling has stopped) the solution should be returned to marker level, by the addition of water and salts. The proportion of salt to water that should be added varies a bit according to the temperature of the bath just before it was shut off. If it was boiling high, then a greater proportion of water to salts should be made; if it was boiling low, then additions of each should be made as prescribed for an initial charging.

The idea of replenishing the hot dip bath after each usage rather than just before starting it up is recommended because the operator knows the status of the bath when he takes out the last batch of work and therefore can make an addition, favoring salts or water as the instance indicates. Also, the added salts or water will go into solution more readily in a bath that has just been shut off than in one that is at room temperature and hence in a semi-solid state.

A note of caution: a hot dip bath that has ceased to boil looks to be quite inert; however, for some time its temperature is higher than that of boiling water. Thus, if water is poured in

too rapidly during this period, a very sizable eruption will occur. Moral: put the water in very, very slowly or take a few
lessons in how to dodge hot blueing solution as it flies through
the air.

Dragout. Dragout is the term applied to the transfer of blueing solution from the blueing bath to the tank in which parts are
rinsed after they are colored. Dragout cannot be avoided since
a certain amount of blueing solution remains on, or in, holes,
crevices, et cetera, of parts that are taken from the hot dip to
the rinse tank. But dragout can be reduced to a minimum if the
gunsmith will acquire the habit of tilting work as it is lifted
from the blueing tank prior to rinsing. Tilting, when done correctly, will empty most of the highly concentrated liquid from
the bore and receiver of any weapon. Always lift the receiver
end of a rifle or shotgun first so the solution will tend to flow
out of the muzzle end as the unit is lifted from the tank. Parts
having exceptionally deep holes or recesses should be so wired
that when suspended in the blueing tank they will be positioned
like an inverted cup.

For the gunsmith who is inclined to pooh pooh such ideas as
work tilting and work positioning to minimize dragout, attention is drawn to the fact that dragout is the chief way in which
blueing salts are expended in hot dip process. In a commercial
or military setup, where a blueing plant operates all day, the
dragout sometimes runs as high as 15 or 20 pounds. The loss of
a pound per complete rifle is not uncommon if a small bath is
inefficiently operated. However, tilting and the like will reduce
it to a quarter of that amount.

Tank Layouts. Although a complete weapon can be colored in
the hot dip process by using just one tank, such a method of
operation is strictly a home-workshop proposition and neither
practical nor sensible for the professional gunsmith. At least a
three-tank setup is required for smooth and efficient operation
in the smallest professional shop and even this includes only
the minimum essentials, leaving much wiping and oiling to be
done by hand.

In Figure 96 there are illustrated in basic form nine possible
layouts for blueing firearms and their component parts by the
hot dip process, ranging from the one-tank home style to an
eight-tank layout which is very practical even when used on a
comparatively small scale.

Because rifle tanks are of necessity long, it is not always possible, due to space limitation, for the gunsmith to position his tank in flow line fashion as illustrated in Figure 96. Actually it is not necessary to lay out tanks in any particular way just so long as the ones to be heated are grouped together when a single heating stand (gas stove) is employed. Figure 96 (a) shows two variations of tank layout. There are many ways of positioning tanks in a small shop so that all space will be utilized, and the individual gunsmith is of course the best judge as to how that is to be done.

When the gunsmith is in doubt as to what sort of heating apparatus should be purchased, this writer would recommend that lengths of drilled pipe, equipped with gas pipe connection (for natural, bottled or city gas) be positioned under a stand made of angle iron, as in Figure 94. If gas of some type is not available, then heating can be done with kerosene, gasoline or electric stoves or heaters. Since specific conditions, governed by locality, building regulations, local laws and personal choice, will in most cases guide the gunsmith in deciding what type of heating arrangement is best for his needs, there is little worth in going into a lengthy dissertation on the relative efficiency of the various fuels. Safe to say, though, that gas is the preferred method of heating blueing tanks where fine adjustment of the valve, and consequently flame, can be of great help in maintaining an even temperature bath.

Although Figure 96 is of itself self-explanatory, perhaps it might be well to comment on each layout so that no possible misunderstanding will be allowed to present itself to the reader.

Layout A. This is the simplest layout possible. The parts to be blued must be freed of dirt by hand cleaning with a volatile solvent, and then wiped dry. After required immersion in the blueing bath the parts must be rinsed under a running faucet. Rinsing "just blued" parts under a faucet, tap, spigot, or whatever one chooses to call it, is a poor practice since much of the concentrated salts solidifies on parts while they are transferred from the tank to the running water. Large units such as barrels, which must be cooled piecemeal under a faucet, are difficult and tricky to handle since their rinsing is invariably accompanied by splattering and spluttering as bits of hot salts fly out of the bore and other repositories.

Layout B. Similar to "A" except that the presence of the

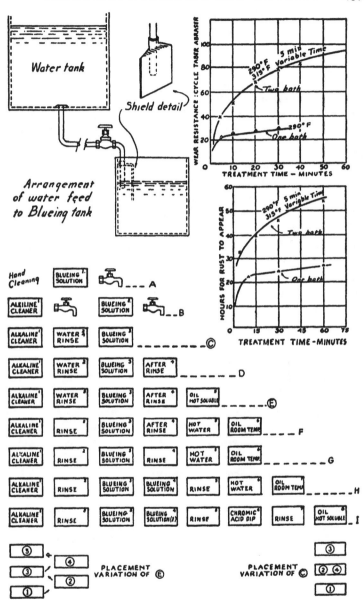

LAYOUT OF BLUEING TANKS
Hot Dip Process

FIGURE 96

alkaline cleaner tank assures that work will go into the blueing tank clean and more likely to "wet" better. Rinsing after cleaning and after blueing still must be done under the faucet, though, so this layout is only a little bit better than one tank.

Layout C. The addition of the water rinse tank makes this a passable professional layout. Note that the rinse tank illustrated bears the numbers 2 and 4 encircled; this means the parts to be processed are dipped, after cleaning and after blueing, in the same tank.

Layout D. The after-rinse tank in this layout is a convenience since the gunsmith can let blued work lay in this tank for a few extra minutes for complete rinsing without interfering with after-cleaning rinsing, as would be the case if only one rinse tank were used.

Layout E. The hot soluble oil in this layout makes it possible for work to be completely processed from the buffed state to the ready-for-assembly state without being handled, rubbed, et cetera. Too, work that is processed near closing time, or for that matter, any time, can be left in the oil tank without fear that it will rust as long as it is completely submerged. Hot soluble oil will wash away from inaccessible recesses blueing salts that remain even after the water rinse.

Layout F. In this layout Tank 5 contains boiling water in which the blued parts are put a few minutes after they have been rinsed in cold water (Tank 4). As the parts are lifted from the boiling water they dry by heat of evaporation. They are then plunged into Tank 6, which is filled with a light-bodied, acid-free oil. Parts should be allowed to remain in oil until they cool or, as a general rule, about 15 minutes.

Layout G. In this layout two blueing tanks are used instead of the customary one. This two-bath method is recommended by the Alrose Chemical Co. (owners of the Jetal Process) for use when firearms are being blued. The Heatbath Corporation (owners of the Pentrate Process) recommend the two-bath process for blueing anything. Both organizations explain that superior penetration, and therefore superior wearing qualities, are obtained when the two-bath method is used. And to back up the explanation Mark Weisberg, president of the Alrose Chemical Co., and one of the originators of the hot dip blueing process (he holds patents on the original process) has kindly allowed the graphs in Figure 96 to be reproduced here.

In the two-bath method one blueing tank (the first) has a lower concentration of salts and therefore boils at a lower temperature than the other. Concentration is such that the first tank boils from 285°–290° F. and the second from 310°–315° F.

This writer cannot recommend proportions for salts, such as Black Diamond, for the two-bath method. However, if the gunsmith is interested in knowing more about the two-bath method, he should not hesitate to write Mr. Weisberg of the Alrose Co.

Layout H. This is a variation of the two-bath method which corresponds to "F" in that a boiling water rinse and acid-free oil are used rather than hot soluble oil.

Layout I. This is a variation of "G" but differs from all others in that a chromic acid dip (1 ounce chromic acid to 1 gallon of water) is employed to counteract the strong alkaline film that remains on processed work even after it has been rinsed thoroughly.

The chromic acid dip can be used to advantage in any tank layout because, by reducing the after-blue alkaline, it helps to do away with the unpleasant burns one receives from handling work that has been colored by the hot dip process.

From the foregoing comment on tank layouts the gunsmith should be able to devise an arrangement that best suits his particular circumstances. No matter what his decision might be, though, he should not forget that a few dollars put initially in an additional tank or two is money wisely invested. The true value of a rinse tank or oil dip tank is often not realized by the mechanic who has never availed himself of their helpfulness. In short, this writer gives wholehearted support to the idea of having as many *necessary* tanks in a blueing layout as space permits.

Layouts "F" and "I" are so designed as to make blueing a clean, profitable phase of gunsmithing rather than a drudgery to be put off as one would a visit to the dentist.

"Blossoming." Many a person who has had a gun blued by the hot dip process is often surprised, if not alarmed, upon seeing a sizable deposit of white or yellow powder, formed around the juncture of the barrel and receiver, a few days after it has been received from the gunsmith in allegedly tip-top condition. Wiping the accumulated powder off with a rag and then oiling is sometimes all the corrective action that is required. In other instances wiping and oiling only serve as a temporary measure for another "blossom" is apt to come forth after a few more days, at the same place on the gun or at some other juncture, possibly around the edges of the front sight base. This blossoming, or efflorescence as it might more technically be referred to, is a result of insufficient rinsing after blueing. And the reason it appears at such places as those mentioned above is because it is forced in, so to speak, while a hot liquid, between threaded sections, drive fitted parts and similar close fitted units, and is not dislodged by a minute or two under running water or in a rinse tank.

"Blossoming" can be cut to a minimum, if not eliminated entirely, by:

1) use of the boiling rinse;
2) use of the hot soluble oil bath;
3) use of the chromic acid rinse.

Some types of weapons require more rinsing than others due to their style of construction. As a rule, the more close-fitting joints, or deep dead-end holes, there are in a unit, the greater the chance for "blossoming." A little experimenting by the individual gunsmith will more often than not demonstrate the necessity for using any or all of the above listed baths for reducing excessive alkalinity and subsequent "blossoming."

"Blossoming" is of itself not detrimental to a blued surface but it certainly does spoil the overall appearance of an otherwise nicely finished weapon. In addition it (the salts) can blemish stock finish and rot the wood if it oozes out between metal and wood sections of a gun. The powder of which a blossom is made up will, in contact with an open wound, cause a very uncomfortable sensation—something of the intensity of iodine poured into a deep cut.

In deep, narrow coil spring wells, as for example in the recoil spring plug of a .45 Government Automatic pistol, blueing salts cannot always be rinsed out if they have caked to any extent. Therefore, it is a good practice to check deep hole parts before assembling them and make certain that there are no caked salts present. If there are, dip the part in boiling water for a few minutes to soften the deposit so it can be poured out. Never attempt to chip or scrape away caked blueing salts as there is too great a danger of damaging surrounding metal.

Summation on Hot Dip Blueing

As a means of incorporating the high points of operation already discussed, with a few minor points worthy of special mention, it might be well to consider briefly the blueing of, say, a .30 caliber Springfield rifle by the hot-dip method in tank layout "F" (Figure 96). In the interest of brevity it is to be assumed that all tanks are filled to their proper level and that they are at operating temperatures.

First Step. Wire all parts in the prescribed manner with non-coated iron or steel wire. Wire should be so affixed that it does not bear too heavily against a surface that must be blued and so possibly prevent the point of contact from being colored. Small parts like the cut-off screw, the striker, the bolt sleeve lock pin, et cetera, should be placed in a basket for blueing. *Do not blue any of the springs.*

Second Step. When the alkaline cleaner is boiling vigorously, lower the wired parts into Tank 1, making certain that all metal surfaces are submerged. All the work should remain in the cleaner for at least five minutes. After the work has been in this tank for a couple of minutes, swish it up and down gently by the wires. This will break away any foreign matter that might be adhering to a surface. As the work is lifted from this tank, it should be tilted to reduce to a minimum the dragout of cleaning solution and, more important, the introduction of greasy matter into the rinse tank (Tank 2).

Third Step. Rinse parts in Tank 2 by swishing them up and down vigorously to wash away any loose adhering polishing or buffing compound. If after thorough rinsing, water does not adhere to the surface of the metal at all, but rather tends to break away and leave it dry, then the work should be put back in the cleaner to remove the greasy film present. Work going from the rinse tank to the blueing tank should also be freed of excess water by tilting or shaking.

The water in the No. 2 rinse tank should be changed after every use of the blueing facilities because of the oily skim that collects on top of the water and tends to stick to work being withdrawn from the tank. Actually the most desirable construction of an after-cleaning rinse tank is one that has an overflow about 2" below the top of the tank, and a method of introducing running water into the tank. In this setup the oily skim (which is lighter than water and floats on top of the bath) is always being drained off.

Fourth Step. Gently lower the work into the blueing tank. Try to lower the barrel in evenly (i.e., do not have either the muzzle or breech end pointing upward at a sharp angle) as the boiling solution has a tendency to "climb up" the bore of any long tube and belch out the end exposed to the air.

Watch the thermometer very closely while the parts are in this tank and if the temperature drops appreciably when cold work is introduced into it, do not be alarmed or tempted to turn up the gas valve or reduce the tank inflow (if you have this set-up). Almost without fail the temperature will jump back quickly to normal.

After the work has been in this tank for a few minutes, lift it out for just an instant and see if the color is starting to take or if a red stain is present. If the latter condition is noted, then the bath is boiling at too high a temperature and must be lowered. Introduce water immediately, but slowly, and so force the temperature down. It is not necessary to pull the work from a blueing tank instantly if a red stain is present on it. It is better to concentrate on restoring the proper boiling temperature to the bath since an extra minute in the bath will not make the red stain any worse, and there is always the possibility that the lowering of the temperature will eliminate it.

Though most manufacturers of gun blueing salts recommend a timed period of immersion (as a rule about 20 minutes) for work, this writer recommends that the gunsmith learn to know the salts and bath he is working with and rely on quick looks every five minutes at the work in the blueing tank as a means of adjudging proper immersion time. Some steels will color fully and achieve the high depth of penetration, from a practical standpoint, in 10 minutes, while others will scarcely color in half an hour. Too, the idea of inspecting work being colored, at periodic intervals, is a good way to double-check on the coloring status of the bath.

Fifth Step. When the work has colored properly, lift it from the blueing tank (tilt it) and quickly plunge it into the after-rinse tank (No. 4), at the same time swishing the work around.

Inasmuch as this tank layout (F) has a hot water rinse (Tank 5) it is not necessary to leave the work in the cold rinse tank very long—just long enough to cool the work is sufficient. Note, however, that in a layout that does not include a hot water rinse, the work should remain in the cold rinse for a few minutes at least, and the water should be changed very frequently to keep the alkalinity of this rinse at a minimum.

Sixth Step. Introduce the work into the hot water rinse and let it remain there for about two or three minutes, withdraw it, eliminate any accumulated water by tipping or shaking, and finally plunge it into the oil bath (Tank 6).

Seventh Step. After a sufficient interval in the oil bath, lift out the work and suspend it over the oil tank (attach the wires to a bar or wire rigged up from the ceiling) for five or 10 minutes to permit draining off of the excess oil. Though this might appear to be a rather unnecessary step, it is actually a practical one since much oil that would be otherwise wasted is recovered and, more important, the shop and workbench are not messed up by guns dripping with oil being shifted around.

Note on Oils. Whether the gunsmith uses a soluble oil or a mineral oil is primarily a matter of choice based on personal opinion. However, it might be well to point out that some types and brands of mineral oil, because of the way they are manufactured, are injurious to a newly-blued surface. And this includes some of the cheaper grades of motor oil. There are on the market today special oils, which are not too expensive, made for use on oxidized metal. See dealers listed in Chapter Twenty.

Linseed oil or any such rapid oxidizing oil should not be used on parts that have been blued by the hot dip process, or for that matter, by any process. Linseed oil has no place on the metallic portions of a gun unless one wants to put on a film for preserving the outside surfaces of a barrel or receiver. If a gun that has been blued is coated, while hot, with linseed oil and is left exposed to the air for a day or two, it is one tough job to dissolve away the coating that forms in every crevice and cut of the gun and its parts. There is no particular reason for using linseed oil after blueing and the gunsmith who does so is just inviting a lot of extra work. And if by chance the linseed is not completely wiped away there is always that lurking possibility that parts will act sluggishly and perhaps stick fast when the film oxidizes completely.

Once the gunsmith has selected a reliable after-blueing oil, he can use it on all guns, whether they have been blued by the rusting process, the hot dip process, or the niter bath process.

CHAPTER SEVENTEEN

Buying and Selling Used Guns

IT IS not always possible, because of financial reasons, for a gunsmith to have on hand even a small stock of the various manufacturers' new guns. Yet, since a gunsmith's shop is a very logical place for a man to buy a gun, the matter of dealing in secondhand firearms should receive the consideration of every mechanic interested in supplementing his regular income derived from repair work. Like many other phases of the gun business, not all the details incident to dealing in secondhand guns can be covered by a set of hard and fast rules. Yet there are tricks to every trade and to that end the suggestions made in this chapter are advanced.

General Factors Affecting Price

Unlike a used automobile, which may have defects that cannot be discovered unless it is subject to an inspection that might take many hours, if not days, the condition of most any used gun can be determined in a matter of minutes. This is indeed a boon for the gunsmith because it is this factor that he must take into account before making an estimate as to what the gun is worth. True, other factors enter into the picture and we shall deal with them in due order.

Repairs. When repairs are to be necessary before a used gun can be made fit for resale the cost of the repairs should be computed at full price. Otherwise the gunsmith will soon discover he is not making a good margin of profit on each secondhand gun transaction. For example, suppose that a particular used gun in perfect condition will ordinarily bring a price of $18.00, but needs parts that will cost the gunsmith $3.00, and he desires to realize a 20% profit on the final sale price. While at first analysis it might seem reasonable to pay about $12.50 for the weapon as is, further consideration indicates that this would be a poor bargain, for the gunsmith has not included in his estimate a deduction for the time (at a regular per hour rate) that it will take to install the $3.00 worth of parts. In some cases this might mean a difference of only 50¢ or 60¢ but in others it might represent $3.00 or $4.00, or the difference between profit and loss on the transaction.

Thus it can be clearly seen that all secondhand gun repairs must be computed on the basis of the gunsmith's regular rates. This must be especially noted when appraising weapons which retail, even when new, at a very low price. If the cost of repairing an inexpensive gun, plus profit margin, will bring the resale price within 15% of list price, then, generally speaking, it is a poor risk to bother with such a weapon unless, when put up for sale, it can be truthfully represented as being like new.

Refinishing. If a gun being considered for purchase is in need of refinishing, the gunsmith can afford to be a little on the generous side in allowing for the cost of reblueing the gun since there is a good margin of profit on this sort of work. If it is a nickel-plated or chrome-plated gun and requires refinishing, then the weapon will in all likelihood have to be sent to a commercial plating firm. In instances of this sort, the gunsmith must deduct not only for the plating fee but also for his time in disassembling, reassembling and making minor adjustments usually necessitated by the addition of the plating material on certain parts. While on this topic, it might be well to point out that the resale value of any gun is greatly enhanced by a reblueing or replating job. Often there are no pits or rust on the exterior of a gun but the blueing is worn off from holster use or handling. As such the gun does not have to be reground prior to blueing (See Chapter Sixteen). This greatly reduces the amount of time that must be spent on the operation, and, consequently, it is possible to figure on a little less than the usual full blueing job price.

In preference to renickeling an inexpensive revolver or pistol, it is often just as well to buff those sections of the gun where the plating has peeled off. A cloth buff coated with chrome tripoli gives a nice finish and the entire gun should be treated so that there will not be any high color spots. If there are traces of pitting or rust on the backstrap, trigger, hammer, et cetera of a plated gun, then a fiber wheel coated with No. 200 grit emery should be used to dress them down prior to buffing.

Barring very unusual economic conditions, such as those

brought about by the advent of World War II and its effect on the overall gun business, the price of small arms, both new and used, remains pretty steady year in and year out.

Specific Factors Affecting Price

Age of Guns. Generally speaking, the age of a gun has very little bearing on its value unless, of course, it is either a dated or obsolete weapon. By dated, we mean a gun that is of a design that has since its origination been radically modified and the newer models have features that were not a part of and cannot be incorporated in the older version. An example of this type is the old .38 Colt automatic pistol (Model 1902) which was a forerunner of the now well known .38 Super automatic. Many of these old 1902 models are still kicking around, but under normal circumstances they do not command a price anywhere near that brought by a .38 Super auto. Often guns of the dated type can be purchased and sold to a collector who is assembling a complete line of one make or type of firearm; or if a gun is in such a condition that it is beyond the stage of profitable repair, it can be used as a source of parts for other guns of the same model needing only minor repair.

Obsolete Guns. An obsolete weapon might generally be described as a gun of a model no longer manufactured and for which commercial ammunition is not available. This is not a hard and fast definition, but for purposes of reference it will suffice. An example of an obsolete gun would be a pin fire pistol or a needle rifle. As a matter of fact, muzzle-loading small arms, for all practical consideration, are also obsolete weapons.

To try and outline a specific method for evaluating either dated or obsolete weapons would be an almost impossible task and definitely not within the scope of this writing. When dealing with guns in these categories, the individual gunsmith must learn to judge their value from a purely selfish point of view. In other words, he must consider just what they are worth to him as items which have very little resale value, unless to a limited special class of customer. There is always the possibility that an obsolete or dated gun might turn out to be a valuable antique or rare item, but this is so remote that it should never enter into an appraisal consideration unless the gunsmith has a thorough knowledge of antique guns and can readily recognize the genuine article. Dealing in antique and old guns is a business in itself and the gunsmith, who usually has enough trouble conducting his repair shop, should avoid the pitfalls of this phase of gun trading unless he has time and money to spare—both in appreciable quantities.

Antique Guns. If antique guns are such a lure that the gunsmith feels he must dabble in them, then there are a few very important precautions that must be observed.

In restoring antiques that are battered, rusty, and in overall poor condition, a certain amount of work must, of necessity, be performed on them before they can be offered for sale. Before proceeding with the repair process, however, a little research work should be done to ascertain just how the gun looked when it was originally made. Was it blued or was it browned? Was it highly finished or was it replete with tool marks from the hand fitting of parts? Was the wood oil finished, or covered with a stain or varnish? In short, enough should be known about the original appearance of the weapon so that any work performed upon it will not result in overembellishment or tend to destroy its value as a true collector's item. Under no circumstances whatsoever should identifying trade marks, letters, symbols, proof marks, or numbers be obliterated, defaced or altered in any manner, so that certification as to the authenticity of an antique will be made difficult or impossible.

In dealing with popular make and model guns, the gunsmith does not have to reckon with the unknowns and unpredictables that are part and parcel of the antique gun business, for the old reliable Stoeger catalog can be consulted for current list prices.

Foreign Guns. If the gunsmith is considering the purchase of a foreign gun, and there will be many of these war souvenirs making the rounds in the next 10 years, he must be very, very careful and not be deceived by external appearances.

Choice engravings and special gadgets do not necessarily make a good gun. As a matter of fact, on some cheap foreign made guns, engraving is used extensively to cover up otherwise sloppy fitting work between side plates, bottom plates, and other sections of a receiver where assemblies are joined together; while some gadgets, such as pins, which indicate when the gun is cocked, are so designed that they get out of order when subject to any degree of hard usage.

Now this does not mean that all engraving or special devices on foreign guns are detrimental to its value but it does mean that they are not points upon which the gunsmith should judge the true value of the weapon.

For the past 10 or 15 years Germany has been very prolific in the matter of introducing and making new guns, some of them good and others just run-of-the-mill. Good, bad or indifferent, though, indications are that the Germans will not be engaged to any appreciable degree in making small arms for at least the next decade. Hence, parts for German guns will be near impossible to obtain. Although certain parts for the Luger, P.38, Mauser rifle, and other very popular German guns might be manufactured and distributed by some American companies, they will be quite expensive since they will not be completely mass produced.

Other parts for these and other German guns will, of course, have to be made by the gunsmith himself. In either case, the cost of parts will be high and a major factor to be considered if a foreign gun being bought is in need of repair.

With foreign weapons there can also be the problem of ammunition. This will not be true of all weapons made in the late Herr Hitler's land because some of the ammunition for German rifles and shotguns is manufactured by American cartridge companies, e.g., the 9mm Luger and the 8mm Mauser cartridge. However, some of the German three barrel guns and other weapons are chambered for cartridges which are not made in this country and for which there is little demand; nor can they be reloaded with American components. At best, the value of weapons in this category should only be considered from the standpoint of a collector's item.

The gunsmith should very carefully inspect each foreign gun that is offered to him. No point is too small to be overlooked or checked off as insignificant, for it can be safely stated that, as a rule, foreign guns bring no better price than a domestic gun of a corresponding type and model, and the demand for them is no greater. Add to this the high cost of putting a foreign made weapon in first class condition and we have enough good reasons to regard them with caution and buy them at rock bottom prices.

The "Like New" Gun. Sometimes a gun will be offered to the gunsmith for sale that is virtually new—perhaps only holster-worn on the outside and perfect otherwise. Customers usually feel that a gun of this sort should be worth almost list price, maybe $2.00 or $3.00 off, at most. Ethically and technically the gun is secondhand and must be judged accordingly for it will not command list price. Suppose this gun we are speaking about listed for, say, $32.00 new. This means it cost the dealer about $25.60, or 20% less. Now the gunsmith, knowing that he cannot get $32.00 for this gun on resale, must of business necessity offer less than $25.60 for it if he expects to realize his 20% profit. Therefore, it is safe to say that no used gun, irrespective of its fine condition, should be worth more than 70% of list.

Setting the Price

The Customer's Estimate. In buying a used gun from a customer, the gunsmith should try at all times to have the customer state just how much he expects to get for the piece. However, not all customers are willing to ask a set price, choosing rather to hear what the gunsmith is willing to pay and then haggling with him for more money. This latter is a poor method and when possible should be avoided, for it is not infrequently the cause of hard feelings between both parties since each feels the other is out to get the best price without regard for fair dealing.

The Dealer's Estimate. In computing the approximate value of any used gun of standard domestic manufacture, the gunsmith must consider the following factors:

1) The top price the gun, in first class condition, will bring.
2) The amount of work, in terms of dollars and cents, that will be necessary to put the gun in first class condition.
3) The advisability of putting the gun in first class shape. In other words, is a gun that costs only $12.00 new, worthy of being reblued and fitted with new sights if it will bring a top price of $8.50, or could it be sold as is, mechanically O.K., for $6.00?
4) Would it be easier to sell the gun as being in passable condition with say, a slightly cracked stock and worn finish, neither defect being the type which would affect the safety or operation of the piece, or would it be better to remedy them and ask a much higher price?
5) What are the sale possibilities for a particular weapon under consideration? Does a gun of this sort, for instance an autoloading rifle in a shop serving a community where shotguns are the primary hunting weapon, have a ready market, or will it have to stay in stock until a transient customer buys it?

Sale Possibilities

Local Conditions. In connection with this last factor, the gunsmith who likes to realize every dollar he possibly can, should investigate the possibility of making connections with a dealer located in a large city who can, by virtue of his cosmopolitan and mail order trade, dispose of any type gun very rapidly. By having an outlet of this sort, the gunsmith can purchase most any weapon that is offered to him at a reasonable price, fix it up and forward it to the bigger dealer. When operating under this method, a smaller profit per gun must be expected. However, this should not deter one from trying it, for it will be a means of making a profit not only on a transaction that might not otherwise have been practical, but also it will afford a method for a full measure of profit on any repair work incident to putting the piece in salable condition. In addition, the gunsmith is assured of a rapid turnover, which means that his gun-buying capital will not be tied up to the extent where he might have to pass up other buying opportunities because of lack of money.

Advertising. Hard-to-sell or unusual guns can also be sold by advertising them through the classified sections of sporting magazines, the best for this sort of selling being "The American Rifleman," virtually all of whose readers are gun prospects. If the gunsmith is working on a narrow margin of profit with an inexpensive gun he must not fail to take into account the cost (minimum $1.50) of the advertisement.

File of Potential Buyers. In a neighborhood where hunters, shooters or collectors are constantly in the market for a special or odd type of weapon, the gunsmith should make a point to learn of each one's specific desires and catalog them. When one of these "wanted" weapons comes to the gunsmith's attention, he can then contact the interested party who might want the gun revamped or modified to suit his particular taste. Naturally, before proceeding with any such work, an estimate as to what the finished product will cost should be submitted and agreed to by the prospective purchaser. In the absence of any previous dealings with a customer who requests special work on a gun not yet actually sold to him, a deposit should be collected, amounting to at least the original cost of the gun to the gunsmith.

Describing Condition. To get a good idea of what a used gun of popular make will sell for in different stages of condition, it is well to study the classified ad section of recent issues of "The American Rifleman." This magazine uses clearly-defined terms to describe the condition of guns advertised in its classified columns, which should leave little doubt in the dealer's mind as to approximately what a particular gun is worth.

Special Work. When a gunsmith has a pet idea as to how a gun can be fixed up as a special purpose target or defense weapon—perhaps with special grips, sights or action—he can profitably utilize a secondhand piece to make his brainchild a reality. He will not only be satisfying a desire to do creative work, but also he might be opening a possible field for his particular specialty when a proud purchaser shows the special weapon to fellow shooters and gun lovers. Work done on a model gun should be of the highest order and finely finished. On a pilot job, an extra hour or two can be devoted to little details without regard to every penny, for when a gunsmith's special work is being shown among gun lovers the gun as is must speak for itself. Little overlooked details in workmanship that the gunsmith might ordinarily be able to justify, or at least explain, if he were present, are apt to be judged harshly by disinterested gun critics who are forming opinions on the basis of what they see—not what the gunsmith *meant to do*. All of which should remind one that good work makes for satisfied customers and better business; while inferior work makes for fewer customers, bad business and often ultimate failure.

The value of doing each job correctly and having it ready when promised cannot be overstressed, for it is this basic phase of daily operation that will decide in no small way the gunsmith's ultimate integrity and prosperity.

CHAPTER EIGHTEEN

Specialty Work

IN ADDITION to the revenue from regular repair and refinishing jobs, many gunsmiths derive extra monetary compensation, at a high hourly rate, by doing special work. Some of these craftsmen are recognized as expert stockmakers, some as master barrelmakers and others are specialists on working over target pistols—to mention a few. As specialists, they can ask and get a better price for their work than they could possibly expect if they were just doing general repair work.

These specialists are definitely more made than born. They have learned to recognize their weaknesses and deficiencies in doing certain types of work and in so doing also noted that there were other phases of gunsmithing at which they excel. Often this is the result of special training in some field such as cabinet making or tool and die making; sometimes it is the offshoot of specialized employment at an armory or gun factory.

Not every gunsmith gets the opportunity to develop a specialty trade, for the nature of the work in some localities is such that only the run-of-the-mill type repair jobs are encountered and he is not able to discover his latent possibilities. However, there are some services which can be offered by any gunsmith that should allow him to realize a few extra dollars with a minimum of hard shop work. While it is not expected that a gunsmith will wish to neglect his regular work by putting these services in operation, he will certainly enhance his reputation and become better known as a gun repairman if he does include them.

In every town or city where banks, express companies, finance companies or similar organizations are located, there is a potential market for the Number One Service to be described. Usually these firms have pistols or revolvers, and occasionally shotguns, which are used by guards, clerks and tellers in protecting money, securities and valuables. More often than not these weapons are given very little, if any, care by the persons using them, with the result that most of the guns are in very poor condition.

This writer has had many opportunities to examine such weapons and found the following conditions to exist:

1) Cartridges so badly corroded in the chambers of a revolver that it was necessary to clean the barrel, discharge the cartridges and then pound the empty shells loose.

2) Cartridges left in the magazine of an automatic pistol so long that after the top one had been stripped off the others would not move up into place, necessitating such vigorous action to remove them that the magazine was rendered useless.

3) Barrels of pistols and revolvers badly rusted or so filled with clothing, lint and dust that light was barely visible through the bore.

4) Cylinders in revolvers and magazines in pistols frozen so tightly that they resisted removal by all means ordinarily available to the person who would have occasion to use the gun.

5) Dried oil or grease in the mechanism of a revolver to such an extent that the cylinder would not turn or the hammer fall with sufficient force to set off the cartridge.

6) Revolver cylinders so badly out of alignment that the gun when fired "spit lead" out the side, of sufficient size and with enough velocity to seriously injure any person standing within five to 10 feet of the firer.

7) Guns chambered for the .32 S&W cartridge with .32 Automatic ammunition in them.

8) Guns with broken or weak mainsprings, broken firing pins, and grips broken or chipped so badly that the mechanism was filled with dust or lint—in all cases rendering them inoperative.

In addition to the aforementioned conditions rendering such guns unserviceable, many company-owned weapons used by personnel unfamiliar with firearms suffer from more conventional deficiencies, such as bent front sights, bad magazines, broken extractors and ejectors and rust where blueing once was.

Many companies, both large and small, have guns which, for the purpose of protection are worthless, and in most cases are in such condition because no one in authority in the organization is aware of the situation, or does not fully understand the company's liability should innocent persons be injured or shot as a result of the gun being in bad condition.

Service Number One

For correcting such conditions Service Number One is the answer. The gunsmith's approach and the handling of the situation may vary to suit local conditions but for general purposes it should run along the following lines.

Soliciting Business. List all the companies within reasonable traveling distance that use guns for protective purposes and either by mail or in person (preferably the latter) contact an individual with authority in each organization, outlining your qualifications as a gunsmith and facilities for putting guns in first class condition. If a letter is sent, it should be typewritten on letterhead stationery and be as brief as possible. The suggested Form Letter Number One contains all the information necessary to convey the thought and yet is not so lengthy that a busy executive will become disinterested before he has read the full text.

Reference to the exact cost of the service is not mentioned in the letter because to some it might appear to be too expensive, yet after hearing from the gunsmith first hand precisely what will be done for the amount charged, the prospective customer will feel more cordial towards the plan.

Talking It Up. When talking to a prospective customer about this service, the gunsmith should strive to impress upon him the importance of a gun being in good working order at all times, not only from the protection standpoint but also the trouble and liability which might be visited upon an organization if an employee or bystander should be injured by a gun bursting from a clogged barrel, or is hit by a lead sliver from a revolver out of alignment. Too, it is well to point out how a well cared for gun will last indefinitely, while rust and corrosion in a barrel or on the surface means replacement or refinishing at no small cost.

Initial Steps. Before contracting to service the guns of any organization, the gunsmith should request that he be allowed to inspect all weapons that will normally come under his care so that he can report on their condition as is, and make recommendations for putting them in first-class shape at the outset. Thus he will be able to start with a clean slate and henceforth devote his main efforts to preventive maintenance.

After examining the guns for broken parts, worn barrels, rust or worn finish, et cetera, he should then submit an estimate of what it will cost to put the guns in good order. Nothing should be overlooked at this inspection, for when the gunsmith returns them they must be as nearly perfect as possible, and unless they are greatly mishandled it will be assumed that the guns will not require any such major overhaul again for some time to come.

Charges on this initial work should be at standard rates and no more for, irrespective of how big an organization might be, they are not given to doing business with people who overcharge or take advantage of them in business dealings.

Permanent Set-Up. After the initial inspection and overhaul work the gunsmith should make arrangements to return every three months to reinspect and thoroughly clean each gun. The price for this periodic maintenance service might vary in different localities but a fair price is $1.00 per gun when there are less than 10 guns and $.75 per gun if there are more. For this fee the gunsmith should thoroughly clean the gun, as described in Chapter Six, and inspect it for any defects that would affect its efficiency or usefulness as an instrument of protection.

If any repairs are necessary, the approval of someone in authority should be obtained and a price agreed upon, so that collection of money for work performed can be accomplished later without quibbling.

After each quarterly inspection, a report, either verbal or written, should be submitted to the company, indicating any unusual conditions on the guns inspected. For example, if .32 shorts are in a gun chambered for the .32 S&W long cartridge; or a front sight is badly bent; or the muzzle damaged, indicating the gun had been dropped, the fact should be noted. In this way the company will know just what guns are being mishandled and, since they are issued out to the guards by serial number, who is abusing the gun.

There are many variations of this service and it can often be expanded to include local police departments and post offices, to say nothing of merchants, such as jewelers or storekeepers. In the case of local merchants having only one or two guns, the inspection fee will of necessity have to be more than that charged banks or it would not pay to service them.

This service can also be operated so as to include a course in the handling, care and cleaning of guns for guards and other persons using weapons. Also, the gunsmith can offer to act as agent in the purchase of any new guns or ammunition that might be required by the companies he is servicing.

Local conditions might necessitate the gunsmith altering his method of operation with this cleaning and maintenance service but the thought of rendering good service at a fair price should always be the main point of guidance.

When a gunsmith puts down any gun as finished he should always feel and know that he could trust his own life with it. If he cannot honestly say that the gun is safe and dependable, then he had better mend his ways or go to work in another business, where a job half done or almost right will not put the lives of others in jeopardy.

SUGGESTED FORM LETTER
(NUMBER ONE)

MARINE PARK GUN WORKS

3 Centre Market Place
New York City

Federal Firearms   Telephone
Lic. No. 207   Canal 6–2794

Mr. Harold J. Roddin, Manager
Flatlands Bank & Trust Company
4730 Hendrickson Street
New York, New York

My dear Mr. Roddin:

For the past five years we have been serving the hunters, target shooters and peace officers of this community in the matter of gun repair and refinishing. In our well equipped shop we have the trained personnel and most up to date facilities for accomplishing every type of small arms inspection and maintenance work.

Within a few weeks we intend to inaugurate in this area an inspection service for companies which must use firearms as a means of protecting money, securities, valuables and property.

A gun, not unlike an automobile, requires periodic inspection and, when necessary, repair, if it is to be ready for best operation at any and all times.

We shall be pleased to call upon you at your convenience to explain in detail the merits of our reasonable service.

Very truly yours,

MARINE PARK GUN WORKS

Service Number Two

A pre-hunting and pre-storage cleaning and preserving service for shooters who use their guns only a few days out of each year during the hunting season and then put them away for next year can be operated to the most profitable extent in cities and towns where there is little need for a man to have his hunting weapon ready for use other than during the hunting season.

Advertising. About a month or two before gunning season the gunsmith should have letters printed similar to Form Letter Number Two and send them to all the hunters in his locality. The total cost for printing and mailing, say 150 of these circulars, should not exceed $10.00 and the results will more than justify the expenditure.

SUGGESTED FORM LETTER
(NUMBER TWO)

MARINE PARK GUN WORKS
3 Centre Market Place
New York City

Federal Firearms
Lic. No. 207

Telephone
Canal 6–2794

Dear Fellow Sportsman:

When you take your gun out of storage this year will you be sure that it is in A1 shape for getting that big buck you missed last season? Or will the action be sluggish or bore rusted from the improper oil that you thought would not dry up or evaporate?

Before hunting season draws another day nearer, why not look at your pet shooting irons and see if they are ready for the "first day."

If you have any doubt about their readiness condition bring them to us for inspection and cleaning.

We have in stock at all times a complete selection of parts and accessories for popular and many old makes of shotguns and rifles.

Don't wait until it is too late for us to give quick service. Bring your guns in before the seasonal rush.

Then when the season is over and you are ready to put the guns away, bring them to our shop and we will clean and prepare them for storage so that next year, or if needed sooner, when you want to use them, it will only be necessary to wipe our special preservative from the bore and metallic surfaces of the gun.

Inquire about our modest prices for either of these services— don't let a bad gun spoil the fun and sport that you have waited for all year.

Yours for better hunting,

MARINE PARK GUN WORKS

It should be noticed that the letter invites the customer to bring his gun in before, as well as after, the hunting season. In this way the letter will attract some shooters who prefer to do their own oiling and greasing but like to have their weapons checked before they go afield, as well as those who want their gun inspected and prepared prior to storage.

Price. For either or both services no fixed price can be here listed, for there are entirely too many extenuating factors to be taken into consideration. Nevertheless, the main gage for price fixing on work of this sort is the basic hourly rate as determined in Chapter One.

Of course, if the gunsmith prefers, he can charge a definite amount for completely cleaning and greasing a gun prior to storage on a flat rate basis, say, for example, $3.00 for double barrel shotguns; $2.50 for repeating shotguns and rifles; and $2.00 for bolt action guns.

Service Number Two (Special)

In connection with this service, it might be well if the gunsmith's location is such that it is accessible to a wealthy residential neighborhood, to include a sort of super-special cleaning and checking service. Such a service—designed primarily for hunters and shooters who either do not care enough, know enough, or have not the time to clean their guns—should include the following:

1) Complete disassembly of the gun, including all small springs, parts, et cetera.
2) Complete cleaning of all the metallic parts in a solvent such as carbon tetrachloride, white gasoline (acid free), or a water soluble cleaner like trisodium phosphate or Oakite (See Chapter Six for details).
3) Complete cleaning of the gun barrel, including the removal of leading or metal fouling from rifle barrels and dents from shotgun tubes.
4) Removal of burrs from the edges and surfaces of working parts.
5) Reslotting or replacement of any screws whose heads are marked or in any way deformed.
6) Reworking the ends of any holding pins that show signs of deformation or extreme wear.
7) Reblueing of any screws or small pins that have been reworked; in cases where such parts have been case-hardened originally,

they should be case-hardened for colors instead of being blued.

8) Checking of the trigger pull and adjustment of same if it is required. Note: Before fooling around with the trigger pull of anybody's gun, find out first if they like the pull as it is; perhaps some shooters might not want the pull changed. However, if pull is so light or so adjusted that there is danger of the gun being jarred off, then call this fact to the gun owner's attention. (Double barrel shotguns should have a uniform and equal pull on each trigger and not be so sensitive that the gun might double fire when one trigger is pulled.)

9) Checking with dummy cartridges, the function of the magazine, extractor, ejector, et cetera, and protrusion, shape and condition of the firing pin.

10) Preparing the gun for storage, either short-term storage (a few months) or long-time storage (a year). When preparing the gun for storage up to and including a year, grease should not be put in the mechanism of the gun unless the customer specifically requests it. The presence of grease in the mechanism of most guns means that the entire gun must be again disassembled before it can be used.

It is all right to use Sheath or Hoppe's Gun Grease in the bore of the gun and on the exterior metal surfaces, but a good protective oil like Hoppe's Gun Oil will protect the mechanism adequately if it is applied immediately after the parts have been cleaned. Do not put any more than a very light film of oil on the parts and handle the parts with clean cotton gloves prior to oiling. As a matter of fact, after the gun has been cleaned, and before it is greased and oiled, gloves should be worn so that ole debbil perspiration will not leave the gunsmith's trademark in the form of rust colored fingerprints.

So, checked and preserved by a gunsmith, the owner's gun should be returned to him covered with waxed paper or other special moisture-proof covering, carefully wrapped around the weapon. Should the customer want to remove the waxed paper that is his business, but if the paper is put on properly the gun can be put in a case or in a closet safe from the ravages of corrosion. Too often a stored gun is robbed of much of its protective oil by the owner putting it in a case that absorbs the oil, or on a closet shelf where the wood absorbs the oil and subsequently helps in promoting rust.

For this super-special service on a hunting weapon the gunsmith should not feel bashful in charging from $5.00 to $10.00, depending somewhat on the type of gun serviced and the amount of work performed.

It is surprising how much revenue and attendant good reputation a gunsmith can realize by operating this type of service; but, as always, the workmanship must be first-class and the smallest details not overlooked.

In this particular class of work small details mean, among other things, using good oil and grease. Preservatives that will not gum up or that do not contain chemicals which are deleterious to gun metal or wood must be used.

Sperm oil, which has the reputation of being the oil of oils for gun lubrication, may be all right but this writer does not care to boost it very much because there are many kinds of sperm oil and most of them are unsuited for gun lubrication work. Without going into details incident to the manufacture and distribution of sperm oil, suffice to say that too much of it that is procurable through ordinary local supply channels is adulterated, misnamed or just downright fake.

There are many reliable oils and greases made by arms and gun specialty companies which can be used with confidence, so that the gunsmith should not resort to using preservatives which are made for so-called all around use.

Special Work on Revolvers

No matter how many different models of revolvers the gun manufacturers put on the market there are always gun bugs who want something that is just a little bit different. Fortunately for all concerned, the revolver lends itself very well to a multitude of modifications, most of which can be accomplished without special or expensive equipment. Cut down barrels, abbreviated trigger guards, reshaped grips and spurless hammers are a few of the operations that are performed on six-guns to make them into pocket or belly guns.

Colt revolvers, because of their basic design, are more easily converted than any other make of revolver. Still this does not mean that barrel cutting or trigger guard alteration is impossible on guns of S&W manufacture.

Cutting Down Barrel. Cutting down the barrel of the revolver is a simple job but one that requires a bit of careful preparatory work to insure that the modified gun will be capable of accuracy normally expected of a short barrelled weapon. Before cutting

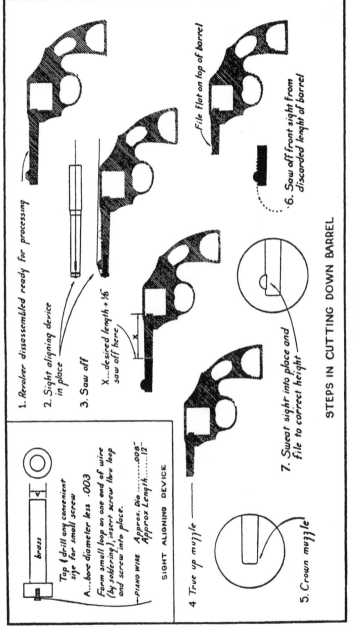

1. Revolver disassembled ready for processing

2. Sight aligning device in place

3. Saw off

X...desired length + ⅛" saw off here

4 True up muzzle

5. Crown muzzle

File flat on top of barrel

6. Saw off front sight from discarded lenght of barrel

7. Sweat sight into place and file to correct height

brass

Tap (drill any convenient size for small screw

A...bore diameter less .003

Form small loop on one end of wire (by soldering) insert screw thru loop and screw into place.

PIANO WIRE Approx. Dia ....008"
Approx Length........12"

SIGHT ALIGNING DEVICE

STEPS IN CUTTING DOWN BARREL

FIGURE 97

off the barrel to within ⅛″+ of the desired finish length it is first necessary to predetermine the height of the front sight that will be needed for the shorter barrel. To do this the gun should be placed in a vise having leather or wooden jaws and the sight aligning device (Figure 97) inserted in the gun barrel. By laying fine piano wire across the top of the front sight and drawing it back until it lays in the center of the rear sight groove, the proper height for the front sight, to be placed at any point on the barrel, can be determined, Figure 97 illustrates this operation in detail.

It should be noticed from the illustration that the wire is not allowed to lay at the bottom of the rear sight groove but at a plane even with an imaginary line drawn across the top of the frame of the rear sight point. Height measurement is secured by using a pair of outside calipers and leaving them set after the measurement has been taken from the bottom of the barrel to the top of the stretched wire, so that the height of the newly installed sight can be checked. For true accuracy, the thickness of the wire being used should be deducted from the total height measurement, since it is included in the original height determination and would tend to make the gun shoot a bit low.

Next comes the cutting off of the barrel, which is best accomplished with a hacksaw having a fine toothed blade, preferably about 24 teeth per inch. If it is desired that the finished barrel be 2″ long, then it should be cut off at 2⅛″, the extra ⅛″ being allowed for trueing up and crowning. Every effort should be made to saw the barrel off as straight as possible so that a minimum of cutting and filing will be necessary.

It is necessary to square the cut off barrel so that the bullet will not, upon leaving the muzzle, be subject to an uneven push of gas, which would send the slug off at an angle to the line of sight. Trueing up can be accomplished with a file, or if a great number of guns are to be processed, with a cutting tool as illustrated in Figure 98. In either case the trueness of the muzzle surface can be checked with the gage illustrated in Figure 99. The gage is easily turned from either drill rod or tool steel and should be polished and hardened. So made, it will last a lifetime. A separate gage can be made for the .32 caliber S&W, .38 caliber S&W, .38 caliber Special and .45 caliber, or brass bushings to fit over a basic ¼″ pilot can be utilized so that one gage will suffice for all calibers.

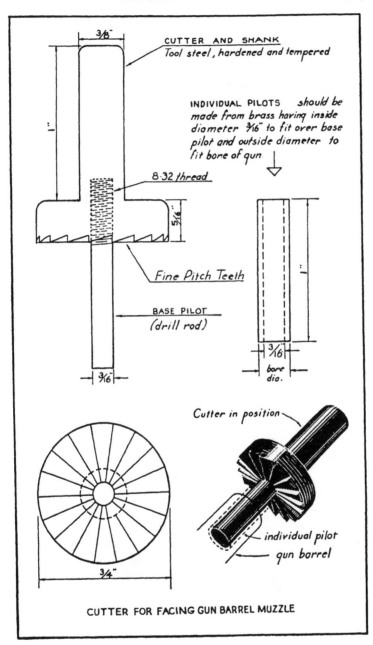

CUTTER AND SHANK
Tool steel, hardened and tempered

INDIVIDUAL PILOTS should be
made from brass having inside
diameter 3/16" to fit over base
pilot and outside diameter to
fit bore of gun

8·32 thread

Fine Pitch Teeth

BASE PILOT
(drill rod)

3/16"

3/16"
bore
dia.

Cutter in position

individual pilot
gun barrel

3/4"

CUTTER FOR FACING GUN BARREL MUZZLE

FIGURE 98

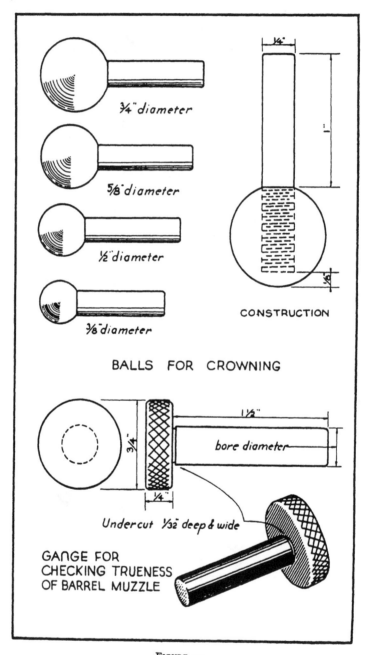

¾" diameter

⅝" diameter

½" diameter

⅜" diameter

CONSTRUCTION

BALLS FOR CROWNING

bore diameter

Undercut ⅟₃₂" deep & wide

GANGE FOR
CHECKING TRUENESS
OF BARREL MUZZLE

FIGURE 99

To use this gage for checking after the barrel has been cut off and trued, it is only necessary to fit the proper adapter to the pilot, lightly coat the undersurface of the gage head, where it will rest on the muzzle, with prussian blue, and drop it into the bore of the gun. The gage should then be pressed down upon lightly and rotated. In this way the prussian blue will be transferred to the muzzle of the gun on the high spots. If the entire muzzle is covered with blue, then the trueness of the surface will be evident; otherwise, if the blue appears only on one part, this would indicate a high spot in need of dressing down.

It is imperative that the pilot for each caliber be as close to the exact dimension as possible and only so much minus tolerance be allowed that will permit it to enter the gun bore with that amount of force that can be applied with the fingers. About three or four thousandths of an inch less than bore diameter is ideal.

Crowning Barrel. The barrel cut off and trued, we next come to the crowning operation. Barrels are crowned as a means of protecting the rifling should the gun be dropped on its muzzle. Crowning is best accomplished on any gun by putting the barrel in a lathe and machining it. However, since this method is impractical with revolvers, where removal and installation of the barrel is a major operation, an alternate but no less efficient method can be employed.

In Figure 100 the phases of the crowning process are illustrated. The first operation is accomplished with an ordinary 60° countersink having sharp cutting edges free of nicks and held in an ordinary carpenter's or breast drill. With this gun firmly held in the vise, the barrel being in a horizontal position, the countersink is inserted in the gun bore and rotated a few times until it breaks the edges of the rifling to a depth of between $\frac{1}{32}''$ and $\frac{1}{16}''$. It is absolutely necessary that the axis of the barrel and the axis of the countersink be in line during this operation so that the edges of the rifling will be cut evenly.

The second phase of the crowning job is done with either a file or fine grinding wheel, and consists of a simple operation on the outside edge of the muzzle, the bevel extending evenly all around the muzzle. No definite size or shape for the bevel can be given here because of the different wall thicknesses of various models and calibers of barrels but the crowned-muzzle on the discarded cut-off section serves as an excellent guide.

Final finish is given to the interior part of the crown by means of a brass ball attached to a short shaft (Figure 99). A paste made of powdered abrasive (No. 200 grit) and light oil serves as the cutting medium when interposed between the ball and muzzle. The ball can be rotated by hand drill power or chucked in a drill press and run at low speed.

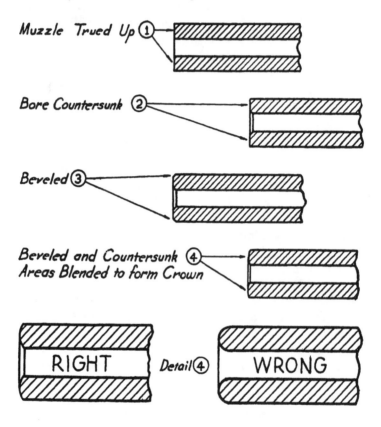

STEPS IN CROWNING A BARREL MUZZLE

FIGURE 100

The exterior surface of the muzzle crown can be polished and blended with a piece of fine emery cloth held between the thumb and fore finger.

Another type of crowning tool is illustrated in Figure 101. The blade in this tool must be made from hardened and tempered tool steel or drill rod.

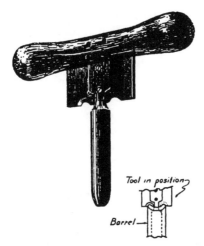

BARREL CROWNING TOOL

FIGURE 101

Putting Front Sight On. The barrel crowned, we now saw the old front sight from the cut-off section of the barrel. This cutting should be done with a fine toothed thin hacksaw blade so as to leave a maximum of sight base for sturdiness. The sight base must then be filed flat so that it will lay evenly on a similar flat filed on top of the gun barrel (Figure 97). The sight base and flat on the barrel should then be cleaned with alcohol or gasoline so that solder will adhere to these surfaces, thus insuring a satisfactory pair of tinned surfaces for sweating.

The easiest and best way to tin the components for sweating is to heat up the soldering iron and, when it becomes hot enough to melt the solder, file all four faces of the copper. This done, a piece of acid core solder is rubbed over any face of the soldering iron and then transferred to the surface of the metal being tinned. To distribute the solder evenly on the sight base or barrel flat the soldering iron should be moved back and forth under the pressure of the hand. In this way the heat from the iron is conducted to the metal being tinned and makes for better adhesion of the solder. After tinning, all excess solder should be filed off so that only a bare surface covering remains. Then the sight should be placed on the barrel flat and direct heat from a Bunsen burner or alcohol torch applied. When the melting point of the solder has been reached, little beads will be noticed forming between the sight and barrel. At this point the torch should be laid aside and a flat piece of steel (a small file serves well for this purpose) pressed down on top of the sight. By this action the sight is fixed more firmly in place and all excess solder is squeezed out. Care must be taken during this operation lest the sight be tipped over to one side or the other.

It is necessary to hold the sight down for about 30 seconds until the solder cools and sets. In the beginning, the novice gunsmith will have a tendency to overheat the components being sweated, with the result that he will have to hold the sight in place for a long period of time while cooling takes place.

For those who do not relish the prospect of holding the sight in place by hand a "C" clamp arrangement can be employed. However, it will be found from experience gained by the former method, after a few tries that a clamp will be unnecessary.

Although this writer has cut down some 400-odd revolvers and put their sights on with a lead base solder, there are some gun owners who do not believe that lead-tin solder is strong enough for the job. In such cases commercial silver solder can be used instead. If a milling machine is available, then a very shallow half-moon slot (cut with a T slot cutter) can be milled in the barrel, similar to the front sight slot in the barrel of most Colt revolvers, as made at the factory.

The writer does not recommend that revolver front sights be brazed on because the heat required to melt brass often causes scale to form on the rifling. True, sights are brass-brazed in place at the Colt factory, but like everything else concerned with revolver making, the Colt outfit has the "know how" and equipment to do an excellent job on a production basis.

The gun cut-down, crowned, and sight in place, there remains only the task of scraping off the excess solder with a chisel and filing down the front sight to the predetermined height. The top of the sight, when filed to correct height, should not be left flat on top but rather blended into the general half-round contour of a commercial sight.

If a sight is found to be canted slightly to one side after being affixed, it is an easy matter to straighten it by placing the thin part of the sight blade between protected vise jaws with the gun in the butt up position. Using the frame at the butt section as a point of leverage the sight blade can be bent slightly in the desired direction. If the soldering job is done right this bending action will not dislodge or loose the sight itself from the base.

Incidentally, any bending that might be necessary should be performed before the height of the front sight is reduced so that more of the blade will be available for holding in the vice. For front sights of target width, that is $\frac{1}{8}''$ or $\frac{1}{10}''$ size, bending after soldering is almost out of the question. However, this should prove to be of very little consequence since target style revolvers are rarely submitted to a gunsmith for cutting-down.

At any rate, a sight that is canted, or off center very much, should be loosened up by heat and resoldered in place. Sight bending should not be resorted to as a cure-all for all sights that do not shape up correctly after they have been soldered-on. Rather it is to be used only when the sight appears to be a hair or two off and where chances are that reheating and replacing would not be likely to produce a better setting.

To remove stubborn chips and burrs that might be turned up on the muzzle rifling, a proper size brass-bristled cleaning brush should be pushed back and forth through the barrel a few times.

Bits of solder clinging to the sight or barrel can be cleaned off with a wire wheel attached to a polishing head or motor shaft. The gun should be held lightly against the wheel during this operation so that the sight itself will not be scored by the wheel.

Blueing the Cut-Down Barrel. Where complete blueing of the barrel is not practical or indicated some method of coloring the sight and bright surrounding area should be used; there are many touch-up blueing methods widely advertised which will be found all right for this purpose.

The quick method rusting process can be used advantageously to blue the muzzle end and sight of a cut-down gun. It is not necessary to swab solution over the entire gun in such cases, but rather only on the barrel and sight. Generally four or five applications of the solution and an equal number of cardings will produce a very professional looking job. To preclude any rusting, the frame should be dipped in oil, while still hot, and then dried off with a soft cloth.

Nevertheless, it is better, if the gunsmith has facilities for quick method blueing available, to include an extra fee in the cost estimate and reblue the entire weapon. This makes for a much neater all around job and goes toward making the gun more pleasing to the customer's eyes.

In the case of chrome or nickel-plated guns, a good buffing treatment as described in Chapter Sixteen will make for a very well finished looking appearance after a barrel cut-down job.

Special Considerations. There are special problems common to certain models of revolvers that will be encountered in doing this cut-down barrel work, but none of them so complex or involved that they defy solution. For example, certain S&W revolvers can be cut down only so far, due to the presence of the extractor rod locking lug. In such instances the extreme length of the abbreviated barrel will be governed by the position of this piece. Also, when the Colt Police Positive Special is cut to 2″ or less, the end of the extractor rod will protrude beyond the muzzle of the gun. Again the solution is simple; the extractor rod tip should be screwed off and the rod threaded down to about ¼″ beyond the limit of the factory threading. Then about ¼″ can be sawed off the rod and the tip screwed back on. This will bring the end of the rod to a point behind the gun muzzle.

Sometimes the customer will want a special type of front sight on his belly gun and in rare instances no sight at all. In either case the gunsmith should be prepared to cope with the situation and give the customer what he wants.

Cut-Away Trigger Guard. The advisability of cutting out trigger guards on revolvers has always been a point of hot discussion. This consideration, however, does not affect the gunsmith and his mechanical workings to any great extent for it is his job to carry out the wishes of his customers to the best of his ability within the limits of ethics and the law. One of the main advantages claimed for a cut-out trigger guard is that it allows the shooter who has a glove on his hand to operate the weapon in an easier and more positive manner.

At any rate, there is very little work to the job for it entails only the cutting off of the guard at the points indicated in Figure 102 and the blending and smoothing up of the surface left rough by the hacksaw. Under no circumstances whatsoever should the guard be cut in such a manner that the remaining edge is behind the tip of the trigger, for this would only be inviting trouble in the way of malfunction should the guard become bent up, even the slightest bit, and interfere with the trigger being pulled back for double action shooting. To preclude this undesirable condition from happening with any revolver having a cut-out guard, some gunsmiths grind off between ¹⁄₁₆″ and ⅛″ from the tip of the trigger to compensate for any possible bending of the guard. The idea is not without merit but the owner of the gun should be consulted before going ahead with such an additional modification.

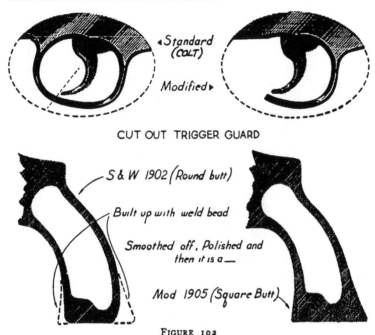

Standard (COLT)

Modified ▸

CUT OUT TRIGGER GUARD

S & W 1902 (Round butt)

Built up with weld bead

Smoothed off, Polished and then it is a —

Mod 1905 (Square Butt)

FIGURE 102

Work on Grip Frame. Considering the many different sizes and shapes of hands that men have there are few revolver grips that are satisfactory for all shooters. In addition, some peace officers and lawful gun toters like powerful guns for pocket use but dislike the large grips that are a feature of the weapon's basic design. In some cases, thinning out the wooden grips serves to partially correct the situation, but in other cases it is necessary to perform a more drastic operation.

As with cutting down barrels, not all revolver grip frames can be made smaller or re-shaped to any extent because of the location of certain parts. In the S&W, for example, the mainspring prevents it. One type of frame though—the Colt Police Positive —lends itself very well to reduction in size and either the Colt P.P. .38 short, Colt P.P. .32 long or Colt Bankers Special .38 short or .22 rim fire are excellent pieces for converting their grip frame to Colt Pocket Positive size.

Figure 103 illustrates the five steps incident to this conversion job.

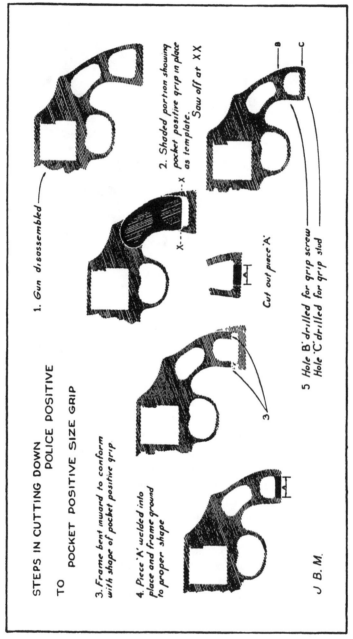

STEPS IN CUTTING DOWN
        POLICE POSITIVE
TO   POCKET POSITIVE SIZE GRIP

1. Gun disassembled

2. Shaded portion showing pocket positive grip in place as template.
Saw off at XX

3. Frame bent inward to conform with shape of pocket positive grip

4. Piece 'A' welded into place and frame ground to proper shape

Cut out piece 'A'

5 Hole 'B' drilled for grip screw
  Hole 'C' drilled for grip stud

J. B. M.

FIGURE 103

In Step One the gun is pictured completely stripped—this includes removal of the bolt and bolt spring, as well as the other parts.

In Step Two the small Pocket Positive grip is pictured as laid in place on the frame and the line "X-X" scribed across the front and back strap indicating where the sawing off should be done.

In Step Three the straps are shown as bent inward so that they conform more closely to the outline of the smaller grip. Also "Y," which is saved from the discarded butt piece trimmed up to fill in as the new butt base, is shown in place.

In Step Four the revolver is shown with the piece welded in place and the grip frame filed and ground to the contour of the Pocket Positive grip. If welding facilities are not available the piece can be brazed into place. However, this latter method does not produce as neat a job as welding since traces of brass will show through after the gun is blued. Some gunsmiths may even wish to sweat (solder) the piece in place in the absence of means for producing the high temperature needed for welding or brazing.

When using this method more filing will have to be done so that a perfect bearing surface will be present between the ends of the inserted piece and the places at which the union must be made on the inside of the straps. To insure full strength for the grip frame on a sweated joint, it is advisable for the gunsmith to pin the front and back straps to the inserted piece. This is done by drilling a $3/32''$ hole through the back strap, inserted piece, and front strap of the gun, after the surfaces have been filed, fitted and tinned, and then forcing a $3/1000''$ oversize pin into the hole through the three sections.

Then, when heat is applied to fuse the tinned surfaces, the pin, which should also have been lightly tinned before insertion, will be firmly in place. This pin should be made of cold rolled steel or any steel which will not become hard with the application of that amount of heat used to melt the solder. This precaution is necessary so that when it comes time to drill the hole for the stock pin the drill will not strike a hardened piece of metal as would be the case if drill rod or tool steel was used as a fastening pin.

In Step Five the revolver is shown with a hole drilled through the web of the frame to accommodate the stock screw and the stock pin hole with the pin inserted. The location for both of these holes is easily determined by using the Pocket Positive grip as a template and laying out the center of the holes accordingly.

As will be quite obvious, it is necessary to reblue the entire gun frame after doing this modification job.

Although the Colt Police Positive in the calibers and styles previously mentioned is the model of revolver best suited to grip abbreviation, it is by no means the only one. From the foregoing description, however, the gunsmith should be able to get a good idea of the possibilities of this class of work.

Additions to grips can also be made; for example, the Model 1902 S&W Military & Police revolver with the round butt can be converted to the Model 1905 by building up the butt straps with steel flowed on with an acetylene torch. This is not a job which will be too often encountered by the gunsmith but this writer was called upon frequently to do it for dealers who find it easier to sell the square butt (1905 Model) S&W than the S&W Model 1902.

In the work of grip alteration, as in other phases of special repair work, skill, plus imagination will open up a great field of possibilities for the progressive gunsmith who realizes that there is more to gunsmithing than just putting a mainspring or firing pin in an heirloom shotgun.

Hammer Alteration. For peace officers and other persons who, by virtue of their occupation, must carry a small pocket weapon available for quick draw at any time, the revolver with a spurless hammer is a great advantage, for it does not have the tendency to catch or foul on pocket lining. Figure 104 illustrates the approximate position at which the hammer spur should be cut off, as well as the method of serrating the remaining section so the hammer can be cocked for single action after it is brought backward part way by pressing on the trigger. After serrating or checkering the top of the hammer, the gunsmith should check to see that the firing pin has not been staked in place by the filing action, for, as mentioned in Chapter Eleven, the firing pin in modern Colt and S&W revolvers must always be free to move in an up and down direction in the hammer.

While the spurs can be hacksawed off hammers of Colt manufacture, those of S&W make must be ground off, since they are surface-hardened and resist all cutting by saw blades. After cutting off the spur, all ragged and rough edges should be dressed down with emery cloth or, better still, by means of a soft back abrasive wheel of the type described in Chapter Sixteen.

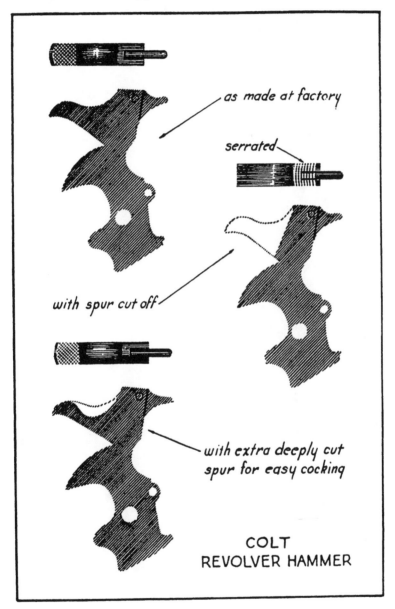

as made at factory

serrated

with spur cut off

with extra deeply cut spur for easy cocking

COLT
REVOLVER HAMMER

FIGURE 104

In addition to the special methods and services covered in this chapter, each individual gunsmith will, in the course of time, no doubt "discover" certain other phases of his work which can be elevated to a specialty plane and afford him a chance to derive extra income from it.

CHAPTER NINETEEN

TABLES OF MECHANICAL REFERENCE

DECIMAL EQUIVALENTS

Fraction	Decimal Equivalent	Fraction	Decimal Equivalent	Fraction	Decimal Equivalent	Fraction	Decimal Equivalent
1/64	0.015625	17/64	0.265625	33/64	0.515625	49/64	0.765625
1/32	.03125	9/32	.28125	17/32	.53125	25/32	.78125
3/64	.046875	19/64	.296875	35/64	.546875	51/64	.796875
1/16	.0625	5/16	.3125	9/16	.5625	13/16	.8125
5/64	.078125	21/64	.328125	37/64	.578125	53/64	.828125
3/32	.09375	11/32	.34375	19/32	.59375	27/32	.84375
7/64	.109375	23/64	.359375	39/64	.609375	55/64	.859375
1/8	.125	3/8	.375	5/8	.625	7/8	.875
9/64	.140625	25/64	.390625	41/64	.640625	57/64	.890625
5/32	.15625	13/32	.40625	21/32	.65625	29/32	.90625
11/64	.171875	27/64	.421875	43/64	.671875	59/64	.921875
3/16	.1875	7/16	.4375	11/16	.6875	15/16	.9375
13/64	.203125	29/64	.453125	45/64	.703125	61/64	.953125
7/32	.21875	15/32	.46875	23/32	.71875	31/32	.96875
15/64	.234375	31/64	.484375	47/64	.734375	63/64	.984375
1/4	.25	1/2	.5	3/4	.75	1	1.

TABLES OF DECIMAL EQUIVALENTS

			7ths, 14ths, and 28ths of an Inch				
7th	14th	28th	Decimal	7th	14th	28th	Decimal
		1	.035714			15	.535714
	1		.071429	4			.571429
		3	.107143			17	.607143
1			.142857		9		.642867
		5	.178571			19	.678571
	3		.214286	5			.714286
		7	.25			21	.75
2			.285714		11		.785714
		9	.321429			23	.821429
	5		.357143	6			.857143
		11	.392857			25	.892857
3			.428571		13		.928571
		13	.464286			27	.964286
	7		.5				

			6ths, 12ths, and 24ths of an Inch				
6th	12th	24th	Decimal	6th	12th	24th	Decimal
		1	.041667			13	.541666
	1		.083333		7		.583333
		3	.125			15	.625
1			.166666	4			.666666
		5	.208333			17	.708333
	3		.25		9		.75
		7	.291666			19	.791666
2			.333333	5			.833333
		9	.375			21	.875
	5		.416666		11		.916666
		11	.458333			23	.958333
3			.5				

INCHES INTO MILLIMETERS

In.	0	1/16	1/8	3/16	1/4	5/16	3/8	7/16	1/2	9/16	5/8	11/16	3/4	13/16	7/8	15/16
0	0.0	1.6	3.2	4.8	6.4	7.9	9.5	11.1	12.7	14.3	15.9	17.5	19.1	20.6	22.2	23.8
1	25.4	27.0	28.6	30.2	31.7	33.3	34.9	36.5	38.1	39.7	41.3	42.9	44.4	46.0	47.6	49.2
2	50.8	52.4	54.0	55.6	57.1	58.7	60.3	61.9	63.5	65.1	66.7	68.3	69.8	71.4	73.0	74.6
3	76.2	77.8	79.4	81.0	82.5	84.1	85.7	87.3	88.9	90.5	92.1	93.7	95.2	96.8	98.4	100.0
4	101.6	103.2	104.8	106.4	108.0	109.5	111.1	112.7	114.3	115.9	117.5	119.1	120.7	122.2	123.8	125.4
5	127.0	128.6	130.2	131.8	133.4	134.9	136.5	138.1	139.7	141.3	142.9	144.5	146.1	147.6	149.2	150.8
6	152.4	154.0	155.6	157.2	158.8	160.3	161.9	163.5	165.1	166.7	168.3	169.9	171.5	173.0	174.6	176.2
7	177.8	179.4	181.0	182.6	184.2	185.7	187.3	188.9	190.5	192.1	193.7	195.3	196.9	198.4	200.0	201.6
8	203.2	204.8	206.4	208.0	209.6	211.1	212.7	214.3	215.9	217.5	219.1	220.7	222.3	223.8	225.4	227.0
9	228.6	230.2	231.8	233.4	235.0	236.5	238.1	239.7	241.3	242.9	244.5	246.1	247.7	249.2	250.8	252.4
10	254.0	255.6	257.2	258.8	260.4	261.9	263.5	265.1	266.7	268.3	269.9	271.5	273.1	274.6	276.2	277.8
11	279.4	281.0	282.6	284.2	285.7	287.3	288.9	290.5	292.1	293.7	295.3	296.9	298.4	300.0	301.6	303.2
12	304.8	306.4	308.0	309.6	311.1	312.7	314.3	315.9	317.5	319.1	320.7	322.3	323.8	325.4	327.0	328.6
13	330.2	331.8	333.4	335.0	336.5	338.1	339.7	341.3	342.9	344.5	346.1	347.7	349.2	350.8	352.4	354.0
14	355.6	357.2	358.8	360.4	361.9	363.5	365.1	366.7	368.3	369.9	371.5	373.1	374.6	376.2	377.8	379.4
15	381.0	382.6	384.2	385.8	387.3	388.9	390.5	392.1	393.7	395.3	396.9	398.5	400.0	401.6	403.2	404.8
16	406.4	408.0	409.6	411.2	412.7	414.3	415.9	417.5	419.1	420.7	422.3	423.9	425.4	427.0	428.6	430.2
17	431.8	433.4	435.0	436.6	438.1	439.7	441.3	442.9	444.5	446.1	447.7	449.3	450.8	452.4	454.0	455.6
18	457.2	458.8	460.4	462.0	463.5	465.1	466.7	468.3	469.9	471.5	473.1	474.7	476.2	477.8	479.4	481.0
19	482.6	484.2	485.8	487.4	488.9	490.5	492.1	493.7	495.3	496.9	498.5	500.1	501.6	503.2	504.8	506.4
20	508.0	509.6	511.2	512.8	514.3	515.9	517.5	519.1	520.7	522.3	523.9	525.5	527.0	528.6	530.2	531.8
21	533.4	535.0	536.6	538.2	539.7	541.3	542.9	544.5	546.1	547.7	549.3	550.9	552.4	554.0	555.6	557.2
22	558.8	560.4	562.0	563.6	565.1	566.7	568.3	569.9	571.5	573.1	574.7	576.3	577.8	579.4	581.0	582.6
23	584.2	585.8	587.4	589.0	590.5	592.1	593.7	595.3	596.9	598.5	600.1	601.7	603.2	604.8	606.4	608.0

MILLIMETERS TO DECIMALS OF AN INCH
From 1 to 99 Units

Millimeters	0	1	2	3	4	5	6	7	8	9
	0	0.03937	0.07874	0.11811	0.15748	0.19685	0.23622	0.27559	0.31496	0.35433
10	0.39370	.43307	.47244	.51181	.55118	.59055	.62992	.66929	.70866	.74803
20	.78740	.86614	.90551	.90551	.94488	.98425	1.02362	1.06299	1.10236	1.14173
30	1.18110	1.22047	1.25984	1.29921	1.33858	1.37795	1.41732	1.45669	1.49606	1.53543
40	1.57480	1.61417	1.65354	1.69291	1.73228	1.77165	1.81102	1.85039	1.88976	1.92913
50	1.96850	2.00787	2.04724	2.08661	2.12598	2.16535	2.20472	2.24409	2.28346	2.32283
60	2.36220	2.40157	2.44094	2.48031	2.51968	2.55905	2.59842	2.63779	2.67716	2.71653
70	2.75590	2.79527	2.83464	2.87401	2.91338	2.95275	2.99212	3.03149	3.07086	3.11023
80	3.14960	3.18897	3.22834	3.26771	3.30708	3.34645	3.38582	3.42519	3.46456	3.50393
90	3.54330	3.58267	3.62204	3.66141	3.70078	3.74015	3.77952	3.81889	3.85826	3.89763

HUNDREDTHS OF AN INCH TO MILLIMETERS
From 1 to 99 Hundredths

Hundredths of an Inch	0	1	2	3	4	5	6	7	8	9
	0	0.254	0.508	0.762	1.016	1.270	1.524	1.778	2.032	2.286
10	2.540	2.794	3.048	3.302	3.556	3.810	4.064	4.318	4.572	4.826
20	5.080	5.334	5.588	5.842	6.096	6.350	6.604	6.858	7.112	7.366
30	7.620	7.874	8.128	8.382	8.636	8.890	9.144	9.398	9.652	9.906
40	10.160	10.414	10.668	10.922	11.176	11.430	11.684	11.938	12.192	12.446
50	12.700	12.954	13.208	13.462	13.716	13.970	14.224	14.478	14.732	14.986
60	15.240	15.494	15.748	16.002	16.256	16.510	16.764	17.018	17.272	17.526
70	17.780	18.034	18.288	18.542	18.796	19.050	19.304	19.558	19.812	20.066
80	20.320	20.574	20.828	21.082	21.336	21.590	21.844	22.098	22.352	22.606
90	22.860	23.114	23.368	23.622	23.876	24.130	24.384	24.638	24.892	25.146

TABLE OF TAPERS
Diametrical Variation for a Given Length

Length of Tapered Portion Inches	Taper per Foot-Inches					
	1/16	3/32	1/8	1/4	3/8	1/2
1/32	.0002	.0002	.0003	.0007	.0010	.0013
1/16	.0003	.0005	.0007	.0013	.0020	.0026
1/8	.0007	.0010	.0013	.0026	.0039	.0052
3/16	.0010	.0015	.0020	.0039	.0059	.0078
1/4	.0013	.0020	.0026	.0052	.0078	.0104
5/16	.0016	.0024	.0033	.0065	.0098	.0130
3/8	.0020	.0029	.0039	.0078	.0117	.0156
7/16	.0023	.0034	.0046	.0091	.0137	.0182
1/2	.0026	.0039	.0052	.0104	.0156	.0208
9/16	.0029	.0044	.0059	.0117	.0176	.0234
5/8	.0033	.0049	.0065	.0130	.0195	.0260
11/16	.0036	.0054	.0072	.0143	.0215	.0286
3/4	.0039	.0059	.0078	.0156	.0234	.0312
13/16	.0042	.0063	.0085	.0169	.0254	.0339
7/8	.0046	.0068	.0091	.0182	.0273	.0365
15/16	.0049	.0073	.0098	.0195	.0293	.0391
1	.0052	.0078	.0104	.0208	.0312	.0417
2	.0104	.0156	.0208	.0417	.0625	.0833
3	.0156	.0234	.0312	.0625	.0937	.1250
4	.0208	.0312	.0417	.0833	.1250	.1667
5	.0260	.0391	.0521	.1042	.1562	.2083
6	.0312	.0469	.0625	.1250	.1875	.2500
7	.0365	.0547	.0729	.1458	.2187	.2917
8	.0417	.0625	.0833	.1667	.2500	.3333
9	.0469	.0703	.0937	.1875	.2812	.3750
10	.0521	.0781	.1042	.2083	.3125	.4167
11	.0573	.0859	.1146	.2292	.3437	.4583
12	.0625	.0937	.1250	.2500	.3750	.5000
13	.0677	.1016	.1354	.2708	.4062	.5417
14	.0729	.1094	.1458	.2917	.4375	.5833
15	.0781	.1172	.1562	.3125	.4687	.6250
16	.0833	.1250	.1667	.3333	.5000	.6667
17	.0885	.1328	.1771	.3542	.5312	.7083
18	.0937	.1406	.1875	.3750	.5625	.7500
19	.0990	.1484	.1979	.3958	.5937	.7917
20	.1042	.1562	.2083	.4167	.6250	.8333
21	.1094	.1641	.2187	.4375	.6562	.8750
22	.1146	.1719	.2292	.4583	.6875	.9167
23	.1198	.1797	.2396	.4792	.7187	.9583
24	.1250	.1875	.2500	.5000	.7500	1.0000

NUMBER SIZES OF DRILLS

Drill No.	Deci.	Drill No.	Deci.	Drill No.	Deci.	Drill No.	Deci.
80	.0135	60	.0400	40	.098	20	.161
79	.0145	59	.0410	39	.0995	19	.166
78	.0160	58	.0420	38	.1015	18	.170
77	.0180	57	.0430	37	.1040	17	.173
76	.0200	56	.0465	36	.1065	16	.177
75	.0210	55	.0520	35	.1100	15	.180
74	.0225	54	.0550	34	.1110	14	.182
73	.0240	53	.0595	33	.1130	13	.185
72	.0250	52	.0635	32	.116	12	.189
71	.0260	51	.0670	31	.120	11	.191
70	.0280	50	.0700	30	.129	10	.194
69	.0292	49	.0730	29	.136	9	.196
68	.0310	48	.0760	28	.141	8	.199
67	.0320	47	.0785	27	.144	7	.201
66	.0330	46	.0810	26	.147	6	.204
65	.0350	45	.0820	25	.150	5	.206
64	.0360	44	.0860	24	.152	4	.209
63	.0370	43	.0890	23	.154	3	.213
62	.0380	42	.0935	22	.157	2	.221
61	.0390	41	.0960	21	.159	1	.228

LETTER SIZES OF DRILLS

Drill No.	Deci.	Drill No.	Deci.	Drill No.	Deci.	Drill No.	Deci.
A	.234	H	.266	O	.316	V	.377
B	.238	I	.272	P	.323	W	.386
C	.242	J	.277	Q	.332	X	.397
D	.246	K	.281	R	.339	Y	.404
E	.250	L	.290	S	.348	Z	.413
F	.257	M	.295	T	.358		
G	.261	N	.302	U	.368		

METRIC DRILLS AND DECIMAL EQUIVALENTS

Diameter mm.	Diameter Inches	Diameter mm.	Diameter Inches	Diameter mm.	Diameter Inches
0.30	0.0118	2.75	0.1082	6.70	0.2637
0.35	0.0137	2.80	0.1102	6.75	0.2657
0.40	0.0157	2.90	0.1141	6.80	0.2677
0.45	0.0177	3.00	0.1181	6.90	0.2716
0.50	0.0196	3.10	0.1220	7.00	0.2755
0.55	0.0216	3.20	0.1259	7.10	0.2795
0.60	0.0236	3.25	0.1279	7.20	0.2834
0.65	0.0255	3.30	0.1299	7.25	0.2854
0.70	0.0275	3.40	0.1338	7.30	0.2874
0.75	0.0295	3.50	0.1378	7.40	0.2913
0.80	0.0314	3.60	0.1417	7.50	0.2952
0.85	0.0334	3.70	0.1456	7.60	0.2992
0.90	0.0354	3.75	0.1476	7.70	0.3031
0.95	0.0374	3.80	0.1496	7.75	0.3051
1.00	0.0393	3.90	0.1535	7.80	0.3070
1.05	0.0413	4.00	0.1574	7.90	0.3110
1.10	0.0433	4.10	0.1614	8.00	0.3149
1.15	0.0452	4.20	0.1653	8.10	0.3228
1.20	0.0472	4.25	0.1673	8.20	0.3230
1.25	0.0492	4.30	0.1692	8.25	0.3248
1.30	0.0511	4.40	0.1732	8.30	0.3268
1.35	0.0531	4.50	0.1771	8.40	0.3307
1.40	0.0551	4.60	0.1811	8.50	0.3346
1.45	0.0570	4.70	0.1850	8.60	0.3385
1.50	0.0590	4.75	0.1870	8.70	0.3425
1.55	0.0610	4.80	0.1889	8.75	0.3444
1.60	0.0629	4.90	0.1929	8.80	0.3464
1.65	0.0649	5.00	0.1968	8.90	0.3504
1.70	0.0669	5.10	0.2007	9.00	0.3453
1.75	0.0688	5.20	0.2047	9.10	0.3583
1.80	0.0708	5.25	0.2066	9.20	0.3622
1.85	0.0728	5.30	0.2086	9.25	0.3641
1.90	0.0748	5.40	0.2126	9.30	0.3661
1.95	0.0767	5.50	0.2165	9.40	0.3701
2.00	0.0787	5.60	0.2204	9.50	0.3740
2.05	0.0807	5.70	0.2244	9.60	0.3779
2.10	0.0826	5.75	0.2263	9.70	0.3818
2.15	0.0846	5.80	0.2283	9.75	0.3838
2.20	0.0866	5.90	0.2322	9.80	0.3858
2.25	0.0885	6.00	0.2362	10.00	0.3937
2.30	0.0905	6.10	0.2401	10.50	0.4133
2.35	0.0925	6.20	0.2441	11.00	0.4330
2.40	0.0944	6.25	0.2460	11.50	0.4527
2.45	0.0964	6.30	0.2480	12.00	0.4724
2.50	0.0984	6.40	0.2519	12.50	0.4921
2.60	0.1023	6.50	0.2559		
2.70	0.1063	6.60	0.2598		

TAPER PIPE TAP SIZES

Tap Size Inches	Threads per Inch NPT	Drill Size Inches
1/8	27	11/32
1/4	18	7/16
3/8	18	37/64
1/2	14	23/32
3/4	14	59/64
1	11½	1 5/32
1¼	11½	1½
1½	11½	1 47/64
2	11½	2 7/32
2½	8	2 5/8
3	8	3¼
3½	8	3¾
4	8	4¼

COMMON METRIC THREADS

Diameter of Screw mm.	Pitch mm.
3	0.5
4	0.75
5	0.75
6	1.0
7	1.0
8	1.0
8	1.25
9	1.0
9	1.25
10	1.5
11	1.5
12	1.5
12	1.75
14	2.0
16	2.0
18	2.5
20	2.5
22	2.5
22	3.0
24	3.0

COMPARISON OF ENGLISH AND METRIC PITCHES

Common English Pitches			*Common Metric Pitches*		
Threads per Inch	Pitch		Pitch		Threads per Inch
	Inches	mm.	mm.	Inches	
4	0.2500	6.350	8.0	0.3150	3.2
4½	.2222	5.644	7.5	.2953	3.4
5	.2000	5.080	7.0	.2756	3.6
6	.1667	4.233	6.5	.2559	3.9
7	.1429	3.629	6.0	.2362	4.2
7½	.1333	3.387	5.5	.2165	4.6
8	.1250	3.175	5.0	.1968	5.1
9	.1111	2.822	4.5	.1772	5.6
10	.1000	2.540	4.0	.1575	6.4
11	.0909	2.309	3.5	.1378	7.3
11½	.0870	2.209	3.0	.1181	8.5
12	.0833	2.117	2.5	.0984	10.2
13	.0769	1.954	2.0	.0787	12.7
14	.0714	1.814	1.75	.0689	14.5
16	.0625	1.588	1.50	.0591	16.9
18	.0556	1.411	1.25	.0492	20.3
20	.0500	1.270	1.00	.0394	25.4
24	.0417	1.058	.90	.0354	28.2
27	.0370	.941	.75	.0295	33.9
28	.0357	.907	.60	.0236	42.3
32	.0312	.794	.45	.0177	56.4
36	.0278	.706	.42	.0165	60.5
40	.0250	.635	.39	.0154	65.1
44	.0227	.577	.36	.0142	70.6
48	.0208	.529	.33	.0130	77
56	.0179	.454	.30	.0118	85
64	.0156	.397	.27	.0106	94
72	.0139	.353	.24	.0094	106
80	.0125	.318	.21	.0083	121
			.19	.0075	134
			.17	.0067	149
			.15	.0059	169
			.13	.0051	195
			.11	.0043	231

TAP DRILL SIZES
(FRACTIONAL SIZES)

Nominal Size of Tap in Inches	Threads Per Inch		Tap-Drill		Actual % Full Thread Tap-Drill Will Give
	NC	NF	Nominal Size	Decimal Equiv.	
¼	20		#8	.1990	79
			#7	.2010	75
			13⁄64″	.2031	72
¼		28	#3	.2130	80
			7⁄32″	.2187	67
5⁄16	18		F	.2570	77
			G	.2610	71
5⁄16		24	I	.2720	75
			J	.2770	66
⅜	16		5⁄16″	.3125	77
			O	.3160	73
⅜		24	Q	.3320	79
			R	.3390	67
7⁄16	14		U	.3680	75
			⅜″	.3750	67
7⁄16		20	W	.3860	79
			25⁄64″	.3906	72
			X	.3970	62
½	13		27⁄64″	.4219	78
			7⁄16″	.4375	62
½		20	29⁄64″	.4531	72
9⁄16	12		31⁄64″	.4844	72
9⁄16		18	½″	.5000	87
			33⁄64″	.5156	65
⅝	11		17⁄32″	.5312	79
			35⁄64″	.5469	66

TAP DRILL SIZES
(FRACTIONAL SIZES)
(*Continued*)

Nominal Size of Tap in Inches	Threads Per Inch		Tap-Drill		Actual % Full Thread Tap-Drill Will Give
	NC	NF	Nominal Size	Decimal Equiv.	
5/8		18	9/16″ 37/64″	.5625 .5781	87 65
3/4	10		41/64″ 21/32″	.6406 .6562	84 72
3/4		16	11/16″ 45/64″	.6875 .7031	77 58
7/8	9		49/64″ 25/32″	.7656 .7812	76 65
7/8		14	51/64″ 13/16″	.7969 .8125	84 67
1	8		7/8″ 57/64″	.8750 .8906	77 67
1		14	59/64″ 15/16″	.9218 .9375	84 67

TAP DRILL SIZES
(MACHINE SCREW SIZES)

Nominal Size of Tap Mach. Screw Nos.	Threads Per Inch		Tap-Drill		Actual % Full Thread Tap-Drill Will Give
	NC	NF	Nominal Size	Decimal Equiv.	
0		80	3/64"	.0469	81
1	64		#53	.0595	66
1		72	#53	.0595	75
2	56		#51	.0670	82
			#50	.0700	69
2		64	#50	.0700	79
			#49	.0730	64
3	48		5/64"	.0781	77
			#47	.0785	75
			#46	.0810	66
3		56	#46	.0810	78
4	40		#44	.0860	80
			#43	.0890	71
4		48	3/32"	.0937	68
5	40		#39	.0995	79
			#38	.1015	72
			#37	.1040	65
5		44	#37	.1040	71
			#36	.1065	63
6	32		#36	.1065	78
			7/64"	.1094	70
			#33	.1130	62
6		40	#33	.1130	77
			#32	.1160	68
8	32		#29	.1360	69

TAP DRILL SIZES
(MACHINE SCREW SIZES)
(Continued)

Nominal Size of Tap Mach. Screw Nos.	Threads Per Inch		Tap-Drill		Actual % Full Thread Tap-Drill Will Give
	NC	NF	Nominal Size	Decimal Equiv.	
8		36	#29 ⁹⁄₆₄″	.1360 .1406	78 65
10	24		#26 #24	.1470 .1520	79 70
10		32	⁵⁄₃₂″ #21 #20	.1562 .1590 .1610	83 76 71
12	24		11⁄₆₄″ #17 #16 #15	.1719 .1730 .1770 .1800	82 79 72 67
12		28	#15 ³⁄₁₆″	.1800 .1875	78 61

AMERICAN NATIONAL SPECIAL (N.S.) SCREW THREAD PITCHES AND RECOMMENDED TAP DRILL SIZES

Sizes	Threads per Inch	Outside Diameter of Screw	Tap Drill Sizes	Decimal Equivalent of Drill
1/4	24 27 32	0.250	4 3 7/32	0.2090 .2130 .2187
5/16	20 27 32	.3125	17/64 J 9/32	.2656 .2770 .2812
3/8	20 27	.375	21/64 R	.3281 .3390
7/16	24 27	.4375	X Y	.3970 .4040
1/2	12 24 27	0.500	27/64 29/64 15/32	0.4219 .4531 .4687
9/16	27	.5625	17/32	.5312
5/8	12 27	.625	35/64 19/32	.5469 .5937
3/4	12 27	.750	43/64 23/32	.6719 .7187
7/8	12 18 27	.875	51/64 53/64 27/32	.7969 .8281 .8437
1	12 27	1.000	59/64 31/32	.9219 .9687

SIZES OF WIRE NAILS

Size (d = penny)	Length (Inches)	Number per Pound
2-d	1	900
3-d	1¼	615
4-d	1½	322
5-d	1¾	250
6-d	2	200
7-d	2¼	154
8-d	2½	106
9-d	2¾	85
10-d	3	74
12-d	3¼	57
16-d	3½	46
20-d	4	29
30-d	4½	23
40-d	5	17
50-d	5½	13+
60-d	6	10+

TABLES FOR COMPUTING WEIGHT OF STEEL
Weight in Pounds of a Lineal Foot of Round, Square and Octagon Stock

Size in Inches	Round	Octagon	Square
¹⁄₁₆	.010	.011	.013
⅛	.042	.044	.053
³⁄₁₆	.094	.099	.120
¼	.168	.177	.214
⁵⁄₁₆	.262	.277	.334
⅜	.378	.398	.481
⁷⁄₁₆	.514	.542	.655
½	.671	.708	.855
⁹⁄₁₆	.850	.896	1.082
⅝	1.049	1.107	1.336
¹¹⁄₁₆	1.270	1.339	1.616
¾	1.511	1.594	1.924
¹³⁄₁₆	1.773	1.870	2.258
⅞	2.056	2.169	2.618
¹⁵⁄₁₆	2.361	2.490	3.006
1	2.686	2.833	3.420
1⅛	3.399	3.585	4.328
1¼	4.197	4.427	5.344

WEIGHTS OF SHEET STEEL AND IRON
U. S. Standard Gage

Gage Number	Approx. Thickness (Inches)	Pounds per Sq. Ft.		Gage Number	Approx. Thickness (Inches)	Pounds per Sq. Ft.	
		Steel	Iron			Steel	Iron
0000000	.5	20.4	20.	17	.05625	2.295	2.25
000000	.46875	19.125	18.75	18	.05	2.04	2.
00000	.4375	17.85	17.5	19	.04375	1.785	1.75
0000	.40625	16.575	16.25	20	.0375	1.53	1.5
000	.375	15.3	15.	21	.03438	1.403	1.375
00	.34375	14.025	13.75	22	.03125	1.275	1.25
0	.3125	12.75	12.5	23	.02813	1.148	1.125
1	.28125	11.475	11.25	24	.025	1.02	1.
2	.26563	10.838	10.625	25	.02188	.8925	.875
3	.25	10.2	10.	26	.01875	.765	.75
4	.23438	9.563	9.375	27	.01719	.7013	.6875
5	.21875	8.925	8.75	28	.01563	.6375	.625
6	.20313	8.288	8.125	29	.01406	.5738	.5625
7	.1875	7.65	7.5	30	.0125	.51	.5
8	.17188	7.013	6.875	31	.01094	.4463	.4375
9	.15625	6.375	6.25	32	.01016	.4144	.4063
10	.14063	5.738	5.625	33	.00938	.3825	.375
11	.125	5.1	5.	34	.00859	.3506	.3438
12	.10938	4.463	4.375	35	.00781	.3188	.3125
13	.09375	3.825	3.75	36	.00703	.2869	.2813
14	.07813	3.188	3.125	37	.00664	.2709	.2656
15	.07031	2.869	2.813	38	.00625	.255	.25
16	.0625	2.55	2.5				

SURFACE SPEED OF WHEEL IN FEET PER MINUTE

Speed of Arbor	DIAMETER OF WHEEL								
	2″	4″	6″	8″	10″	12″	14″	16″	18″
800	420	850	1250	1680	2150	2500	2900	3250	3700
900	470	950	1400	1900	2400	2800	3250	3700	4100
1000	525	1050	1575	2100	2600	3100	3600	4100	4550
1200	630	1260	1950	2550	3200	3750	4400	5000	5550
1400	730	1470	2250	2950	3650	4400	5100	5800	6500
1600	840	1680	2550	3400	4200	5000	5900	6600	7500
1800	940	1890	2900	3800	4750	5650	6600	7500	8500
2000	1050	2100	3200	4200	5250	6250	7300	8400	9300
2200	1150	2300	3450	4550	5750	6900	8000	9100	10300
2400	1260	2500	3750	5000	6300	7500	8800	10000	11200
2600	1360	2700	4100	5450	6800	8200	9600	10900	12200
2800	1470	2950	4400	5900	7400	8900	11000	12500	13200
3000	1570	3140	4700	6250	7900	9400	11000	12500	14100
3200	1680	3350	5000	6650	8400	10000	11800	13400	15100
3400	1780	3560	5250	7000	8900	10600	12500	14300	16000
3600	1880	3780	5600	7500	9500	11300	13200	15100	17000

FUNCTIONS OF NUMBERS

Number	Square	Cube	Square root	Logarithm	Number	Square	Cube	Square root	Logarithm
1	1	1	1.0000	0.00000	51	2601	132651	7.1414	1.70757
2	4	8	1.4142	.30103	52	2704	140608	7.2111	1.71600
3	9	27	1.7321	.47712	53	2809	148877	7.2801	1.72428
4	16	64	2.0000	.60206	54	2916	157464	7.3485	1.73239
5	25	125	2.2361	.69897	55	3025	166375	7.4162	1.74036
6	36	216	2.4495	.77815	56	3136	175616	7.4833	1.74819
7	49	343	2.6458	.84510	57	3249	185193	7.5498	1.75587
8	64	512	2.8284	.90309	58	3364	195112	7.6158	1.76343
9	81	729	3.0000	.95424	59	3481	205379	7.6811	1.77085
10	100	1000	3.1623	1.00000	60	3600	216000	7.7460	1.77815
11	121	1331	3.3166	1.04139	61	3721	226681	7.8102	1.78533
12	144	1728	3.4641	1.07918	62	3844	238328	7.8740	1.79239
13	169	2197	3.6056	1.11394	63	3969	250047	7.9373	1.79934
14	196	2744	3.7417	1.14613	64	4096	262144	8.0000	1.80618
15	225	3375	3.8730	1.17609	65	4225	274625	8.0623	1.81291
16	256	4096	4.0000	1.20412	66	4356	287496	8.1240	1.81954
17	289	4913	4.1231	1.23045	67	4489	300763	8.1854	1.82607
18	324	5832	4.2426	1.25527	68	4624	314432	8.2462	1.83251
19	361	6859	4.3589	1.27875	69	4761	328509	8.3066	1.83885
20	400	8000	4.4721	1.30103	70	4900	343000	8.3666	1.84510
21	441	9261	4.5826	1.32222	71	5041	357911	8.4261	1.85126
22	484	10648	4.6904	1.34242	72	5184	373248	8.4853	1.85733
23	529	12167	4.7958	1.36173	73	5329	389017	8.5440	1.86332
24	576	13824	4.8990	1.38021	74	5476	405224	8.6023	1.86923
25	625	15625	5.0000	1.39794	75	5625	421875	8.6603	1.87506
26	676	17576	5.0990	1.41497	76	5776	438976	8.7178	1.88081
27	729	19683	5.1962	1.43136	77	5929	456533	8.7750	1.88649
28	784	21952	5.2915	1.44716	78	6084	474552	8.8318	1.89209
29	841	24389	5.3852	1.46240	79	6241	493039	8.8882	1.89763
30	900	27000	5.4772	1.47712	80	6400	512000	8.9443	1.90309
31	961	29791	5.5678	1.49136	81	6561	531441	9.0000	1.90849
32	1024	32768	5.6569	1.50515	82	6724	551368	9.0554	1.91381
33	1089	35937	5.7446	1.51851	83	6889	571787	9.1104	1.91908
34	1156	39304	5.8310	1.53148	84	7056	592704	9.1652	1.92428
35	1225	42875	5.9161	1.54407	85	7225	614125	9.2195	1.92942
36	1296	46656	6.0000	1.55630	86	7396	636056	9.2736	1.93450
37	1369	50653	6.0828	1.56820	87	7569	658503	9.3274	1.93952
38	1444	54872	6.1644	1.57978	88	7744	681472	9.3808	1.94448
39	1521	59319	6.2450	1.59106	89	7921	704969	9.4340	1.94939
40	1600	64000	6.3246	1.60206	90	8100	729000	9.4868	1.95424
41	1681	68921	6.4031	1.61278	91	8281	753571	9.5394	1.95904
42	1764	74088	6.4807	1.62325	92	8464	778688	9.5917	1.96379
43	1849	79507	6.5574	1.63347	93	8649	804357	9.6437	1.96848
44	1936	85184	6.6332	1.64345	94	8836	830584	9.6954	1.97313
45	2025	91125	6.7082	1.65321	95	9025	857375	9.7468	1.97772
46	2116	97336	6.7823	1.66276	96	9216	884736	9.7980	1.98227
47	2209	103823	6.8557	1.67210	97	9409	912673	9.8489	1.98677
48	2304	110592	6.9282	1.68124	98	9604	941192	9.8995	1.99123
49	2401	117649	7.0000	1.69020	99	9801	970299	9.9499	1.99564
50	2500	125000	7.0711	1.69897	100	10000	1000000	10.0000	2.00000

TABLE OF THE CHEMICAL ELEMENTS WITH THEIR SYMBOLS, ATOMIC NUMBERS AND ATOMIC WEIGHTS

Name	Symbol	Atomic Number	Atomic Weight	Name	Symbol	Atomic Number	Atomic Weight
Aluminum	Al	13	26.97	Molybdenum	Mo	42	95.95
Antimony	Sb	51	121.76	Neodymium	Nd	60	144.27
Argon	A	18	39.944	Neon	Ne	10	20.183
Arsenic	As	33	74.91	Nickel	Ni	28	58.69
Barium	Ba	56	137.36	Nitrogen	N	7	14.008
Beryllium	Be	4	9.02	Osmium	Os	76	190.2
Bismuth	Bi	83	209.00	Oxygen	O	8	16.000
Boron	B	5	10.82	Palladium	Pd	46	106.7
Bromine	Br	35	79.916	Phosphorus	P	15	30.98
Cadmium	Cd	48	112.41	Platinum	Pt	78	195.23
Calcium	Ca	20	40.08	Potassium	K	19	39.096
Carbon	C	6	12.010	Praseodymium	Pr	59	140.92
Cerium	Ce	58	140.13	Protoactinium	Pa	91	231.
Cesium	Cs	55	132.91	Radium	Ra	88	226.05
Chlorine	Cl	17	35.457	Radon	Rn	86	222.
Chromium	Cr	24	52.01	Rhenium	Re	75	186.31
Cobalt	Co	27	58.94	Rhodium	Rh	45	102.91
Columbium	Cb	41	92.91	Rubidium	Rb	37	85.48
Copper	Cu	29	63.57	Ruthenium	Ru	44	101.7
Dysprosium	Dy	66	162.46	Samarium	Sm	62	150.43
Erbium	Er	68	167.2	Scandium	Sc	21	45.10
Europium	Eu	63	152.0	Selenium	Se	34	78.96
Fluorine	F	9	19.00	Silicon	Si	14	28.06
Gadolinium	Gd	64	156.9	Silver	Ag	47	107.880
Gallium	Ga	31	69.72	Sodium	Na	11	22.997
Germanium	Ge	32	72.60	Strontium	Sr	38	87.63
Gold	Au	79	197.2	Sulfur	S	16	32.06
Hafnium	Hf	72	178.6	Tantalum	Ta	73	180.88
Helium	He	2	4.003	Tellurium	Te	52	127.61
Holmium	Ho	67	163.5	Terbium	Tb	65	159.2
Hydrogen	H	1	1.0080	Thallium	Tl	81	204.39
Illinium	Il	61	?	Thorium	Th	90	232.12
Indium	In	49	114.76	Thulium	Tm	69	169.4
Iodine	I	53	126.92	Tin	Sn	50	118.70
Iridium	Ir	77	193.1	Titanium	Ti	22	47.90
Iron	Fe	26	55.85	Tungsten	W	74	183.92
Krypton	Kr	36	83.7	Uranium	U	92	238.07
Lanthanum	La	57	138.92	Vanadium	V	23	50.95
Lead	Pb	82	207.21	Xenon	Xe	54	131.3
Lithium	Li	3	6.940	Ytterbium	Yb	70	173.04
Lutecium	Lu	71	174.99	Yttrium	Y	39	88.92
Magnesium	Mg	12	24.32	Zinc	Zn	30	65.38
Manganese	Mn	25	54.93	Zirconium	Zr	40	91.22
Mercury	Hg	80	200.61				

MELTING POINTS OF COMMON METALS

Metal	° Fahr.
Mercury	−38
Sulphur	236
Tin	450
Bismuth	520
Cadmium	610
Lead	621
Zinc	787
Antimony	1166
Magnesium	1204
Aluminum	1218
Silver	1761
Gold	1945
Copper	1981
Manganese	2300
Silicon	2588
Nickel	2646
Cobalt	2696
Chromium	2768
Pure Iron	2800
Wrought Iron	2700–2750
Stainless Steel	2400–2700
Carbon Steel	2400–2750
Cast Iron	2100–2350
Cast Steel	2600–2750
Palladium	2820
Zirconium	3090
Vanadium	3128
Platinum	3191
Molybdenum	4595
Tantalum	5252
Tungsten	6152
Carbon	6332
Brass	1700–1850
Bronze	1675
Solder (50–50)	450
Babbitt Metals	350–450
Zinc Die Casting Alloy	715–720

APPROXIMATE MELTING POINT OF COMMON SALTS
(Used for Tempering Baths)

Salt	°F.
Sodium Chloride (Table Salt)	1480° F.
Sodium Nitrate	590° F.
Sodium Sulphate	1620° F.
Potassium Nitrate	640° F.

CONVERSION OF FAHRENHEIT AND CENTIGRADE SCALES

Cen.	Fah.	Cen.	Fah.	Cen.	Fah.	Cen.	Fah.	Cen.	Fah.	Cen.	Fah.	Cen.	Fah.
0	32	230	446	460	860	690	1274	920	1688	1150	2102	1380	2516
5	41	235	455	465	869	695	1283	925	1697	1155	2111	1385	2525
10	50	240	464	470	878	700	1292	930	1706	1160	2120	1390	2534
15	59	245	473	475	887	705	1301	935	1715	1165	2129	1395	2543
20	68	250	482	480	896	710	1310	940	1724	1170	2138	1400	2552
25	77	255	491	485	905	715	1319	945	1733	1175	2147	1405	2561
30	86	260	500	490	914	720	1328	950	1742	1180	2156	1410	2570
35	95	265	509	495	923	725	1337	955	1751	1185	2165	1415	2579
40	104	270	518	500	932	730	1346	960	1760	1190	2174	1420	2588
45	113	275	527	505	941	735	1355	965	1769	1195	2183	1425	2597
50	122	280	536	510	950	740	1364	970	1778	1200	2192	1430	2606
55	131	285	545	515	959	745	1373	975	1787	1205	2201	1435	2615
60	140	290	554	520	968	750	1382	980	1796	1210	2210	1440	2624
65	149	295	563	525	977	755	1391	985	1805	1215	2219	1445	2633
70	158	300	572	530	986	760	1400	990	1814	1220	2228	1450	2642
75	167	305	581	535	995	765	1409	995	1823	1225	2237	1455	2651
80	176	310	590	540	1004	770	1418	1000	1832	1230	2246	1460	2660
85	185	315	599	545	1013	775	1427	1005	1841	1235	2255	1465	2669
90	194	320	608	550	1022	780	1436	1010	1850	1240	2264	1470	2678
95	203	325	617	555	1031	785	1445	1015	1859	1245	2273	1475	2687
100	212	330	626	560	1040	790	1454	1020	1868	1250	2282	1480	2696
105	221	335	635	565	1049	795	1463	1025	1877	1255	2291	1485	2705
110	230	340	644	570	1058	800	1472	1030	1886	1260	2300	1490	2714
115	239	345	653	575	1067	805	1481	1035	1895	1265	2309	1495	2723
120	248	350	662	580	1076	810	1490	1040	1904	1270	2318	1500	2732
125	257	355	671	585	1085	815	1499	1045	1913	1275	2327	1505	2741
130	266	360	680	590	1094	820	1508	1050	1922	1280	2336	1510	2750
135	275	365	689	595	1103	825	1517	1055	1931	1285	2345	1515	2759
140	284	370	698	600	1112	830	1526	1060	1940	1290	2354	1520	2768
145	293	375	707	605	1121	835	1535	1065	1949	1295	2363	1525	2777
150	302	380	716	610	1130	840	1544	1070	1958	1300	2372	1530	2786
155	311	385	725	615	1139	845	1553	1075	1967	1305	2381	1535	2795
160	320	390	734	620	1148	850	1562	1080	1976	1310	2390	1540	2804
165	329	395	743	625	1157	855	1571	1085	1985	1315	2399	1545	2813
170	338	400	752	630	1166	860	1580	1090	1994	1320	2408	1550	2822
175	347	405	761	635	1175	865	1589	1095	2003	1325	2417	1555	2831
180	356	410	770	640	1184	870	1598	1100	2012	1330	2426	1560	2840
185	365	415	779	645	1193	875	1607	1105	2021	1335	2435	1565	2849
190	374	420	788	650	1202	880	1616	1110	2030	1340	2444	1570	2858
195	383	425	797	655	1211	885	1625	1115	2039	1345	2453	1575	2867
200	392	430	806	660	1220	890	1634	1120	2048	1350	2462	1580	2876
205	401	435	815	665	1229	895	1643	1125	2057	1355	2471	1585	2885
210	410	440	824	670	1238	900	1652	1130	2066	1360	2480	1590	2894
215	419	445	833	675	1247	905	1661	1135	2075	1365	2489	1595	2903
220	428	450	842	680	1256	910	1670	1140	2084	1370	2498	1600	2912
225	437	455	851	685	1265	915	1679	1145	2093	1375	2507	1605	2921

CONVERSION FORMULAE

From—° Cen. to ° Fah. → Degrees Centigrade $\times 1.8 + 32$ = degrees Fahrenheit

From —° Fah. to ° Cen. → $\dfrac{\text{Degrees Fahrenheit} - 32}{1.8}$ = degrees Centigrade

S.A.E. STEEL SPECIFICATIONS

CARBON STEELS

SAE Number	Nominal Chemical Ranges			
	Carbon Range	Manganese Range	Phosphorus Max.	Sulfur Max.
1008	0.10 max.	0.30–0.50	0.040	0.050
1010	0.08–0.13	0.30–0.50	0.040	0.050
1015	0.13–0.18	0.30–0.50	0.040	0.050
1016	0.13–0.18	0.60–0.90	0.040	0.050
1020	0.18–0.23	0.30–0.50	0.040	0.050
1022	0.18–0.23	0.70–1.00	0.040	0.050
1024	0.20–0.26	1.35–1.65	0.040	0.050
1025	0.22–0.28	0.30–0.50	0.040	0.050
1030	0.28–0.34	0.60–0.90	0.040	0.050
1035	0.32–0.38	0.60–0.90	0.040	0.050
1036	0.32–0.39	1.20–1.50	0.040	0.050
1040	0.37–0.44	0.60–0.90	0.040	0.050
1045	0.43–0.50	0.60–0.90	0.040	0.050
1050	0.48–0.55	0.60–0.90	0.040	0.050
1052	0.47–0.55	1.20–1.50	0.040	0.050
1055	0.50–0.60	0.60–0.90	0.040	0.050
1060	0.55–0.65	0.60–0.90	0.040	0.050
1066	0.60–0.71	0.80–1.10	0.040	0.050
1070	0.65–0.75	0.70–1.00	0.040	0.050
1080	0.75–0.88	0.60–0.90	0.040	0.050
1085	0.80–0.93	0.70–1.00	0.040	0.050
1095	0.90–1.05	0.30–0.50	0.040	0.050

MANGANESE STEELS

SAE Number	Nominal Chemical Ranges				
	Carbon Range	Manganese Range	Phosphorus Max.	Sulfur Max.	Silicon Range
1320	0.18–0.23	1.60–1.90	0.040	0.040	0.20–0.35
1330	0.28–0.33	1.60–1.90	0.040	0.040	0.20–0.35
1335	0.33–0.38	1.60–1.90	0.040	0.040	0.20–0.35
1340	0.38–0.43	1.60–1.90	0.040	0.040	0.20–0.35

FREE CUTTING STEELS

SAE Number	Nominal Chemical Ranges			
	Carbon Range	Manganese Range	Phosphorus Range	Sulfur Range
Bessemer				
1111	0.08–0.13	0.60–0.90	0.09–0.13	0.10–0.15
1112	0.08–0.13	0.60–0.90	0.09–0.13	0.16–0.23
1113	0.08–0.13	0.60–0.90	0.09–0.13	0.24–0.33
Open Hearth				
1115	0.13–0.18	0.70–1.00	0.045 max.	0.10–0.15
1117	0.14–0.20	1.00–1.30	0.045 max.	0.08–0.13
1118	0.14–0.20	1.30–1.60	0.045 max.	0.08–0.13
1132	0.28–0.34	1.35–1.65	0.045 max.	0.08–0.13
1137	0.32–0.39	1.35–1.65	0.045 max.	0.08–0.13
1141	0.37–0.45	1.35–1.65	0.045 max.	0.08–0.13
1145	0.42–0.49	0.70–1.00	0.045 max.	0.04–0.07

NICKEL STEELS

SAE Number	Nominal Chemical Ranges					
	Carbon Range	Manganese Range	Phosphorus Max.	Sulfur Max.	Silicon Range	Nickel Range
2315 2317	0.15–0.20	0.40–0.60	0.040	0.040	0.20–0.35	3.25–3.75
2330	0.28–0.33	0.60–0.80	0.040	0.040	0.20–0.35	3.25–3.75
2340	0.38–0.43	0.70–0.90	0.040	0.040	0.20–0.35	3.25–3.75
2345	0.43–0.48	0.70–0.90	0.040	0.040	0.20–0.35	3.25–3.75
2515	0.12–0.17	0.40–0.60	0.040	0.040	0.20–0.35	4.75–5.25

NICKEL CHROMIUM STEELS

SAE Number	Nominal Chemical Ranges						
	Carbon Range	Manganese Range	Phosphorus Max.	Sulfur Max.	Silicon Range	Nickel Range	Chromium Range
3115	0.13–0.18	0.40–0.69	0.040	0.040	0.20–0.35	1.10–1.40	0.55–0.75
3120	0.17–0.22	0.60–0.80	0.040	0.040	0.20–0.35	1.10–1.40	0.55–0.75
3130	0.28–0.33	0.60–0.80	0.040	0.040	0.20–0.35	1.10–1.40	0.55–0.75
3135	0.33–0.38	0.60–0.80	0.040	0.040	0.20–0.35	1.10–1.40	0.55–0.75
3140	0.38–0.43	0.70–0.90	0.040	0.040	0.20–0.35	1.10–1.40	0.55–0.75
3141	0.38–0.43	0.70–0.90	0.040	0.040	0.20–0.35	1.10–1.40	0.70–0.90
3145	0.43–0.48	0.70–0.90	0.040	0.040	0.20–0.35	1.10–1.40	0.70–0.90
3150	0.48–0.53	0.70–0.90	0.040	0.040	0.20–0.35	1.10–1.40	0.70–0.90
3240	0.38–0.45	0.40–0.60	0.040	0.040	0.20–0.35	1.65–2.00	0.90–1.20
3312 } 3310	0.08–0.13	0.45–0.60	0.025	0.025	0.20–0.35	3.25–3.75	1.40–1.75

MOLYBDENUM STEELS

SAE Number	Nominal Chemical Ranges							
	Carbon Range	Manganese Range	Phosphorus Max.	Sulfur Max.	Silicon Range	Nickel Range	Chromium Range	Molyb. Range
4023	0.20–0.25	0.70–0.90	0.040	0.040	0.20–0.35	....	....	0.20–0.30
4027	0.25–0.30	0.70–0.90	0.040	0.040	0.20–0.35	....	....	0.20–0.30
4032	0.30–0.35	0.70–0.90	0.040	0.040	0.20–0.35	....	....	0.20–0.30
4037	0.35–0.40	0.75–1.00	0.040	0.040	0.20–0.35	....	....	0.20–0.30
4042	0.40–0.45	0.75–1.00	0.040	0.040	0.20–0.35	....	....	0.20–0.30
4047	0.45–0.50	0.85–1.00	0.040	0.040	0.20–0.35	....	....	0.20–0.30
4063	0.60–0.67	0.75–1.00	0.040	0.040	0.20–0.35	....	....	0.20–0.30
4068	0.64–0.72	0.75–1.00	0.040	0.040	0.20–0.35	....	....	0.20–0.30
4119	0.71–0.22	0.70–0.90	0.040	0.040	0.20–0.35	....	0.40–0.60	0.20–0.30
4125	0.23–0.28	0.70–0.90	0.040	0.040	0.20–0.35	....	0.40–0.60	0.20–0.30
4130	0.28–0.33	0.40–0.60	0.040	0.040	0.20–0.35	....	0.80–1.10	0.15–0.25
4137	0.35–0.40	0.70–0.90	0.040	0.040	0.20–0.35	....	0.80–1.10	0.15–0.25
4140	0.38–0.43	0.75–1.00	0.040	0.040	0.20–0.35	....	0.80–1.10	0.15–0.25
4145	0.43–0.48	0.75–1.00	0.040	0.040	0.20–0.35	....	0.80–1.10	0.15–0.25
4150	0.46–0.53	0.75–1.00	0.040	0.040	0.20–0.35	....	0.80–1.10	0.15–0.25
4320	0.17–0.22	0.45–0.65	0.040	0.040	0.20–0.35	1.65–2.00	0.40–0.60	0.20–0.30
4340	0.38–0.43	0.60–0.80	0.040	0.040	0.20–0.35	1.65–2.00	0.70–0.90	0.20–0.30
4615	0.13–0.18	0.45–0.65	0.040	0.040	0.20–0.35	1.65–2.00	....	0.20–0.30
4620	0.17–0.22	0.45–0.65	0.040	0.040	0.20–0.35	1.65–2.00	....	0.20–0.30
4640	0.38–0.43	0.60–0.80	0.040	0.040	0.20–0.35	1.65–2.00	....	0.20–0.30
4815	0.13–0.18	0.40–0.60	0.040	0.040	0.20–0.35	3.25–3.75	....	0.20–0.30
4820	0.18–0.23	0.50–0.70	0.040	0.040	0.20–0.35	3.25–3.75	....	0.20–0.30

CHROMIUM STEELS

SAE Number	Nominal Chemical Ranges					
	Carbon Range	Manganese Range	Phosphorus Max.	Sulfur Max.	Silicon Range	Chromium Range
5120	0.17–0.22	0.70–0.90	0.040	0.040	0.20–0.35	0.70–0.90
5140	0.38–0.43	0.70–0.90	0.040	0.040	0.20–0.35	0.70–0.90
5150	0.48–0.55	0.70–0.90	0.040	0.040	0.20–0.35	0.70–0.90
5210	0.95–1.10	0.30–0.50	0.025	0.025	0.20–0.35	1.20–1.50

CHROMIUM VANADIUM STEEL

SAE Number	Nominal Chemical Ranges						
	Carbon Range	Manganese Range	Phosphorus Max.	Sulfur Max.	Silicon Range	Chromium Range	Vanadium Min.
6150	0.48–0.55	0.65–0.90	0.040	0.040	0.20–0.35	0.80–1.10	0.15

SILICON MANGANESE STEEL

SAE Number	Nominal Chemical Ranges				
	Carbon Range	Manganese Range	Phosphorus Max.	Sulfur Max.	Silicon Range
9260	0.55–0.65	0.70–0.90	0.040	0.040	1.80–2.20

CHAPTER TWENTY

SOURCES OF SUPPLY

THE main purpose of this chapter is to provide the gunsmith with a pertinent listing of places where he can get the tools, equipment and supplies he needs but *which cannot be supplied by local dealers*. Trading in one's community is an old American custom and an invaluable way of gaining a favorable reputation, which is most desirable for anyone, especially a gunsmith.

Although this writer has not had personal dealings with every firm listed in this chapter, he has no reason to believe that any of them are less than honest and reputable. The mere fact that a supplier or organization is not listed is no indication that its standing is in any way inferior to those listed. Space limitations and the desire to suggest those firms with whom the writer is best acquainted has been the deciding factor.

The Classified Telephone Directory. Because many gunsmiths do not have the equipment for doing welding, plating and, in some cases, heat treatment on large units, they must find a place where work in need of such processing can be sent.

Where possible it is best to have special work farmed out locally because of transportation costs, speed in delivery, et cetera and the quickest way to find out where in any community welding, machine shop, heat treatment, plating and other similar services are available is to consult the local Classified Telephone Directory. In this book, which is given to every telephone subscriber, there is listed alphabetically almost every conceivable source of supply and service for many miles around. If a local Directory by chance does not list the type of services the gunsmith is interested in, he should not hesitate to write the telephone company and ask how he might go about securing a copy of a Classified Directory covering a local large city. With a Classified Directory on hand the gunsmith can pretty well rest assured that he has the most complete general register of local craftsmen and tradespeople—in which he too should be listed. After all, maybe the doctor in a nearby town might want to know where he can get a gun fixed.

Jobbers. When a gunsmith decides to expand his business by selling new guns, ammunition and accessories, he should contact a jobber in his territory who will discuss the matters of credit, delivery, display, et cetera in a manner adapted to the gunsmith's financial condition and surroundings. The small shop gunsmith should not waste his time trying to bypass the jobber and deal directly with the gun or ammunition factories, for they do not as a rule sell directly to small retail outlets.

If the gunsmith is in doubt about who his nearest jobber for any particular item is, he need only drop a post card to the "SPORTING GOODS DEALER DIRECTORY," 10th & Olive St., St. Louis, Missouri, and he will be favored with a prompt and accurate answer.

A gunsmith should never feel slighted if a manufacturer refers him to a jobber for merchandise to be sold at retail. This is an established method of doing business in the sporting goods as well as most other fields. An understanding jobber is frequently the small shop gunsmith's best friend, for he will extend credit and lend display material to help him over those inevitable rough spots that occur in every business.

Firearms Manufacturers (Gunsmiths should request parts catalogue)

Ithaca Gun Co. (Ithaca, Western and Lefever Shotguns)
Ithaca, New York

Winchester Repeating Arms Co. (Rifles and Shotguns)
New Haven, Conn.

Savage Arms Corp. (Rifles, Shotguns, Fox Shotguns)
Utica 1, New York

Remington Arms Co. (Rifles, Shotguns, Parker Shotguns)
Ilion, New York

Iver Johnson Arms & Cycle Works (Shotguns, .22 cal. Rifles, Revolvers)
Fitchburg, Mass.

Browning Arms Co. (Autoloading and Overunder Shotguns)
St. Louis 3, Missouri

Smith & Wesson (Revolvers)
Springfield, Mass.

High Standard Mfg. Corp. (Automatic Pistols)
1811 Dixwell Ave.
Hamden, Conn.

Marlin Firearms Co. (Rifles and Shotguns)
New Haven, Conn.

Marble Arms & Mfg. Co. ("Game Getter" Gun)
Gladstone, Michigan

Colts Patent Firearms Mfg. Co. (Revolvers, Pistols, Automatic Pistols)
Hartford, Conn.

Stevens Arms Co. (Shotguns, Rim-Fire Rifles)
Chicopee Falls, Mass.

Hunter Arms Co. (Hunter & Fulton Shotguns, L. C. Smith Shotguns)
Fulton, New York

Harrington & Richardson Arms Co. (.22 cal. Rifles, Revolvers, Single Shot Shotguns)
Worcester, Mass.

C. J. Hamilton & Son (Rim-Fire Rifles)
Plymouth, Michigan

Sight Manufacturers (Gunsmiths should request catalogue)

W. R. Weaver Co. (Telescopic Sights & Mounts for Rifles & Shotguns)
El Paso, Texas

Redfield Gunsight Co. (All Types of Metallic Sights; Mounts for Telescopic Sights)
3315 Gilpin St.
Denver, Colorado

Merit Gunsight Co. (Iris Shutter Peep Disc)
6144 Monadnock Way
Oakland 3, Calif.

J. W. Fecker (Telescopic Sights for Rifles)
2016 Perrysvile Ave.
Pittsburgh, Pa.

King Gunsight Co. (Rifle, Pistol and Revolver Sights)
667 Howard St.
San Francisco, Calif.

Lyman Sight Corp. (Metallic Sights; Telescopic Sights & Mounts for Rifles)
Middlefield, Conn.

Marble Arms & Mfg. Co. (Metallic Sights)
Gladstone, Michigan

M. L. & M. J. Stith (Special Mounts)
Transit Tower
San Antonio 5, Texas

Pacific Gunsight Co. (Metallic Sights)
355 Hayes St.
San Francisco, Calif.

John Unertl Optical Co. (Telescopic Sights & Mounts for Rifles; Tube Sights)
3551 East Street
Pittsburgh 14, Pa.

O. F. Mossberg & Sons (Telescopic Sights & Mounts for Rifles)
131 St. John St.
New Haven 5, Conn.

R. A. Litschert (Telescopic Sights for Rifles)
Winchester, Indiana

Vaver Sight Co. (Metallic Sights)
4311 West 24th Place
Chicago 2, Illinois

Swain-Nelson Co. (Nydar Sight for Shotguns)
2346 Glenview Rd.
Glenview, Illinois

Choke Manufacturers

Poly Choke Co.
Hartford, Conn.

W. R. Weaver Co.
El Paso, Texas

Compensators

Cutts Compensator
Made by
Lyman Gunsight Co.
Middlefield, Conn.

Cartridge Reloading Tools

Lyman Gunsight Corp. (Ideal Reloading Tools)
90 West St.
Middlefield, Conn.

Pacific Gunsight Co. (Pacific Reloading Tools)
355 Hayes St.
San Francisco, Calif.

Belding & Mull
Philipsburg, Pa.

Potter Engineering Co.
Cazenovia, New York

Star Machine Works
San Diego, Calif.

Modern-Bond Corp.
813 W. 5th St.
Wilmington, Delaware

C. Schmitt (Straight Line Tools)
Washington Avenue
Minneapolis, Minn.

Hollywood Gun Shop
6032 Hollywood Blvd,
Hollywood 28, Calif.

Cameron Mfg. Corp. (Jordan Press)
Emporium, Pa.

Optical Instruments Inspected and Repaired

Mirakel Repair Co.
Mount Vernon, New York

Belz, Opticians
2 East 44th St.
New York 17, N.Y.

All Gunsmiths Supplies (Write for list of supplies available)

Stoeger Arms Corp.
507 Fifth Ave.
New York, N.Y.

Frank Mittermeier
3577 E. Tremont Ave.
Bronx 61, N.Y.

Pacific Gunsight Co.
355 Hayes St.
San Francisco, Calif.

Gun Stocks, Pre-inletted

Stoeger Arms Corp.
507 Fifth Ave.
New York, N.Y.

Dave W. Thomas
Vineland, New Jersey

Stock Blanks, Wood for Gun Stocks, Inletting Service

Dave W. Thomas
Vineland, New Jersey

Filler and Finishes for Gunstocks

Stoeger Arms Corp.
507 Fifth Ave.
New York, N.Y.

Checkering Tools (For working on wood)

E. M. Farris
Portsmouth, Ohio

Frank Mittermeier
3577 E. Tremont Ave.
Bronx 61, New York

Stoeger Arms Corp.
507 Fifth Ave.
New York, N.Y.

Stockmakers Tools

Stoeger Arms Corp.
507 Fifth Ave.
New York, N.Y.

Frank Mittermeier
3577 E. Tremont Ave.
Bronx 61, N.Y.

Checkering Tools (For working on metal)

Stoeger Arms Corp.
507 Fifth Ave.
New York, N.Y.

Barrel Vise

Pacific Gunsight Co.
355 Hayes St.
San Francisco, Calif.

Rifle Barrels (Special)

J. R. Buhmiller
Eureka, Montana

Niedner Rifle Corp.
Dowagiac, Michigan

P. O. Ackley Co.,
160 Elm St.
Trinidad, Colorado

Roy E. Weatherby
8823 Long Beach Blvd.
South Gate, Calif.

Gages (Headspace)

Merit Gunsight Co. (.22 cal. Rim Thickness Gage)
6144 Monadnock Way
Oakland, Calif.

L. E. Wilson
Cashmere, Washington

Blueing Solutions (Hot Rusting Type and Cold Rusting Type)

Stoeger Arms Corp.
507 Fifth Ave.
New York, N.Y.

Pacific Gunsight Co.
355 Hayes St.
San Francisco, Calif.

Browning Arms Co.
St. Louis, Missouri

Ruptured Shell Extractors

Marble Arms & Mfg. Co.
Gladstone, Mich.

Union Hardware Co.
Torrington, Conn.

Chemicals (For blueing solutions)

Merck & Co. (Manufacturing
Chemists)
Rahway, New Jersey

Parts for Firearms (Modern, Obsolete
& Foreign)

Hudson Sporting Goods Co.
52 Warren St.
New York, N.Y.

E. M. Farris (Muzzle Gun Supplies)
210 Chillicothe St.,
Portsmouth, Ohio

Woodworking Machine Tools

The Delta Mfg. Co. (Band Saws,
Lathes, Jig Saws, Circular
Saws)
695 E. Vienna Ave.
Milwaukee 1, Wisconsin

Barron Tool Co. (Drill Press Accessories for Woodworking)
370 Architects Bldg.
Detroit, Mich.

Mead Specialties Co. (Belt Sander)
4114 N. Knox Ave.
Chicago, Illinois

Metal Working Machine Tools

Atlas Press Co. (Lathes, Drill
Presses, Shapers, Milling Machines and Attachments for these
machines)
Kalamazoo 13, Mich.

South Bend Lathe Works (Lathes)
452 E. Madison St.
South Bend, Indiana

Electric Hand Tools

Chicago Wheel & Mfg. Co.
(Handee Grinder)
1101 W. Monroe St.
Chicago, Illinois

Dremel Mfg. Co. (Moto Tool)
Racine, Wisconsin

Burgess Battery Co. (Vibro Tool)
176 N. Wabash Ave.
Chicago, Illinois

**Heat Treating Furnaces, Tempering
Salts and Pressed Steel Pots**

Stewart Industrial Furnace Division
Chicago Flexible Shaft Co.
5600 W. Roosevelt Road,
Chicago, Illinois

Welding (Electric) Machines

Hobart Brothers Co.
Troy, Ohio

John H. Graham Co., Inc. (Magic
Wand Welder)
105 Duane St.
New York, N.Y.

Tweezer Weld Corp. (Spot Welder)
Newark, New Jersey

Lincoln Electric Co.
Cleveland, Ohio

Welding Equipment (Gas)

Linde Air Products Co.
New York, N.Y.

Ammunition (Special)

Hudson Sporting Goods Co. (Cartridges for British & Italian
Rifles)
52 Warren St.
New York, N.Y.

Francis Bannerman & Sons (For
obsolete weapons)
501 Broadway
New York, N.Y.

Files (Metal and Wood Cutting)

Nicholson File Co.
19 Acorn St.
Providence, R.I.

American Swiss File Co. (Special
Files, Rifflers & Swiss Files)
Elizabeth, N.J.

Woodworking Tools (Chisels, Knives, etc.)

Crescent Products Co. (Carving Tools)
440 Fourth Ave.
New York, N.Y.

Greenlee Tool Co. (Chisels, Auger Bits, Gouges)
2124 Columbia Ave.
Rockford, Illinois

Stanley Tool Co.
New Britain, Conn.

Hammacher & Schlemmer
10th St. & 4th Ave.
New York, N.Y.

Precision Measuring Instruments

Ford Motor Co. (Johansson Gage Blocks)
Dearborn, Mich.

Brown & Sharpe
Providence, R.I.

L. S. Starrett
Athol, Mass.

Goodell-Pratt Co.
Greenfield, Mass.

Millers Falls Co.
Greenfield, Mass.

Drills, Taps and Dies

Black Drill Co. (Special Drills for Hard Steel Only)
1390 E. 22nd St.
Cleveland, Ohio

Morse Twist Drill Co.
New Bedford, Mass.

Greenfield Tap & Die Co.
Greenfield, Mass.

Union Twist Drill Co.
Athol, Mass.

Plastic Rods, Sheets, Tubes, Adhesives for Ornamenting Stocks & Grips (Plexiglass, Lucite, etc)

Carmen-Bronson Co.
165 East 3rd St.
Mt. Vernon, N.Y.

Plastic Supply Co.
2618 St. Louis Ave.
St. Louis, Missouri

Plastic Parts Boxes

Bill Dewitt Baits Division (Shoe Form Co.)
Auburn, New York

Metals, (Tool Steel, Drill Rod, Lead, Copper, etc.)

Patterson Brothers
Park Row
New York, N.Y.

Pacific Gunsight Co.
355 Hayes St.
San Francisco 2, Calif.

Small Tools (Distributor & Manufacturer)

Center Tool Co. (Punches, Drills, Pliers, Screwdrivers, Milling Cutters, Toolbits, Taps, Dies, Reamers, Special Steels, Precision Measuring Tools, etc.)
Catalogue to gunsmiths upon request.
152 Center St.
New York, N.Y.

Metal Finishing Supplies

Dealers in All Supplies

Plating Equipment & Supply Co.
182 Grand St.
New York, N.Y.

J. J. Siefen Co.
5657 Lauderdale St.
Detroit 9, Mich.

Beam-Knodel Co.
195 Lafayette St.
New York, N.Y.

Canadian-Hanson & Van Winkle Co. Ltd.
2 Silver St.
Toronto, Canada

Sommers Bros. Mfg. Co.
3443 N. Broadway
St. Louis 7, Missouri

P. R. Mallory & Co.
Indianapolis 6, Ind.

Blackening Processes, Steel

Stoeger Arms Corp.
507 Fifth Ave.
New York, N.Y.

Aeroil Burner Co., Inc.
West New York, N.J.

Alrose Chemical Co.
Providence 1, R.I.

Black-Ox Chemical Co.
756 McCarter Highway
Newark 5, N.J.

Du Lite Chemical Corp.
Middletown, Conn.

The Enthone Co.
442 Elm St.
New Haven 2, Conn.

Heatbath Corp.
Springfield 1, Mass.

E. F. Houghton & Co.
303 W. Lehigh Ave.
Philadelphia 33, Pa.

Cleaners, Metal

American Chemical Paint Co.
Ambler, Pa.

Circo Products Co.
2835 Chester Ave.
Cleveland 14, Ohio

Magnus Chemical Co. Inc.
Garwood, N.J.

Oakite Products, Inc.
20 E. Thames St.
New York 6, N.Y.

Optimus Detergents Co.
276 Church St.
Matawan, N.J.

Pennsylvania Salt Mfg. Co.
1000 Widener Bldg.
Philadelphia 7, Pa.

Compositions, Polishing and Buffing

M. E. Baker Co.
143 Sidney St.
Cambridge, Mass.

E. Reed Burns Mfg. Corp.
40–42 Withers St.
Brooklyn 11, N.Y.

Formax Mfg. Co.
Bellevue & Benson
Detroit 7, Mich.

Hanson-Van Winkle-Munning Co.
Matawan, N.J.

Harrison & Co.
Box 695
Groveland, Mass.

The Lea Mfg. Co.
Waterbury 86, Conn.

Chas. F. L'Hommedieu & Sons Co.
4521 Ogden Ave.
Chicago 23, Ill.

Dipping Baskets

American Hard Rubber Co.
11 Mercer St.
New York 13, N.Y.

American Plating Rack Co.
630 Parkview
Detroit 14, Mich.

American Wire Form Co., Inc.
265–273 Grant Ave.
Jersey City 5, N.J.

The Youngstown Welding & Eng. Co.
Youngstown, Ohio

Felt Polishing Wheels

Bacon Felt Co.
711 Grove St.
Winchester, Mass.

Eastern Felt Co.
80 Canal St.
Winchester, Mass.

Glue, Polishing

J. J. Siefen Co.
5657 Lauderdale St.
Detroit 9, Mich.

Hydrochloric Acid (Muriatic Acid)

General Chemical Co.
40 Rector St.
New York 6, N.Y.

Inhibitors, Acid

American Chemical Paint Co.
Ambler, Pa.

Monsanto Chemical Co.
Merrimac Division, Everett Station
Boston 49, Mass.

Monel Metal Equipment

The Youngstown Welding & Engineering Co.
Oakwood Ave.
Youngstown, Ohio

Nickel Stripper

All-Brite Chemical Co.
P.O. Box 1542
Waterbury 89, Conn.

The Chemical Corp.
93 Broad St.
Springfield, Mass.

Kelite Products, Inc.
909 E. 60th St.
Los Angeles 1, Calif.

Nitric Acid

Lasalco, Inc.
2818–38 La Salle St.
St. Louis 4, Mo.

Seldner & Enequist, Inc.
Brooklyn 22, N.Y.

Platers and Bluers Chemicals

Belke Mfg. Co.
947 N. Cicero Ave.
Chicago, Ill.

The Cowles Detergent Co.
7016 Euclid Ave.
Cleveland 3, Ohio

Frederick Gumm Chemical Co., Inc.
538–542 Forest St.
Kearny, N.J.

Jacob Hay Co.
4014 W. Parker Ave.
Chicago, Ill.

The Lea Mfg. Co.
Waterbury 86, Conn.

Oakite Products, Inc.
20 E. Thames St.
New York 6, N.Y.

Phillips & Jacob
622 Race St.
Philadelphia 6, Pa.

Polishers Brick

American Buff Co.
711 West Lake St.
Chicago 6, Ill.

Divine Brothers Co.
205 Seward Ave.
Utica 1, N.Y.

J. J. Siefen Co.
5657 Lauderdale St.
Detroit 9, Mich.

Polishing Lathes

M. E. Baker Co.
143 Sidney St.
Cambridge, Mass.

Divine Brothers Co.
205 Seward Ave.
Utica 1, N.Y.

The Hisey Wolf Machine Co.
2745 Colerain Ave.
Cincinnati 25, Ohio

J. Holland & Sons Inc.
276 S. 9th St.
Brooklyn 11, N.Y.

Chas. F. L'Hommedieu & Sons Co.
4521 Ogden Ave.
Chicago 23, Ill.

Plating Equipment & Supply Co.
182 Grand St.
New York, N.Y.

Lewis Roe Mfg. Co.
1042–1050 DeKalb Ave.
Brooklyn, N.Y.

Frederic B. Stevens, Inc.
Detroit 26, Mich.

Potassium Cyanide

American Cyanamid & Chemical Corp.
30 Rockefeller Plaza
New York 20, N.Y.

E. I. du Pont de Nemours & Co., Inc.
Wilmington 98, Del.

General Chemical Co.
40 Rector St.
New York 6, N.Y.

Pumice

Tamms Silica Co.
228 N. LaSalle St.
Chicago 1, Ill.

Rouge: Polishing, Buffing, etc.

Apothecaries Hall Co.
Benedict St.
Waterbury 88, Conn.

The Buckeye Products Co.
7020–34 Vine St.
Cincinnati 16, Ohio

E. Reed Burns Mfg. Corp.
40–42 Withers St.
Brooklyn 11, N.Y.

The Matchless Metal Polish Co.
726 Bloomfield Ave.
Glen Ridge, N.J.

The Roberts Rouge Co.
904 Longbrook Ave.
Stratford, Conn.

Rust Preventives (Oils)

Alrose Chemical Co.
Providence 1, R.I.

The Alvey-Ferguson Co.
692 Disney St.
Cincinnati 9, Ohio

The Mitchell Bradford Chemical
Co.
2446 Main St.
Stratford, Conn.

Protective Coatings, Inc.
P.O. Box 56
Strathmoor Station
Detroit 27, Mich.

Valvoline Oil Co.
474 Culvert St.
Cincinnati 2, Ohio

Rust Removers

Int'l Rustproof Corp.
12507–15 Plover Ave.
Cleveland, Ohio

Kelite Products, Inc.
909 E. 60th St.
Los Angeles 1, Calif.

Magnuson Products Corp.
50 Court St.
Brooklyn 2, N.Y.

Oakite Products, Inc.
20 E. Thames St.
New York 6, N.Y.

Sodium Cyanide

American Cyanamid & Chemical
Corp.
30 Rockefeller Plaza
New York 20, N.Y.

The Chemical Corp.
93 Broad St.
Springfield, Mass.

The Harshaw Chemical Co.
1945 E. 97th St.
Cleveland, Ohio

Sodium Hydroxide (Caustic Soda)

Belke Mfg. Co.
947 N. Cicero Ave.
Chicago, Ill.

Frederick Gumm Chemical Co.
538–542 Forest St.
Kearney, N.J.

Merck & Co.
Rahway, N.J.

Puro Chemicals, Inc.
1643 St. Clair Ave.
Cleveland 14, Ohio

The Udylite Corp.
Detroit 11, Mich.

Sodium Nitrite

Croton Chemical Corp.
114 Liberty St.
New York 6, N.Y.

Eaton-Clark Co.
1480 Franklin St.
Detroit 7, Mich.

Solvay Sales Corp.
40 Rector St.
New York 6, N.Y.

Solvents, Degreasing

Bernard Chemical Products
211–213 Patchen Ave.
Brooklyn 33, N.Y.

Solvents, Degreasing

Circo Products Co.
2835 Chester Ave.
Cleveland 14, Ohio

Fidelity Chem. Prod. Corp.
430 Riverside Ave.
Newark 4, N.J.

Stop Off Materials

M. E. Baker Co.
143 Sidney St.
Cambridge, Mass.

Beam Knodel, Inc.
195 Lafayette St.
New York, N.Y.

Sulfuric Acid

General Chemical Co.
40 Rector St.
New York 6, N.Y.

Phillips & Jacob
622 Race St.
Philadelphia 6, Pa.

Tank Linings

The Hauser-Stander Tank Co.
4838 Spring Grove Ave.
Cincinnati 32, Ohio

Heil Engineering Co.
12901 Elmwood Ave.
Cleveland 11, Ohio

Tanks, Ceramic

General Ceramics Co.
Keasbey, N.J.

U.S. Stoneware Co.
Talmadge, Ohio

Tanks, Glass

Alsop Engineering Corp.
Milldale, Conn.

Technichemical Mfg. Co.
1288 Troy Ave.
Brooklyn 3, N.Y.

Tanks, Metal

Aeroil Burner Co., Inc.
West New York, N.J.

Heil Engineering Co.
12901 Elmwood Ave.
Cleveland 11, Ohio

J. Holland & Sons, Inc.
274 South 9th St.
Brooklyn 11, N.Y.

The Carl Mayer Corp.
3030 Euclid Ave.
Cleveland, Ohio

Plating Products Co.
352 Mulberry St.
Newark 2, N.J.

Tanks, Wood

The Hauser-Stander Tank Co.
4838 Spring Grove Ave.
Cincinnati 32, Ohio

Kalamazoo Tank & Silo Co.
508 Harrison St.
Kalamazoo 16, Mich.

Temperature Regulators

American Instrument Co.
8020 Georgia Ave.
Silver Springs, Md.

Barber-Colman Co.
1205 Rock St.
Rockford, Ill.

Beam Knodel, Inc.
195 Lafayette St.
New York, N.Y.

The Brown Instrument Co.
4513 Wayne Ave.
Philadelphia 44, Pa.

The Foxboro Co.
Foxboro, Mass.

Leeds & Northrup Co.
4970 Stenton Ave.
Philadelphia 44, Pa.

Taylor Instrument Companies
95 Ames St.
Rochester 1, N.Y.

Wheels, Rubber Polishing

Belke Mfg. Co.
947 N. Cicero Ave.
Chicago, Ill.

Brightboy Industrial Div.
Weldon Roberts Rubber Co.
6th Ave. & No. 13th St.
Newark 7, N.J.

Wetting Agents

Alrose Chemical Co.
Providence 1, R.I.

Wheels, Polishing

Advance Polishing Wheels
844 W. 49th Pl.
Chicago, Ill.

Beam Knodel, Inc.
195 Lafayette St.
New York, N.Y.

The Bias Buff & Wheel Co.
Division Riegel Textile Corp.
430 Communipaw Ave.
Jersey City 4, N.J.

Behr-Manning Corp.
Troy, N.Y.

E. Reed Burns Mfg. Corp.
40–42 Withers St.
Brooklyn 11, N.Y.

Chicago Wheel & Mfg. Co.
1101 W. Monroe St.
Chicago, Ill.

Divine Brothers Co.
205 Seward Ave.
Utica 1, N.Y.

The Lea Mfg. Co.
Waterbury 86, Conn.

Wheels, Wire

The Black & Decker Mfg. Co.
600 East Penn Ave.
Towson 4, Md.

Periodicals and Books

The more progressive individuals in virtually every field of mechanical, professional and artistic endeavor keep abreast of the latest techniques, doings, methods, personalities and commercial trends by reading trade journals. And in this modern age when new developments come fast and competition is keen, the man who wants to give his customers the best must know as much about his profession as possible.

Although there is no specific gunsmith's trade journal, "The American Rifleman" magazine is the very best source of contemporary technical and commercial information on guns. For those who are interested in guns, "The Rifleman" is a must because it is the individual gunsmith's only connection with thousands of other gunsmiths, both professional and amateur.

"The American Rifleman" (published monthly) goes out to all members of the National Rifle Association and membership in the N.R.A. is just something that every gun lover, gunsmith, gun dealer or gun bug should enjoy and profit from. All inquiries relating to membership in the Association ($3.00 per year) should be addressed to:

The Secretary
National Rifle Association
1600 Rhode Island Avenue,
Washington, D.C.

The gunsmith who wishes to keep abreast of the very latest in Ordnance developments should seek out the magazine that has, since 1920, kept gun technicians and students of preparedness through research informed. The magazine, "JOURNAL OF THE ARMY ORDNANCE ASSOCIATION," is published bi-monthly and sent to members of the Association. On alternate months members receive the Association's Industrial Preparedness Bulletin.

From time to time members are also offered special reports, papers and digests on machine guns, proof marks and similar Ordnance material.

Membership in this non-profit organization, which is open to American male citizens, is $4.00 per year and entitles the member to enjoy whatever facilities and services are available through the various local chapters. For further information address:

Secretary
The Army Ordnance Association
705 Mills Bldg.
Washington, D.C.

The National Muzzle Loading Rifle Association, headquarters Portsmouth, Ohio, is a live wire, "up and coming" outfit. It and its publication "Muzzle Blasts" do a splendid job for shooters and it merits membership support from all active shooters and gunsmiths. For information address:

Muzzle Blasts
Portsmouth, Ohio.

Another magazine which, because of its value to the gunsmith, this writer hastens to recommend is:

The Sporting Goods Dealer
10th & Olive Streets
St. Louis, Missouri

Sporting magazines with a section or department devoted to guns and ammunition

Field & Stream, 515 Madison Ave., New York 22, N.Y.
Fur-Fish-Game, 174 E. Long Street, Columbus 15, Ohio
Hunting & Fishing, 275 Newbury St., Boston 16, Mass.
Outdoor Life, 353 Fourth Ave., New York 10, N.Y.
Outdoors, 729 Boylston St., Boston, Mass.
Outdoorsman, 919 N. Michigan Ave., Chicago 11, Ill.
Sports Afield, 710 Pheonix Bldg., Minneapolis, Minn.

Trade magazines and publications

The Instrument Maker, 1117 Wolfendale St. N.S., Pittsburgh 12, Pa.

The National Hardwood Magazine, P.O. Box 1721, Memphis, Tenn.

Woodworking Digest, 542 S. Dearborn St., Chicago 5, Ill.

American Machinist, 330 West 42nd St., New York 18, N.Y.

Heat Treating & Forging, 108 Smithfield St., Pittsburgh, Pa.

Machine Tool Blue Book, 542 S. Dearborn St., Chicago 5, Ill.

Metal Finishing, 11 West 42nd St., New York 18, N.Y.

The Tool & Die Journal, 2460 Fairmont Blvd., Cleveland 6, Ohio

The Welding Engineer, 506 S. Wabash Ave., Chicago 5, Ill.

Plastics, 274 Madison Ave., New York 16, N. Y.

Books

The following books are suggested because this writer sincerely believes they will help the gunsmith to be a better gun technician and mechanic.

On Gunsmithing, Guns and Ammunition

Modern Gunsmithing—Baker

Advanced Gunsmithing—Vickery

Gunsmith's Manual—Stelle & Harrison (On old weapons)

Firearms Blueing & Browning—Angier

Telescopic Rifle Sights—Whelen

Firearm Design & Assembly (Inletting & Stockmaking Series)—Linden

Small Arms Design & Ballistics (Volumes I & II)—Whelen

Textbook of Firearms Investigation, Identification & Evidence—Hatcher

Textbook of Automatic Pistols—Wilson

Handloaders Manual—Naramore

Complete Guide to Handloading—Sharpe

A History of the Colt Revolver—Haven & Belden

Book of the Springfield—Crossman

Modern Shotguns and Loads—Askins

Gun Collecting—Chapel

The Rifle in America—Sharpe

Smith & Wesson Hand Guns—McHenry & Roper

Automatic Weapons of the World—Johnson and Haven

On Shop Work

American Machinists' Handbook—Colvin & Stanley (McGraw-Hill Book Co. New York, N.Y.)

How to Run a Lathe—South Bend Lathe Co., South Bend, Ind.

The Starrett For Student Machinists—L. S. Starrett Tool Co. Athol, Mass.

Kents Mechanical Engineers Handbook (McGraw-Hill Book Co., New York, N.Y.)

Audels New Machinist & Toolmakers Book—Audel, W. 23rd St., New York, N.Y.

Audels Welders Guide—Audel, W. 23rd St., New York, N.Y.

* Protective Coatings for Metals—Burns & Schuh

* Handbook of Chemistry & Finishing

* Dictionary of Metal Finishing Chemicals—Hall & Hogaboom

Catalogues and Handbooks

Stewart Handbook (Heat Treating Data Book)

Chicago Flexible Shaft Co. 5600 W. Roosevelt Road Chicago, Ill.

Starrett Catalogue (Fine Measuring and Machinists Tools) Athol, Mass.

* (Metal Industry Publishing Co. 11 W. 42nd St., New York, N.Y.

INDEX

Page Numbers in ( ) Indicate Illustrations.
(In view of the profuse number of running heads and illustrations decision
was reached to index *Professional Gunsmithing* by Chapters instead of the
usual treatment).

517

CPSIA information can be obtained
at www.ICGtesting.com
Printed in the USA
BVHW05s0350090718
521073BV00008B/88/P